1st Grade JUMBO Workbook

This book belongs to:

....

US Editors Nancy Ellwood, Margaret Parrish, Allison Singer
Editors Fran Baines, Rohini Deb, Tanya Desai, Camilla Gersh, Jolyon Goddard, Nandini Gupta, Nishtha Kapil, Shahwar Kibria, Cécile Landau, Deborah Lock, Monica Saigal
Art Editors Dheeraj Arora, Jyotsna Julka, Rashika Kachroo, Kanika Kalra, Radhika Kapoor, Pallavi Narain, Tanvi Nathyal, Yamini Panwar, Marisa Renzullo
Managing Editor Soma B. Chowdhury
Managing Art Editors Richard Czapnik, Ahlawat Gunjan
Production Editor Gillian Reid
Production Controller Mandy Inness
Jacket Designer Jomin Johny
Publisher Andrew Macintyre
Associate Publishing Director Liz Wheeler
Publishing Director Jonathan Metcalf

Content previously published in *Math Made Easy Grade 1, Extra Math Practice Grade 1,* and *DK Workbooks: Math, Science, Geography, Language Arts, Spelling 1st Grade*

This Edition published in 2020
First American Edition, 2015
Published in the United States by DK Publishing
1450 Broadway, Suite 801, New York, NY 10018

21 22 23 10 9 8 7 6 5 4 3 2
002–286875–May/2020

A catalog record for this book is available from the Library of Congress.

ISBN 978-0-7440-3295-6

Printed and bound in Canada

For the curious
www.dk.com

Contents

This chart lists all the topics in the book.

Letter to Parents

This book is intended to assist children in first grade. By working through the book, your child will learn all the key concepts taught at this level in a fun and informative way. The exercises and activities will help reinforce his or her understanding of the basic concepts taught in first grade in the following subjects:

- math;
- science;
- geography;
- language arts;
- spelling.

All the activities in the book are intended to be completed by a child with adult support. As you work through the pages with your child, make sure he or she understands what each activity requires. Read the facts and instructions aloud. Encourage questions and reinforce observations that will build confidence and increase active participation in classes at school.

By working with your child, you will understand how he or she thinks and learns. When appropriate, use props and objects from daily life to help your child make connections with the world outside.

In addition, try to help your child connect the content to specific personal experiences. For example, as you read a book together, explore the book cover. Ask your child to retell a story you have read, using temporal words such as "first," "next," "then," and "finally." Encourage your child to practice math, letters, and writing on the practice pages given at the end of the book.

Be sure to praise your child as he or she completes a page, gives a correct answer, or makes progress. This will help build your child's confidence and increase his or her interest in the subjects being studied.

Good luck and remember to have fun!

1st Grade Math

Authors Sean McArdle, Linda Ruggieri
Educational Consultant Alison Tribley

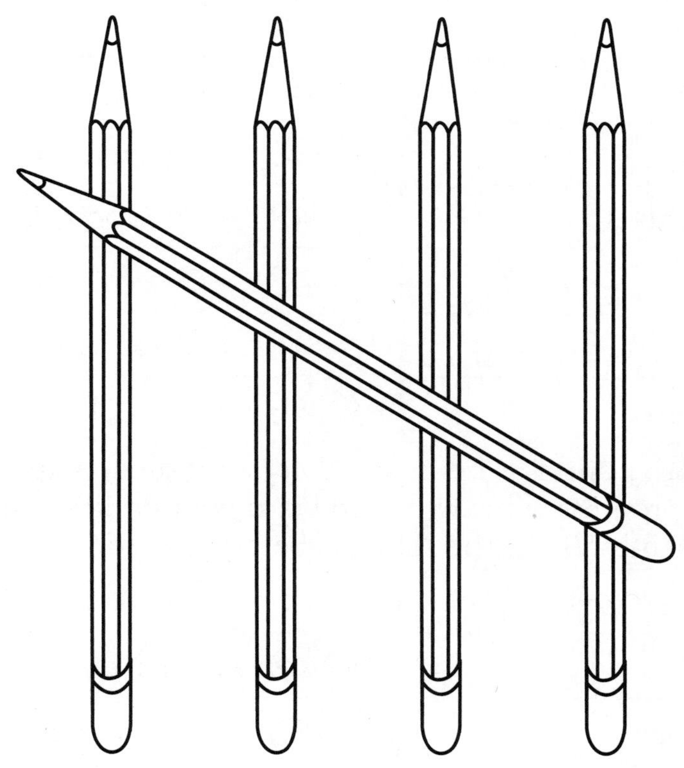

Contents

This chart lists all the topics in the Math section.

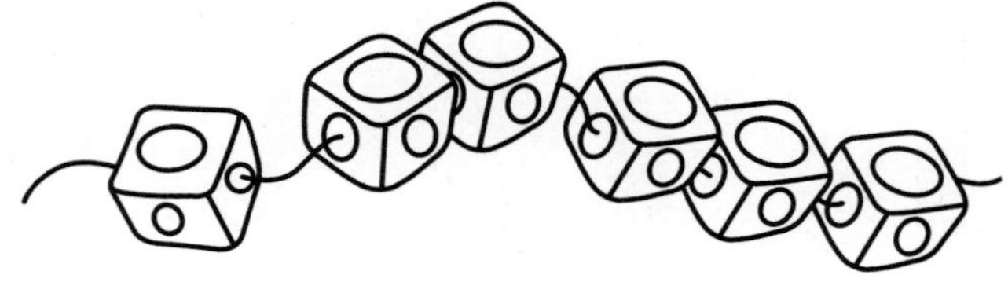

Read, Write, and Draw

Write each number as a word.

4 Four	8	10	3
7	1	5	9
2	6	0	

Write each amount as a number and the word.

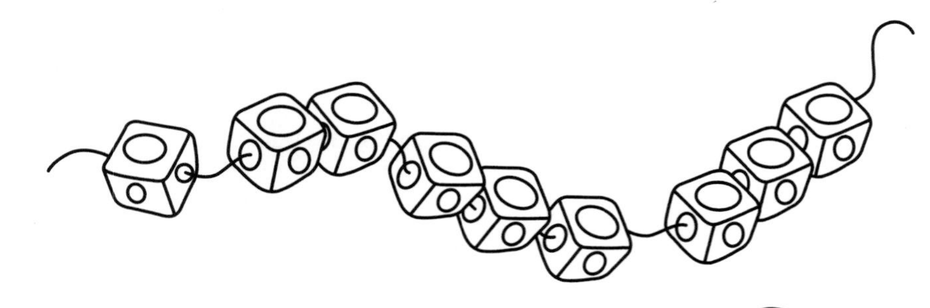

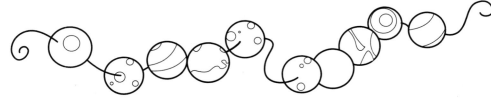

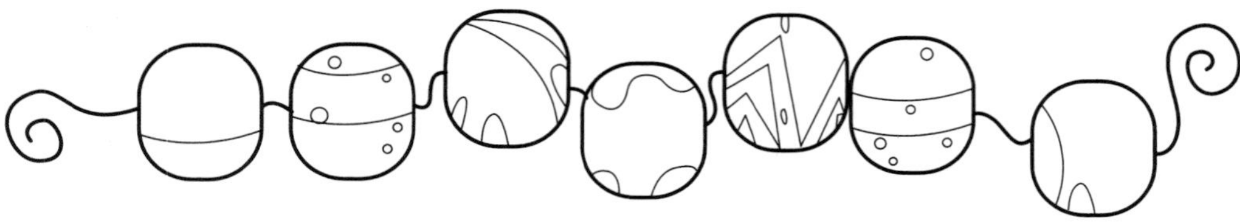

Draw the correct number of things.

Four  Two  Five 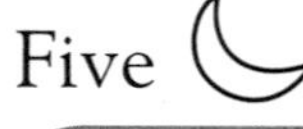 Three 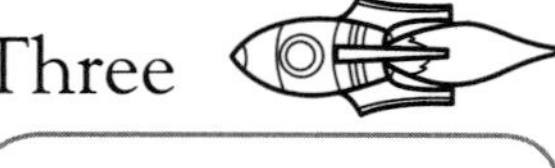

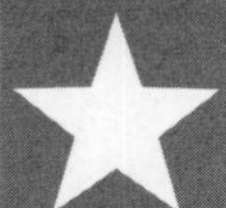

How many in each box?

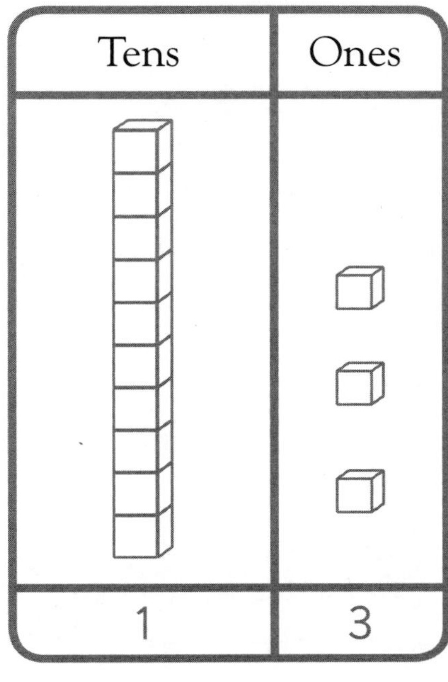

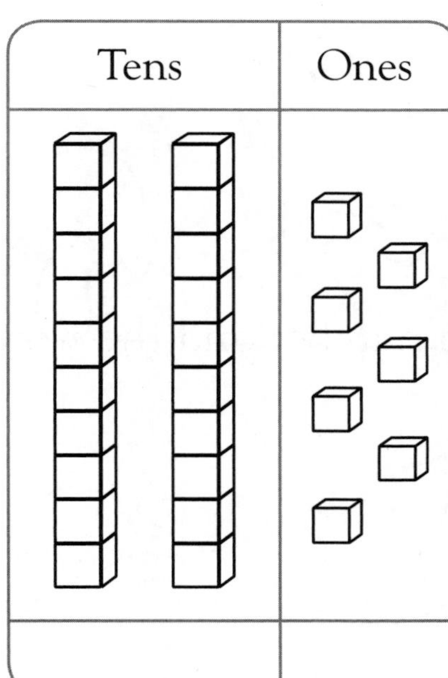

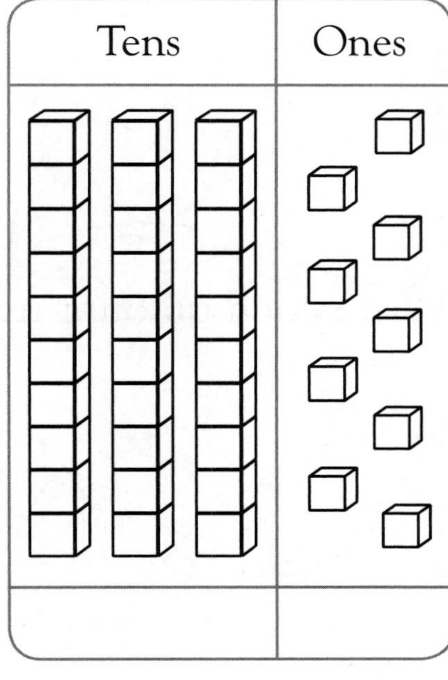

13 ....

Draw each number as tens and ones.

Tens	Ones
1	2

12

Tens	Ones

29

Tens	Ones

36

Count in 3s, 4s, 5s, and 6s.

2 +3 5 +3 8 +3 11 +3 14 +3 17

5 +3 +3

3 +4 +4

7 +5 +5

8 +6 +6

Complete each set.

5 is one more than 

3 is one more than 

6 is one more than

4 is one more than 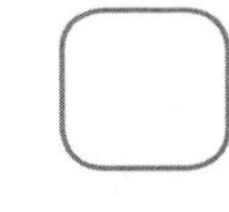

9 is one less than 10

is one less than 15

is one less than 16

is one less than 13

Missing Numbers

Fill in the missing numbers on these train cars.

0 1 2 3 4 5 8 10

8 6 2 0

0 10

8 2

1 5 10

Draw and count the number of times each animal hops.

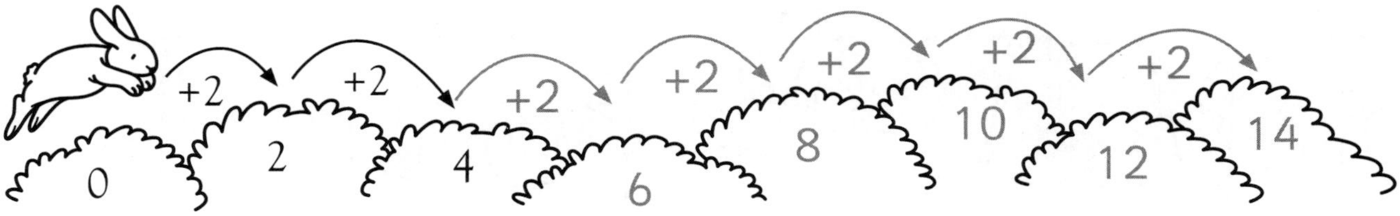

+2 +2 +2 +2 +2 +2 +2

0 2 4 6 8 10 12 14

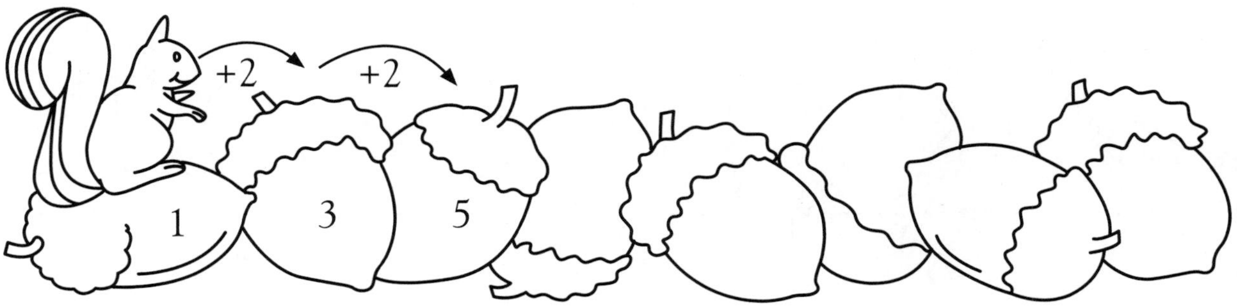

+2 +2

1 3 5

+2 +2

4 6 8

+2 +2

5 7 9

+2 +2

20 22 24 34

Fill in the missing numbers.

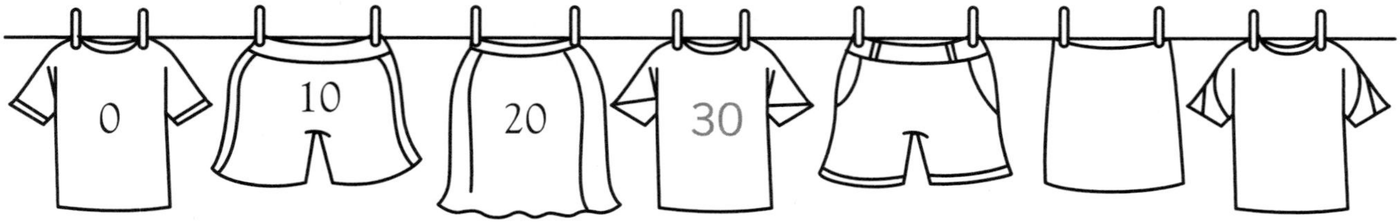

0, 10, 20, 30, ___, ___, ___

50, 60, 70, ___, ___, ___, ___

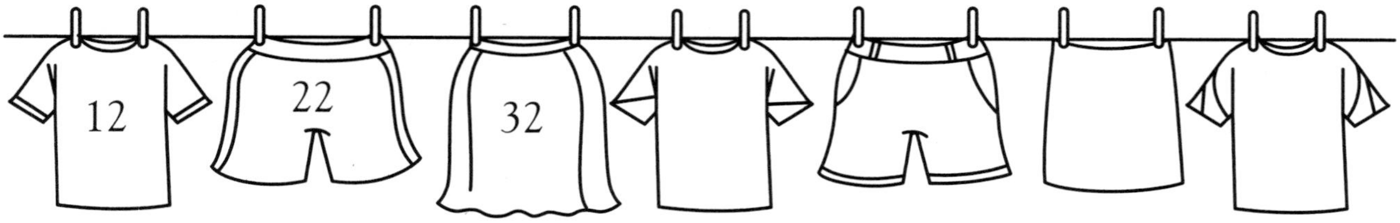

12, 22, 32, ___, ___, ___, ___

4, 14, 24, ___, ___, ___, ___

75, 65, 55, ___, ___, ___, ___

Put the numbers in order, starting with the largest.

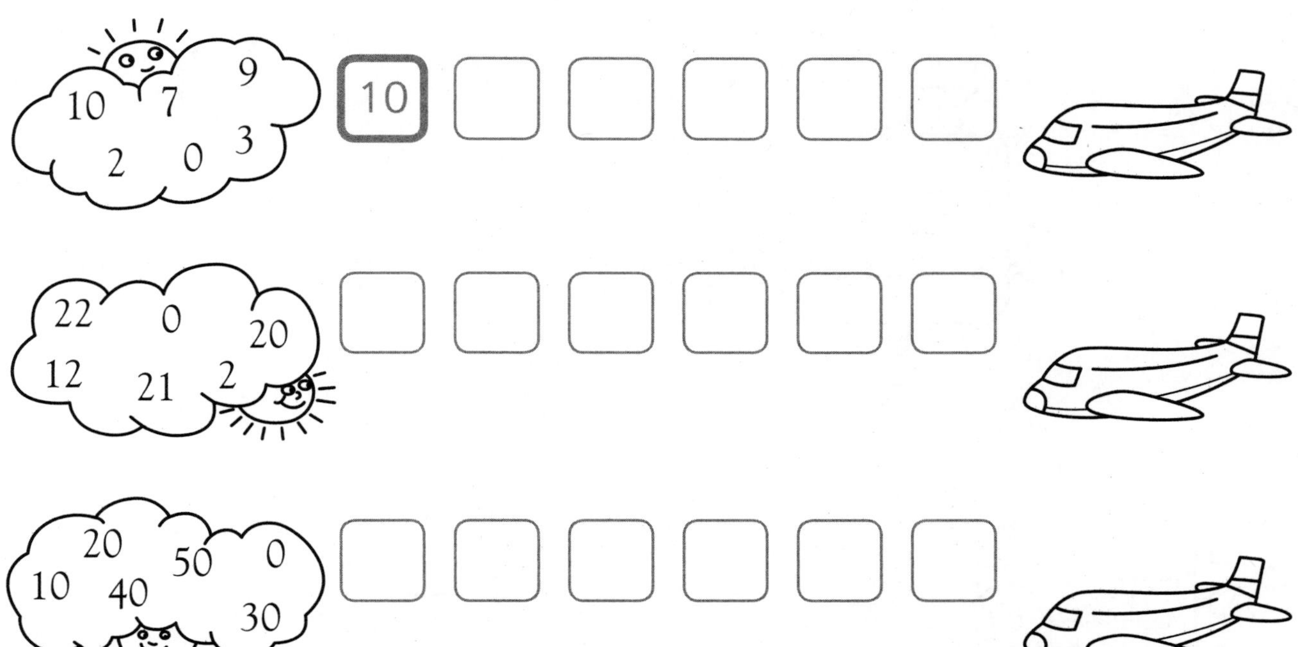

Put the numbers in order, starting with the smallest.

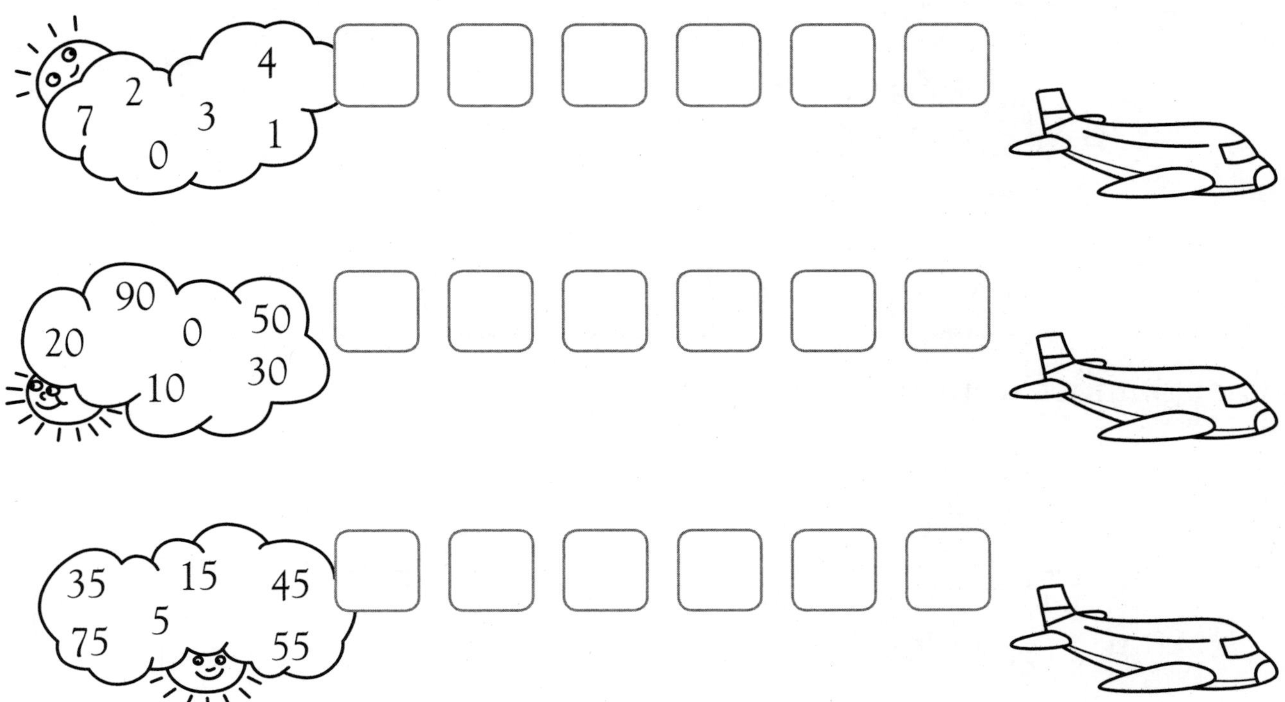

Number Machines

Put 5 into each machine. What comes out?

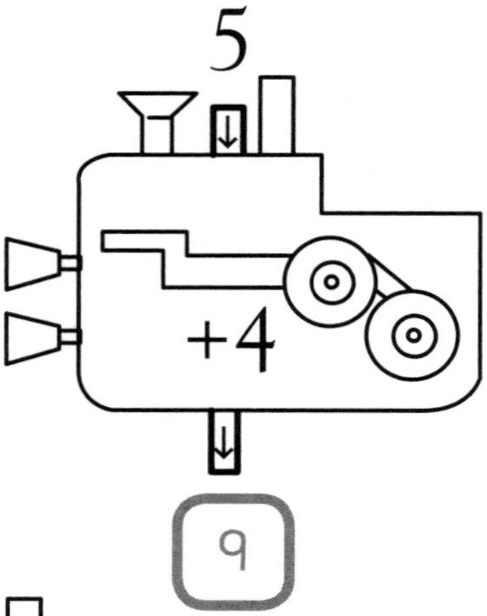

5
+4
9

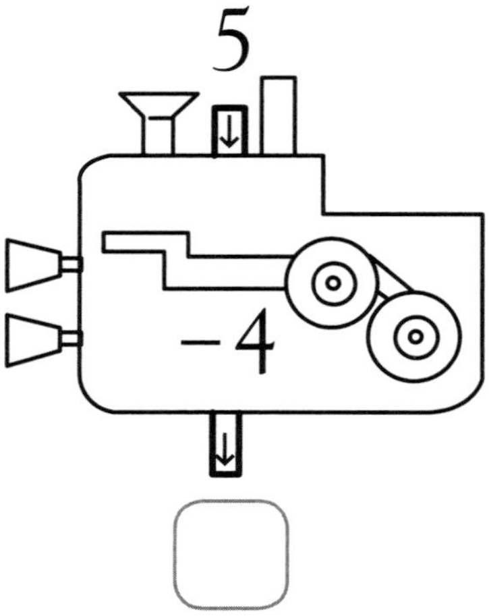

5
−4

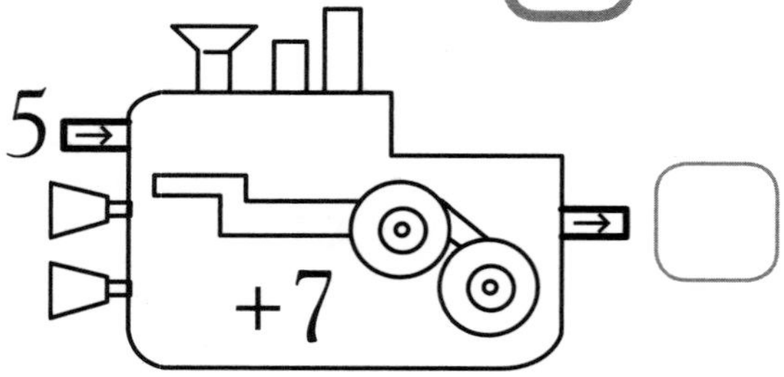

5
+7

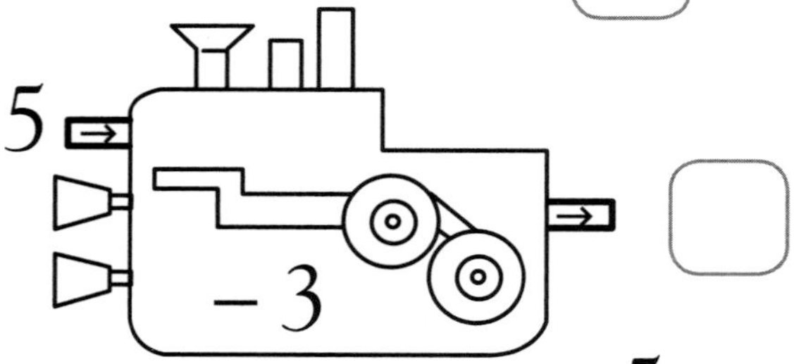

5
−3

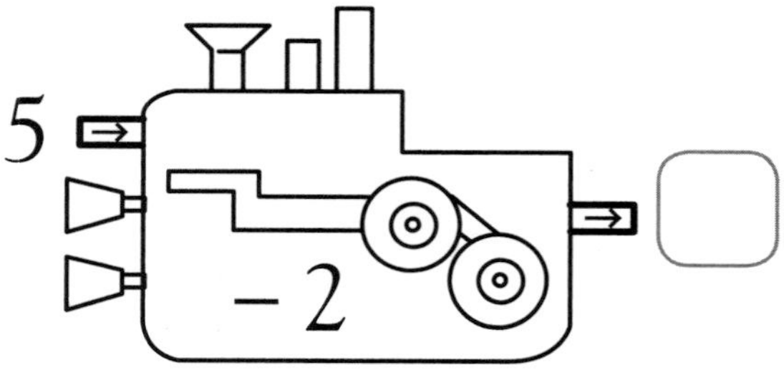

5
−2

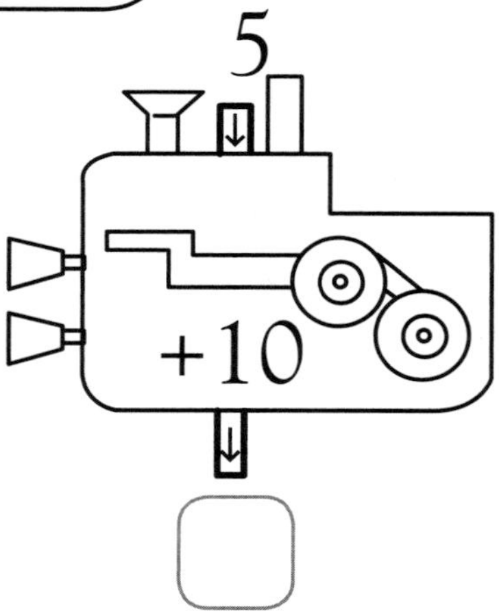

5
+10

What number went into each machine?

Continue these patterns.

□ ☆ □ ☆ □ ☆ □ ....

△ ○ ○ △ ○ ○ ....

□ ▯ □ ▯ □ ▯ ....

○ ◇ ○ ◇ ○ ◇ ....

Continue these number patterns.

2 1 1 2 1 1 ☐ ☐ ☐

3 2 1 3 2 1 ☐ ☐ ☐

4 5 6 4 5 6 4 ☐ ☐

6 6 3 6 6 ☐ ☐ ☐ ☐

Three children are racing.

Which child comes in first (1st)? ....

Which child comes in second (2nd)? ....

Which child comes in third (3rd)? ....

Tim Lewis Darius

Color the path!

Color the 1st, 4th, 7th, 10th stones red.
Color the 2nd, 5th, 8th, 11th stones green.
Color the 3rd, 6th, 9th, 12th stones blue.

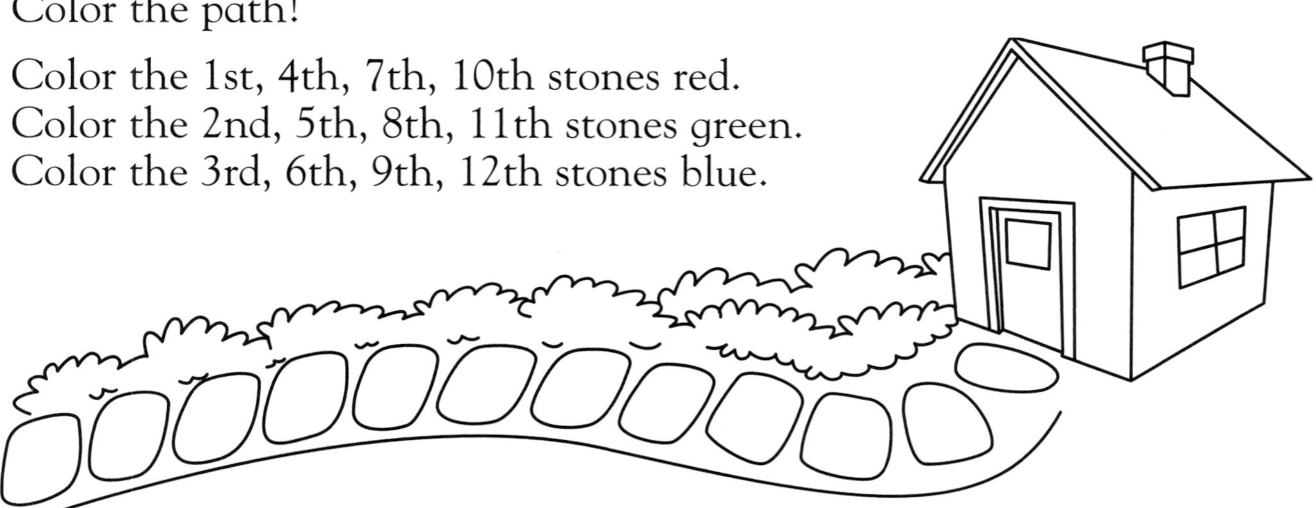

Another race!

What position is each child?

....	....	....	....	....
Shen	Mario	Sally	Jack	Islay

Circle the number that is odd.

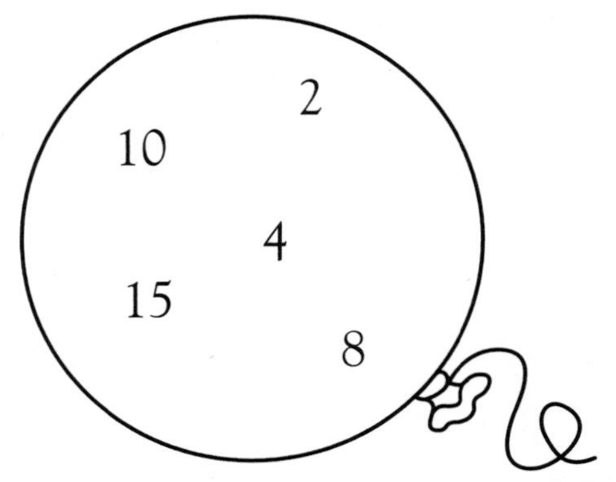

Circle the number that is **not** odd.

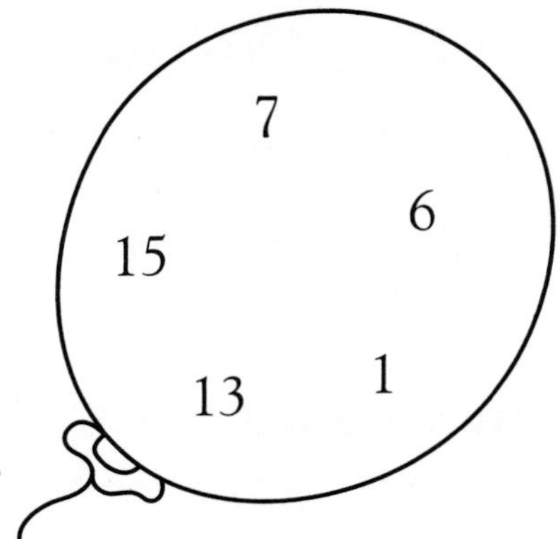

Circle the number that is even.

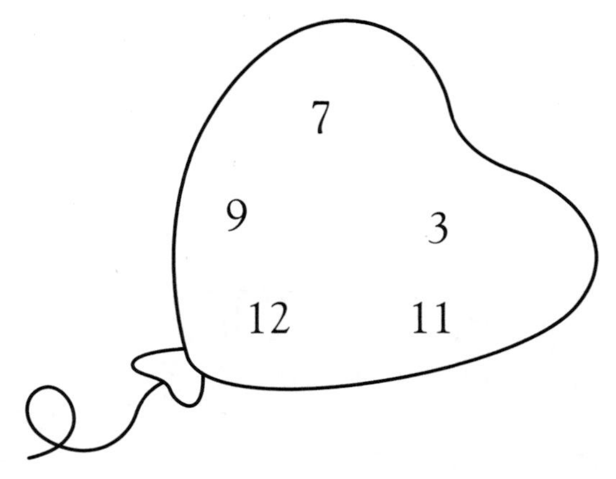

Circle the number that is **not** even.

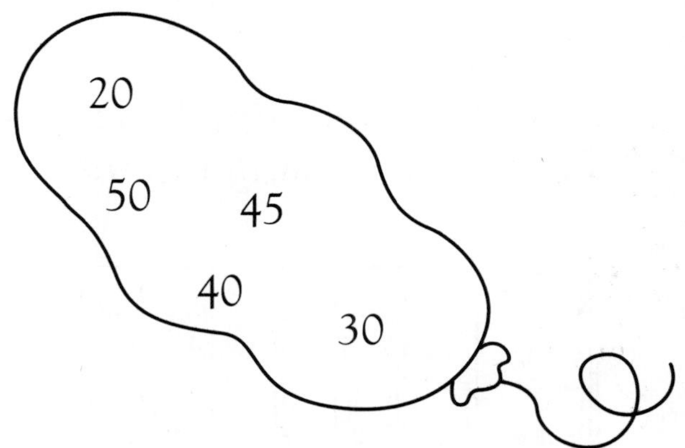

Write the next three odd numbers.

21	23	25	☐	☐	☐
5	7	9	☐	☐	☐

Write the next three even numbers.

24	26	28	☐	☐	☐
66	68	70	☐	☐	☐

Max needs 8 carrots. Cross out (**X**) 8 carrots.

How many carrots are left?

Ann has 15 cupcakes and buys 10 more.
How many cupcakes does Ann have altogether?

Doors on one side of the road have odd numbers.
Fill in the missing numbers.

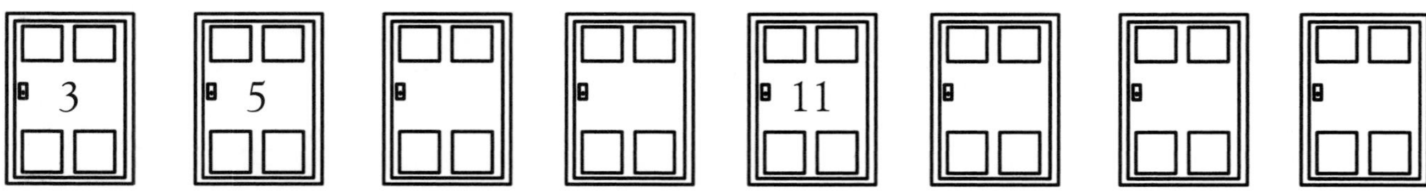

What is next in this sequence?

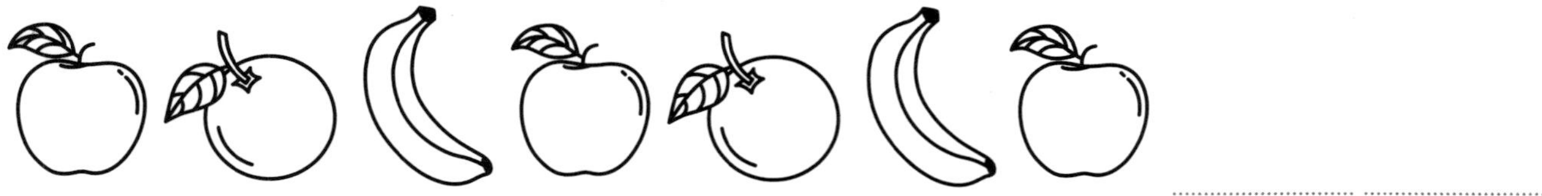

....

How many tens in each number?

14 36 51 20 75

The race!

Smithy Bonnie Dan Sanji

Who is 1st? ....

Who is 2nd? ....

Who is 3rd? ....

Who is 4th? ....

Write the numbers in order, with the smallest number first.

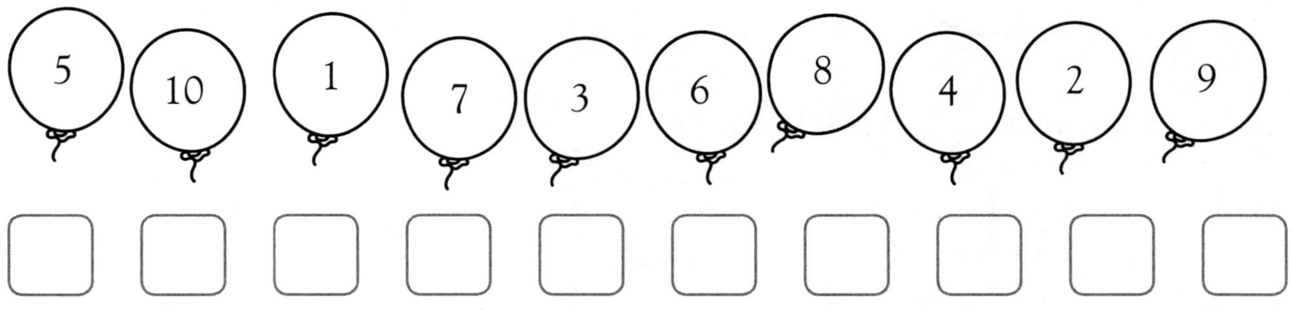

Write the amounts in order with the largest first.

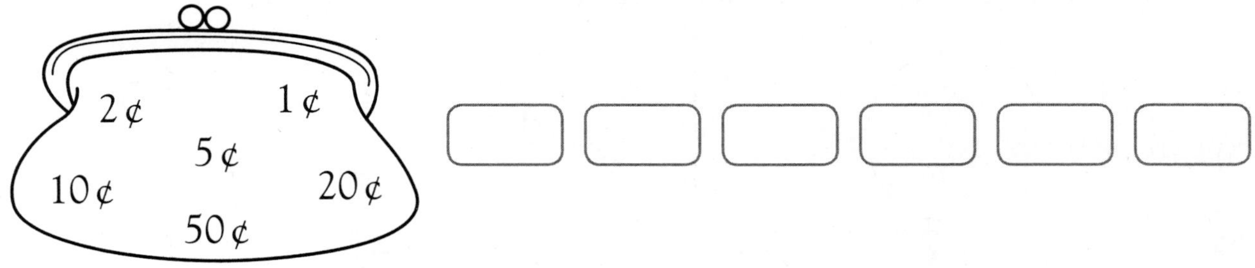

Each group has three chicks.
How many chicks are there in three groups?

Fractions of Shapes

Color half ($\frac{1}{2}$) of each shape.

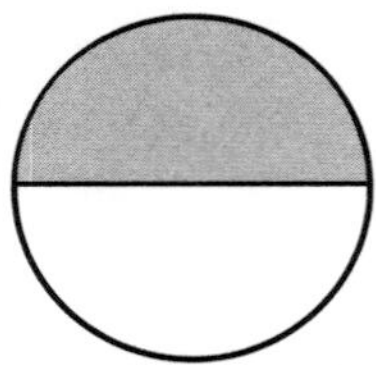 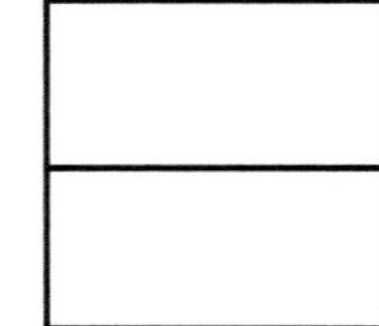 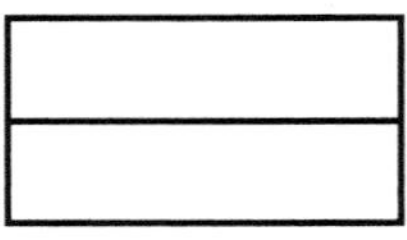

Now color half ($\frac{1}{2}$) of each shape in a different way.

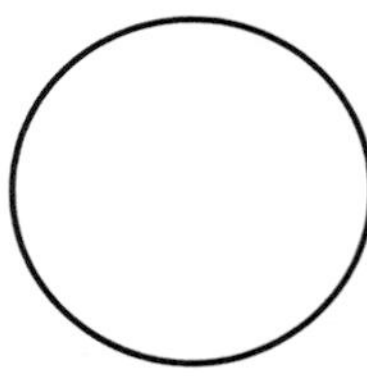 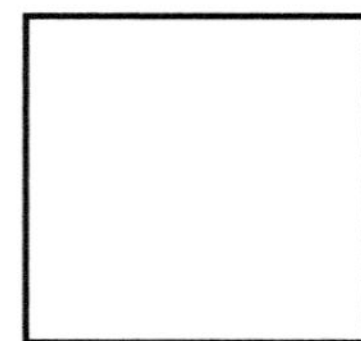 

Color a quarter ($\frac{1}{4}$) of each shape.

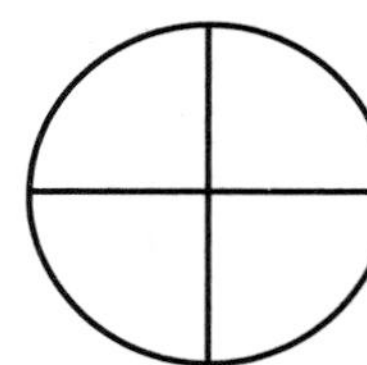 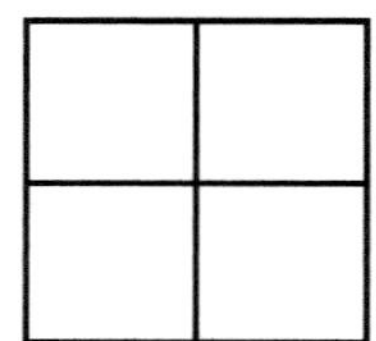 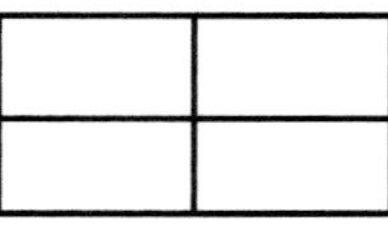

Now color a quarter ($\frac{1}{4}$) of each shape in a different way.

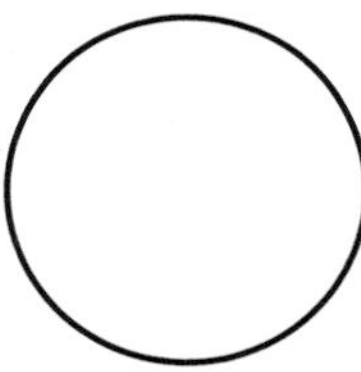 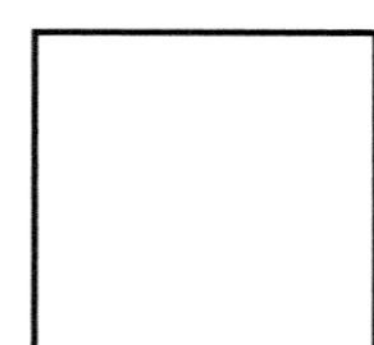 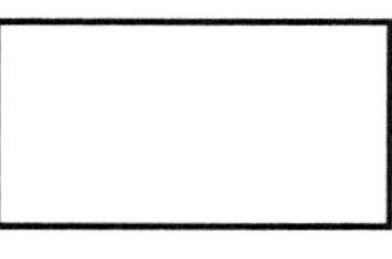

What fraction of each shape is shaded?

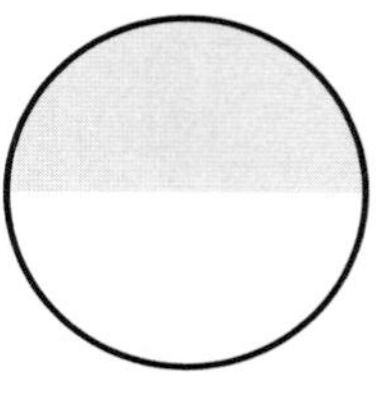  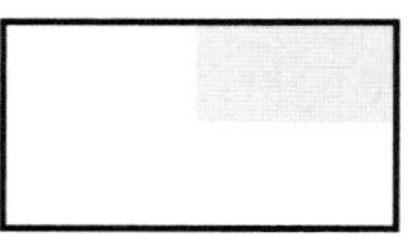

 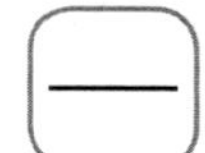 

What is a half ($\frac{1}{2}$) of each number?

10	12	14	16	18	20
5					

What is half ($\frac{1}{2}$) of each amount?

5 ¢

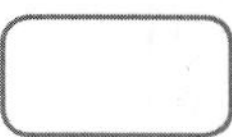

How much is half ($\frac{1}{2}$) of $1.00?

Amy runs 4 miles but Dan runs half ($\frac{1}{2}$) as far. How far does Dan run?

Rajid has to work for one hour but stops halfway. How long is half an hour in minutes?

Using Symbols

< This symbol means less than.
> This symbol means greater than.
= This symbol means equal to or the same as.
Hint: The open end always faces the larger number.

Fill in the boxes with the correct symbol.

56  43

33 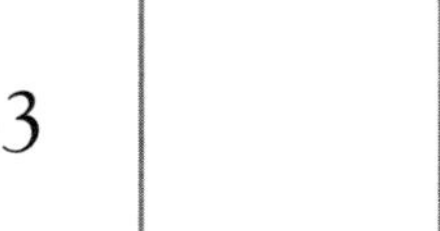 54

15  20

1  4

8  5

26  25

12  12

13  17

Count forward from 109 to 120.

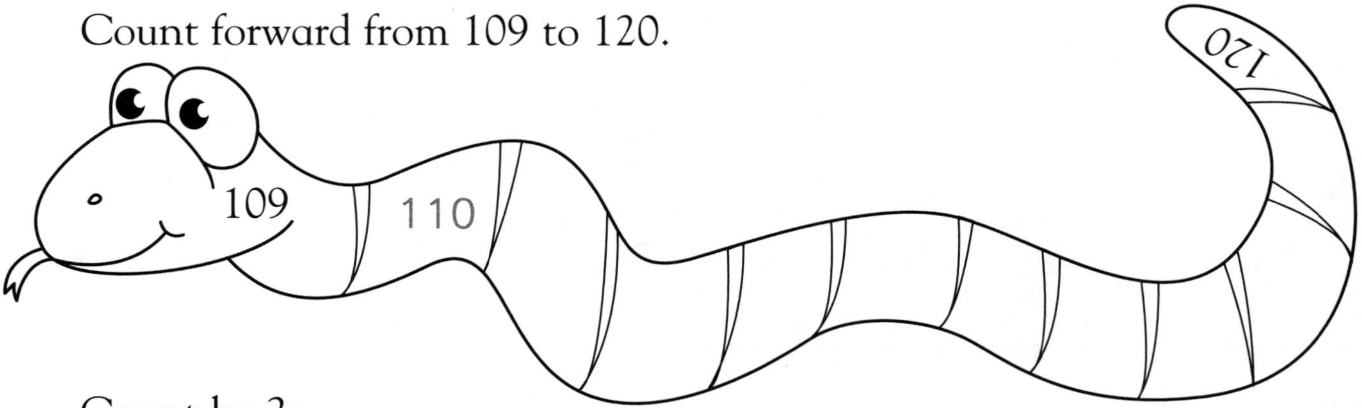

109 110 120

Count by 2s.

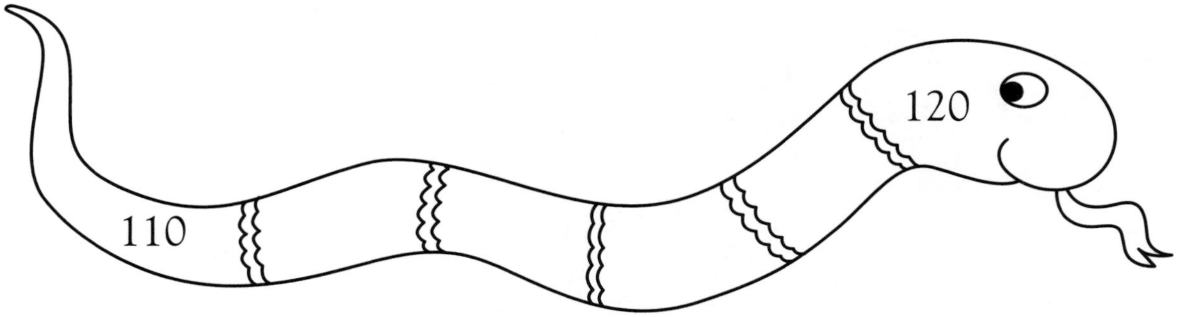

110 120

Count by 5s.

85 120

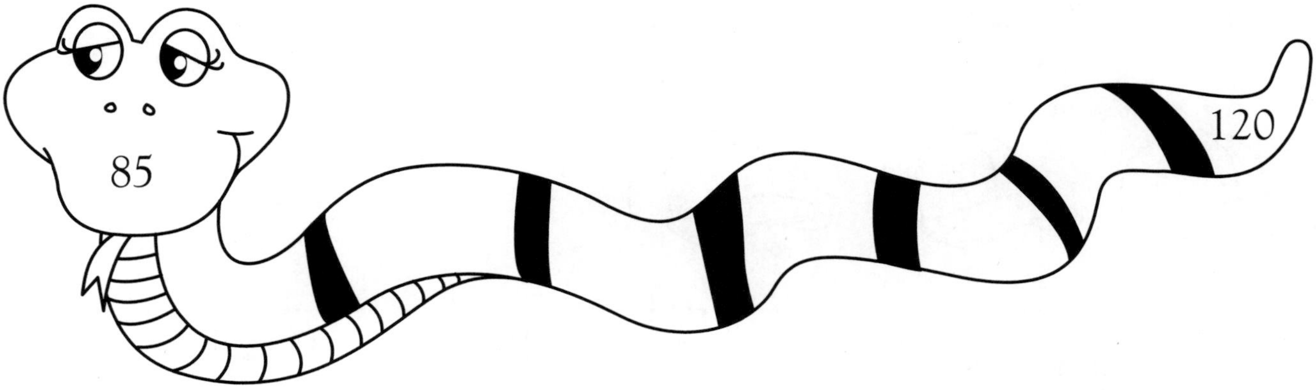

Count backward in 10s from 100 to 0.

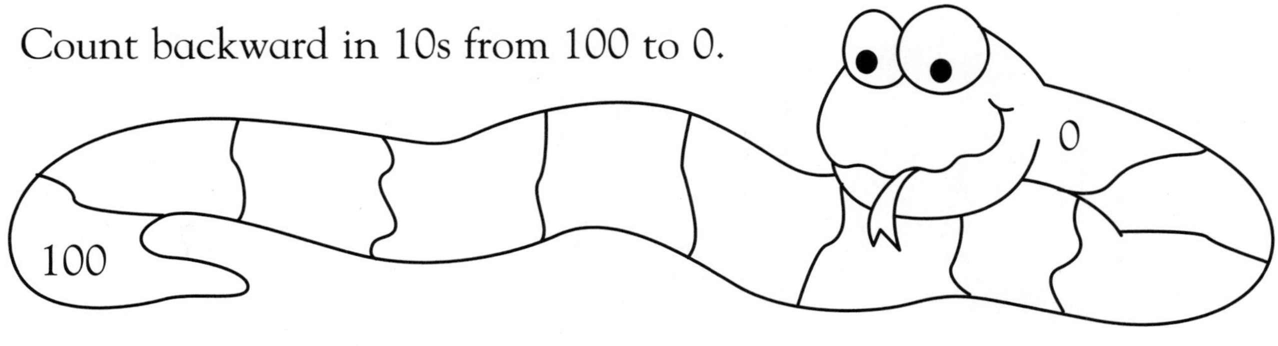

100 0

Adding Up

How many in each row?

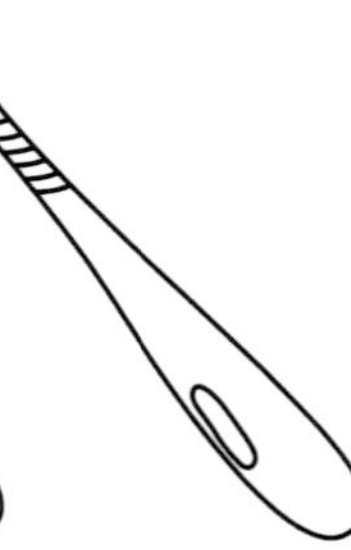
+
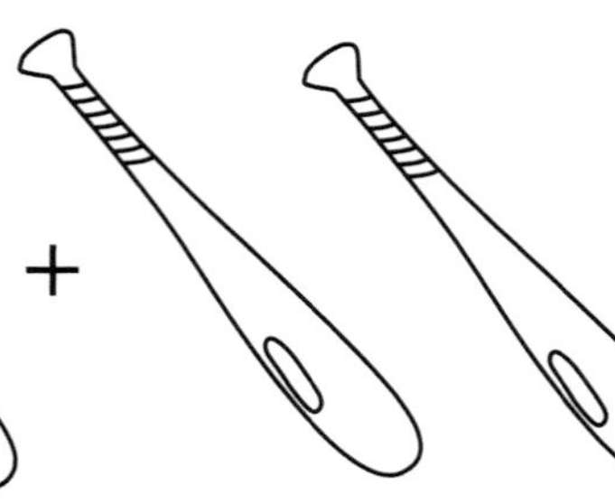
= 6

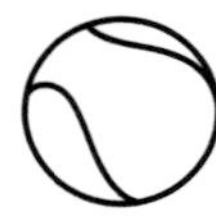

+

=

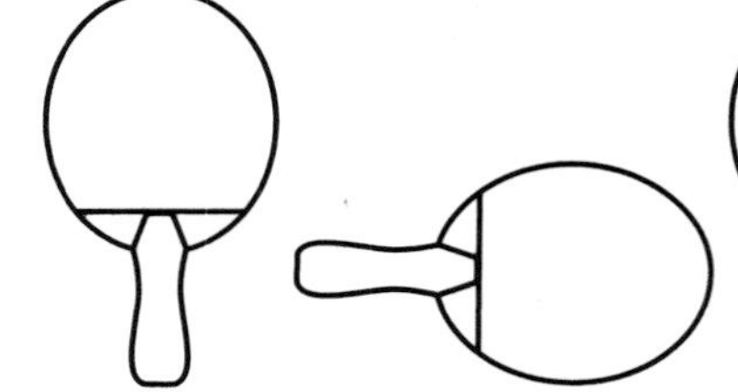
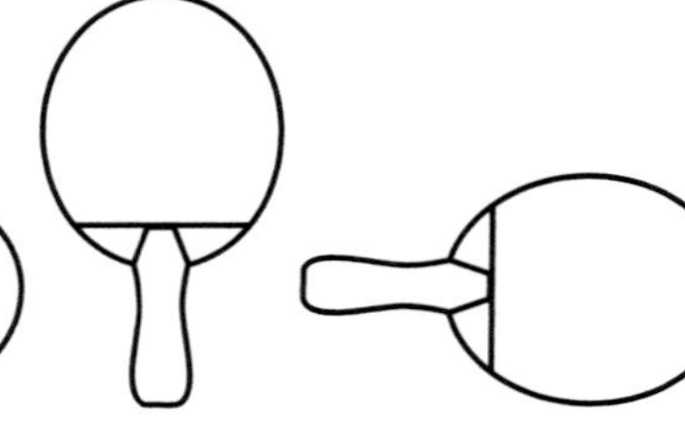
+

=

+

=

Complete each sum.

3 + 1 =	5 + 4 =	7 + 3 =
8 + 0 =	9 + 2 =	10 + 4 =
4 + 8 =	6 + 9 =	13 + 6 =
10 + 10 =	17 + 2 =	4 + 13 =

How many more to make 10?

+ [6] birds

+ [ ] birds

+ [ ] owls

+ [ ] birds

What number is missing?

3 + [ ] = 10

9 + [ ] = 10

[ ] + 5 = 10

[ ] + 6 = 10

4 + [ ] + 5 = 10

[ ] + 3 + 3 = 10

8 + 0 + [ ] = 10

1 + 2 + [ ] = 10

Reduce each amount by 3. **Hint:** Cross out (**X**) 3 and count how many are left.

Make each amount smaller by 2. **Hint:** Cross out (**X**) 2 to help you.

Lessen each amount by 4. **Hint:** Cross out (**X**) 4 to help you.

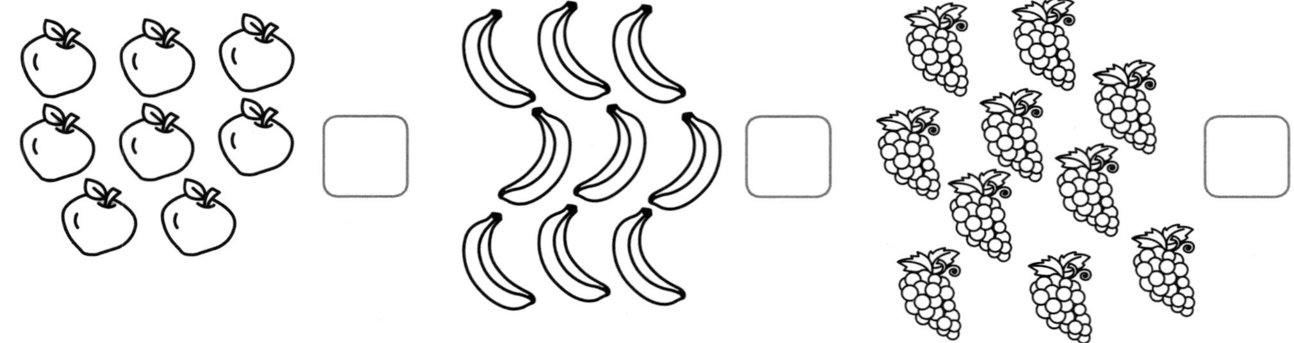

Solve each problem.

10 – 5 = ☐ 9 – 6 = ☐ 12 – 3 = ☐

14 – 10 = ☐ 12 – 12 = ☐ 10 – 8 = ☐

How many are left?

Take 2 dots away from each cap.

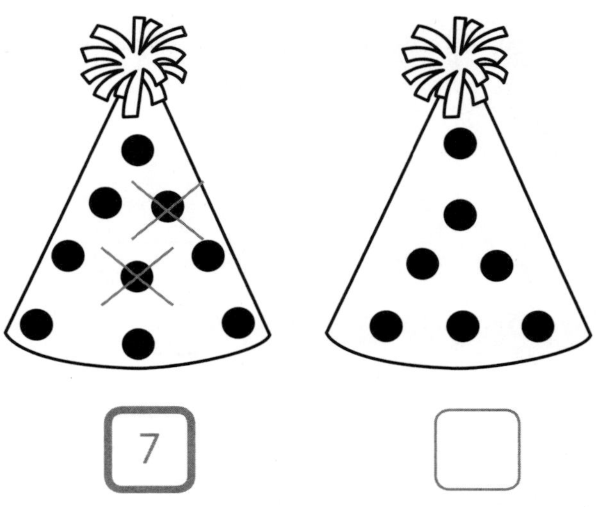

Take 3 candles away from each cake.

Take 4 balloons away from each bunch.

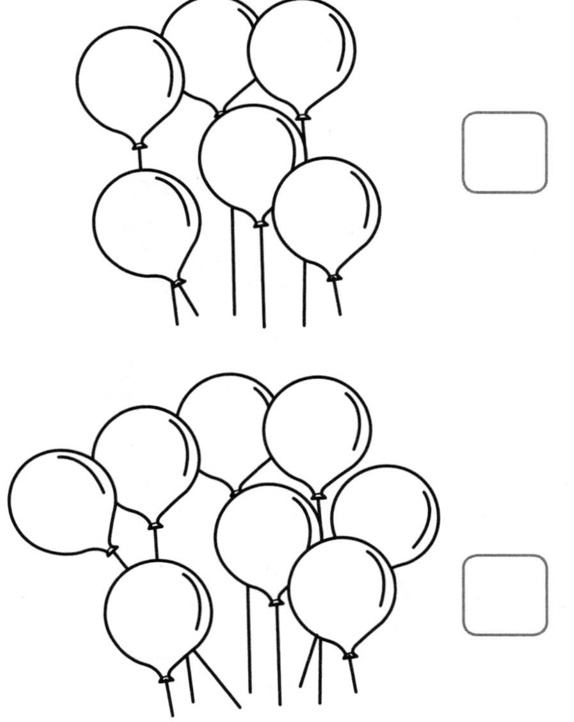

Take 5 presents away from each pile.

Doubles

What is double each number?

2 [4]   3 [ ]   4 [ ]   5 [ ]

1 [ ]   6 [ ]   7 [ ]   8 [ ]

Double each amount.

5¢ [ ]   2¢ [ ]   10¢ [ ]   20¢ [ ]

1¢ [ ]   4¢ [ ]   6¢ [ ]   11¢ [ ]

What were these numbers before they were doubled?

12 [ ]   10 [ ]   8 [ ]   6 [ ]

10¢ [ ]   20¢ [ ]   12¢ [ ]   14¢ [ ]

Try and double these larger numbers.

30 [ ]   40 [ ]   50 [ ]   100 [ ]

15¢ [ ]   25¢ [ ]   60¢ [ ] $6.00 [ ]

Count in groups and write how many.

+ + + = 8

+ + =

+ =

+ =

Now solve these to find each total.

2 groups of 4 =

3 groups of 5 =

4 groups of 3 =

7 groups of 2 =

More Groups

Count in groups and write how many.
Complete the number sentences.

 +  = 12

2 groups of 6 fish = 12

 +  = ☐

☐ groups of ☐ octopuses = ☐

 +  +  = ☐

☐ groups of ☐ crabs = ☐

 +   = ☐

☐ groups of ☐ turtles = ☐

How many paperclips-long is the pencil? 5

How many rulers-tall is the child?

How many shoe boxes-long is the bed?

How many book-lengths is the table?

Keeping Skills Sharp

Molly is going on vacation and can only pack half of her T-shirts.

Cross out (**X**) half of the T-shirts.

Fatima and Nima put their pet mice together.

Fatima has 8 mice and Nima has 6 mice.
How many mice do they have altogether?

Write the answers.

3 + 4 = ☐ 6 + 2 = ☐ 5 + 5 = ☐ 9 + 3 = ☐

10 – 2 = ☐ 8 – 7 = ☐ 5 – 4 = ☐ 3 – 3 = ☐

Fill in the box with the right symbol: <, >, or = .

32 ☐ 12 15 ☐ 15 17 ☐ 21

Clara has a bag with 9 candies.

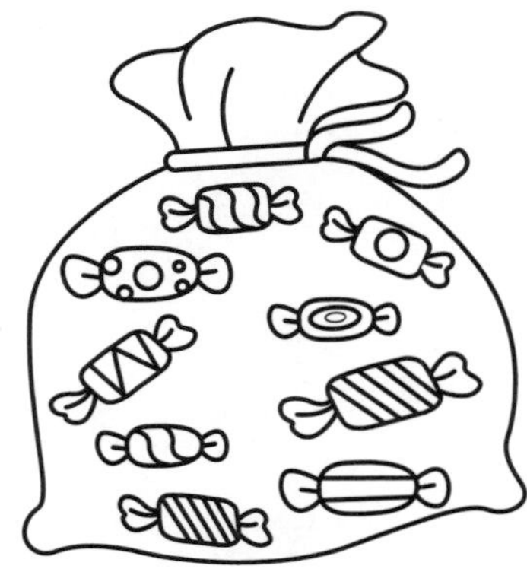

Olly has a bag with 6 candies.

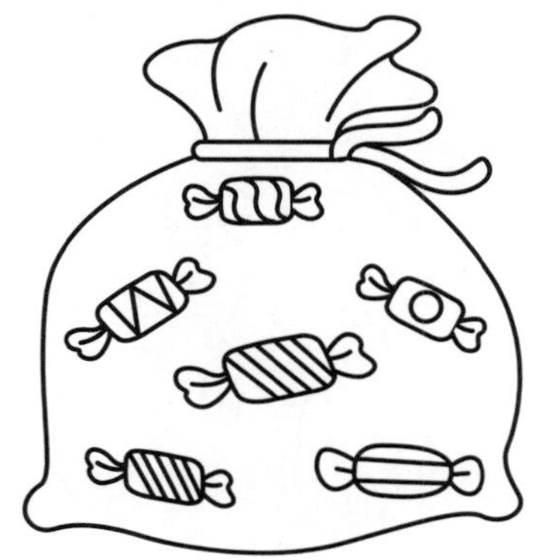

How many more candies does Clara have than Olly? ☐

How many?

Comparing Money

What is the value of each coin?

1 ¢

Draw the coins that make the same amount.

=

=

=

=

=

=

Add the amounts.

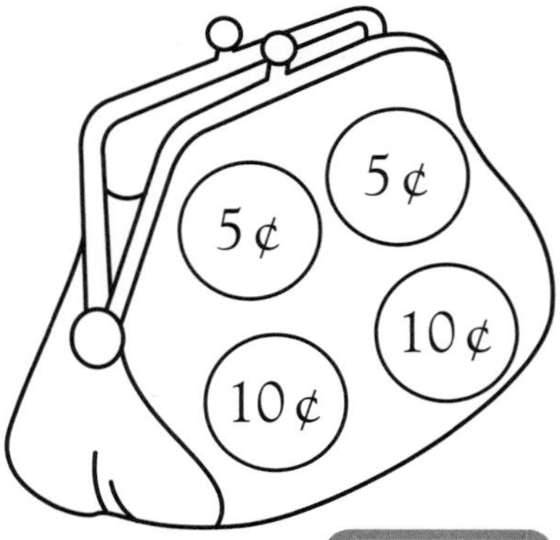

30 ¢

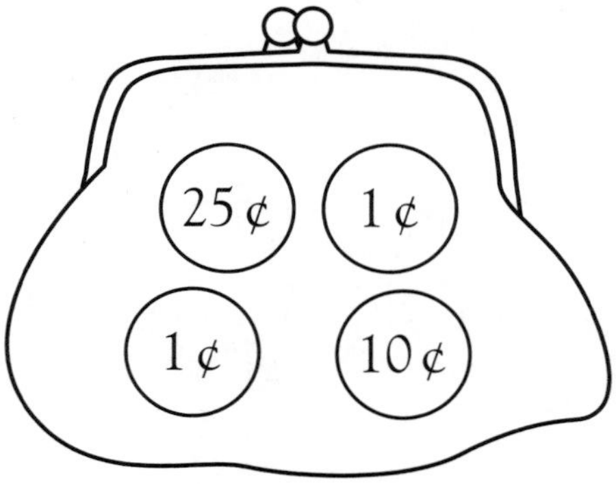

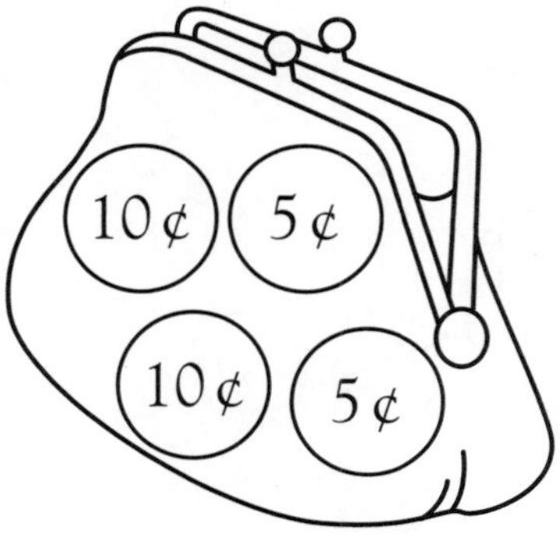

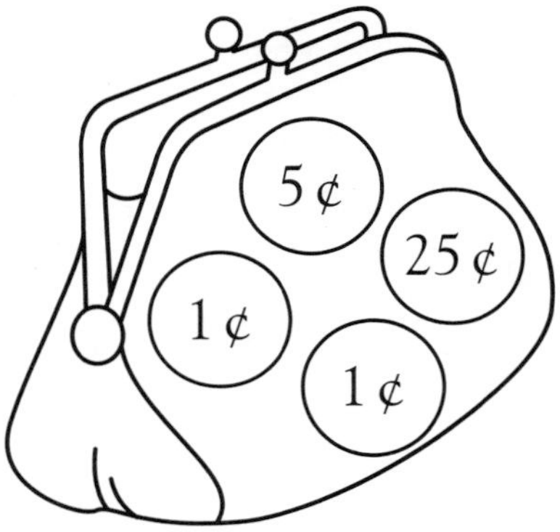

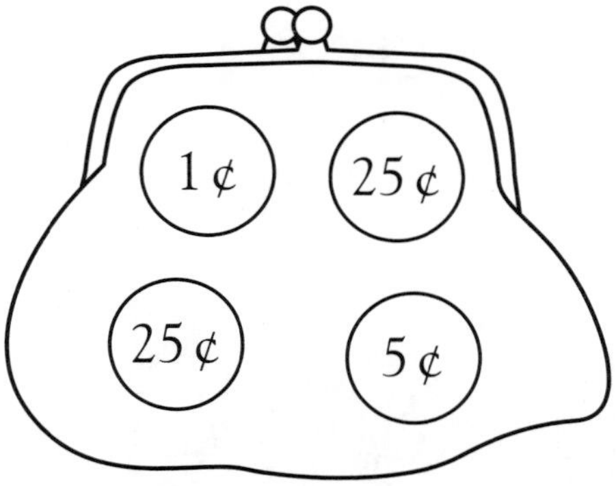

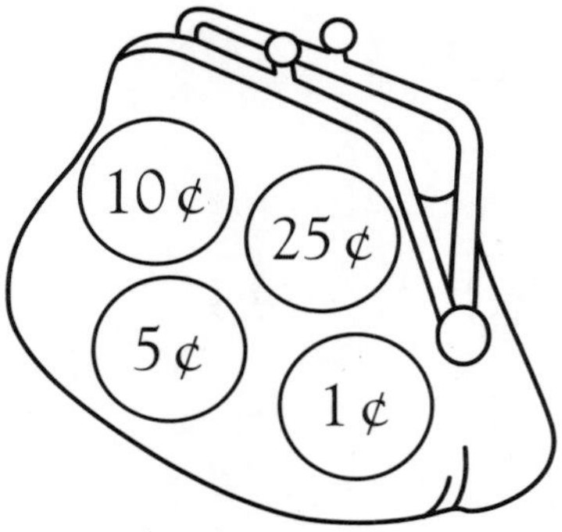

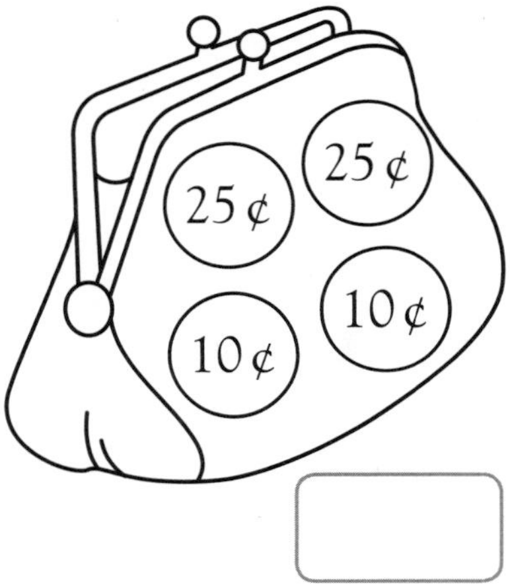

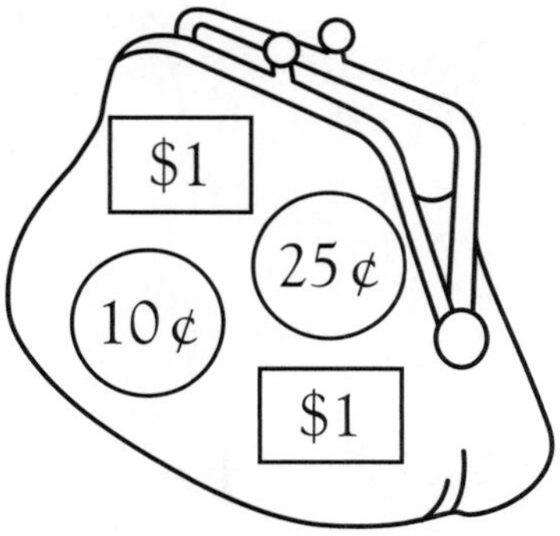

How Much Change?

How much change?

I pay 

my change = 18¢

I pay 

my change = ☐

I pay 

my change = ☐

I pay 

my change = ☐

I pay 

my change = ☐

Who has the most money? ....

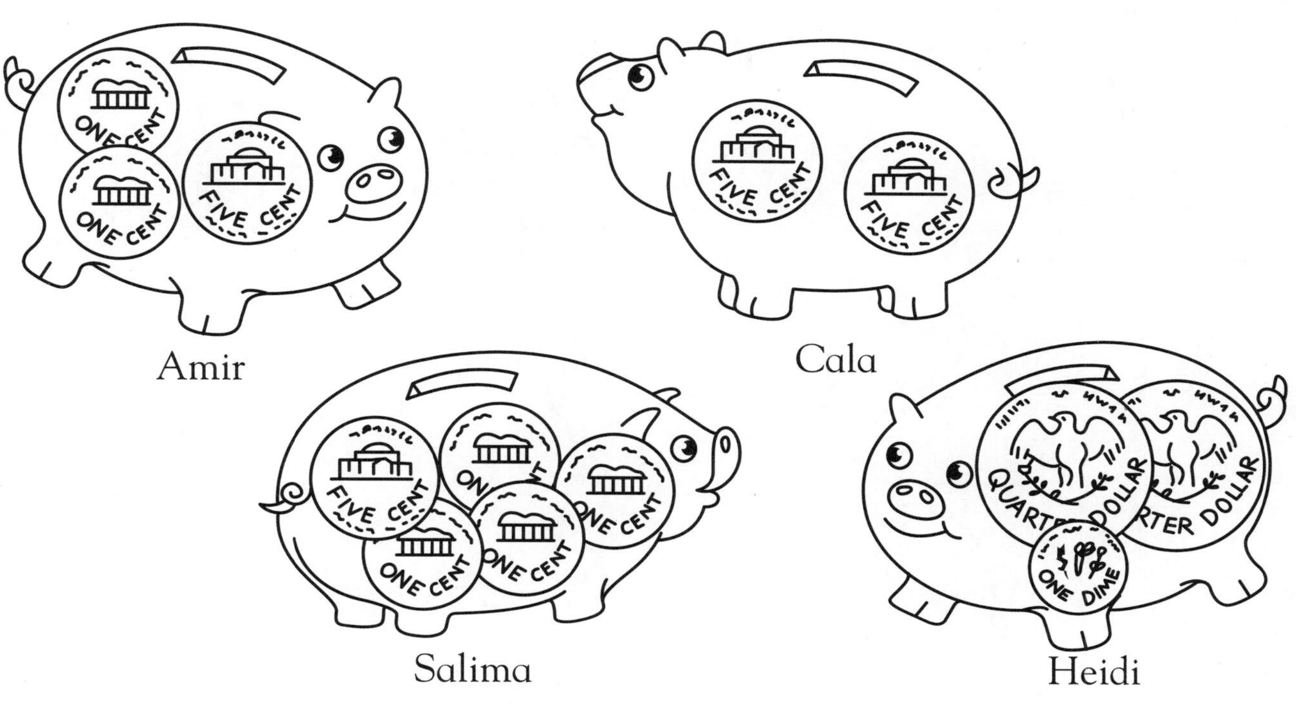

Who has the least money? ....

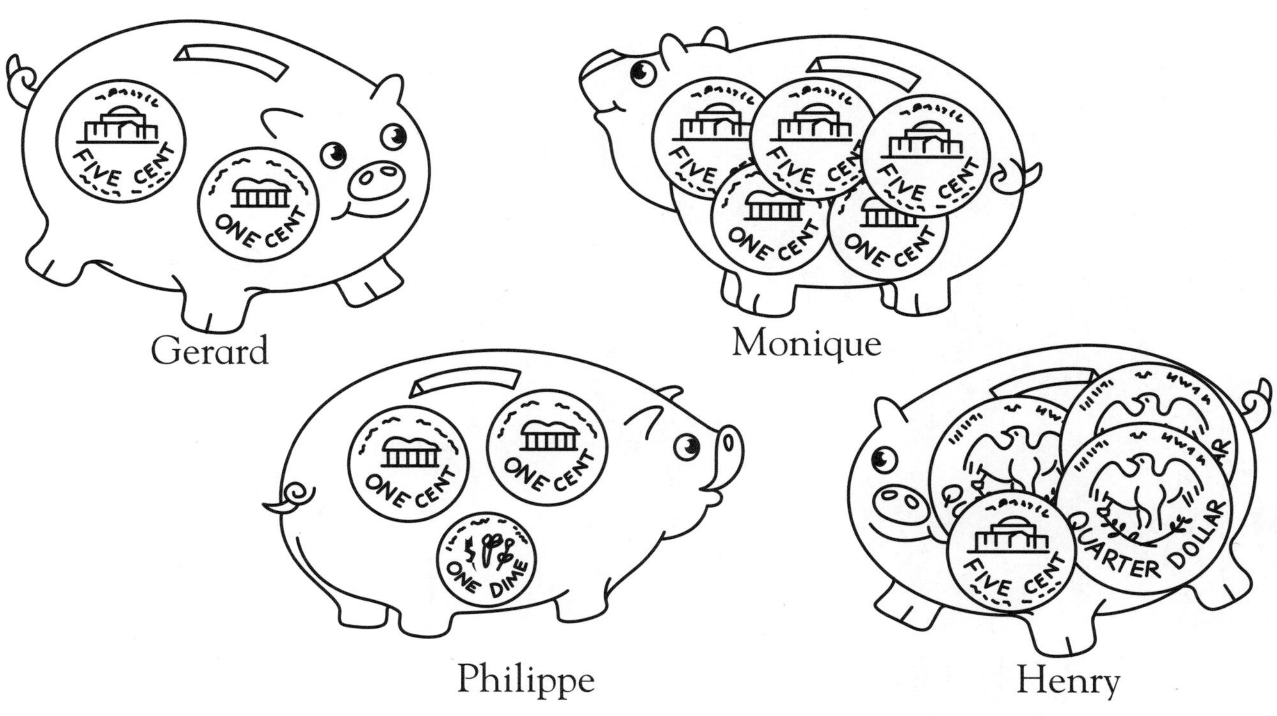

Comparing Sizes

Circle the largest animal in each group.

Circle the smallest animal in each group.

Circle the animal that is the tallest.

Circle the caterpillar that is the longest.

Put these in order from the youngest (1) to the oldest (4).

1

Clock Faces

What time is it?

3 o'clock

Draw the time on each clock.

3 o'clock

7 o'clock

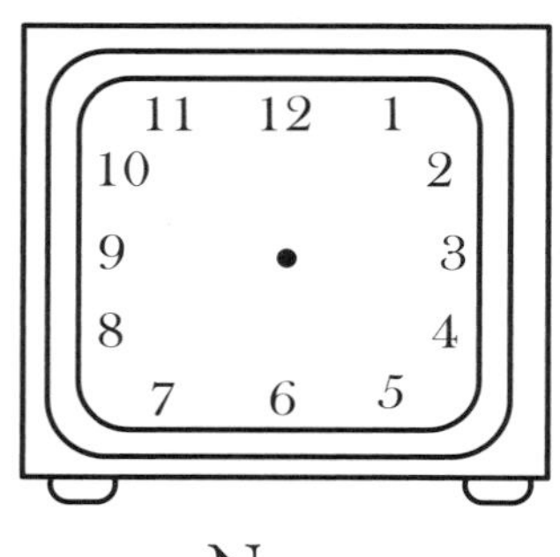

Noon

Draw the time on each clock.

1 o'clock

5 o'clock

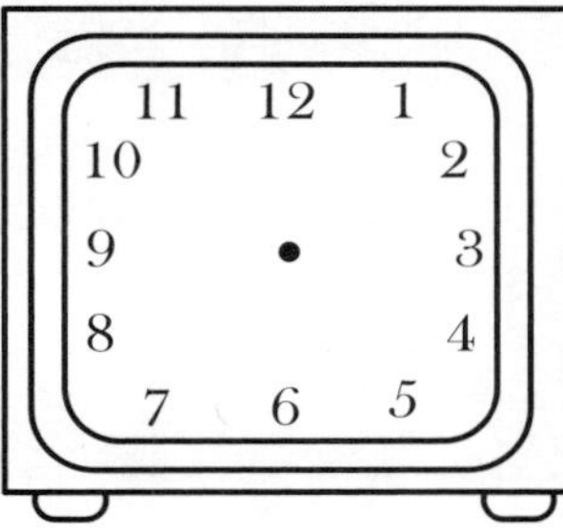

9 o'clock

2 o'clock

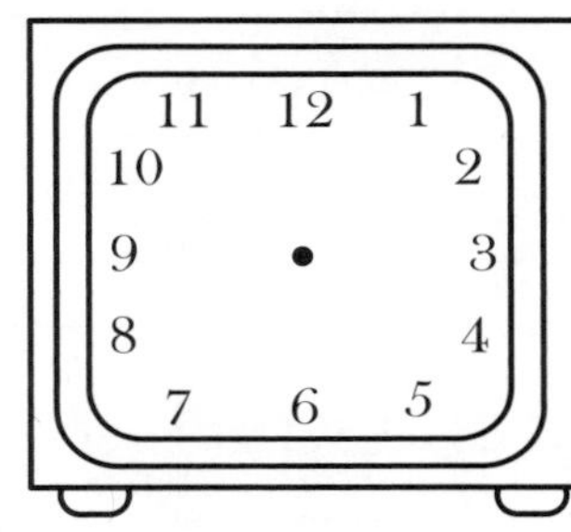

4 o'clock

6 o'clock

Midnight

10 o'clock

8 o'clock

How long between these times?

....

....

Days and Seasons

Which day comes before and which day comes after?

Yesterday	Today	Tomorrow
Monday	Tuesday	Wednesday
	Thursday	
	Monday	
	Saturday	
	Wednesday	
	Sunday	
	Friday	

Which season comes before and which season comes after?

Before	Now	After
	Spring	
	Summer	
	Fall	
	Winter	

Answer these questions.

In which season is Christmas?

In which season do most flowers begin to grow?

In which season do most trees lose their leaves?

Which equations are true and which are false?
Mark each of them with a T for True or an F for False.

$8 = 8$ T

$3 + 4 = 4 + 3$ ☐

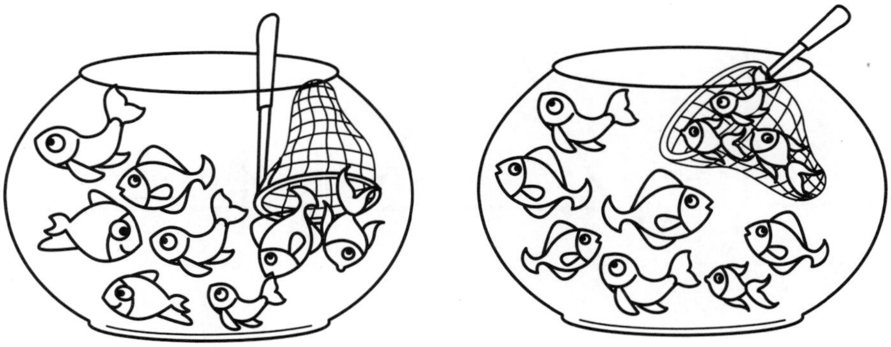

$5 + 3 = 10 - 3$ ☐

$7 = 8 - 2$ ☐

2-D Shapes

Circle the shapes with three sides and cross out (**X**) the shapes with four corners.

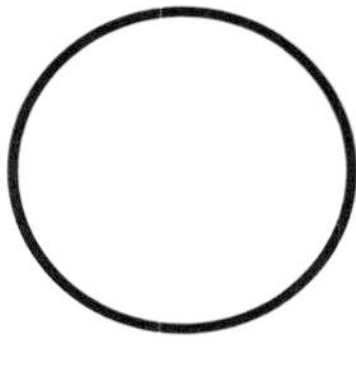  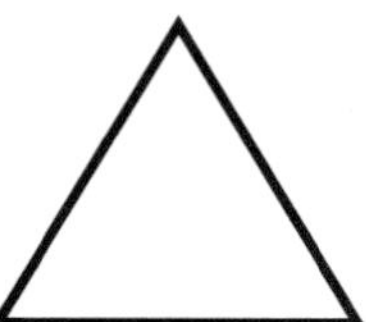 

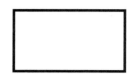

  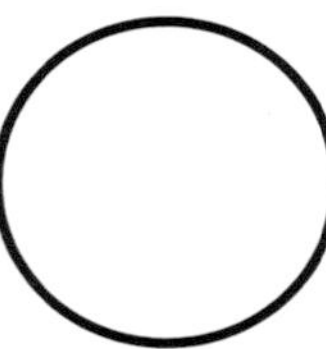 

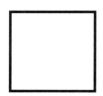

Connect the name to the shape.

Triangle Square Rectangle Circle

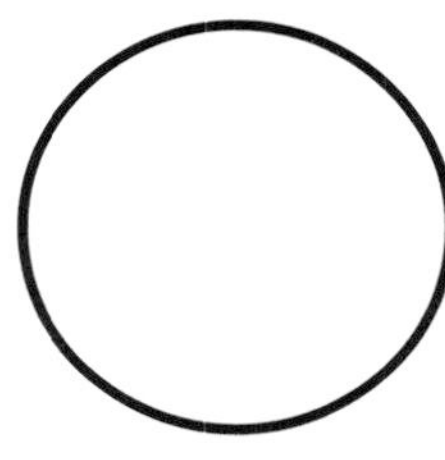 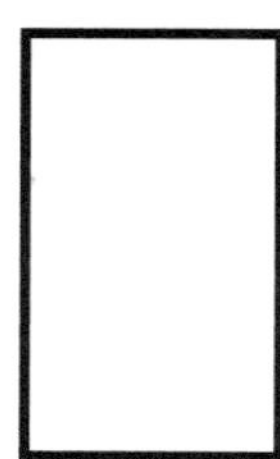  

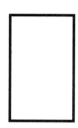

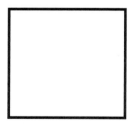

Draw each of these.

Rectangle Square Circle Triangle

Draw the other half.

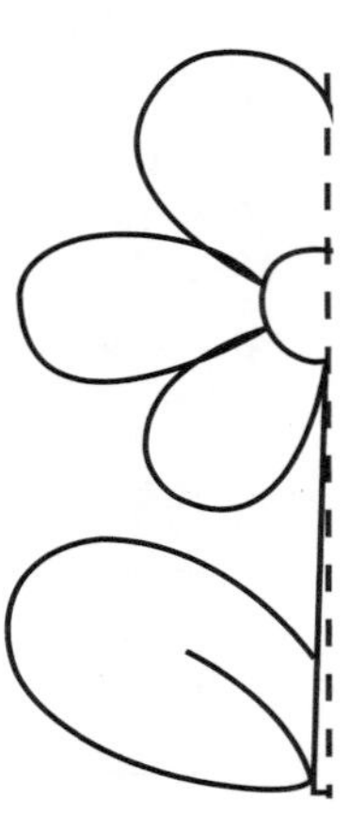

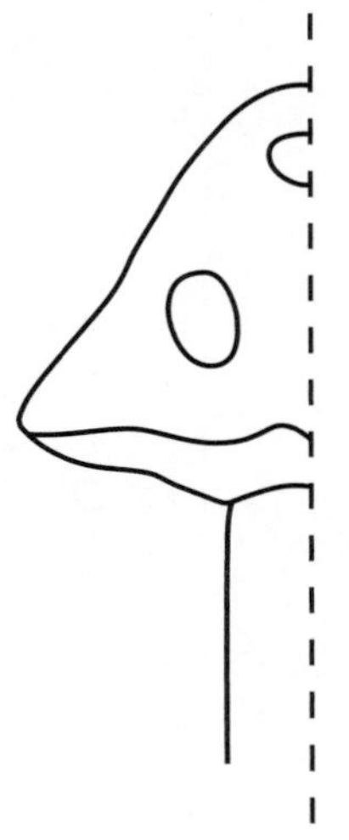

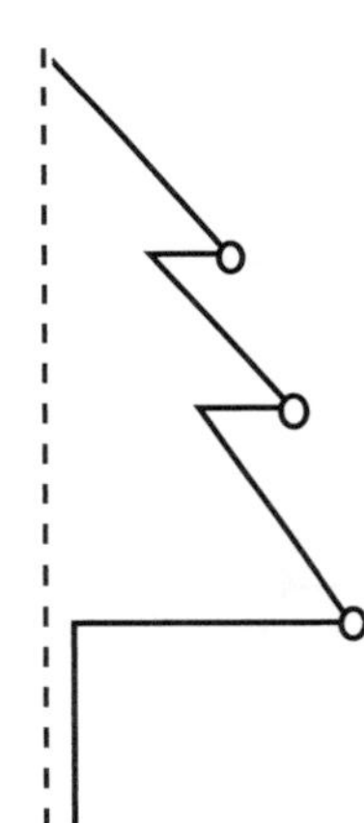

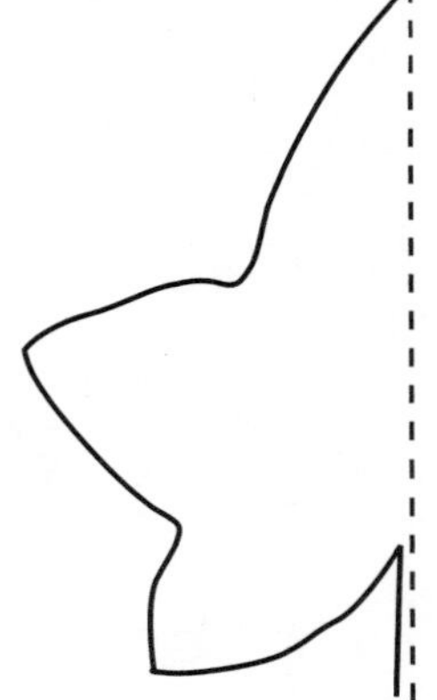

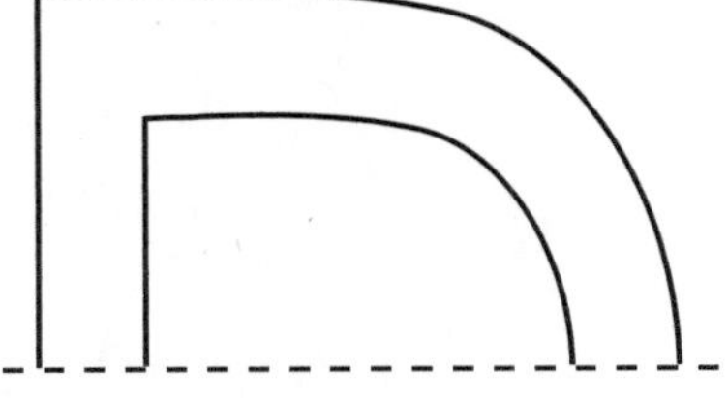

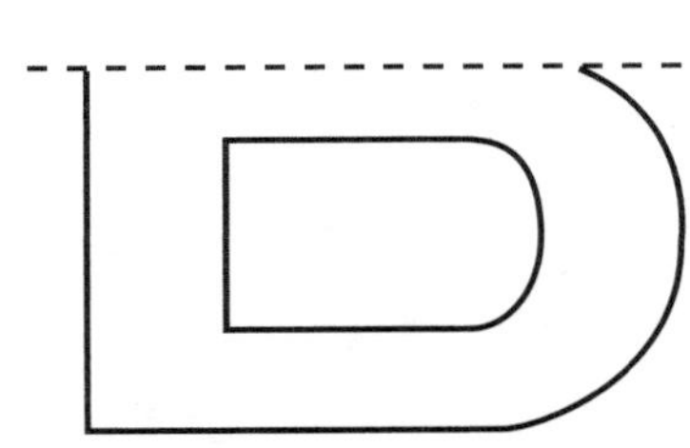

3-D Shapes

Circle the cubes and cross out (**X**) the shapes with curved faces.

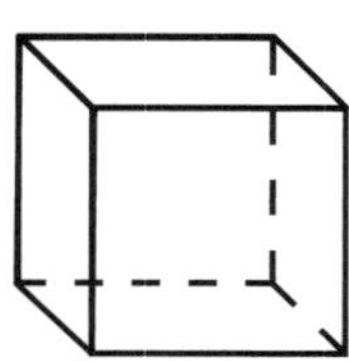  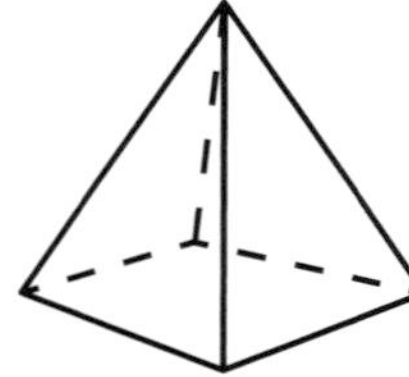 

  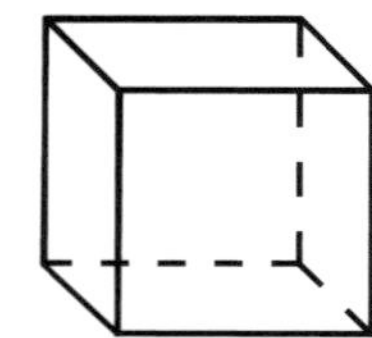 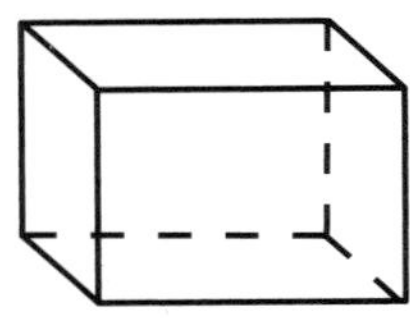

Connect the name to its shape.

Sphere Cone Cube Rectangular prism

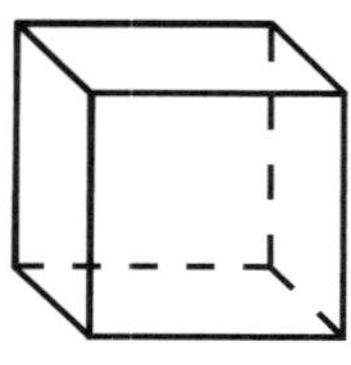  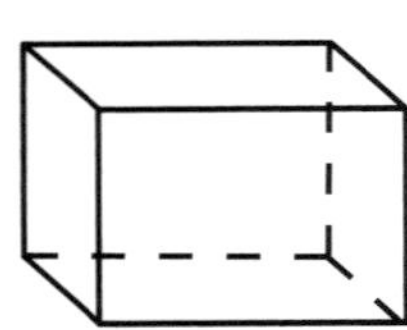 

Draw these shapes as well as you can.

Pyramid Cube Rectangular prism Sphere

Look at the picture.

What is sitting **on** the car? ....

What is **under** the car? ....

What is **in front** of the car? ....

What is **above** the car? ....

What is **between** the birds?

....

What is **inside** the pitcher?

....

Draw a pencil **next to** the notebook.

Draw a dog **outside** the house.

Three children put their money together to buy some fruit.

How much do the children have altogether?

Natasha buys an orange with a 25 ¢ coin.

How much change will Natasha receive?

Pine Bonsai Apple Giant Redwood

Which is the tallest tree?

Which is the shortest tree?

This is the time now.

Darius will go on vacation in four hours.

Draw the time on the clock when Darius goes on vacation.

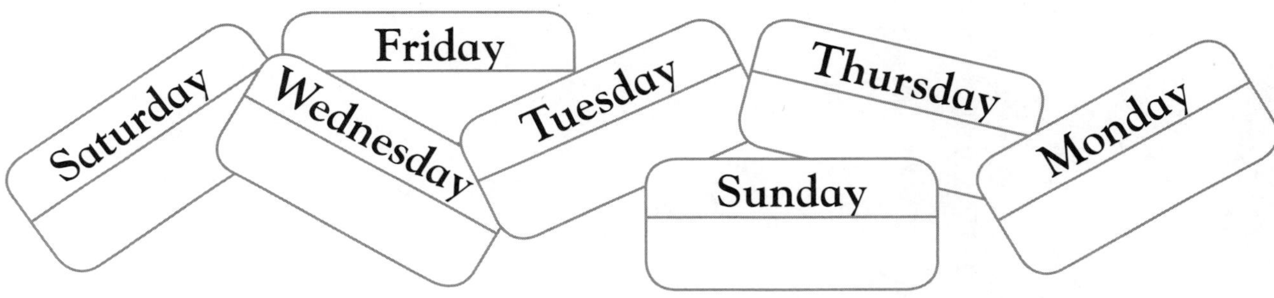

Which are the normal school days?

....

....

Which are the weekend days?

....

Circle the equations that are true.

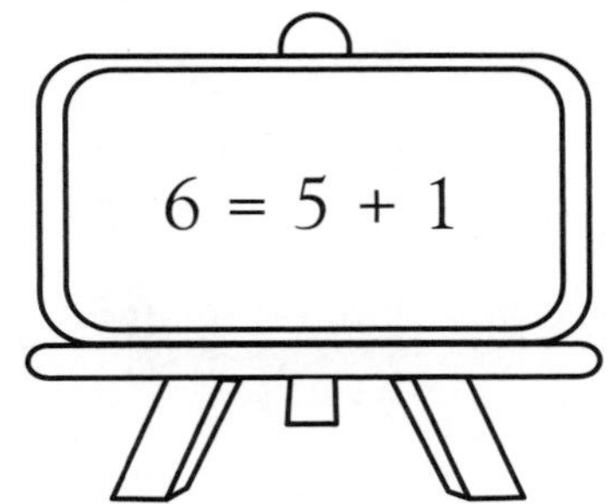

Tens and Ones (Place Value)

GOAL

Learn about groups of tens and ones.

1 ten

3 ones

How many ladybugs are there? **Remember:** First count how many groups of ten there are, then count the ones that are left.

= ☐ tens and ☐ ones

= ☐ tens and ☐ ones

= ☐ tens and ☐ ones

How many ants are there? Circle a group of ten, then count the ants that are left over. Write your answer in terms of tens and ones.

Tens	Ones

GOAL

Learn to find groups of tens and ones.

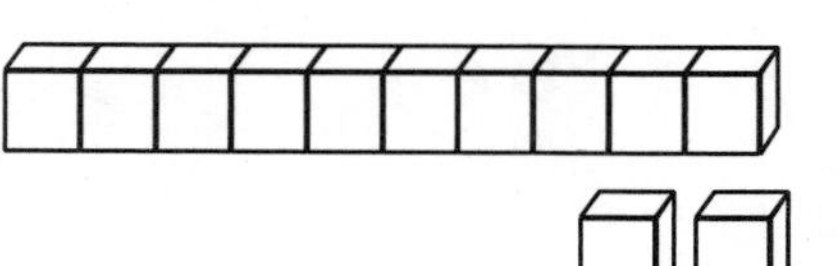

Tens	Ones
1	2

= 12

For each problem, count the number of groups of ten blocks, and write that number under "tens." Then count how many blocks are left, and write that number under "ones." How many total blocks are there in each problem?

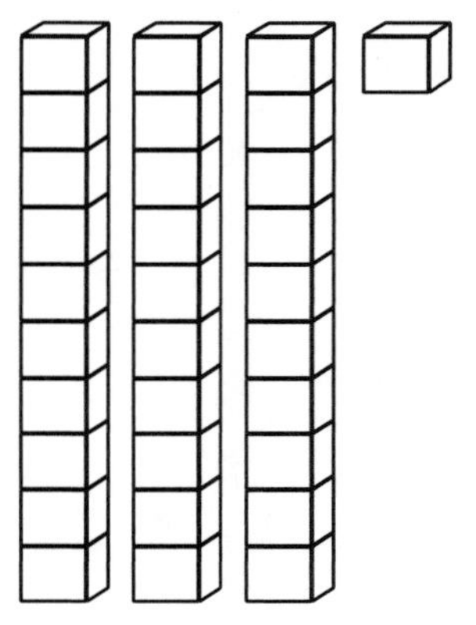

Tens	Ones

=

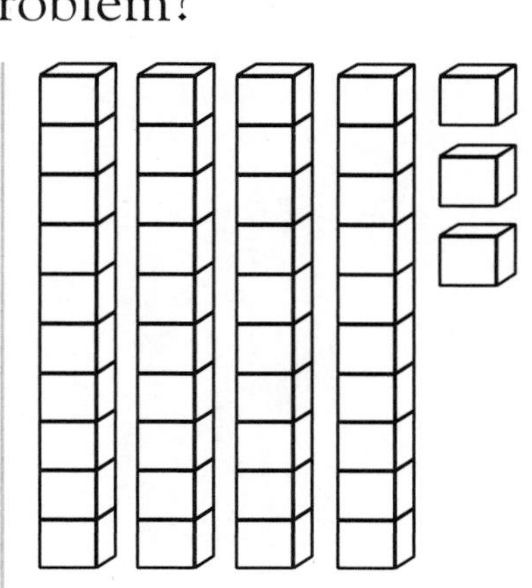

Tens	Ones

=

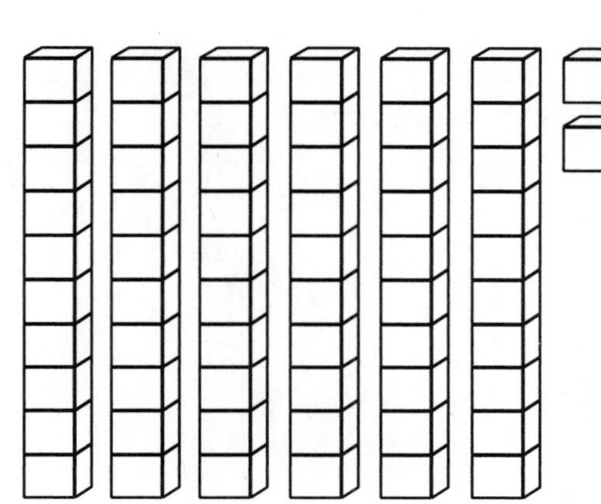

Tens	Ones

=

Fill in the boxes and write the correct number.

	Tens		Ones		Number
2 tens and 8 ones =		+		=	
9 tens and 4 ones =		+		=	
3 tens and 6 ones =		+		=	

Write these numbers as tens and ones.

20 = ☐ tens and ☐ ones

72 = ☐ tens and ☐ ones

35 = ☐ tens and ☐ ones

17 = ☐ tens and ☐ ones

Show One More

GOAL

Learn about adding one more to a number.

5 + 1 = 6

In each row, first count the smiley faces, then draw one more. How many are in each row now? Write the total number.

    + = 

☺ ☺ + = 

☺ + = 

Complete the chart.

Starting Number	Add One More	New Number
9	1	
6	1	
4	1	
5	1	

Add the two groups of hearts. Write the total in the box.

♡ ♡ ♡ ♡ ♡ ♡ ♡ + ♡ =

Find out how to subtract one from a number.

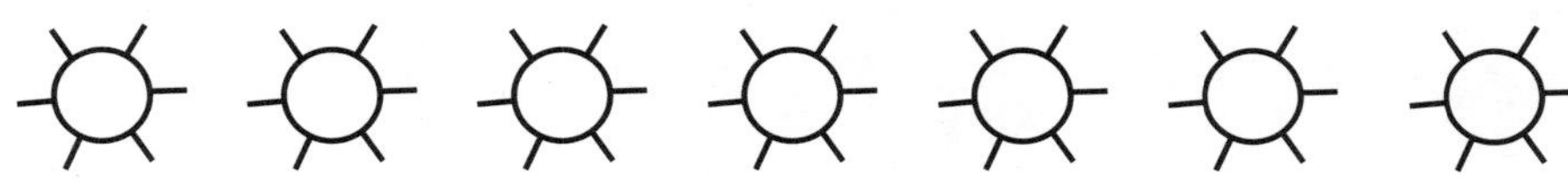

5 – 1 = 4

Count the number of objects in each row. Then cross out (**X**) one. How many are there now?

7 – 1 = ☐

9 – 1 = ☐

Look at the pictures in each column. Circle the picture that shows one less.

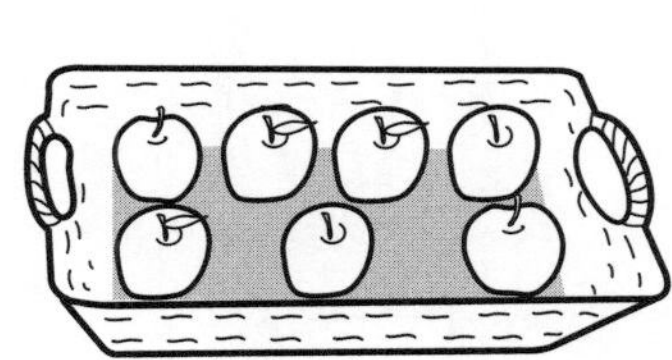

Subtract one from the group of stars below.
Write the subtraction sentence.

☐ – ☐ = ☐

Find Ten More

GOAL

Learn to add ten to a number. 3 add ten = 13

Look at the puzzle pieces. Add ten to each number on the left. Then draw a line from each puzzle piece on the left to its matching number + ten on the right.
Remember: The number on the right must be ten more than the number on the left.

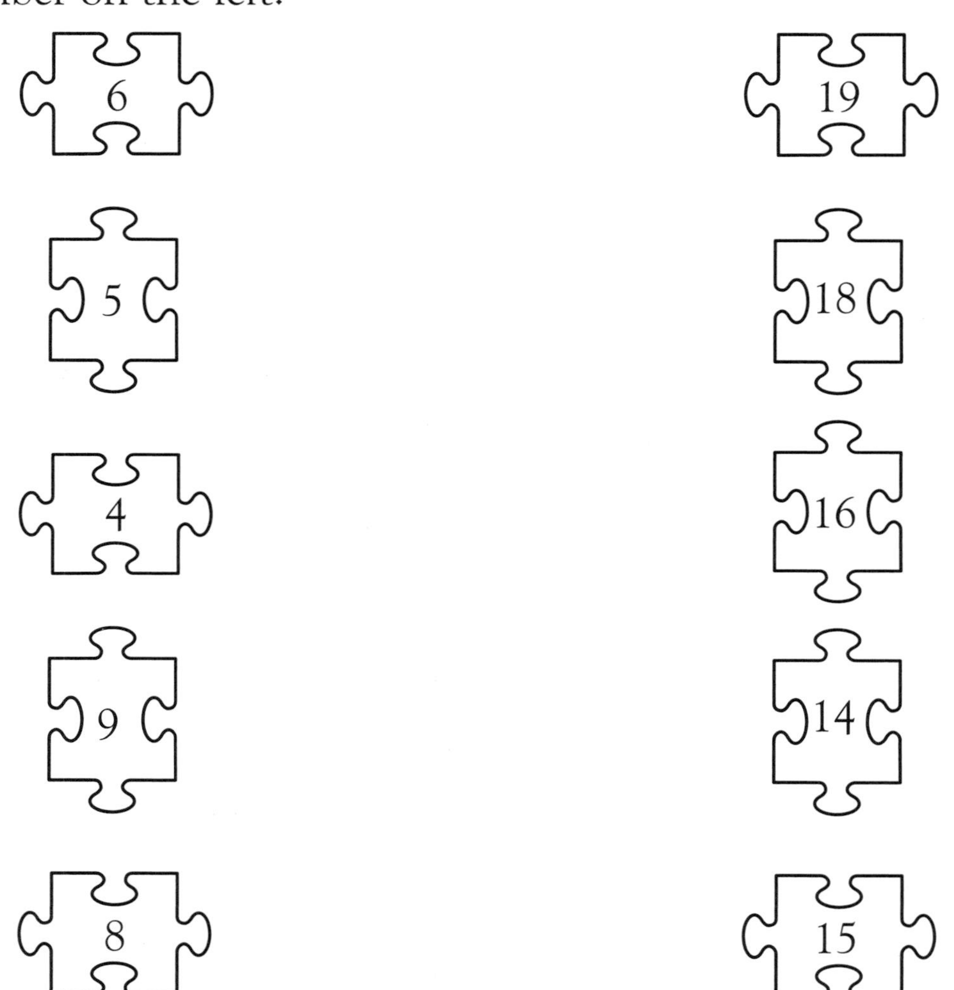

How many groups of ten are there in each number below? Write the answer in the box.

12  35  26 

Find Ten Less ★

GOAL

Learn to subtract ten from a number. 15 subtract ten = 5

Subtract ten from each number in the left column. Then write the subtraction sentence and the answer in the right column.

32 subtract ten	___ = ___
28 subtract ten	___ = ___
25 subtract ten	___ = ___
56 subtract ten	___ = ___
21 subtract ten	___ = ___
36 subtract ten	___ = ___
44 subtract ten	___ = ___
18 subtract ten	___ = ___
68 subtract ten	___ = ___
95 subtract ten	___ = ___

Finish the pattern. Write the number that is ten less each time.

50 40  ___ 10 

Adding Up to 10

GOAL

Learn how to add up to 10.

Read the addition sentences in each row. Then color the flowers using two colors to show the addition sentence.

6 + 4 = 10

8 + 2 = 10

7 + 3 = 10

2 + 8 = 10

3 + 7 = 10

4 + 6 = 10

9 + 1 = 10

5 + 5 = 10

Complete these addition sentences by writing the missing number.

4 + ☐ = 10 ☐ + 2 = 10 3 + 7 = ☐

GOAL

Practice your addition skills.

+ = 20

Help the clown reach the circus tent. First add each number sentence. Then follow the path of the number sentences with answers that are twenty or less.

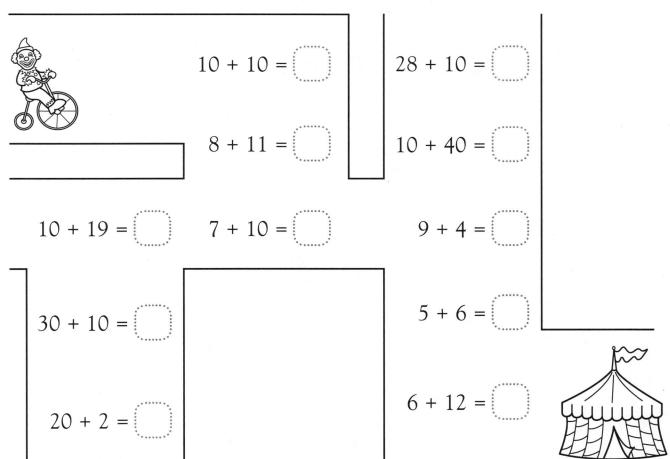

10 + 10 =

28 + 10 =

8 + 11 =

10 + 40 =

10 + 19 =

7 + 10 =

9 + 4 =

30 + 10 =

5 + 6 =

20 + 2 =

6 + 12 =

Draw groups of clown hats to show this number sentence: 3 + 3 = 6.

=

Subtraction from 0 to 10

GOAL

Learn how to subtract with numbers between 0 and 10.

5 − 3 = 2

Look at the groups of fruit in each row. Then write the answer for each subtraction sentence.

7 − 3 =

      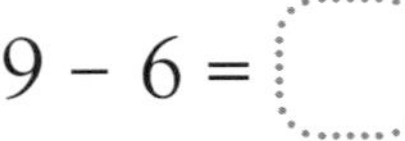

9 − 6 =

       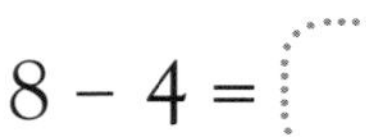

8 − 4 =

        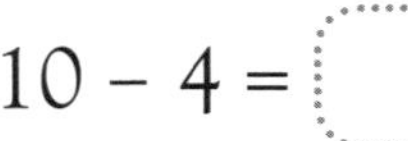

10 − 4 =

    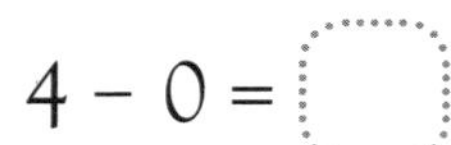

4 − 0 =

Joan counted six oranges in her bowl. She ate two. How many oranges were left?

Write the number sentence.

Practice your subtraction skills.

$$\begin{array}{r} 16 \\ -\ 6 \\ \hline 10 \end{array}$$

Subtract and write the answers in each row.

$$\begin{array}{r} 15 \\ -\ 4 \\ \hline \end{array} \quad \begin{array}{r} 29 \\ -\ 6 \\ \hline \end{array} \quad \begin{array}{r} 18 \\ -\ 5 \\ \hline \end{array} \quad \begin{array}{r} 16 \\ -\ 4 \\ \hline \end{array} \quad \begin{array}{r} 12 \\ -\ 2 \\ \hline \end{array} \quad \begin{array}{r} 19 \\ -\ 3 \\ \hline \end{array}$$

$$\begin{array}{r} 10 \\ -\ 7 \\ \hline \end{array} \quad \begin{array}{r} 9 \\ -\ 5 \\ \hline \end{array} \quad \begin{array}{r} 39 \\ -\ 4 \\ \hline \end{array} \quad \begin{array}{r} 20 \\ -\ 10 \\ \hline \end{array} \quad \begin{array}{r} 16 \\ -\ 8 \\ \hline \end{array} \quad \begin{array}{r} 56 \\ -\ 6 \\ \hline \end{array}$$

$$\begin{array}{r} 14 \\ -\ 7 \\ \hline \end{array} \quad \begin{array}{r} 9 \\ -\ 6 \\ \hline \end{array} \quad \begin{array}{r} 60 \\ -\ 30 \\ \hline \end{array} \quad \begin{array}{r} 89 \\ -\ 9 \\ \hline \end{array} \quad \begin{array}{r} 18 \\ -\ 15 \\ \hline \end{array} \quad \begin{array}{r} 58 \\ -\ 8 \\ \hline \end{array}$$

Read each story. Then write the answer for each subtraction problem.

Juan had thirteen crayons.
He broke two crayons. How many of his crayons were not broken?

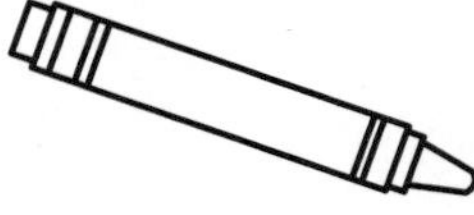

$13 - 2 = \square$

We saw twenty-five bunnies.
Four bunnies ran away.
How many bunnies were left?

$25 - 4 = \square$

Jen made nineteen cupcakes.
She gave away six cupcakes.
How many cupcakes were left?

$19 - 6 = \square$

Seeing Shapes

GOAL

Learn to find the shapes that are alike.

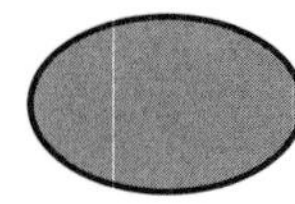 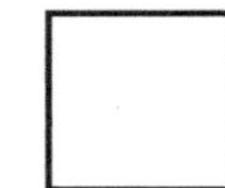 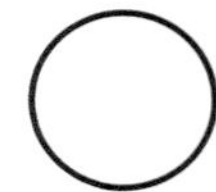  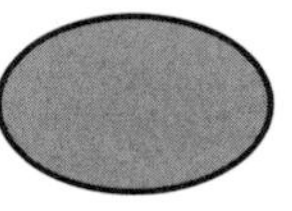

Color in the shape that matches the first one in each row.

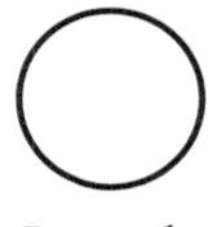    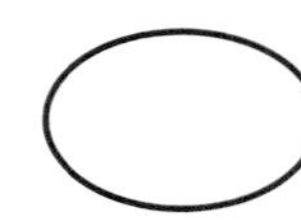 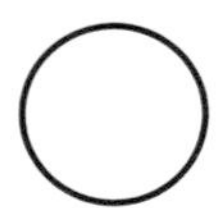

Circle

 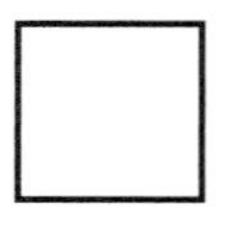 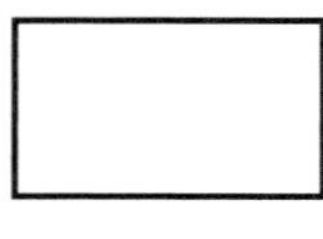 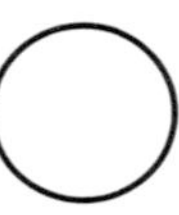  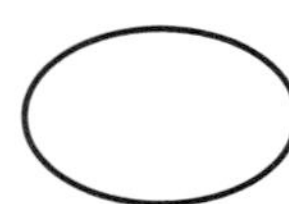

Square

 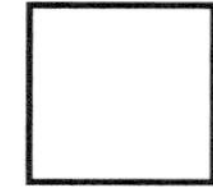 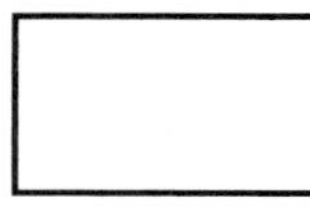  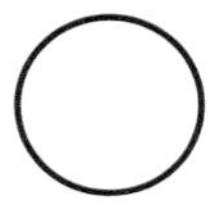 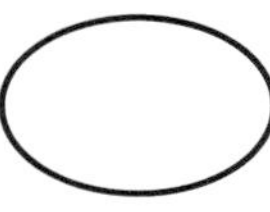

Triangle

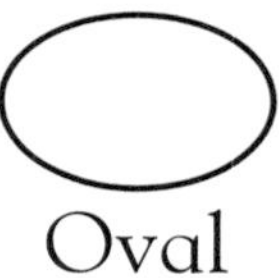 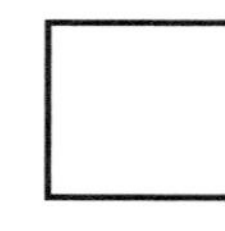 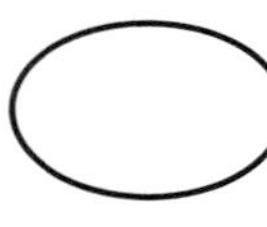  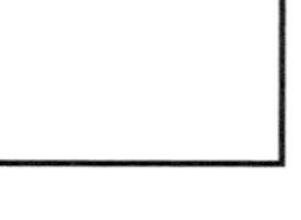 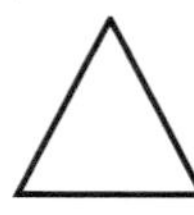 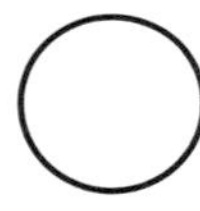

Oval

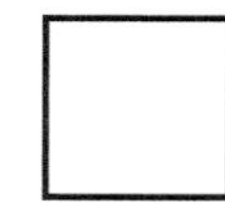 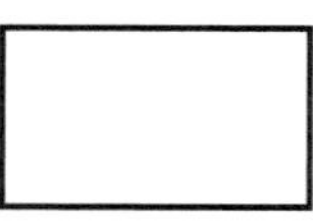  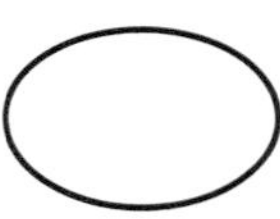 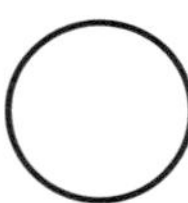

Rectangle

Color the rectangle red. Color the triangle blue.
Put an **S** on the square.

 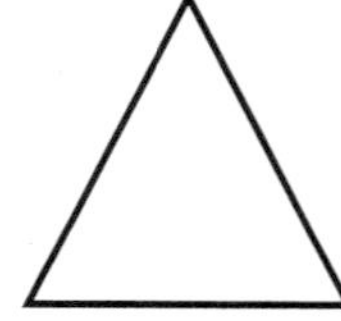 

GOAL

Learn to describe each shape.

A □ has four corners and four sides that are all the same length.
A △ has three sides and three corners.
A ○ is round.
An ⬭ has an egg shape.
A ▭ has four corners and four sides. Two sides are different in length than the other two sides.

Draw a line from each shape on the left to the object on the right with a similar shape.

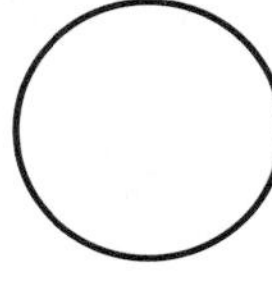

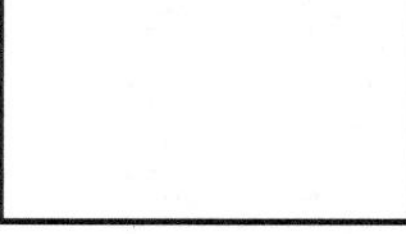

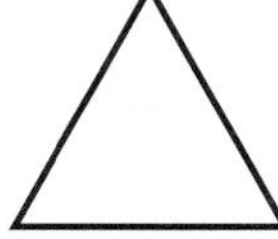

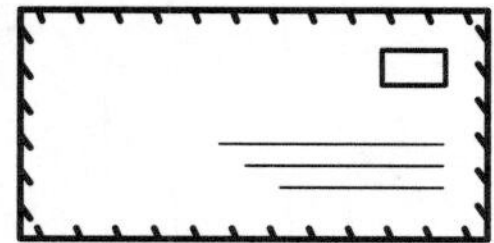

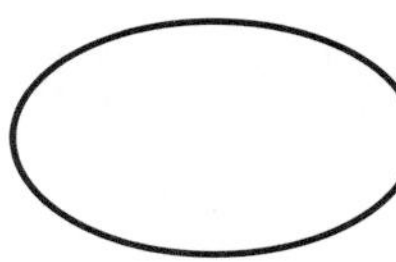

In the box, draw three shapes in this order: square, triangle, circle.

Comparing Shapes

GOAL

Learn how shapes are alike and how they are different.

A ◯ has no corners. A ☐ has four corners.

How many corners and sides does each shape have?
Remember: Some shapes have no corners or sides.
Some have three, four, or more corners and sides.

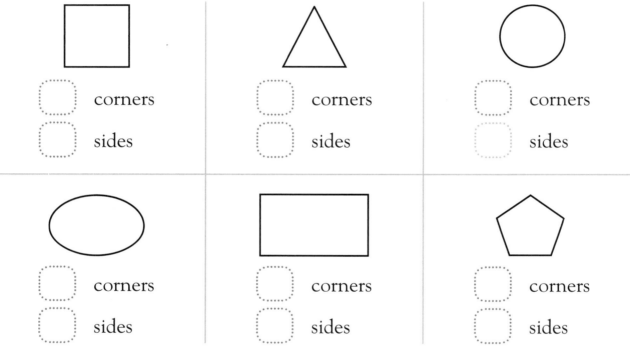

Square	Triangle	Circle
☐ corners	☐ corners	☐ corners
☐ sides	☐ sides	☐ sides

Oval	Rectangle	Pentagon
☐ corners	☐ corners	☐ corners
☐ sides	☐ sides	☐ sides

Read the questions and fill in the missing numbers.

How are squares and rectangles alike? They both have ☐ sides and ☐ corners.

How are circles and triangles different?

Triangles have ☐ corners and ☐ sides.

Circles have ☐ corners and ☐ sides.

How are circles and ovals alike? They both have ☐ sides.

Learn how to sort shapes into groups.

This group has shapes with four sides.

Circle the shapes that belong in each group.

Shapes with no corners

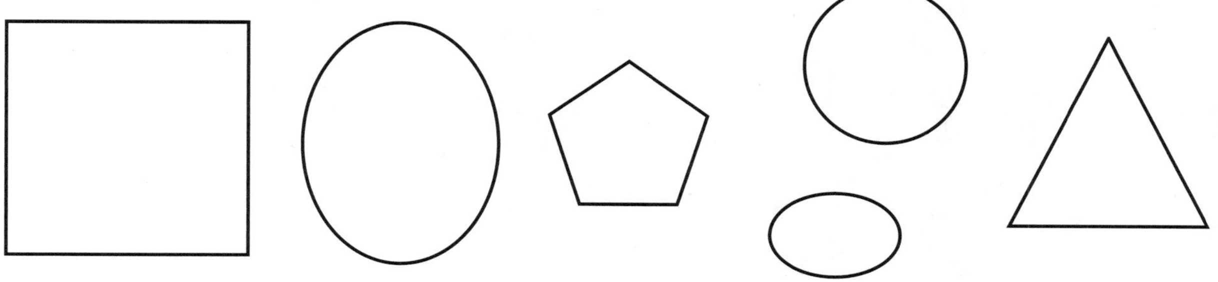

Shapes with four corners

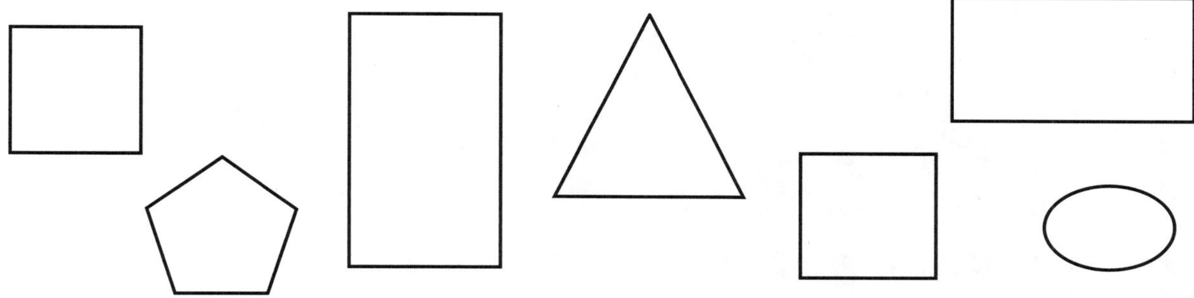

Write the answer to the mystery sentences.

Janette saw a shape with three sides. It looked like a slice of pizza. Which shape did she see? ....

Mike saw a shape with four sides. Two sides were short. The other two sides were longer. Which shape did he see? ....

Peter saw a shape with no sides. It looked like an egg. Which shape did he see? ....

Counting Animals

GOAL

Practice counting. This number line from 1 to 20 may help you.

1 2 3 4 5 6 7 8 9 10 11 12 13 14 15 16 17 18 19 20

Count the animals in each group. Write the number in the box.

Can you count down? Write the missing numbers below the horses.

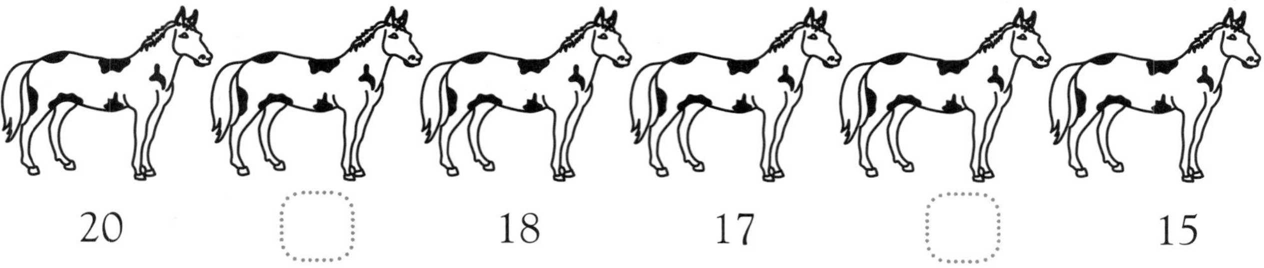

20 ☐ 18 17 ☐ 15

Learn to sort animals into groups.

This group has animals with stripes.

Circle the animals that belong to each group.

Animals with four legs

Animals with two legs

   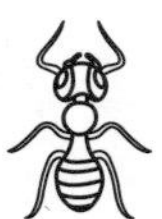

Animals with feathers

Sort the animals by writing the letter **F** under those that can fly.

....

Symmetry

GOAL

Learn that symmetry is when two sides of an object or shape look the same and are equal in size.

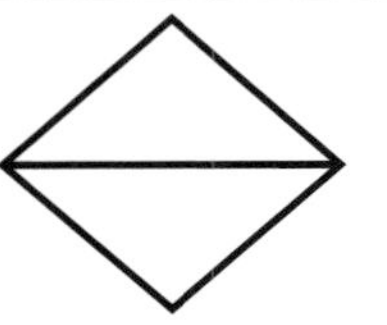

Draw a straight line to divide each shape into two matching parts. Then shade one half of each shape.

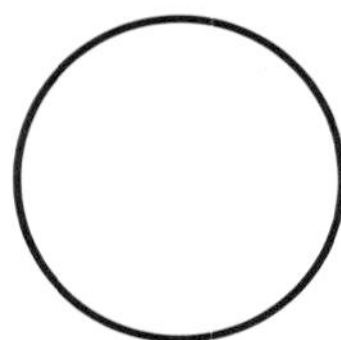  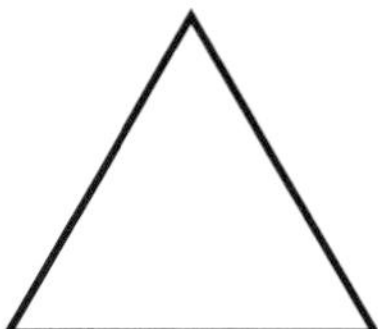  

In each row, circle the shape that has a line of symmetry.

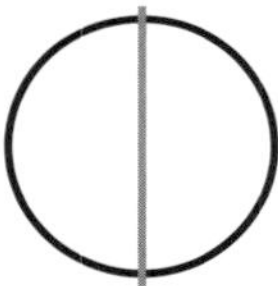 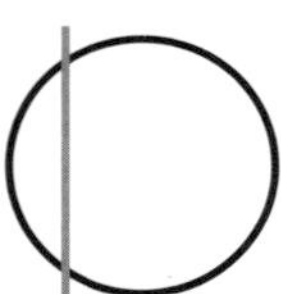 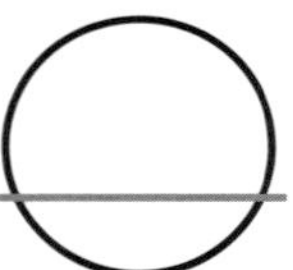 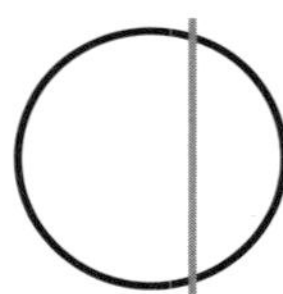

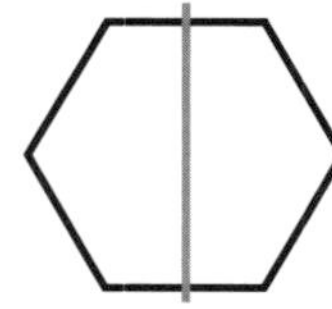 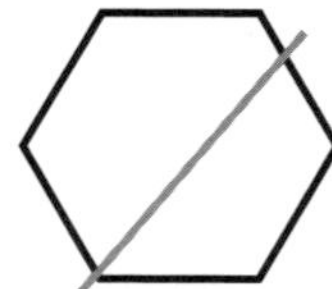 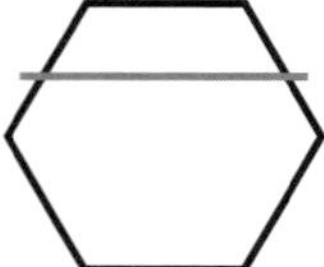 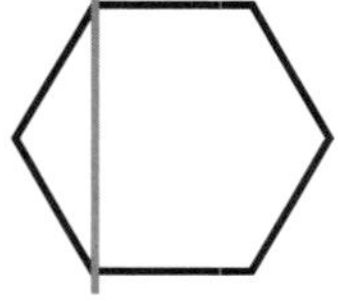

Draw a line of symmetry through each triangle.

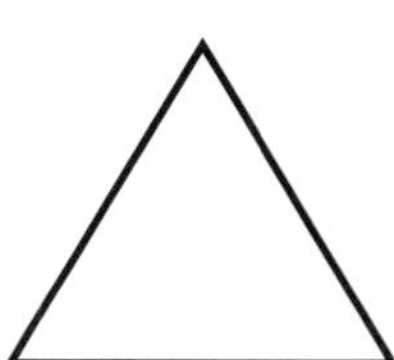 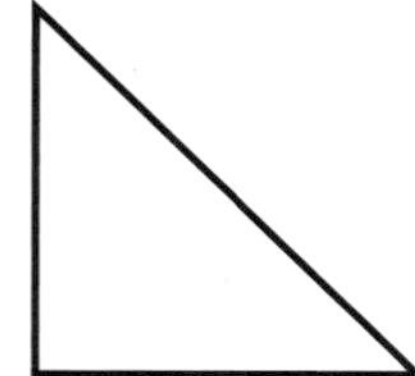

Learn to fold shapes into two matching parts.

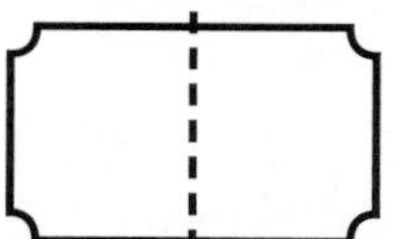

In each row, circle the shape that shows a fold line (----) that makes two matching parts.

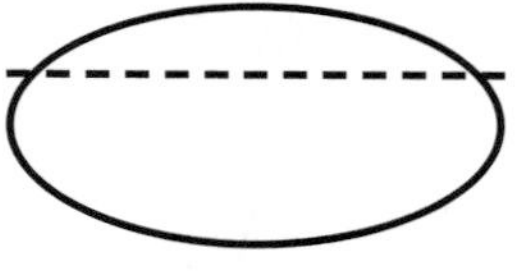 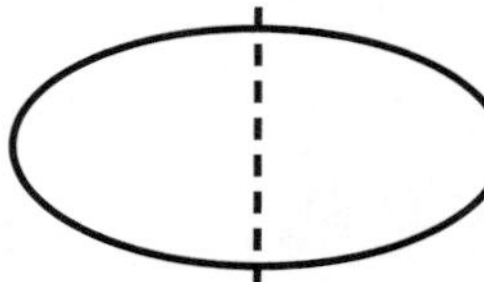 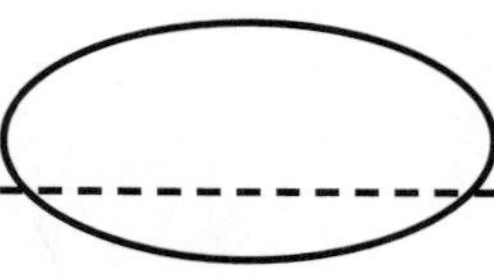 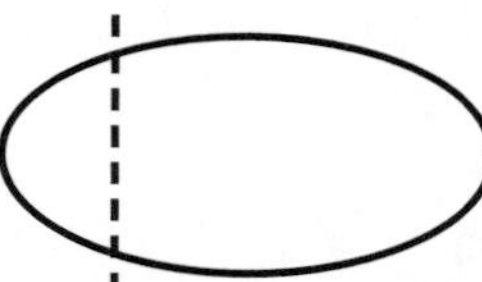

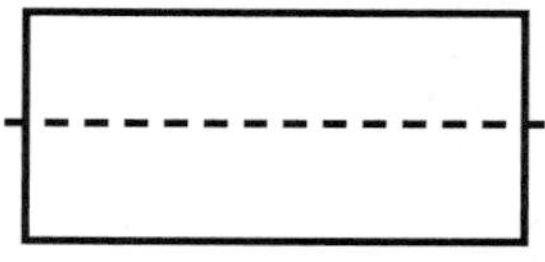  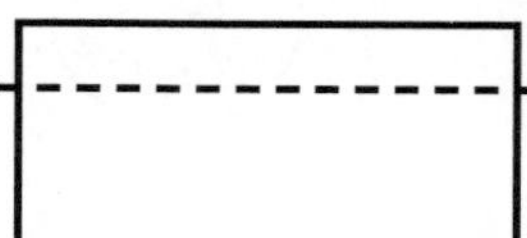 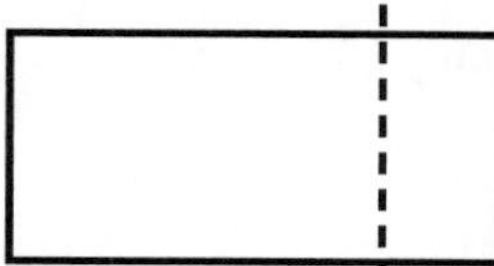

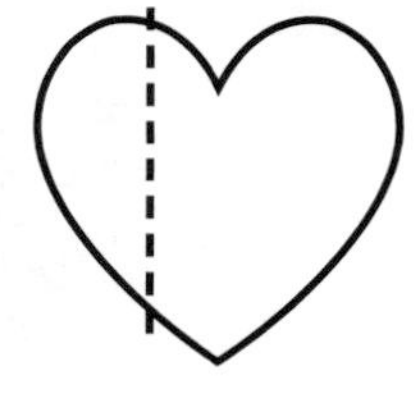   

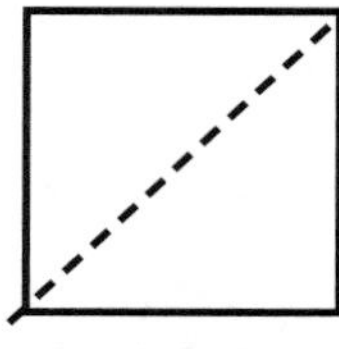 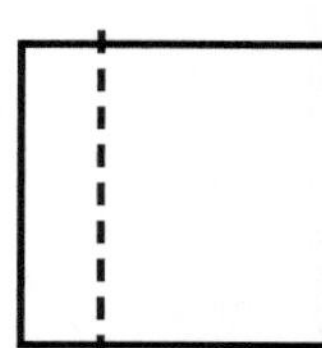 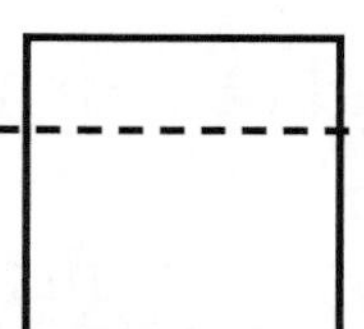 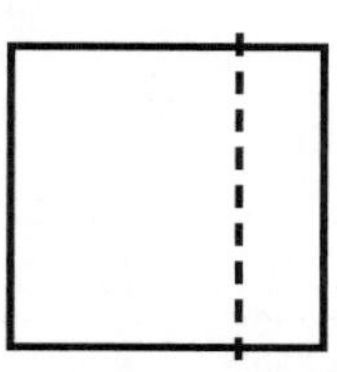

Draw a matching part for each shape.

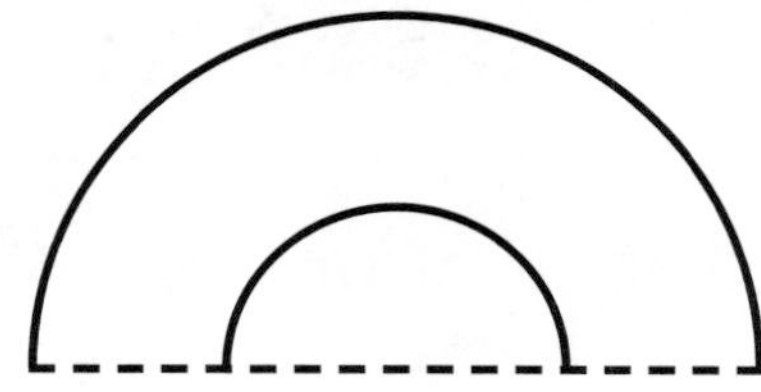

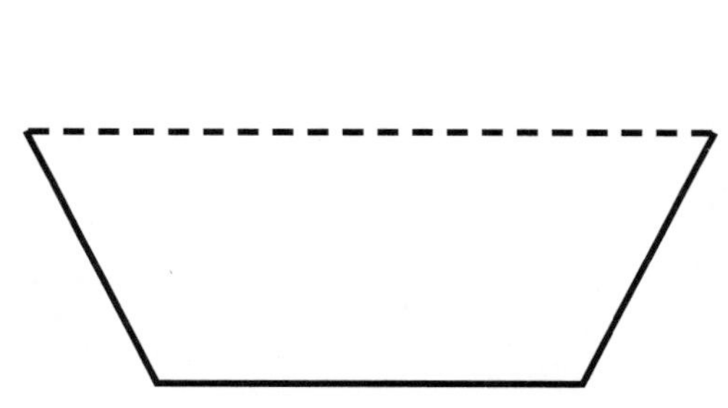

Recognizing Money

GOAL

Learn the names of coins.

1¢ 
Penny

5¢ 
Nickel

10¢ 
Dime

25¢ 
Quarter

Follow the directions in each section.

Circle four pennies.

Circle three nickels.

Circle five dimes.

Circle two quarters.

Circle two pennies and one nickel.

Circle three dimes and one quarter.

Read the amount of cents. Circle the coins that make each amount.

10¢ =

15¢ =

GOAL

Practice adding money.

$$\begin{array}{r} 25¢ \\ +\ 12¢ \\ \hline 37¢ \end{array}$$

Add the amounts of money in each row.

30¢ + 12¢	17¢ + 22¢	33¢ + 25¢	37¢ + 30¢	14¢ + 10¢
50¢ + 30¢	27¢ + 61¢	17¢ + 21¢	35¢ + 13¢	32¢ + 17¢
21¢ + 50¢	16¢ + 11¢	30¢ + 24¢	23¢ + 22¢	18¢ + 20¢
33¢ + 12¢	25¢ + 22¢	40¢ + 23¢	23¢ + 60¢	16¢ + 12¢

Look at each group of coins. Circle the one with the most money.

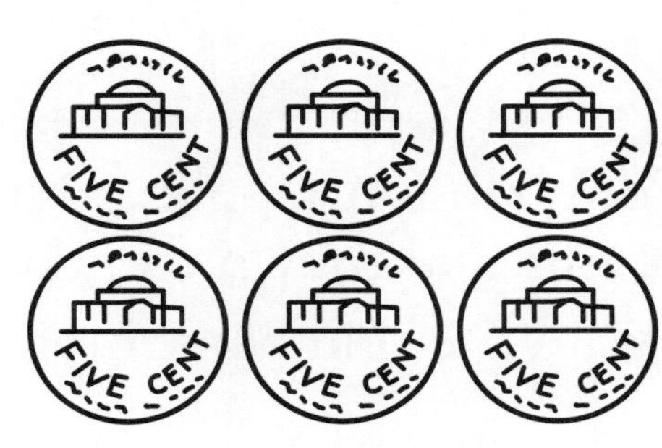

Double Trouble

GOAL

Learn to double amounts.

5¢ + 5¢ = 10¢

	4¢
+	4¢
	8¢

Look at the coins on the left, then draw the coins you need to double each amount. Add to find the total amount in each row.

+  = ☐

+  = ☐

+  = ☐

Write the answer to each addition problem.
Circle the equations that show doubled amounts.

8¢ + 1¢ = ☐ 5¢ + 2¢ = ☐ 5¢ + 5¢ = ☐ 9¢ + 8¢ = ☐

9¢ + 2¢ = ☐ 5¢ + 4¢ = ☐ 6¢ + 3¢ = ☐ 7¢ + 7¢ = ☐

Pam had four apples. Dan bought four peaches. How many pieces of fruit did they have in all?

Write the number sentence. ☐ + ☐ = ☐

Is the answer a double? ....

Find the coins you need to use when buying an item.

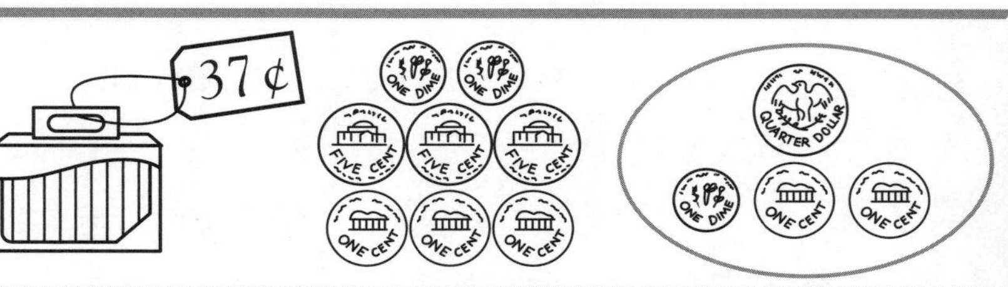

Look at the prices of the items. Circle the coins required to buy the item in each row.

Draw a line to match the treat with the coins you need to buy it.

Figuring Out Change

GOAL

Learn about getting back change.

You have

You buy

Will you get change?

No

Count how much money you have and write the amount in the box. Look at the price of what you buy. Figure out if you will get change, and circle "yes" or "no."

You have		You buy	Will you get change?	
 		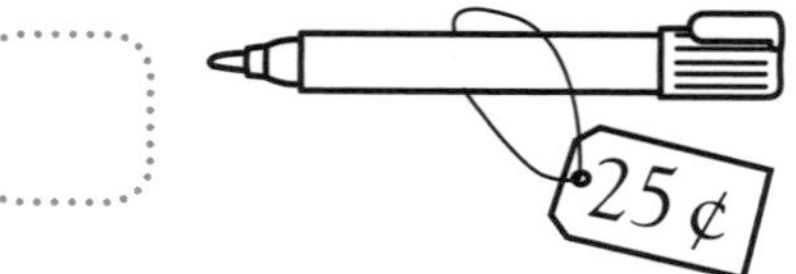 25¢	Yes	No
  		 35¢	Yes	No
  		 15¢	Yes	No
		 55¢	Yes	No

John has 35¢. He buys a toy truck for 24¢.

How much change will John get back?

GOAL

Learn how to calculate change using subtraction.

I have 20¢. I buy one apple. 

I will get 5¢ change.

Read each problem, and write the answer in the last column.

I have	I buy	I will get this much change.
50¢		
70¢		

Look at the prices of snacks given below. Then write the subtraction sentence and answer for each of the problems.

yogurt 30¢	bagel 40¢	bag of pretzels 35¢

Sara has 50¢. She buys a container of yogurt from Mr. Jones. How much change should Mr. Jones give Sara?

Jill has 50¢. She buys a bagel from Mr. Jones. How much change should Mr. Jones give Jill?

Sei has 75¢. She buys a bag of pretzels from Mr. Jones. How much change should Mr. Jones give Sei?

★ Telling the Time: O'Clock

GOAL

Learn to tell what time it is. This clock shows 2 o'clock.

The minute hand moves as the minutes go by.
The hour hand points to the hour of day.

Fill in the number to tell what time each clock shows.

☐ o'clock

☐ o'clock

☐ o'clock

☐ o'clock

☐ o'clock

☐ o'clock

☐ o'clock

☐ o'clock

☐ o'clock

Fill in the correct numbers in the sentence below.

At 3 o'clock, the minute hand points to ☐ and the hour hand points to ☐.

GOAL

Learn to tell the time to the half hour.
"Half past" means that it is 30 minutes past the hour.
When you say "half past one," it is the same as saying "one thirty."

1:30

One thirty

Write the correct time for each clock in numbers and in words.

:

.... thirty

:

.... thirty

:

.... thirty

:

.... thirty

:

.... thirty

:

.... thirty

Write the missing numbers on the clock. Then complete the sentence.

It is half past ....

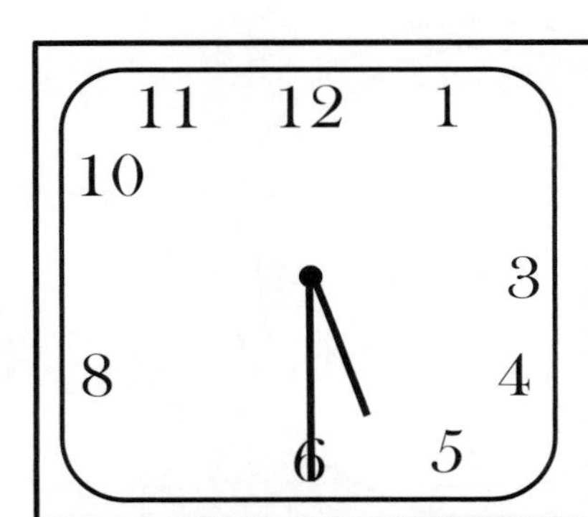

★ Writing the Time: O'Clock

GOAL

Practice using the word *o'clock*.

3 o'clock

Look at each clock. Write the time each clock shows.

Draw the hands on the clock to show the correct time.

5 o'clock

1 o'clock

12 o'clock

GOAL

Learn how to write the time on a digital clock.

Write the time shown on the left onto the digital clock on the right.

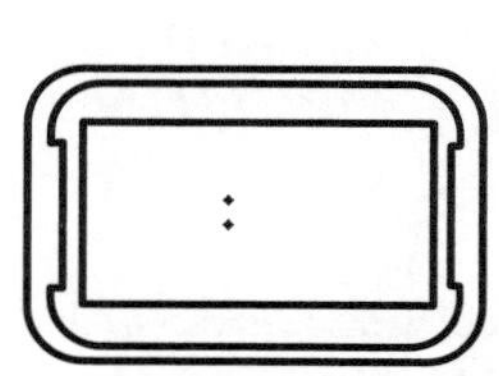

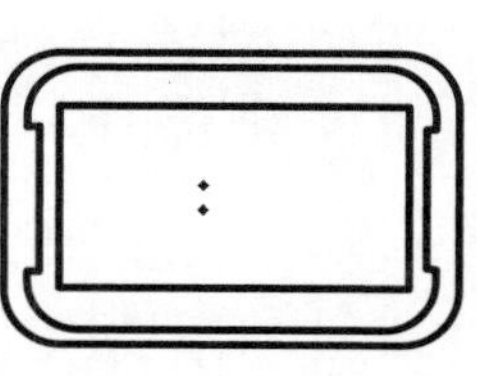

Write the time shown onto the digital clock face.

8 o'clock

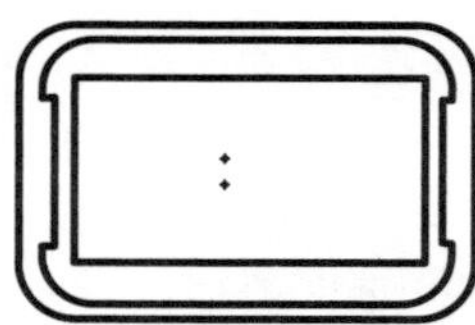

six thirty

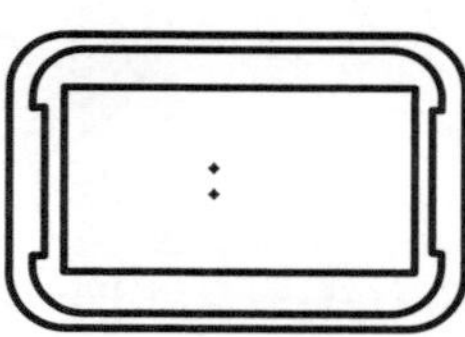

10 o'clock

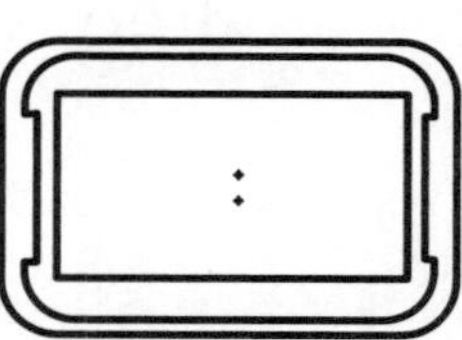

Show half past ten, or ten thirty, on both the clocks.

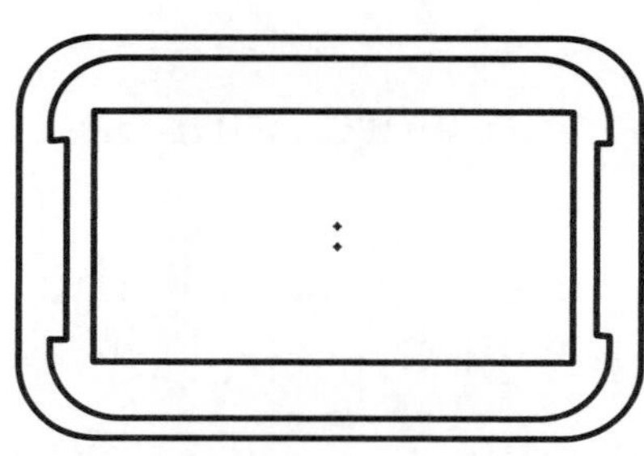

Using Clocks

GOAL

Practice using clocks.

Jamie eats dinner at 5 o'clock.

Is it time for her to eat dinner? Yes 

Circle "yes" or "no" to answer the questions below.

John starts school at 9 o'clock. Does the clock show it is time for John to start school?

Yes No

Look at the time on the clock. It is time for math. Does math start at 10:00?

Yes No

Look at the clock. Reading starts in 1 hour. At what time will reading start?

Sam and his mom went to the store. They left for the store at 4 o'clock. They arrived back at home at 5 o'clock.

How long were Sam and his mother gone? 1 minute 1 hour

Look at the clock on the right. Lunch will start in half an hour. What time will lunch start?

Differences in Time

GOAL

Learn about how long it takes to do some activities.

The activity circled here takes more time than the other.

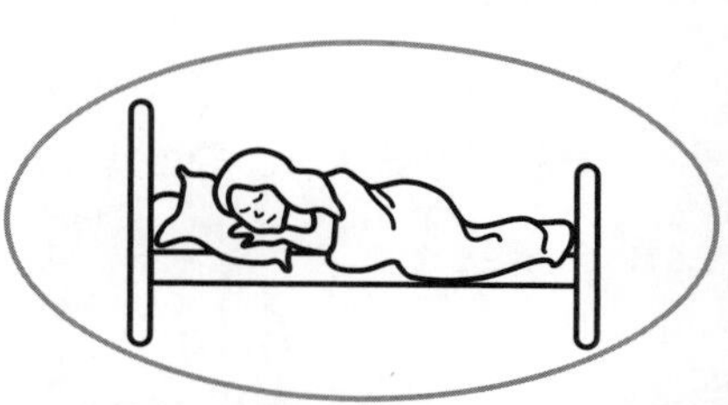

Circle the activity in each group below that takes more time.

Circle the activity in each group below that takes less time.

About how long does each activity take? Circle the best answer.

1 minute 1 hour

1 minute 1 hour

1 minute 1 hour

★ Days of the Week

GOAL

Learn about the days in each week.
These are the names of the seven days of the week in order:

Sunday → Monday → Tuesday → Wednesday → Thursday → Friday → Saturday

Circle the correct answer for each question below.

Which is the first day of the week?	Sunday	Saturday
Which day comes before Wednesday?	Friday	Tuesday
Which day comes after Sunday?	Monday	Wednesday
Which day comes after Friday?	Tuesday	Saturday

July

Sunday	Monday	Tuesday	Wednesday	Thursday	Friday	Saturday
	1	2	3	4	5	6
7	8	9	10	11	12	13
14	15	16	17	18	19	20
☼21	22	23	24	25	26	27
28	29	30	31			

Use the calendar above to answer each question. Circle your answers.

What day of the week is numbered 1?	Thursday	Monday
What is the second Tuesday numbered?	9	16
Which date shows a ☼?	12	21
How many days are there in this month?	28	31
How many Sundays are there in this month?	4	5

Months and Years

GOAL

Learn about the months of the year.

January	February	March	April
31 days	28 days	31 days	30 days
May	June	July	August
31 days	30 days	31 days	31 days
September	October	November	December
30 days	31 days	30 days	31 days

Use the information above to answer each question.

Which month comes after January? ....

Which is the month with the fewest days? ....

How many months begin with the letter J? ☐

How many months have 30 days? ☐

How many months have 31 days? ☐

Which month comes between July and September? ....

Which month comes before June? ....

In the chart above, circle the month of your birthday.

Write the month of your birthday here. ....

How old are you? ☐ years

★ Length

GOAL

Learn to find the length of something using objects, inches, and centimeters.

The crayon is three pennies long.

Each number marks an inch.

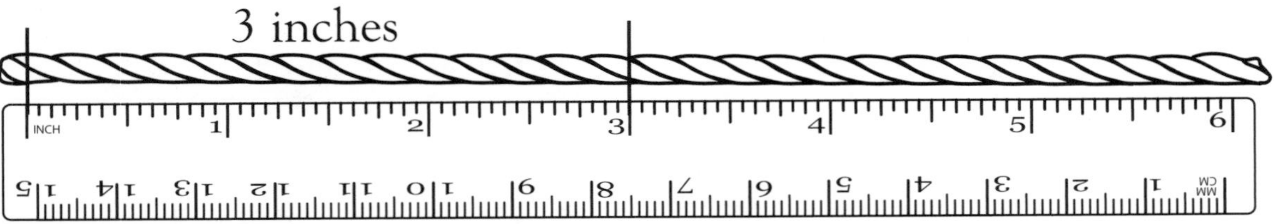

Each number marks a centimeter.

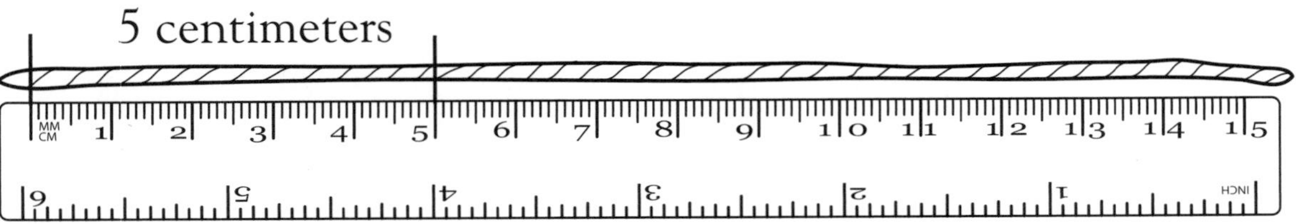

Measure using pennies.

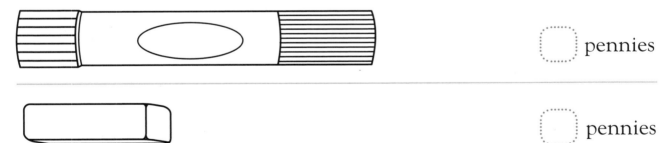

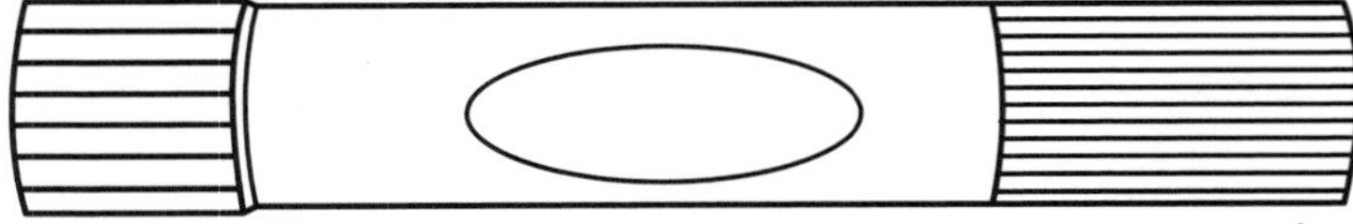

☐ pennies

☐ pennies

Use a ruler to measure this object in inches.

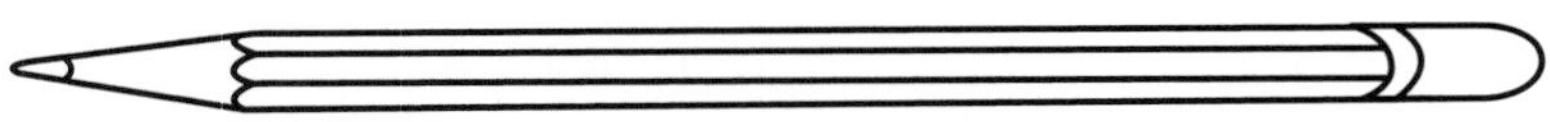

☐ inches long

Use a ruler to measure this object in centimeters.

☐ centimeters long

GOAL

Learn to compare the lengths of things.

This bookcase is short.  This bookcase is long. 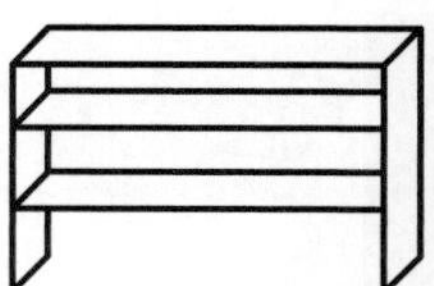

Circle the longer object.

Circle the shorter object.

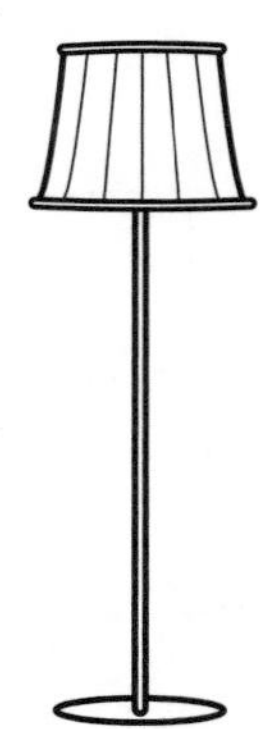

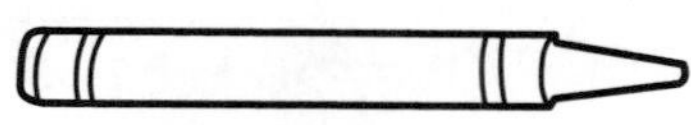

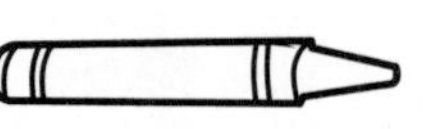

Color the shortest feather blue. Color the longest feather green.
Circle the other feather.

Size

GOAL

Learn about size.

The square with the circle around it is the same size as the first.

Circle the shape that is the same size as the first one.

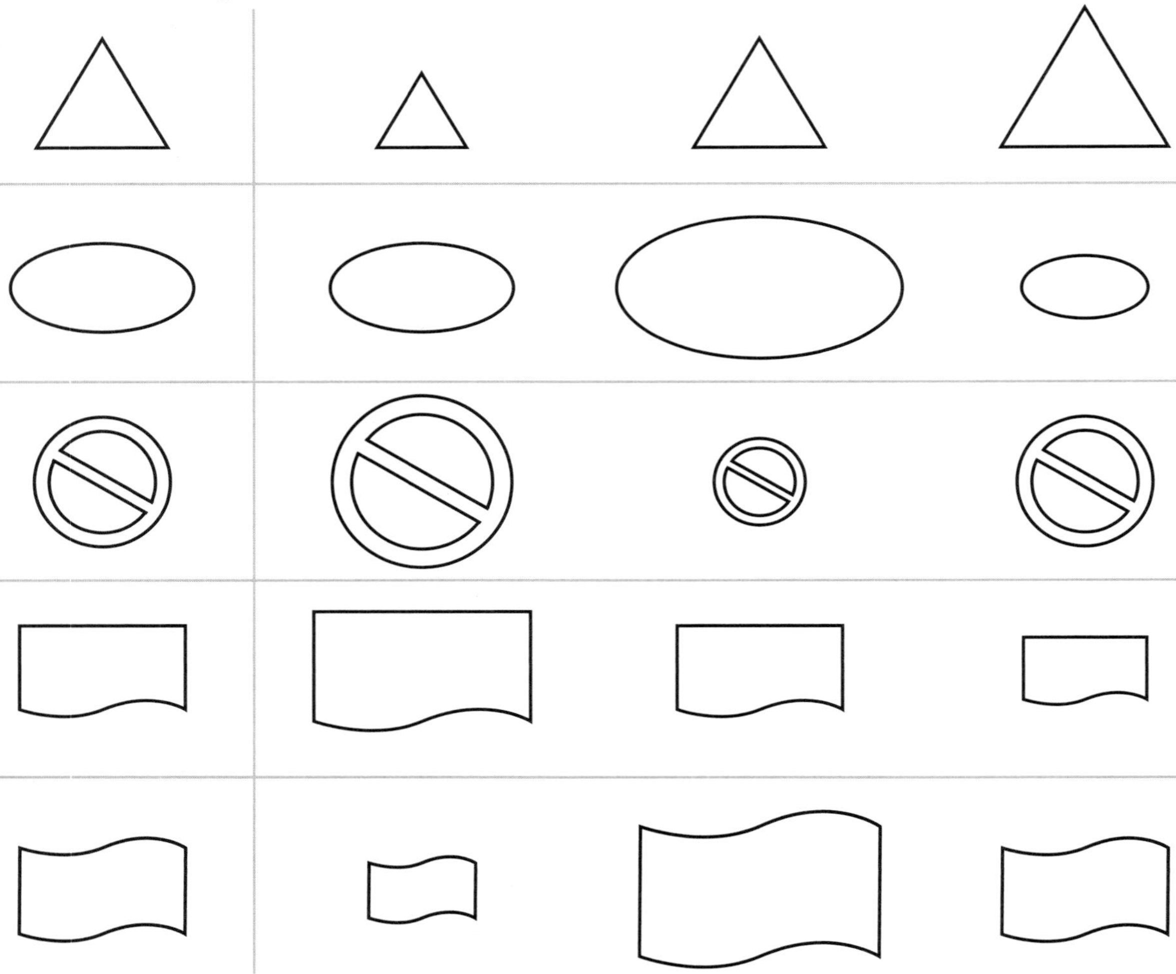

Draw a teddy bear that is about the same size as this one.

Comparing Sizes

Learn to compare sizes, such as long and short.

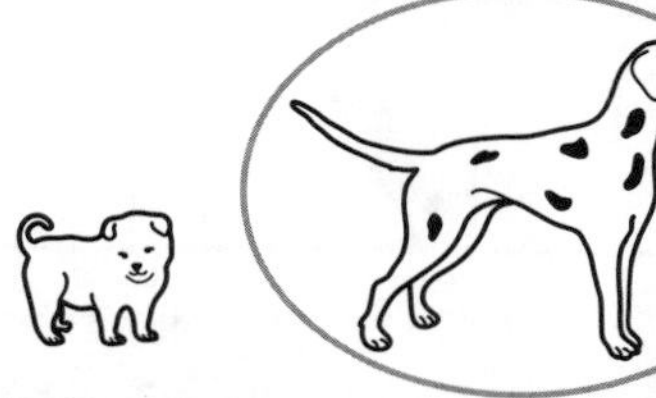

The largest dog is circled.

Look at the animals and performers on the paths to the circus tent.

Path 1. Circle the largest.
Path 2. Circle the shortest.
Path 3. Circle the tallest.
Path 4. Circle the smallest.

Path 1

Path 2

Path 3

Path 4

Read each question, and circle the answer.

Which is heavier?

Which holds more?

Patterns

GOAL

Practice making patterns.

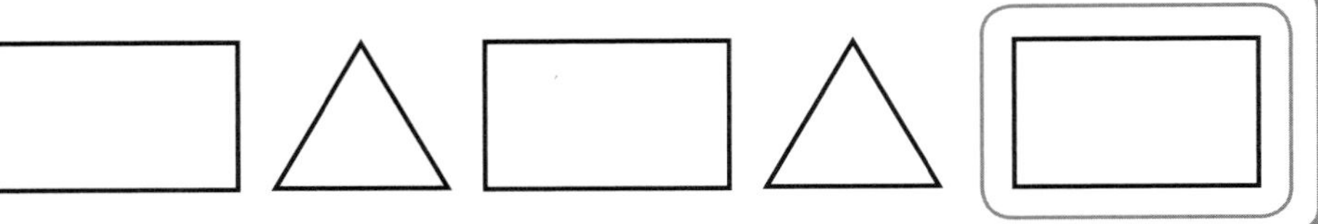

Look at the pattern in each row. Draw the next shape(s) in the pattern.

Write the missing numbers in each pattern.

2	4	6		4		2		
10	20	30		20		10		

Make your own pattern. Use seven shapes or numbers.

A sequence shows the order in which something happens.

1

2

3

Write 1, 2, 3, and 4 to put each story in the correct order.

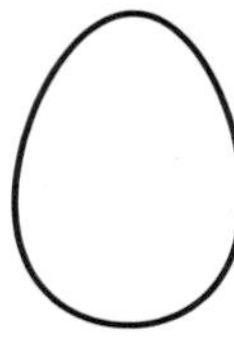

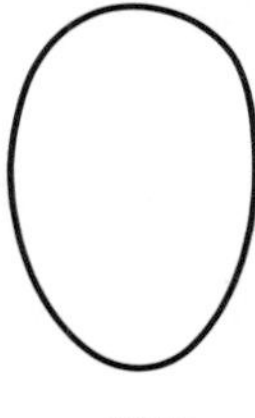

Write the missing numbers in each squence.

20 19 18 ☐ 16 ☐

5 10 ☐ 20 ☐ 30

Picture Graphs

GOAL

Learn to read and use picture graphs to find the answers.

Frogs Tom and Matt Saw at the Pond

Tom	🐸 🐸 🐸
Matt	🐸 🐸 🐸 🐸

Matt saw the most frogs.

Use this picture graph to answer each question.

Dogs in Need of Homes

Black Dogs	🐕 🐕 🐕 🐕
White Dogs	🐕 🐕 🐕
Spotted Dogs	🐕 🐕 🐕
Gray Dogs	🐕 🐕 🐕 🐕 🐕

How many black dogs need homes? ☐

How many spotted dogs need homes? ☐

Which two kinds of dog are the same in number?

....

Of which kind of dog is there the most? ....

How many more gray dogs are there than spotted dogs? ☐

How many black and white dogs need homes? ☐

How many dogs are there in all? ☐

Write the subtraction problem and the answer.
There are 15 dogs in all. People take 4 black dogs home. How many other dogs still need homes? ☐

Bar Graphs

GOAL

Bar graphs show amounts or numbers of things by using bars of different lengths.

The bar graph shows the number of cakes a bakery sold in a day. Use the bar graph to answer the questions.

Cakes Sold in a Day

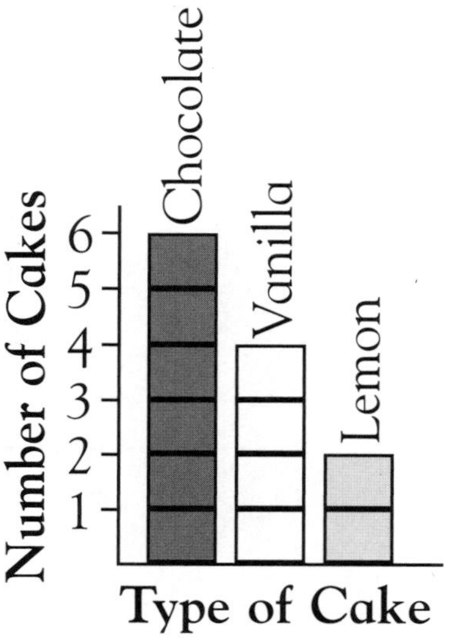

How many lemon cakes were sold?

Which cake did the bakery sell the most? ....

How many vanilla cakes were sold? 

The bar graph shows the number of animals that live on Mr. Jones's farm. Use the bar graph to answer each question.

Animals on Mr. Jones's Farm

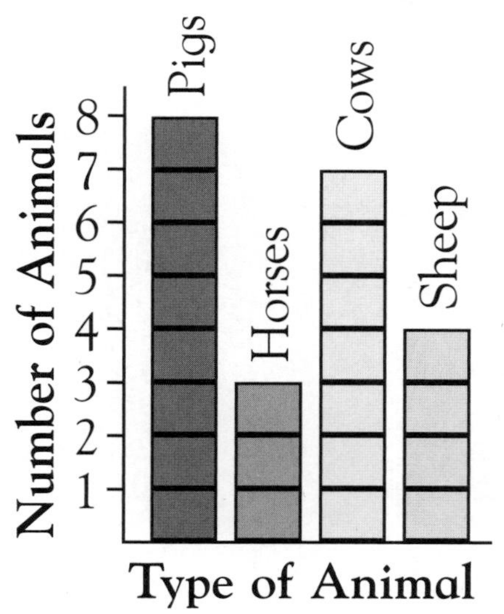

How many pigs live on the farm?

How many cows live on the farm?

Mr. Jones has ☐ sheep.

Mr. Jones has more sheep than ....

Mr. Jones has more .... than cows.

Position Words

GOAL

Use position words to say where things can be found.

The fork is to the left of the plate.

Follow the directions in each sentence.

Draw a cloud above the rocket.

Draw a sun to the left of the rocket.

Draw a planet to the right of the rocket.

Draw a planet below the rocket.

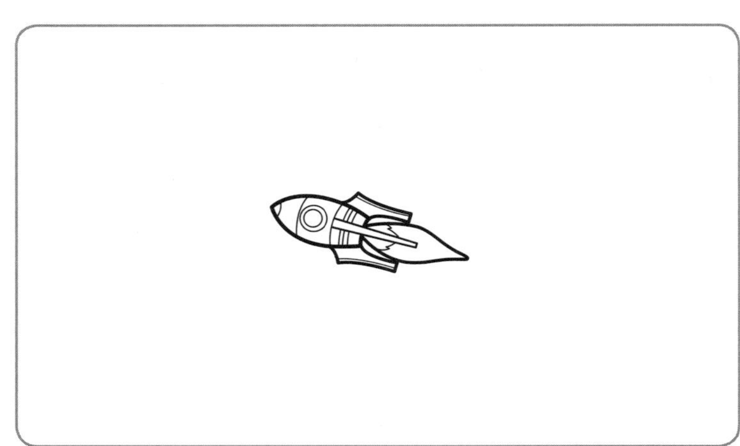

Circle the correct words to complete the sentences.

The bat is .... the ball.

near   far from

The fence is .... the house.

behind   in front of

The girl is walking ....

up the hill   down the hill

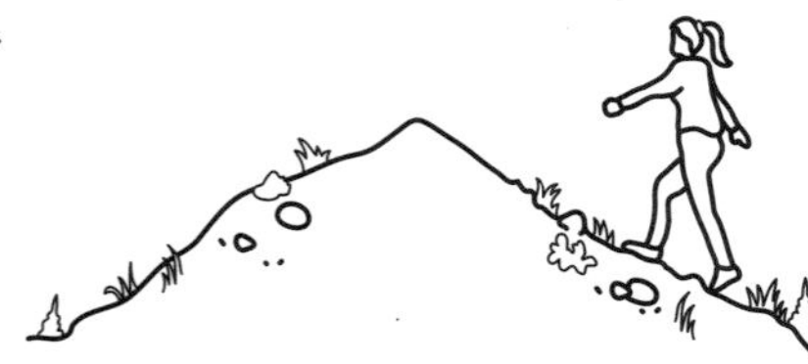

Read the clues, then write each child's name under the correct picture.

Kim is in the middle.

Tom is to the right of Kim.

Bill is to the left of Kim.

....

....

....

Use direction words to find your way. *Behind*, *right*, *left*, *in front of*, *between*, *up*, *down*, *above*, and *below* are some direction words.

Pam's dog has run off into the maze. Can you help her find him? Read the clues and draw a line to show her the way.

Clues

1. At the gate turn right.
2. At the ice cream stand turn left and pass between two apple trees.
3. Turn right and follow the path until you get to a bench.
4. Turn left, then right, and follow the path. Go up the steps.
5. Look behind the goldfish pond.

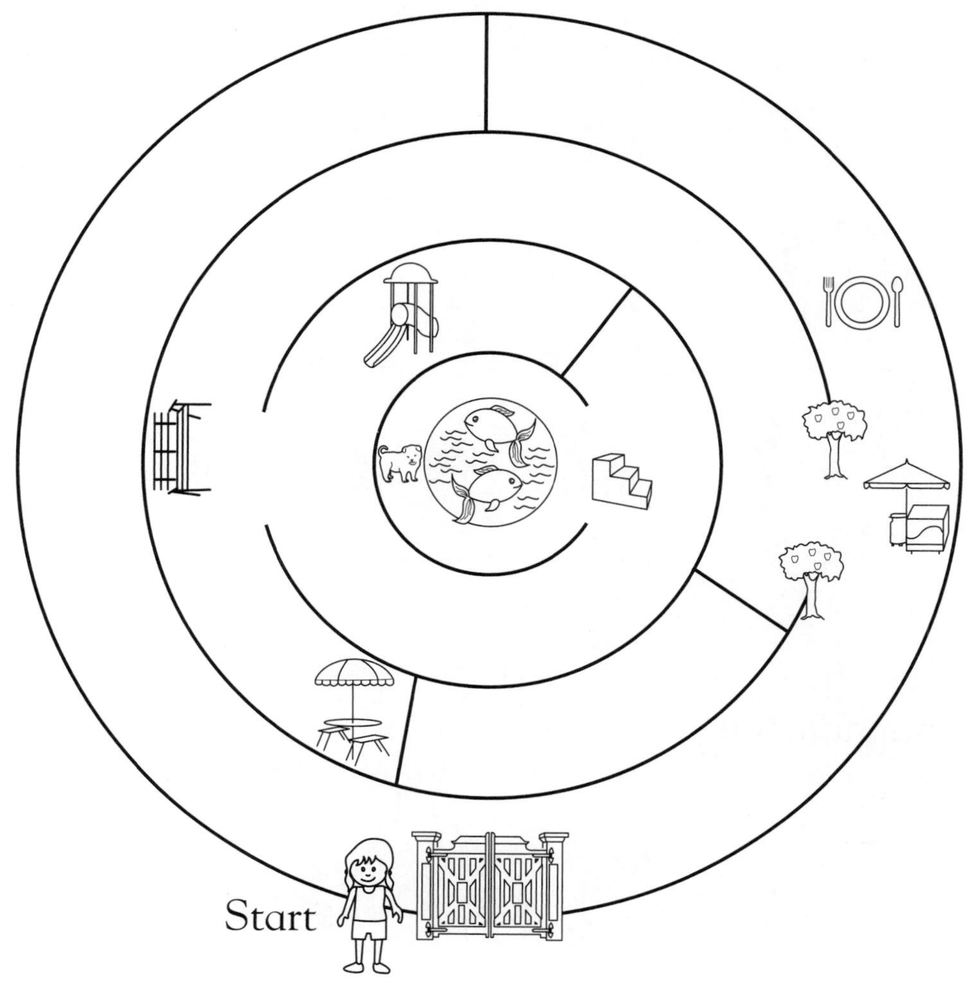

Quick Adding

GOAL

Practice doing quick addition.

$$\begin{array}{r} 5 \\ +\ 5 \\ \hline 10 \end{array}$$

How quickly can you solve these equations? Ready, set, go!

$\begin{array}{r} 10 \\ +10 \\ \hline \end{array}$ $\begin{array}{r} 10 \\ +\ 5 \\ \hline \end{array}$ $\begin{array}{r} 10 \\ +\ 8 \\ \hline \end{array}$ $\begin{array}{r} 10 \\ +\ 7 \\ \hline \end{array}$ $\begin{array}{r} 10 \\ +\ 6 \\ \hline \end{array}$ $\begin{array}{r} 10 \\ +\ 3 \\ \hline \end{array}$

$\begin{array}{r} 8 \\ +\ 8 \\ \hline \end{array}$ $\begin{array}{r} 7 \\ +\ 7 \\ \hline \end{array}$ $\begin{array}{r} 9 \\ +\ 9 \\ \hline \end{array}$ $\begin{array}{r} 4 \\ +\ 4 \\ \hline \end{array}$ $\begin{array}{r} 5 \\ +\ 5 \\ \hline \end{array}$ $\begin{array}{r} 3 \\ +\ 3 \\ \hline \end{array}$

$\begin{array}{r} 6 \\ +\ 2 \\ \hline \end{array}$ $\begin{array}{r} 4 \\ +\ 8 \\ \hline \end{array}$ $\begin{array}{r} 2 \\ +\ 9 \\ \hline \end{array}$ $\begin{array}{r} 1 \\ +\ 4 \\ \hline \end{array}$ $\begin{array}{r} 8 \\ +\ 3 \\ \hline \end{array}$ $\begin{array}{r} 7 \\ +\ 3 \\ \hline \end{array}$

$\begin{array}{r} 9 \\ +\ 8 \\ \hline \end{array}$ $\begin{array}{r} 5 \\ +\ 9 \\ \hline \end{array}$ $\begin{array}{r} 8 \\ +\ 6 \\ \hline \end{array}$ $\begin{array}{r} 5 \\ +\ 7 \\ \hline \end{array}$ $\begin{array}{r} 18 \\ +\ 2 \\ \hline \end{array}$ $\begin{array}{r} 4 \\ +\ 9 \\ \hline \end{array}$

Add the three numbers in each equation.

$\begin{array}{r} 12 \\ 9 \\ +\ 4 \\ \hline \end{array}$ $\begin{array}{r} 6 \\ 5 \\ +\ 8 \\ \hline \end{array}$ $\begin{array}{r} 10 \\ 5 \\ +\ 2 \\ \hline \end{array}$ $\begin{array}{r} 5 \\ 7 \\ +\ 6 \\ \hline \end{array}$

GOAL

Practice doing quick subtraction.

$$\begin{array}{r} 10 \\ -\ 5 \\ \hline 5 \end{array}$$

Solve these equations quickly. You can do it!

$$\begin{array}{r} 6 \\ -\ 3 \\ \hline \end{array} \quad \begin{array}{r} 7 \\ -\ 3 \\ \hline \end{array} \quad \begin{array}{r} 29 \\ -\ 9 \\ \hline \end{array} \quad \begin{array}{r} 9 \\ -\ 6 \\ \hline \end{array} \quad \begin{array}{r} 16 \\ -\ 8 \\ \hline \end{array} \quad \begin{array}{r} 7 \\ -\ 1 \\ \hline \end{array}$$

$$\begin{array}{r} 10 \\ -\ 2 \\ \hline \end{array} \quad \begin{array}{r} 29 \\ -\ 7 \\ \hline \end{array} \quad \begin{array}{r} 12 \\ -\ 6 \\ \hline \end{array} \quad \begin{array}{r} 16 \\ -\ 4 \\ \hline \end{array} \quad \begin{array}{r} 18 \\ -\ 10 \\ \hline \end{array} \quad \begin{array}{r} 16 \\ -\ 6 \\ \hline \end{array}$$

$$\begin{array}{r} 18 \\ -\ 8 \\ \hline \end{array} \quad \begin{array}{r} 9 \\ -\ 5 \\ \hline \end{array} \quad \begin{array}{r} 16 \\ -\ 5 \\ \hline \end{array} \quad \begin{array}{r} 17 \\ -\ 7 \\ \hline \end{array} \quad \begin{array}{r} 16 \\ -\ 3 \\ \hline \end{array} \quad \begin{array}{r} 19 \\ -\ 9 \\ \hline \end{array}$$

$$\begin{array}{r} 14 \\ -\ 6 \\ \hline \end{array} \quad \begin{array}{r} 10 \\ -\ 6 \\ \hline \end{array} \quad \begin{array}{r} 109 \\ -\ 9 \\ \hline \end{array} \quad \begin{array}{r} 47 \\ -\ 7 \\ \hline \end{array} \quad \begin{array}{r} 18 \\ -\ 9 \\ \hline \end{array} \quad \begin{array}{r} 17 \\ -\ 10 \\ \hline \end{array}$$

Circle the number sentence that is related to $10 - 4 = 6$.

$6 - 4 = 2$ $\qquad$ $6 + 4 = 10$ $\qquad$ $10 + 4 = 14$

Parents' Notes

The math covered in this book is very similar to the work children encounter in first grade. The activities are intended to help your child acquire the very basic skills involved in mastering mathematics.

Contents

By working through the math activities in this book, your child will practice:

- reading, writing, and counting numbers to 100;
- counting forward in leaps of up to 10;
- understanding the place values of tens and ones;
- the concept of more than and less than;
- adding and subtracting objects and numbers up to 20;
- understanding of odd and even numbers;
- recognizing simple 2-D shapes, halves and quarters of shapes;
- ordering and comparing numbers up to 100;
- understanding and measuring length;
- using picture and bar graphs;
- recognizing and using position and direction words;
- counting in groups;
- recognizing and using money and telling the time.

How to Help Your Child

Your child's reading abilities may not be up to the level of some of the more specialized math words ("subtraction," for example), so be prepared to assist with the reading of the questions. Working alongside your child also has great benefits in understanding how he or she is thinking and where the stumbling blocks may be.

Often, similar problems will be deliberately worded in different ways such as "what is double each number?" and "what are two groups of…" This is intentional and meant to make children aware that the same basic problem can be expressed in many different ways. If children really understand the math, they will know what needs to be done.

When appropriate, use props to help your child visualize the solutions. For example, have a collection of coins to use for the money problems or find examples of mathematical shapes, such as cubes or spheres, in the objects around your house.

Build your child's confidence with words of praise. If they are getting answers wrong, then encourage them to return to try again another time. Above all, have fun!

Author Hugh Westrup

Educational Consultant Kara Pranikoff

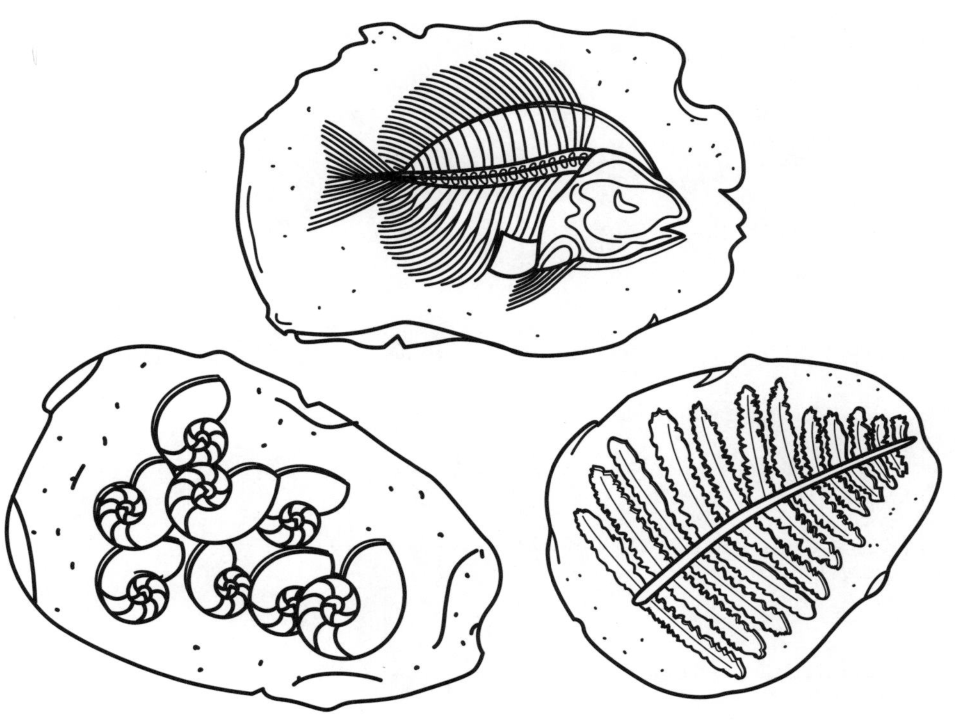

Contents

This chart lists all the topics in the Science section.

Scientists

Scientists study different parts of nature and the universe.

Use the words in the box to complete the sentences.

astronomer	biologist

A scientist who studies living things is a ....

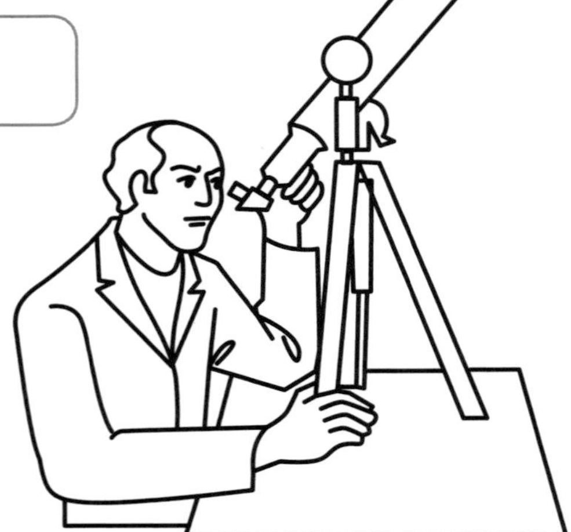

A scientist who studies the stars is an ....

Write **A** near the objects that interest an astronomer and **B** near the ones that interest a biologist.

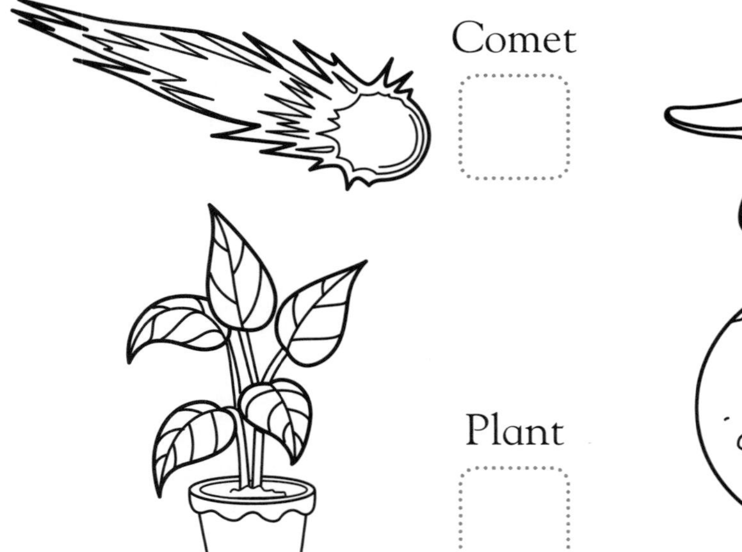

Comet

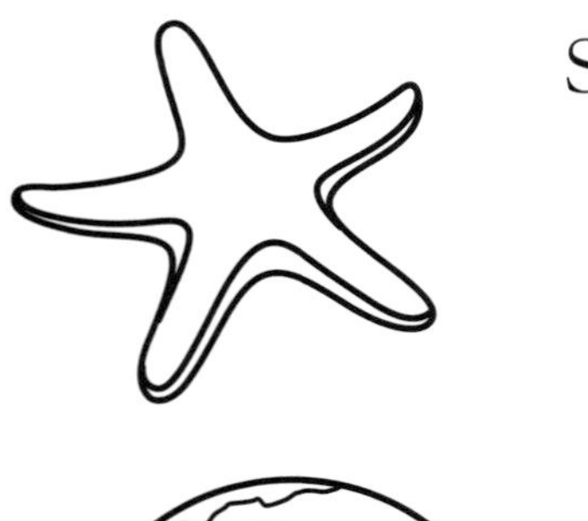

Starfish

Plant

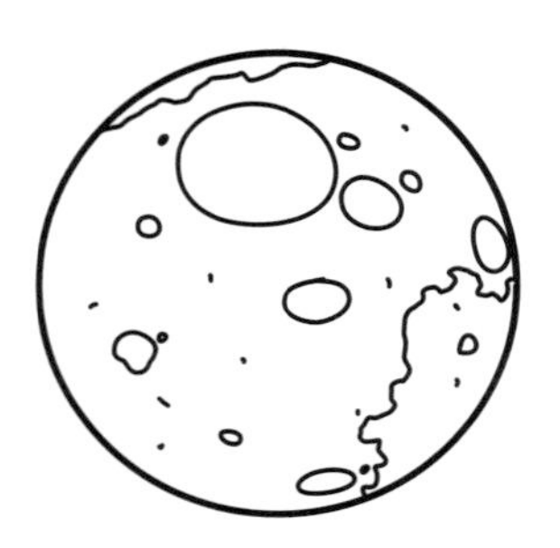

Moon

All living things need food, water, and shelter to survive.

Look at the animals below. Draw a line from each animal to the shelter it lives in.

Animals

Shelters

What kind of food does each animal eat?

Animal Movement

FACTS

Animals move from place to place to find food, seek shelter, and escape from danger. Some animals, such as rabbits, move very quickly, while others, such as snails, move slowly. Some animals run, while others hop, crawl, swim, or fly.

Look at the words beneath each picture below. Circle the word that describes how the animal in the picture is moving.

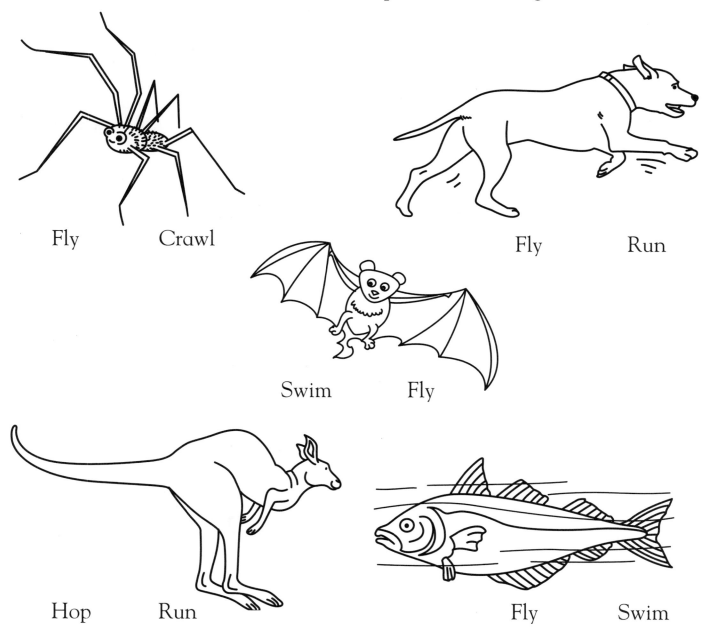

Fly Crawl

Fly Run

Swim Fly

Hop Run

Fly Swim

Plants make their own food inside their leaves by using sunlight, air, and water from the soil. They use this food to grow and make seeds that can grow into new plants.

Read the sentences below. They tell you many facts about an oak tree. Put a check (✓) in the box next to the sentences that are true.

- [ ] The tree makes food inside its leaves.
- [ ] Dogs nest in the branches of the tree.
- [ ] The tree takes in water from the soil through its roots.
- [ ] The tree needs sunlight to make food.
- [ ] The oak tree does not produce any seeds.
- [ ] The seeds an oak tree produces are called acorns.

The Muscles

FACTS

Muscles are stretchy tissues that are attached to the bones. When muscles work, they pull on the bones making them move.

TEST

What You Need:

Chair

What To Do:

1. Sit on the chair. Put both hands around the top of one of your legs.
2. Flex your knee, lifting up the lower part of your leg.
3. Draw an arrow on the picture below, pointing to where you can feel the muscles move and change shape as your leg moves.
4. Stand up. Hold one arm out straight to the side and touch your upper arm.
5. Flex your elbow, lifting up your lower arm.
6. Draw an arrow on the picture below, pointing to where the muscles move and change shape as your lower arm moves.

RESULT

What do you notice about the way your muscles change as you raise your lower leg or arm?

....

Bones support and protect the body.

Read the words in the box. Use them to fill in the blanks around the skeleton below.

elbow	knee	skull	wrist

The .... is where the bones of the upper arm and the lower arm meet.

The .... is where the bones of the upper leg and the lower leg meet.

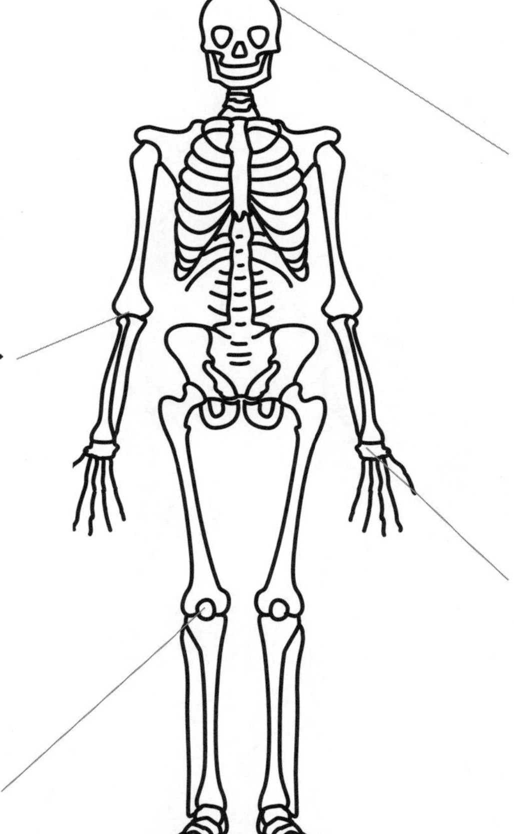

The .... is the bone in the head that protects the brain.

The .... is the part of the body where the bones of the lower arm and the hand meet.

Touch your head. Can you feel your skull? Circle the word that describes how it feels.

Soft Hard

The Organs

An organ is a part of the body that does a special job to help keep you alive. The heart, lungs, stomach, and brain are major organs. The heart pumps blood around the body. The stomach digests food. The lungs absorb oxygen from the air you breathe. The brain is the body's control center.

Use the words in the box to write the labels for the drawing below.

Brain	Heart	Lungs	Stomach

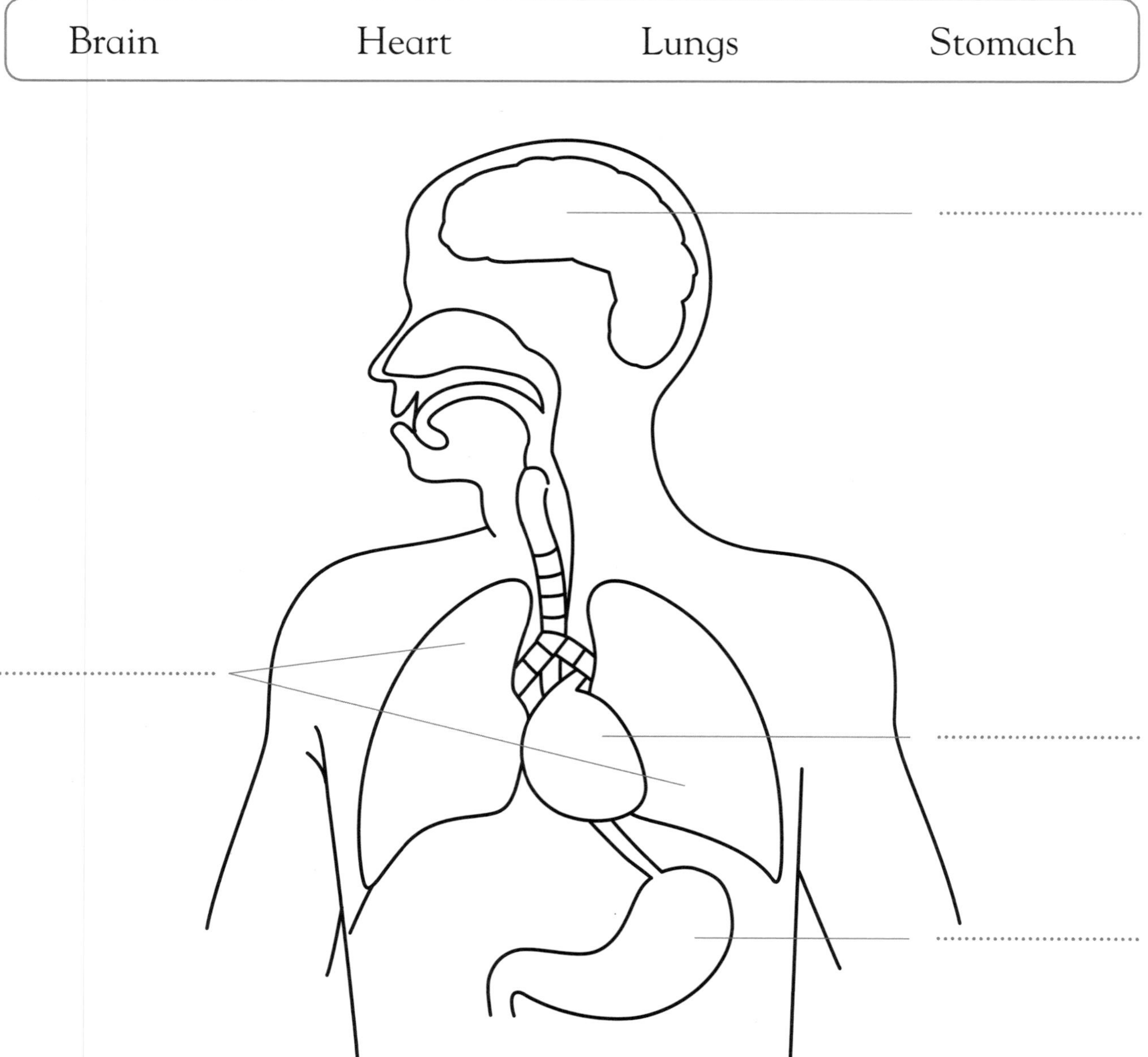

The heart pumps blood around the body. The blood travels in tubes called arteries and veins. Arteries open and close as blood passes through them. If arteries are near the surface of the skin, you can feel them opening and closing. This is called the pulse. How fast your pulse beats, tells you how fast your heart is beating.

TEST **What You Need:**

What To Do:

1. Stand still for about a minute, then find your pulse by placing your fingers on the side of your neck, just underneath your jaw.
2. Sit down in the chair and relax for a few minutes. Find your pulse again. Record whether it is faster or slower than when you were standing.
3. Walk around for a few minutes, then find your pulse again. Record whether it is faster or slower than when you were sitting.
4. Run around for a few minutes, then find your pulse once more. Record whether it is faster or slower than when you were walking.

RESULT Study the results you have recorded for each activity.

Activity	Faster or Slower Pulse
Sitting down	
Walking	
Running	

What do you notice about your results?

....

....

....

★ Teeth

FACTS

When we eat, sometimes food can get stuck between our teeth. If we leave it there, germs can grow and cause tooth decay. So we should regularly brush our teeth to keep them clean and free of germs.

A teacher asks a class of children to do a survey of how often they brush their teeth. The children record their results on a chart:

How Often We Brush Our Teeth

Never					
Not very often	Sean	Sam			
Once a day	James	Amy			
Twice a day	Oliver	Tom	Emily	Maria	Rachel
After every meal	Mina	John	Ling	Kelly	

Which children have the cleanest teeth?

....

The Best Way To Clean Your Teeth

Read the sentences below. Circle the best method of cleaning your teeth.

A. Eat an apple.
B. Rinse your mouth with water.
C. Brush your teeth with toothpaste, then rinse with water.

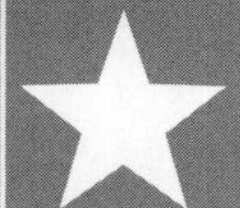

We get our energy and nutrients from the foods we eat. It is important to eat fresh foods from different food groups to be fit and healthy.

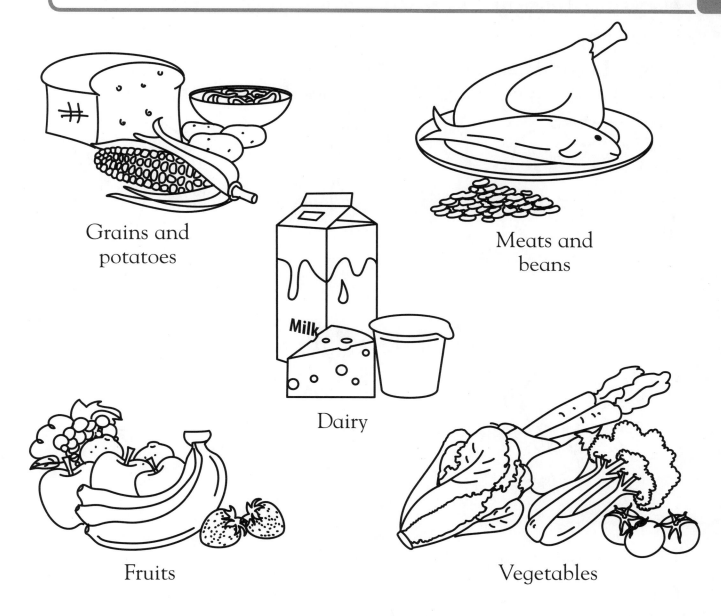

Grains and potatoes

Meats and beans

Dairy

Fruits

Vegetables

Look at the food groups above. Do you eat foods from each of those groups every day? Which are your favorites? Which are your least favorites? Color in the food groups, and add any of your favorite foods that we left out.

Animal Food

FACTS

Animals that eat only plants, like cows and horses, are called herbivores. Animals that eat only meat, like lions, sharks, and snakes, are called carnivores. Animals that eat both meat and plants, like bears, raccoons, and humans, are called omnivores.

Write **H** near the animals that are herbivores, **C** near the animals that are carnivores, and **O** near the ones that are omnivores.

Carnivores catch and kill other animals for food. They have special features that help them do this, such as sharp teeth, beaks, and claws. Many carnivores, like cheetahs and leopards, can also run very fast to catch their prey. Others have good eyesight, like eagles, so they can spot prey from a great distance.

Look at the pictures of the animals below. Circle each part of the animal that will help it to catch and kill prey.

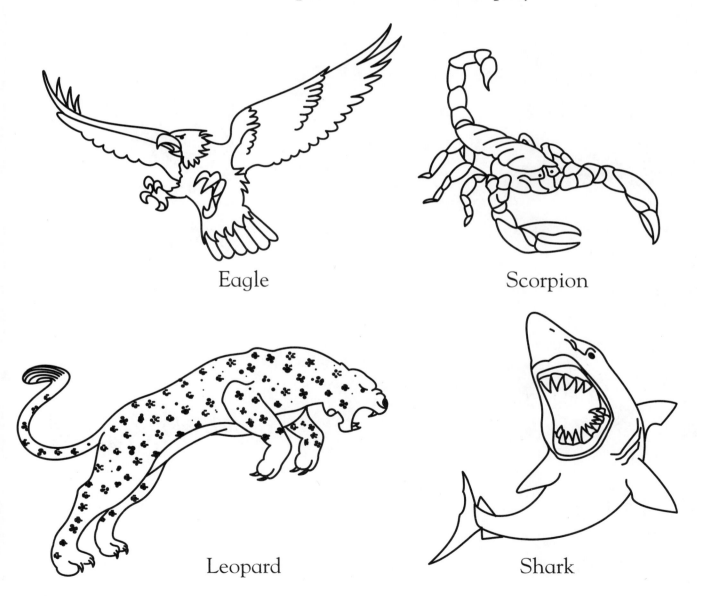

Eagle

Scorpion

Leopard

Shark

Mouths

FACTS

Different animals have different mouth parts that help them eat their favorite foods. Carnivores have sharp, pointed teeth for tearing meat. Herbivores have wide, flat teeth for grinding grass and leaves. Insect-eaters often have long, sticky tongues for catching flying insects. Many birds have sharp, pointed beaks for cracking open nuts and seeds.

Look at the animals and food below. Draw a line from each animal to the food it likes to eat.

Animals

Tiger

Chickadee

Chameleon

Cow

Food

Butterfly

Zebra

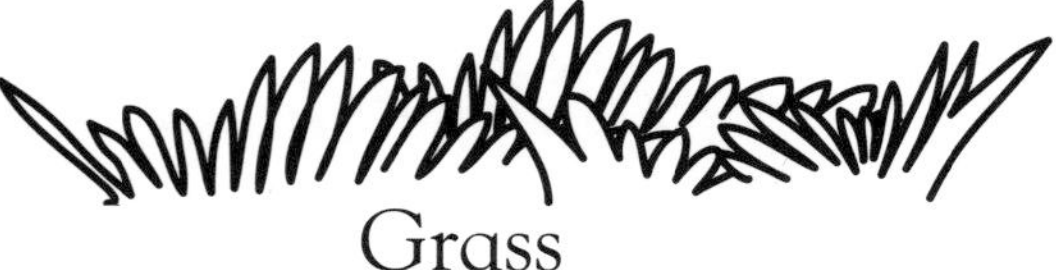

Grass

Seeds

A place where an animal normally lives is called its habitat. Animals are found almost everywhere on Earth, so there are many different kinds of habitats, such as grass, woodland, underground, rivers and lakes, oceans, and the seashore.

Look at the animals and habitats below. Draw a line from each animal to the picture of its habitat.

Animals

Worm

Squirrel

Frog

Crab

Habitats

Seashore

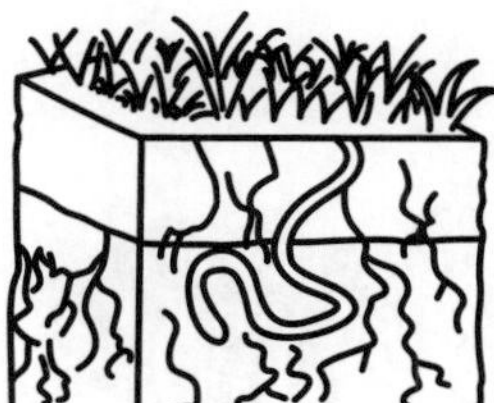

Underground

Forest

Pond

Living in Water

FACTS

Many animals live in water. They have special features, such as fins, flippers, smooth bodies, and flat tails, which help them swim.

Look at the animals below. Circle those that live in water. Point to each animal and say what features it has to help it swim.

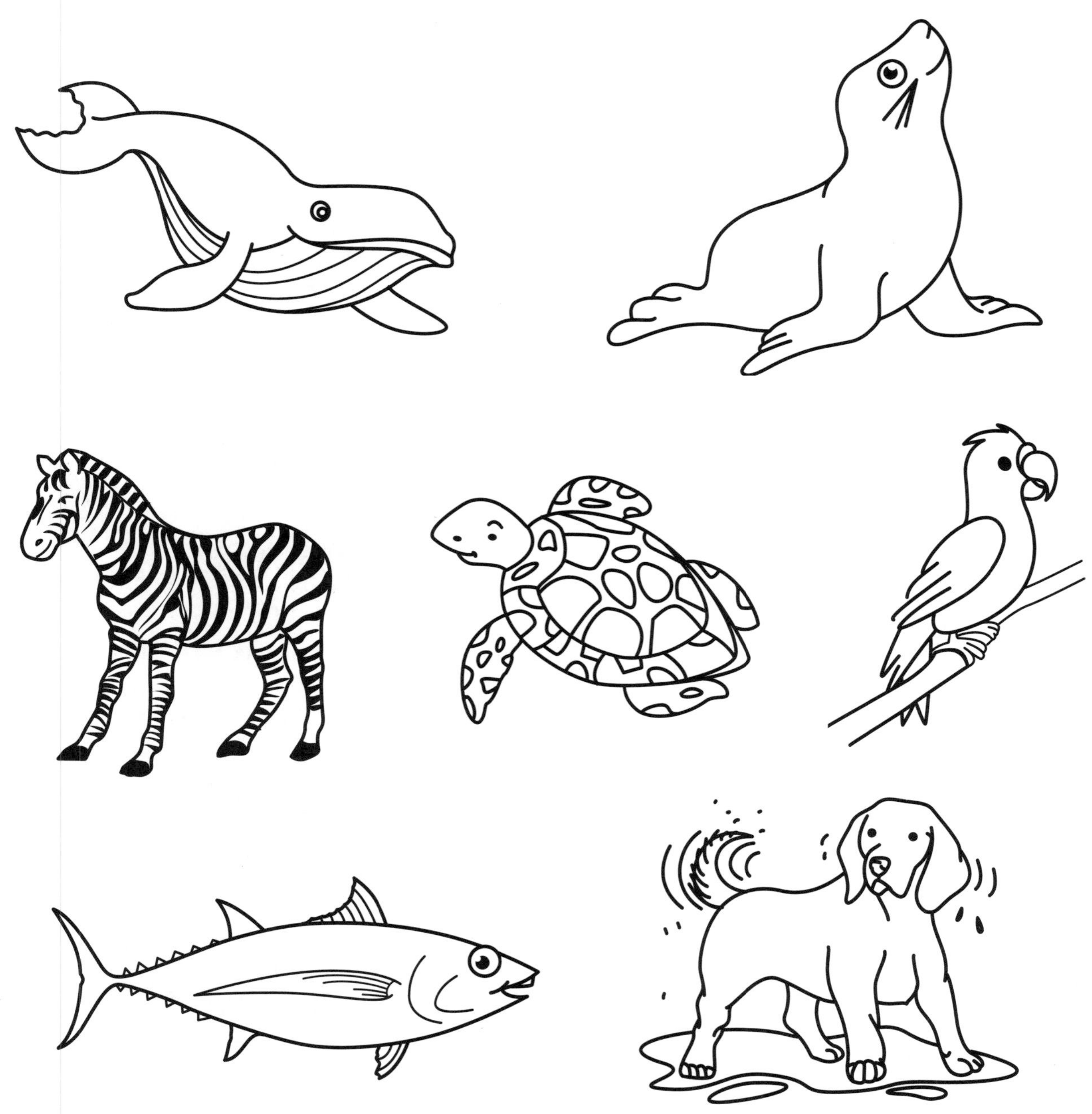

Body Coverings

Different animals have different types of body coverings. Some animals are covered in hair, fur, or feathers, which keep the animal warm and dry. Others have scales, sharp quills, or a hard shell, which help protect the animal's body.

Look at the animals below. Draw a line between each animal and the word that describes the type of body covering it has.

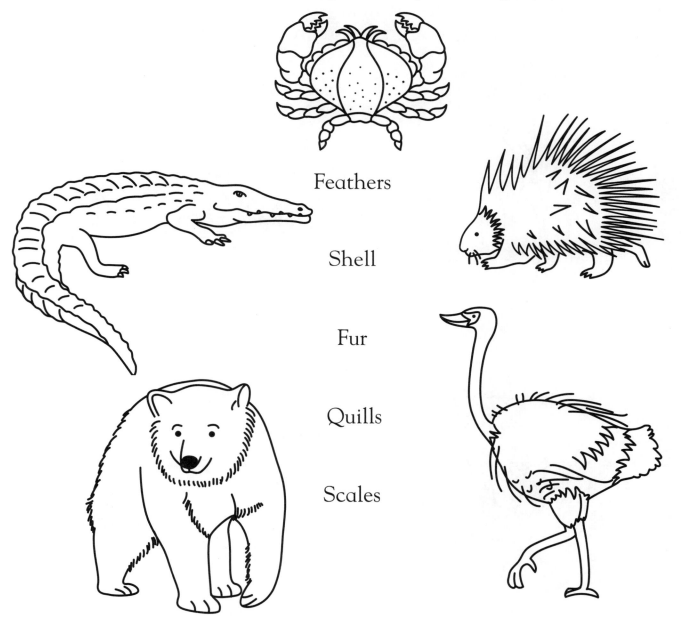

Feathers

Shell

Fur

Quills

Scales

Forest Food Chain

FACTS

A food chain shows how living things get food from the plants and animals around them. Food chains often start with a plant, which is eaten by an animal. Then that animal gets eaten by a bigger animal.

These four living things are part of a forest food chain. Like most food chains, this one begins with a plant. Draw arrows from one animal to the next, showing which animal eats which. **Hint:** Larger animals usually eat smaller animals.

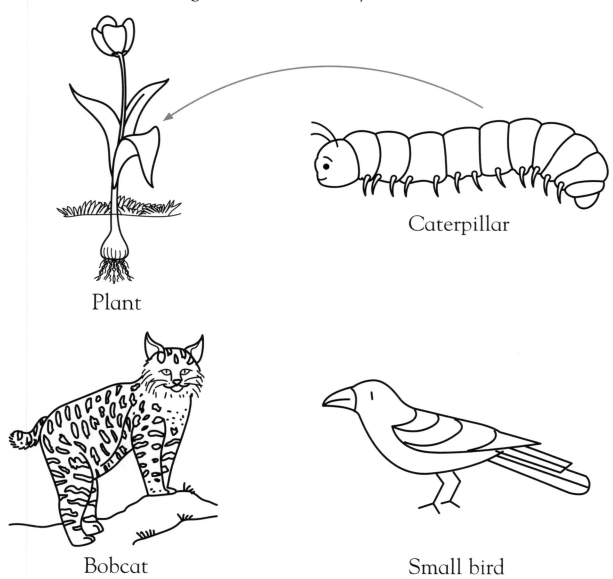

Plant

Caterpillar

Bobcat

Small bird

There are food chains in the ocean as well as on land.

These four animals are part of an ocean food chain that starts with a shrimp. Draw arrows from one animal to the next, showing which animal eats which. **Hint:** Larger animals usually eat smaller animals.

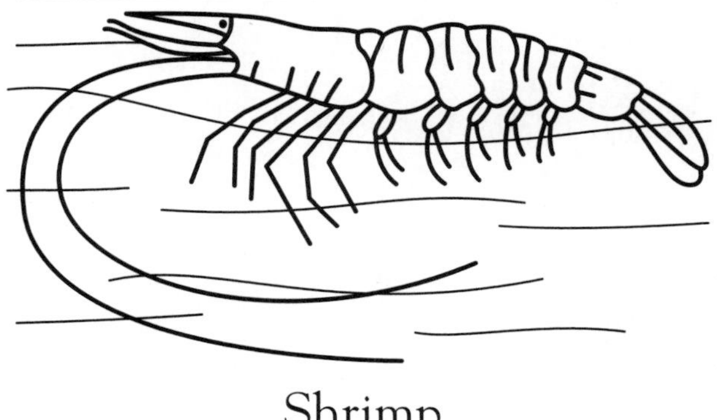

Shrimp

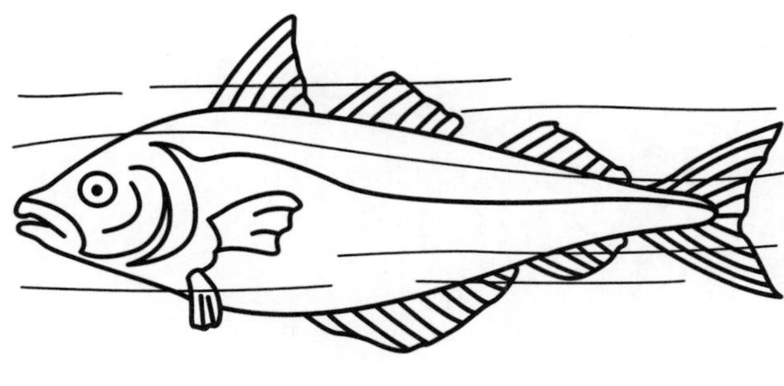

Arctic cod

Polar bear

Seal

Dinosaurs

Dinosaurs and other prehistoric animals lived millions of years ago. Scientists believe there were more than 1,000 different types. Tyrannosaurus rex was a huge fierce meat-eater with lots of sharp teeth. The long-necked Brachiosaurus fed on leaves high up in the trees. Other animals, like Pterodactylus, had wings and could fly.

Connect the dots to reveal the prehistoric animals. Then color them.

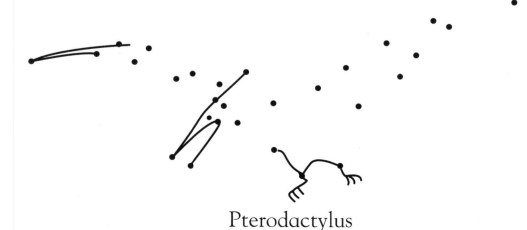

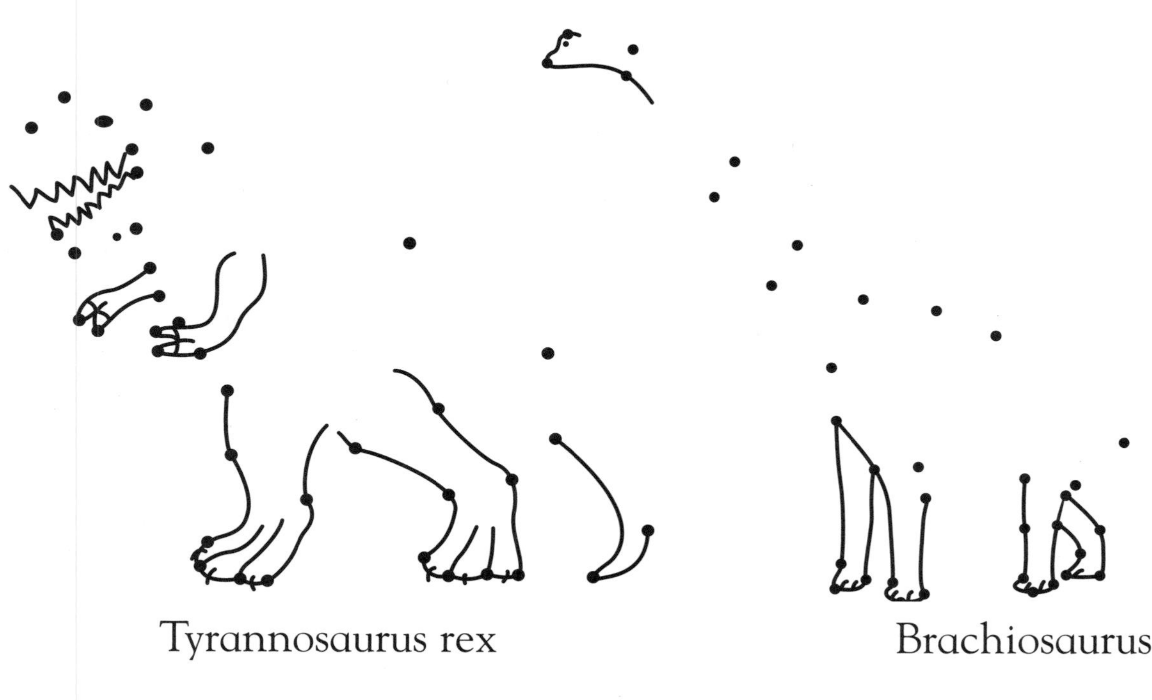

Pterodactylus

Sometimes whole groups of animals die out and no longer appear anywhere on Earth. These animals are called extinct. Many animals alive today are related to animals that are now extinct.

Look at the pictures of animals below. Circle those that are still alive today. Now point to the animals you did not circle. Those animals are extinct.

Dodo

Chickadee

Pterodactylus

Woolly mammoth

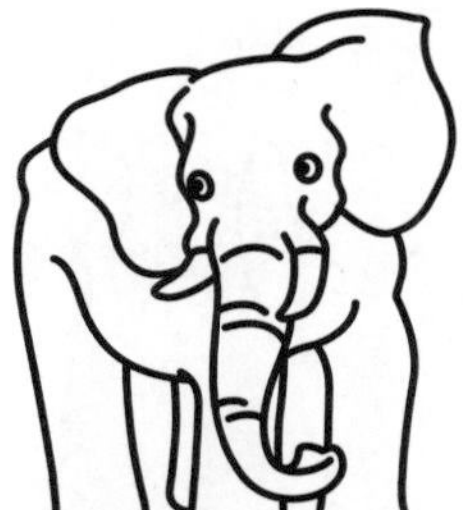

Elephant

Cat

Saber-toothed cat

Fossils

A fossil is the remains of a plant or animal that has been preserved in rock. There are different types of fossils: footprints and plants can make impressions—or indents—in rock. Shells, skeleton, and teeth can be preserved in the rock.

Read the list of different types of fossils given below. Draw a line between the name of each type of fossil and the correct picture.

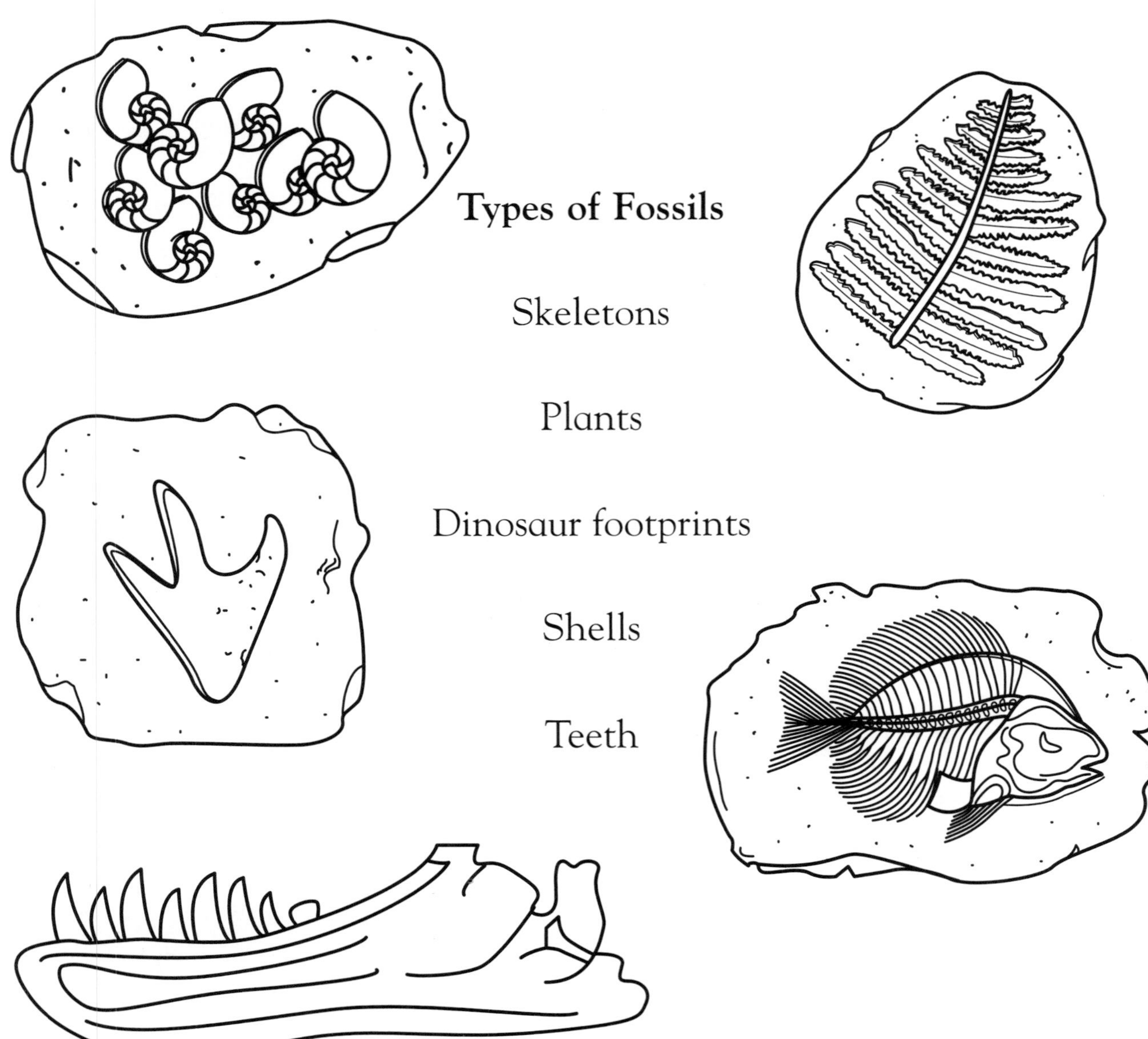

Types of Fossils

Skeletons

Plants

Dinosaur footprints

Shells

Teeth

Humans, plants, and animals share Earth. We need to take care of Earth so that plants, animals, and humans can survive and flourish. There are many ways to take care of Earth. We can recycle metal, plastic, and glass. We can plant trees and flowers. We can use energy from the sun—called solar power. We can use windmills to capture energy from the wind.

Look at the picture. Circle all the things that humans are doing to help the planet.

Natural Resources

Natural resources are things that naturally occur on Earth, which we can use to make other things. Wood is a natural resource that we use to make furniture, buildings, and paper. Oil from deep underground gives us fuel. Water is used for drinking. Sheep give us wool.

Draw a line from each natural resource to the product that is made from it.

Natural Resources	**Products**
 Trees	 Gasoline
 Water	 Wool
 Oil	 Beverages
 Sheep	 Wooden table

The things around you are made from many different materials. Three common materials are wood, metal, and plastic. Metals are usually hard, shiny, and cold to touch. Wood feels warm and often makes a hollow "thud" when you tap it. Plastics come in many forms but are often smooth and shiny.

Write **W** beneath the objects that are made of wood, **M** beneath the ones made of metal, and **P** beneath the ones made of plastic.

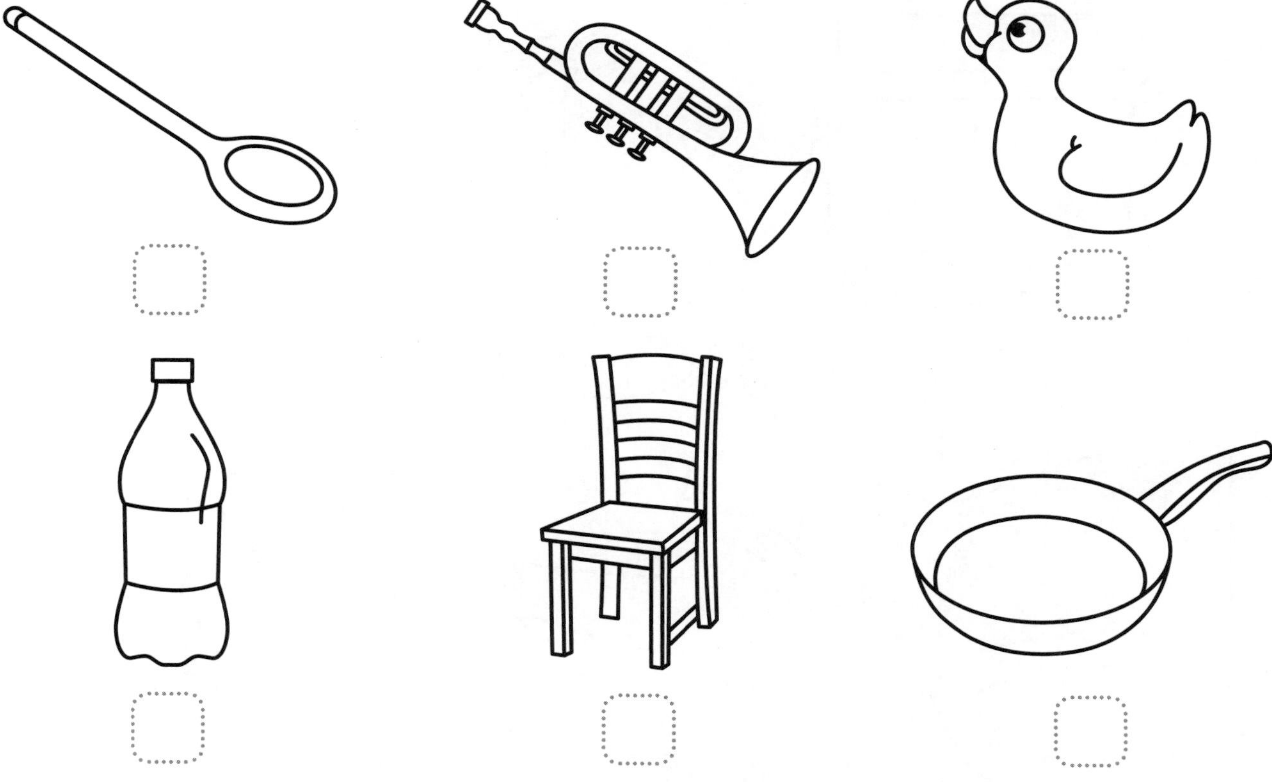

Look around you. Write the name of something made of metal and something made of plastic that you can see.

Metal ....

Plastic ....

Metals

FACTS

Metal is a very useful material and is used to make many different things. Metal objects are usually hard and shiny, and are cold to touch. Some types of metal make a ringing sound when you hit them.

Look at this picture and circle the things made of metal.

Many of the things that we use every day are made of plastic. Plastic is not a natural material, like wood or metal. It is made in a factory. It is strong, lightweight, and can be very useful.

Look at the objects below. Circle those that are made of plastic.

On a separate piece of paper, make a list of all the things in your room that are plastic. How many plastic things did you list?

Wood

FACTS

Wood comes from trees. Lots of the things all around you are made of wood. Wooden things float in water, make a dull sound when you tap them, and often smell nice.

Look at the chart. Put a check (✓) in the correct box next to each object shown on the chart.

Object	Wood	Not Wood
Pencil	☐	☐
Bottle	☐	☐
Spoon	☐	☐
Log	☐	☐
Chair	☐	☐

Paper is also made from wood. You use paper objects every day at home and at school. Books, newspapers, cardboard, notebooks, and tissues are some of the paper things that people use every day.

Look at the objects shown below. Circle the objects that are made of paper.

Length

FACTS

Length is a measure of how long something is.

TEST **What You Need:**

Tape measure

Pencil

What To Do:

Working with an adult, use the tape measure to find the length of the parts of your body listed on the chart. Record the lengths.

RESULT

Body Part	Length
Index finger	inches
Thumb	inches
Foot	inches
Lower leg	inches
Lower arm	inches

Which two body parts are the longest? Which are the shortest?

....

....

Measuring Temperature

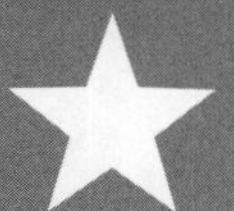

Temperature is a measure of how warm or cold something is. A thermometer is an instrument that measures temperature.

These thermometers measure temperature. Look at each one and write the temperature shown on it in the boxes.

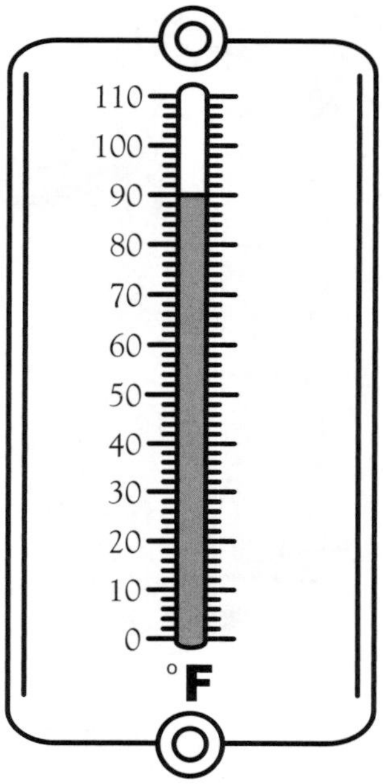

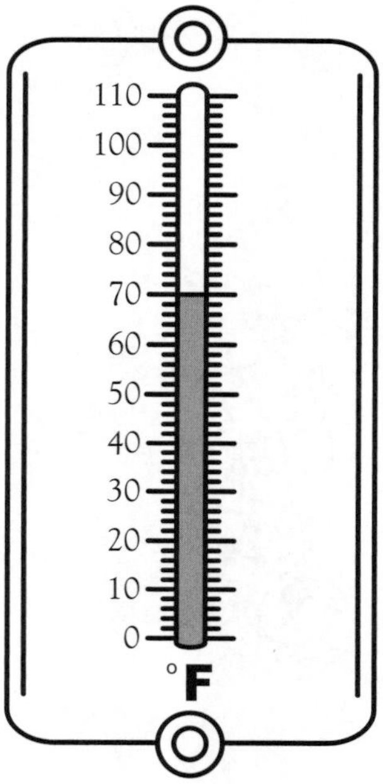

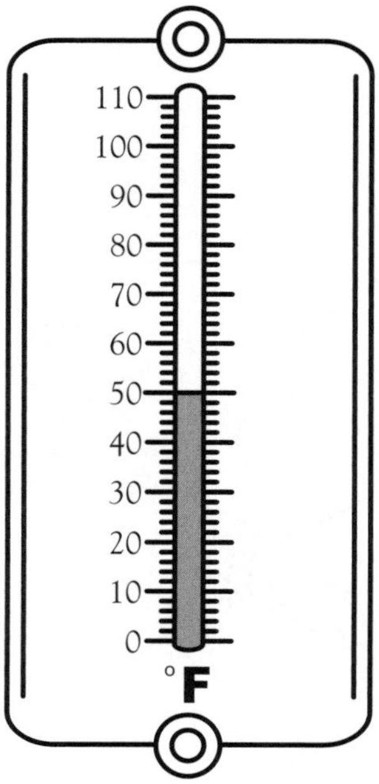

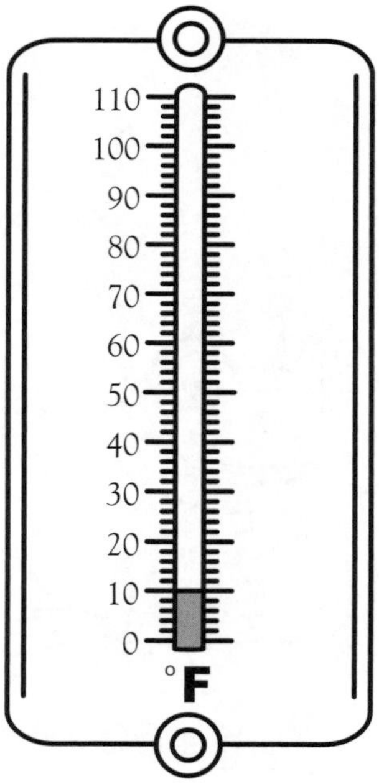

Height

FACTS

Height is a measure of how high or tall something is.

The heights of the four animals shown below are measured using a ruler. The seahorse is 4 in. tall. Write down the height of the other three animals.

4 in.

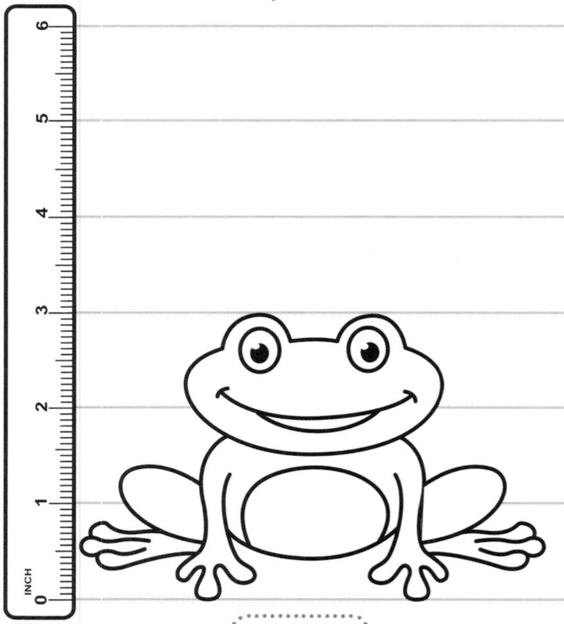

Speed is a measure of how slow or fast something moves.

Write **F** for fast or **S** for slow under each picture.

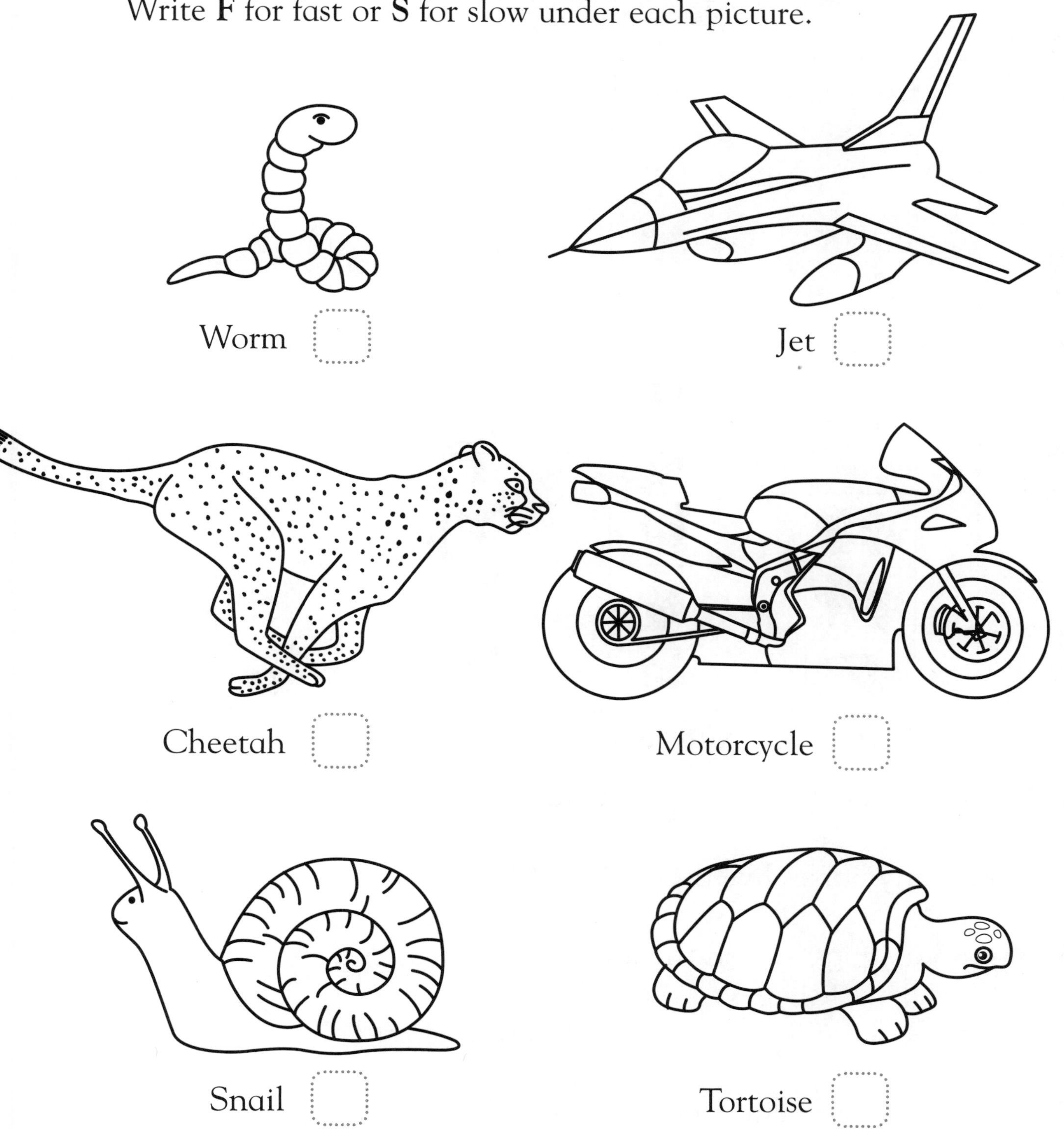

Bar Graph

FACTS

A bar graph is a way of showing information, so you can compare the facts easily.

This bar graph shows how many animals live on a farm. Look at the graph and answer the questions.

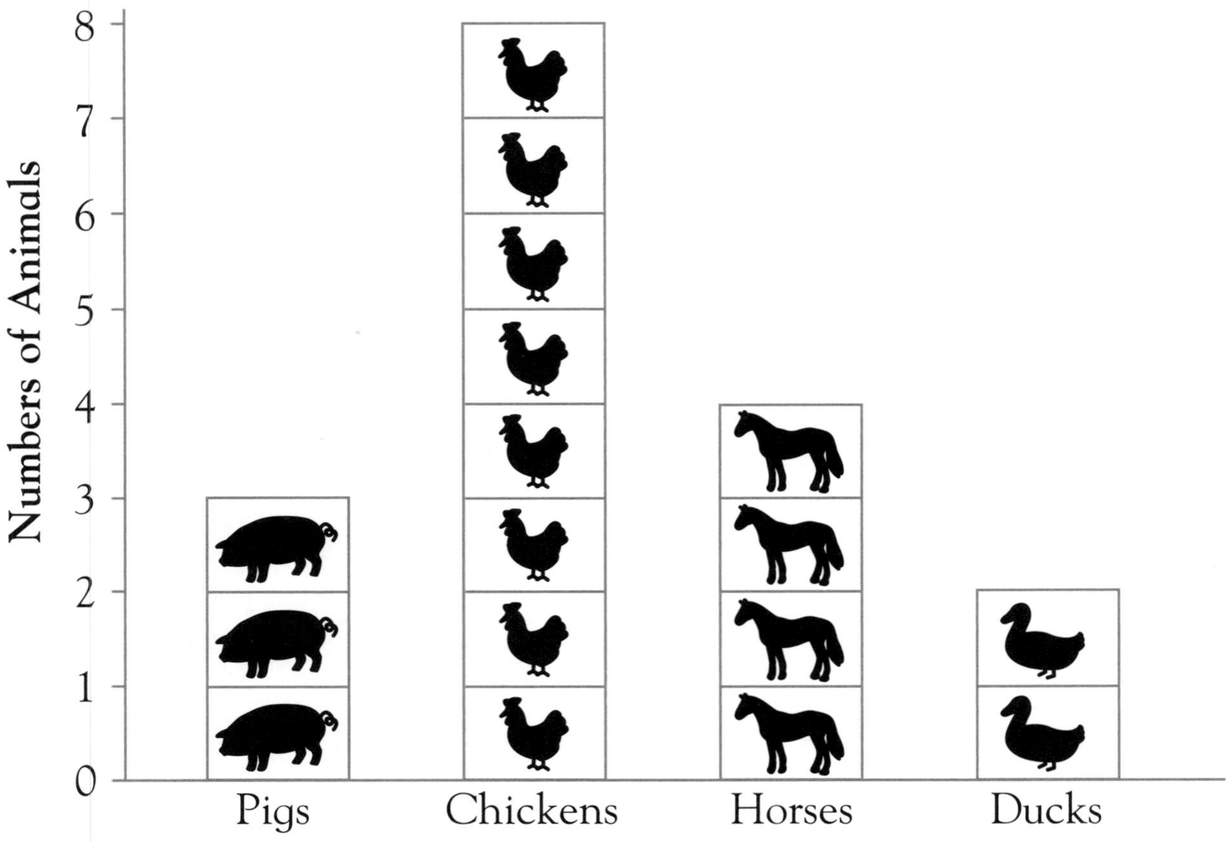

1. How many chickens live on the farm?

2. How many horses live on the farm?

3. How many pigs live on the farm?

4. Are there more pigs or more ducks on the farm? ....

5. How many more chickens than ducks live on the farm?

There are 24 hours in every day, and 60 minutes in each hour.

How do you spend the hours and minutes in your day? Write your name at the top of the chart.

For one day, ask your mom, dad, or other adult to time how long it takes you to do the activities shown on the chart below. Ask the person timing you to write on the chart the number of hours or minutes you spent on each activity.

My Day:............................	
Activities	**Time**
Eat breakfast	
Brush teeth	
Play	
Eat lunch	
Eat dinner	
Watch television	
Read	
Brush teeth/ Get ready for bed	

Matter

FACTS

Matter is the name used to describe all the different material that makes up the universe. All matter exists as a solid, liquid, or gas. A solid keeps its shape. A liquid flows, and takes the shape of the container it is in. A gas will also flow and expand and fill the container that it is in.

Answer the questions on the chart by writing **Yes** or **No** under the name of each substance named at the top of the chart. Then answer the questions under the chart.

Material	**Water**	**Air**	**Penny**
Will it flow?			
Does it keep its shape?			
Will it spread to fill a container?			

1. Which material is a solid? ....

2. Which material is a liquid? ....

3. Which material is a gas? ....

Solids do not change shape by themselves. They will not pour or spread out to fill a space.

Look at the materials shown below. Put a check (✓) in the box next to the name of each one, if you think it is a solid.

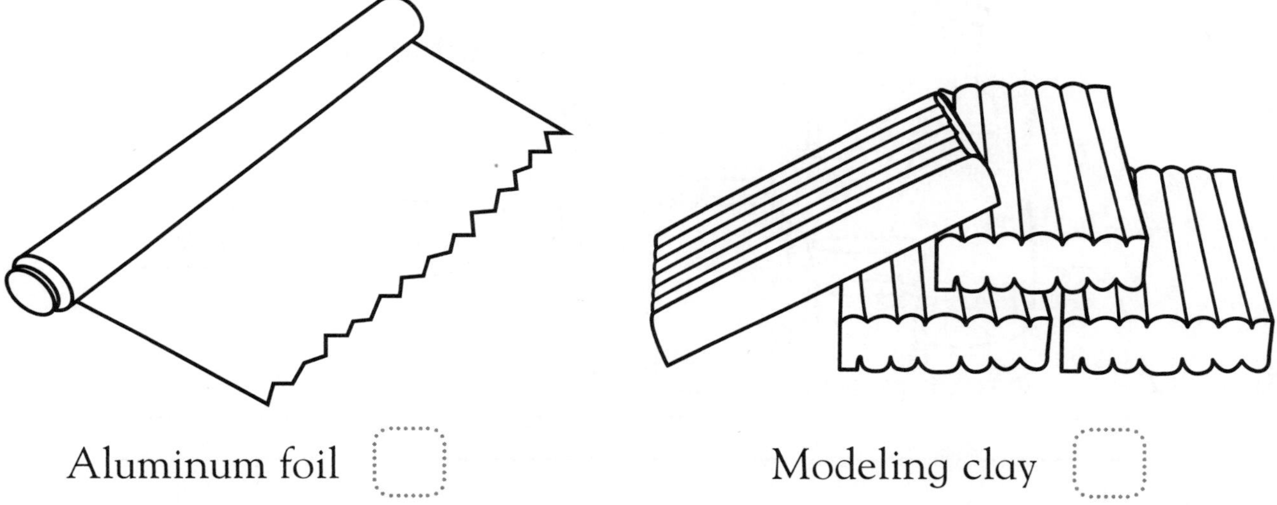

Aluminum foil ☐ Modeling clay ☐

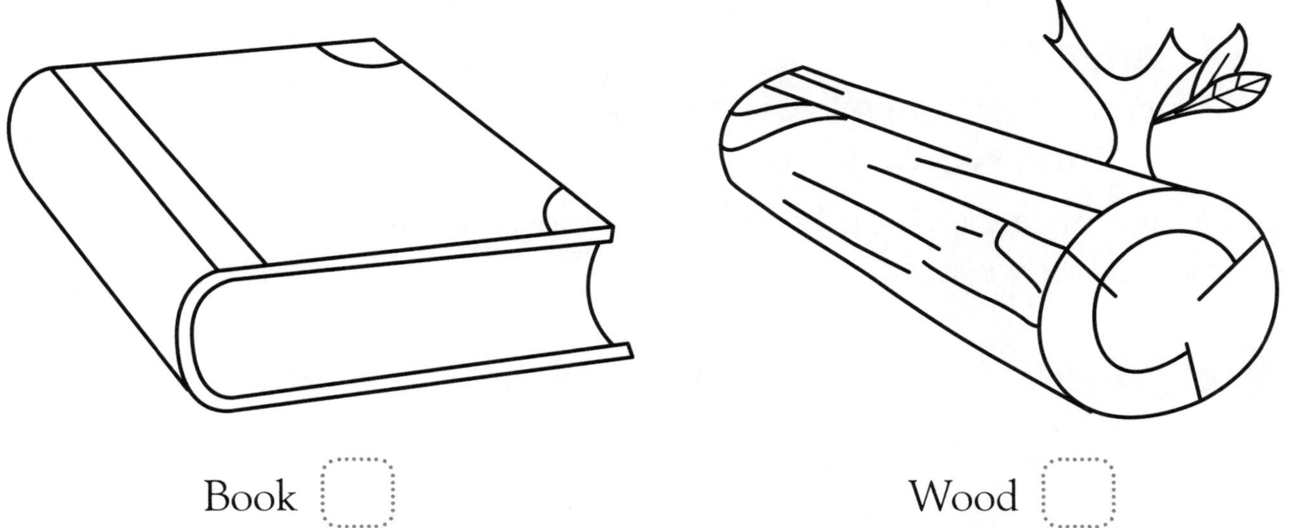

Book ☐ Wood ☐

Liquids

FACTS

Liquids will flow, and take the shape of whatever container they are in. They can also be poured. Some liquids flow faster than others.

TEST **What You Need:**

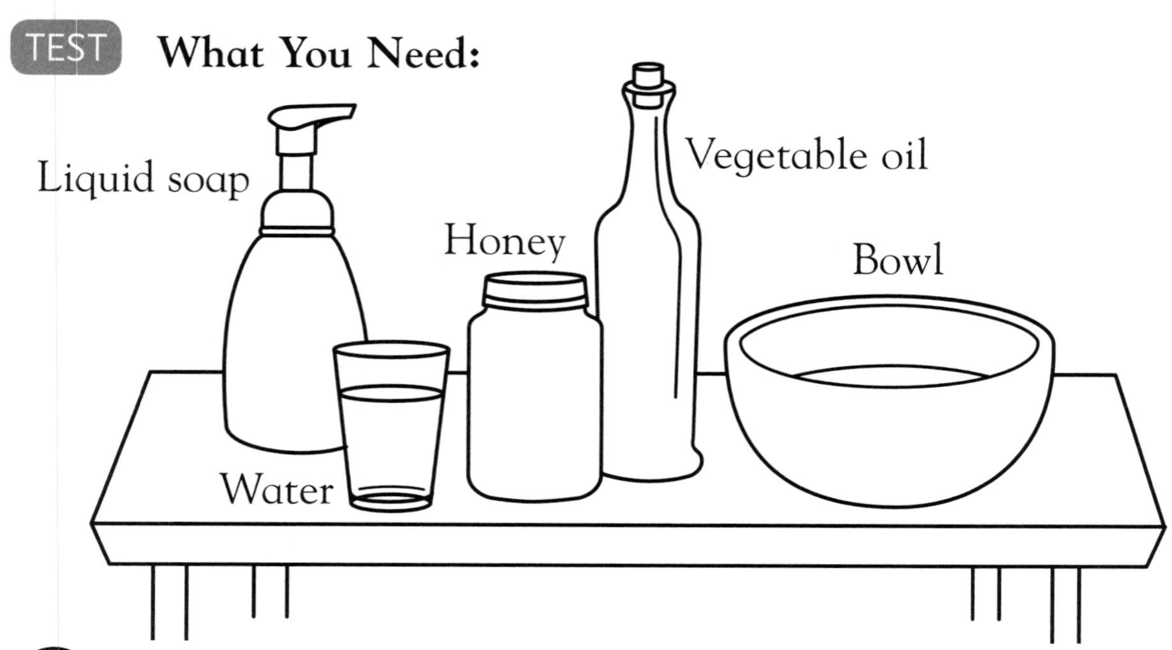

What To Do:

1. Pour a small amount of the liquid soap into the bowl. How quickly did the soap pour? Now pour a small amount of water. How quickly did that pour? Repeat with the honey and vegetable oil.
2. Make note of which liquid poured fastest and which poured slowest.

RESULT

Liquid that pours fastest ....

Liquid that pours slowest ....

Some solids mix into liquids so that the solid seems to disappear. The solid dissolves into the liquid. This happens when you mix sugar into water. You can no longer see the sugar, but you know it is there because the water tastes sweet. Salt is another solid that dissolves in liquids. But some solids, such as pebbles or rice, will not dissolve.

Look at the pictures below. Each one shows a solid next to a liquid. Circle the two solid and liquid pairs where the solid will dissolve into the liquid.

Soup and salt

Water and rice

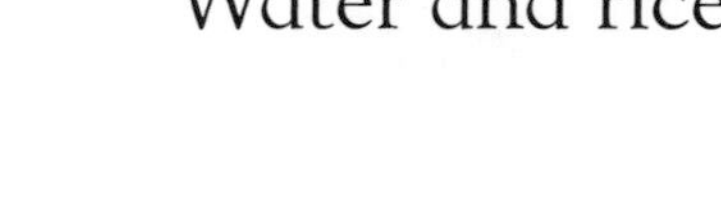

Juice and pebbles

Water and sugar

Heat and Dissolving

FACTS

How hot or cold a liquid is can make a difference to how quickly a solid will dissolve in it.

TEST **What You Need:**

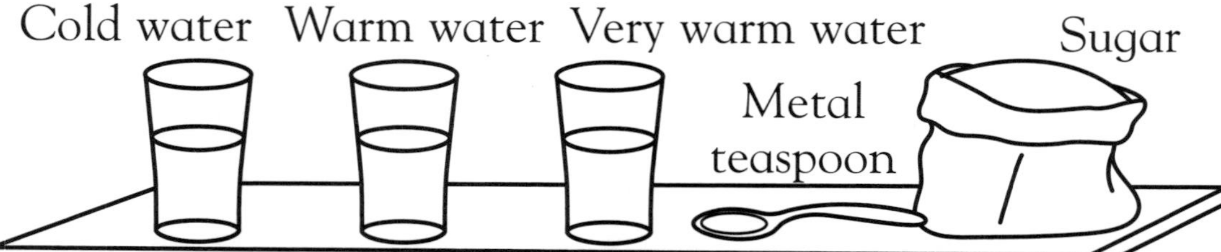

What To Do:

1. Take three glasses. Fill one halfway with cold water, another with warm water, and the third with very warm water.
2. Stir a teaspoon of the sugar into the cold water, counting how many times you have to stir until the sugar has completely dissolved. Make a note of the number of stirs on the chart.
3. Repeat Step 2, stirring a teaspoon of sugar into the warm water. Again count and note the number of stirs it takes for the sugar to completely dissolve. Repeat again, stirring sugar into the very warm water.

RESULT Look at your results on the chart. Answer the question.

Water at Different Temperatures	Number of Stirs
Cold water	
Warm water	
Very warm water	

Does the sugar dissolve faster as the water gets hotter? ....

Air is a mixture of invisible gas. You cannot see it, but you can feel it blowing on a windy day. Just like solids and liquids, gases have weight, and some gases are heavier than others. A balloon filled with a light gas will float up higher than a balloon filled with a heavier gas.

Look at the picture below. The balloon with the swirly dots is filled with a very light gas. The stripy balloon is filled with a heavier gas. The balloon with the clouds on it is filled with the heaviest gas.

1. Point to the balloon with the heaviest gas.

2. Point to the balloon with the lightest gas.

3. Is the stripy balloon heavier or lighter than the balloon with the swirly dots?

....

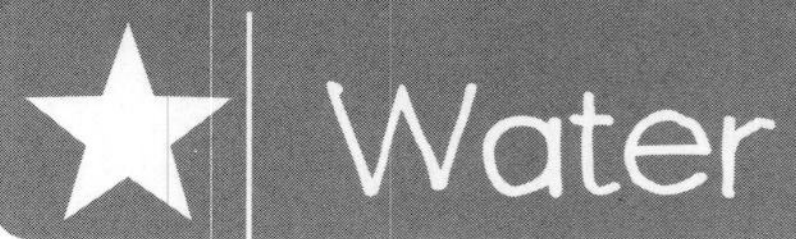

Water

FACTS

Water is usually a liquid, but it can also exist as a solid or gas. When you put water in the freezer, it turns into a solid by becoming ice. When your mom or dad boils water on the stove, it turns into a gas by becoming steam.

Look at the images below. Circle the images where water is a liquid. Make a square around the images where water is a gas. Make a triangle around the images where water is a solid.

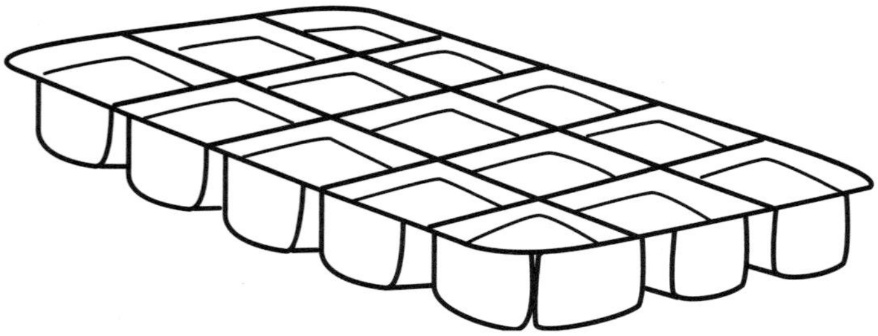

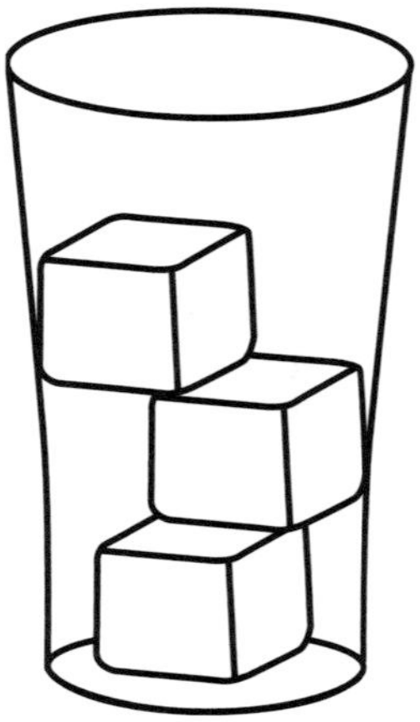

Scientists can tell us what kind of weather we are likely to have in the days and even weeks to come. This helps us prepare for our day, and choose what to wear (and bring) when we go out.

Look at the four scenes below. Then look at the clothes. Draw a line from each scene to the best clothes for the weather shown.

Scenes

Clothes

The Sun

The sun provides light and heat to Earth. The sun is always shining, but we do not always see that. Each day Earth spins around once. As Earth spins, the part facing the sun experiences day time. That part goes through morning and afternoon. As it continues to turn, it slowly turns into night while another part of Earth faces the sun and experiences day time.

Look at the three scenes shown below.

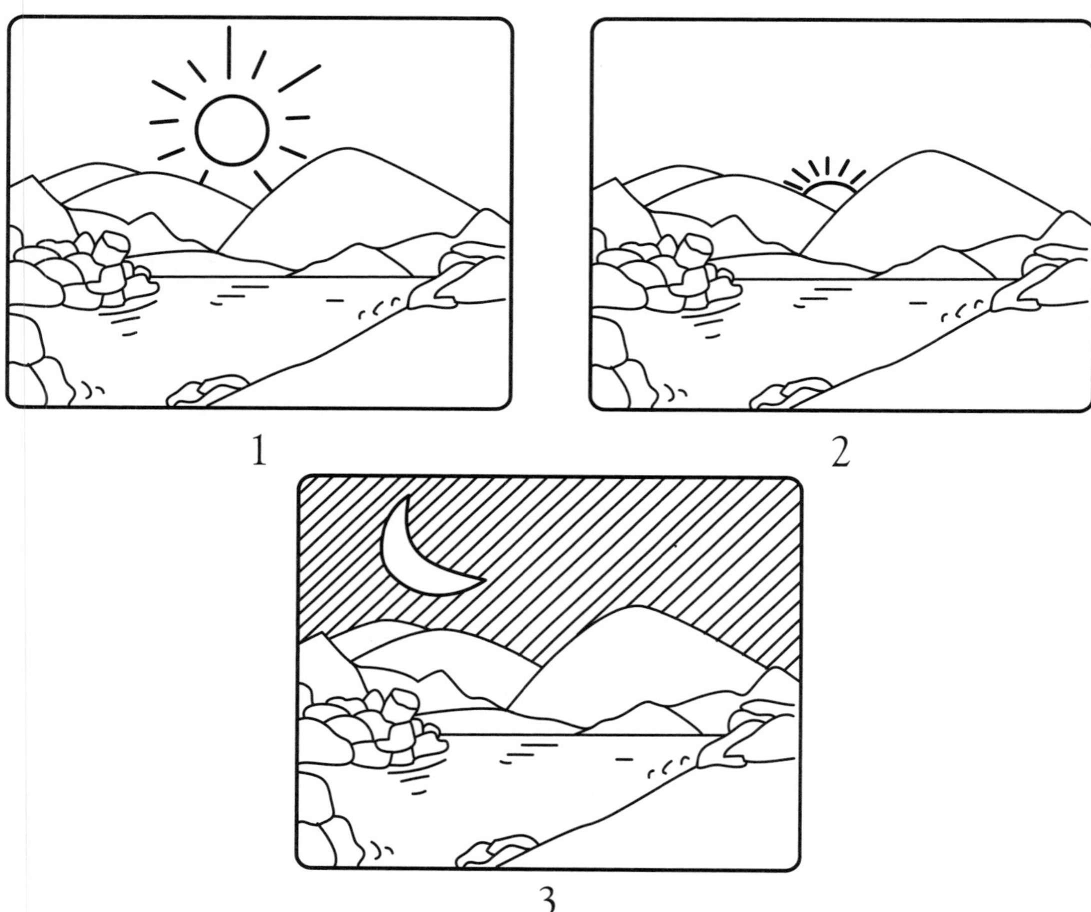

1. In which scene is the hillside facing away from the sun? ....
2. In which scene is the hillside facing the sun? ....
3. In which scene is the hillside turned halfway away from the sun? ....

The moon is a ball of rock that circles Earth about once a month. It looks like it changes shape throughout the month, but it does not. What we see depends on how much light is shining on the moon. The different moon shapes we see are called phases. There are four key phases. A new moon is almost invisible. A full moon looks like a complete circle. A half moon looks like a half circle, and a crescent moon looks like a thin crescent shape.

In the box are the names of the four phases of the moon. Use them to write the labels for the four pictures of the moon below.

Crescent	Full	Half	New

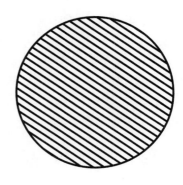

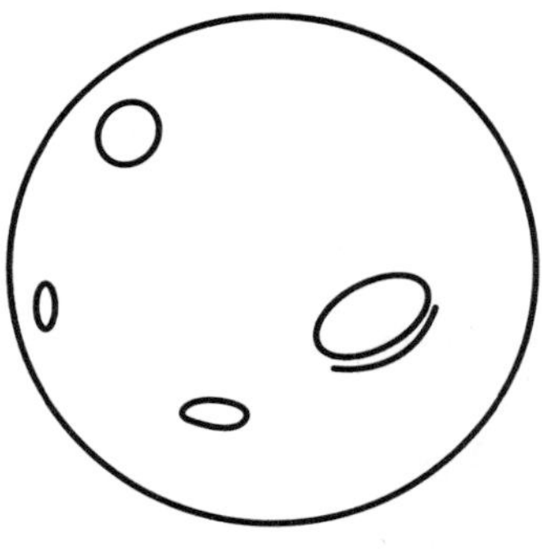

....

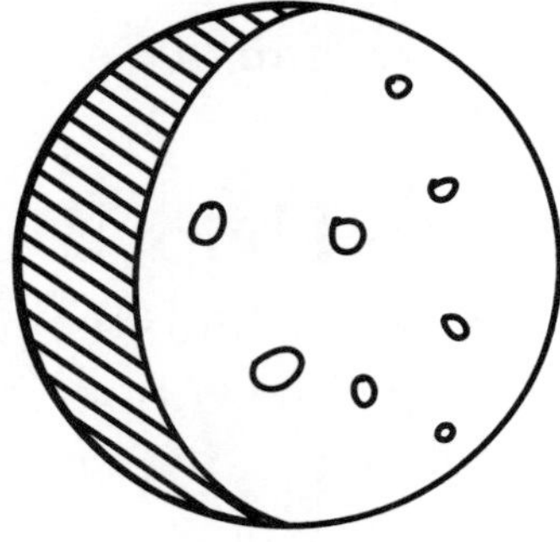

....

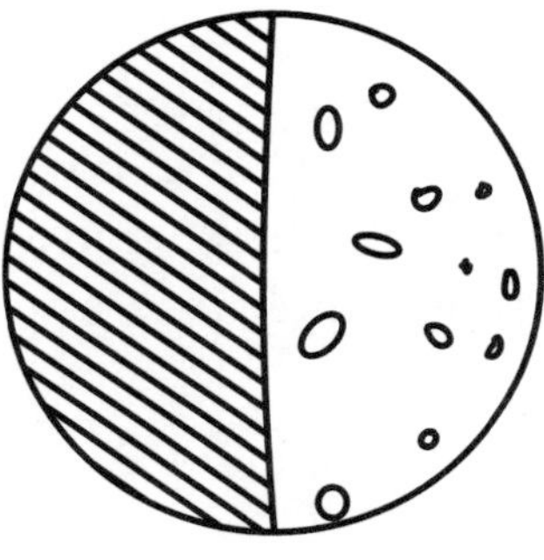

....

....

Parents' Notes

The science covered in this book is similar to the work your child will encounter in first grade. The topics covered are intended to introduce children to basic scientific concepts and ways of thinking about the world.

Contents

Working through this book, your child will gain knowledge about:

- living things;
- animal movement;
- plant life;
- the heart;
- bones and muscles;
- teeth;
- healthy eating;
- animals' mouths and feeding;
- catching prey;
- food chains;
- habitats;
- living in water;
- body coverings;
- extinct animals;
- dinosaurs;
- fossils;
- human activity and the environment;
- natural resources;
- metals, plastic, wood, and paper;
- measuring length;
- temperature;
- speed;
- charts and bar graphs;
- solids, liquids, and gases;
- mixing and dissolving;
- the weather;
- the sun and moon.

How to Help Your Child

First graders will not be able to read many of the instructions. Therefore, there is an expectation that parents, guardians, or helpers will work closely with children as they progress through the activities. Both parents or helpers and children can gain a great deal from working together.

Perhaps the most important thing you can do—both as you go through the activities and in many everyday situations—is encourage children to be curious about the world around them. Whenever possible, ask them questions about what they see and hear. Ask them questions such as "Why?," "What if?," and "What do you think?" Do not be negative about their answers, however silly they may be. There is almost certainly a logic to their response, even if it is not correct. Explore and discuss their ideas with them.

Build your child's confidence with praise and encouragement.

Geography

Author Mark Shulman

Educational Consultant Kara Pranikoff

Contents

This chart lists all the topics in the Geography section.

Geography involves learning about the world around you. Geographers study both the natural world, and the way that humans use and change that world. When you look at a bridge across a river, you see both the natural and the human world. The river is part of the natural world. It was there long before people came to live near it. The bridge is part of the human world. People built the bridge to help them cross the river.

Use the words "natural" or "human" to complete the sentences below.

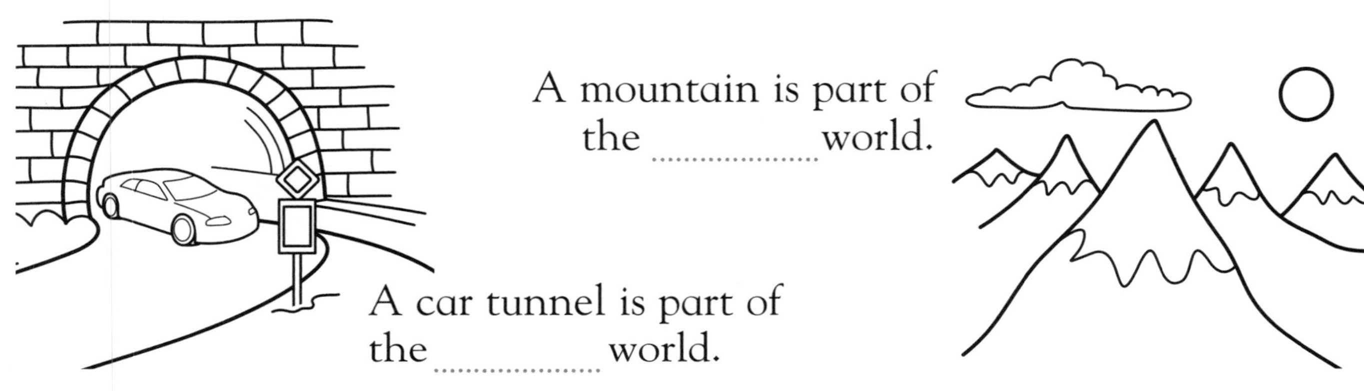

A mountain is part of the .... world.

A car tunnel is part of the .... world.

Write **N** next to the things that are part of the natural world.
Write **H** next to the things that form part of the human world.

Very few places on Earth today have not been affected by human activity. Almost everywhere you look you will see things from both the natural world and the human world.

Look at the picture below. Label the objects that are part of the natural world with the word "Natural" and those that are part of the human world with the word "Human."

Earth

We live on planet Earth. All planets, including Earth, are the shape of a sphere. A sphere is round in every direction, like a ball.

Circle the items that are spheres.

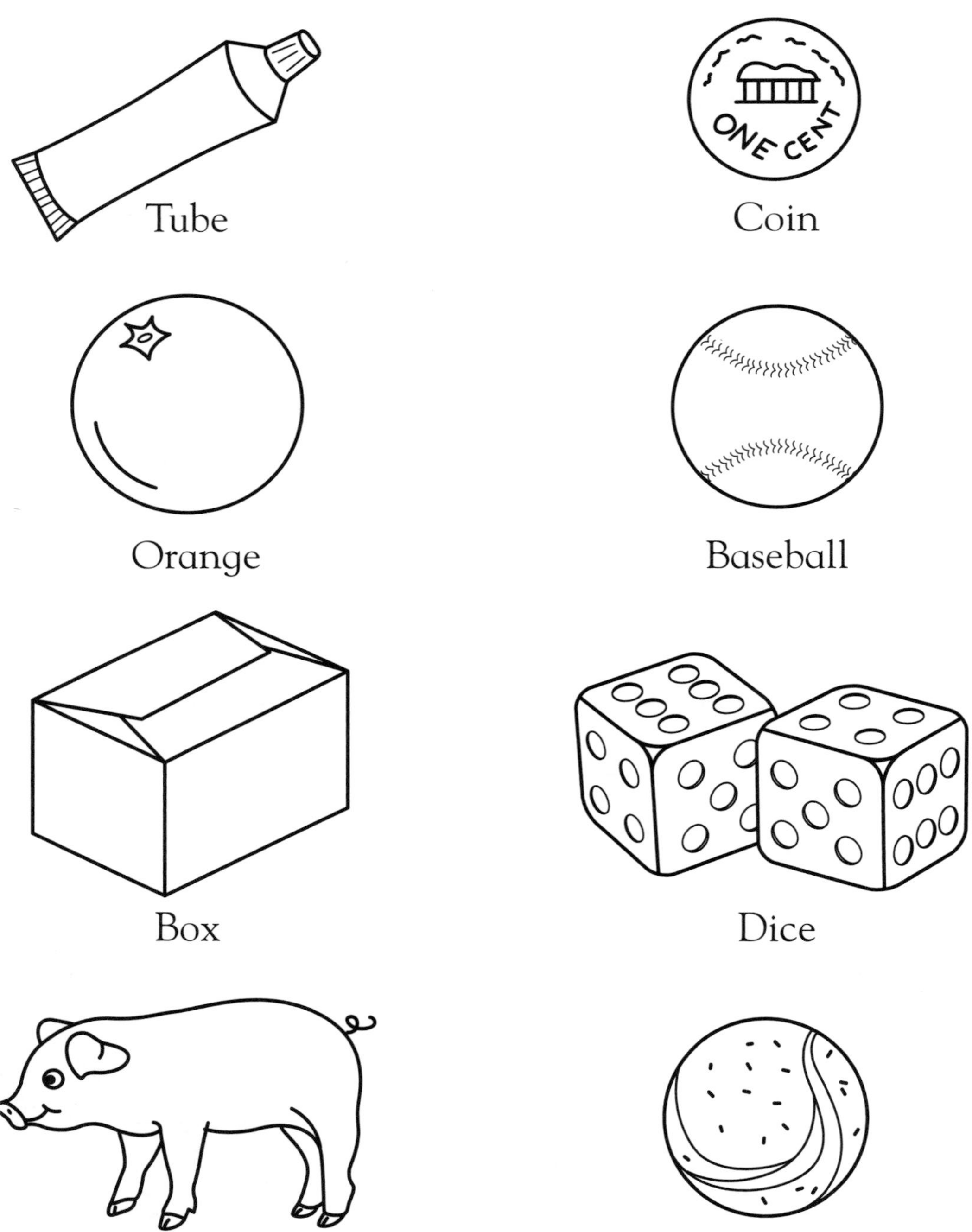

Maps are pictures that help us understand the world. They help us picture many kinds of places. Some maps show only the natural world. Other maps show the human world.

Use the words in the box to label the place shown on each of the maps below.

Bedroom	Country	City	Earth	Island	Mountain

....

....

....

Compass Directions

FACTS

"North," "south," "east," and "west" are words that describe directions. These directions are often marked on a map with a shape called a compass rose. The compass rose tells you in which direction the top of the map is pointing. Most maps have north at the top and south at the bottom, with west on the left and east on the right. The compass rose does not always say north, south, east, and west. Often, it just says **N**, **S**, **E**, and **W**.

Look at the map below. Use the compass rose to answer the questions using the letters **N**, **S**, **E**, or **W**. Your starting point is the house in the middle of the map.

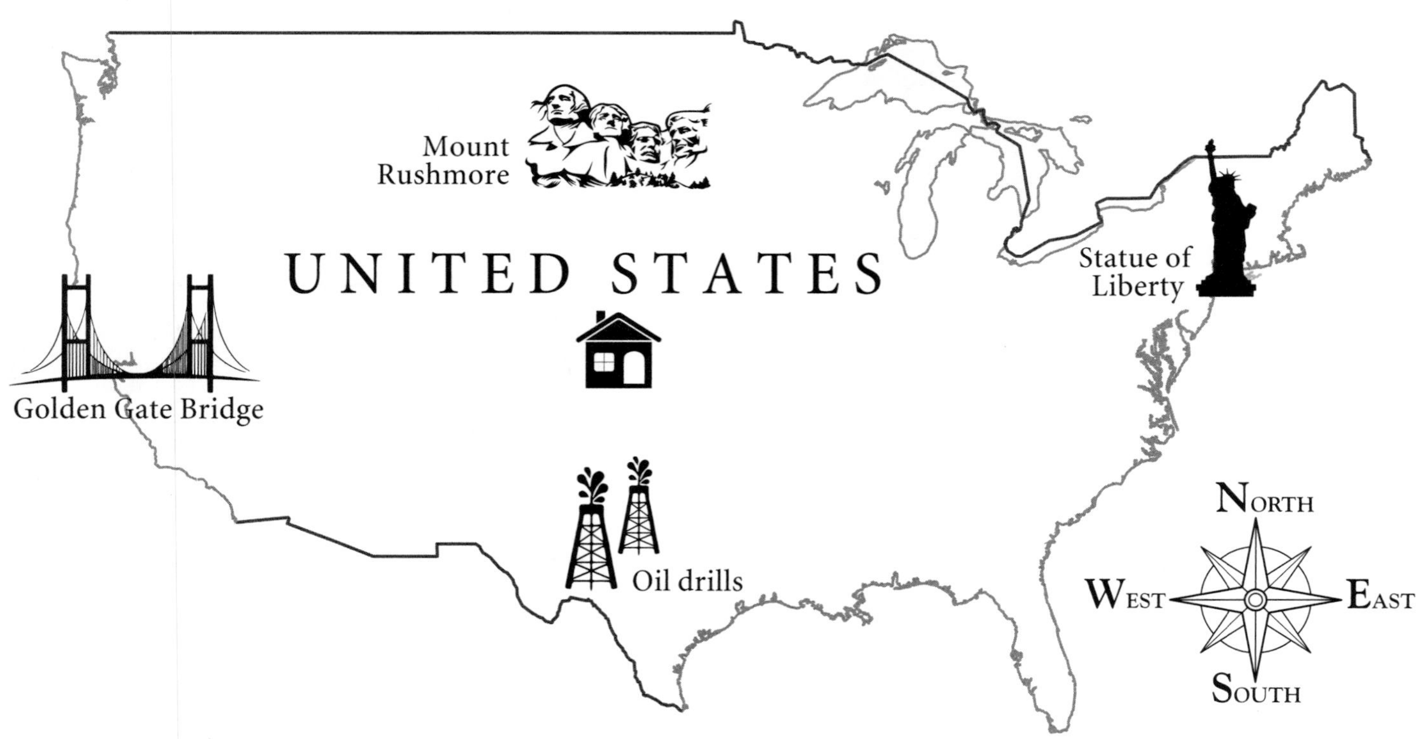

What direction will you travel from the house to the following places?

Oil drills in Texas		Statue of Liberty	
Mount Rushmore		Golden Gate Bridge	

There are seven very large areas of land on Earth. These are called continents. When you look at a map of Earth, you see the seven continents. They are Africa, Antarctica, Asia, Australia, Europe, North America, and South America.

Look at the map carefully and follow the instructions below.

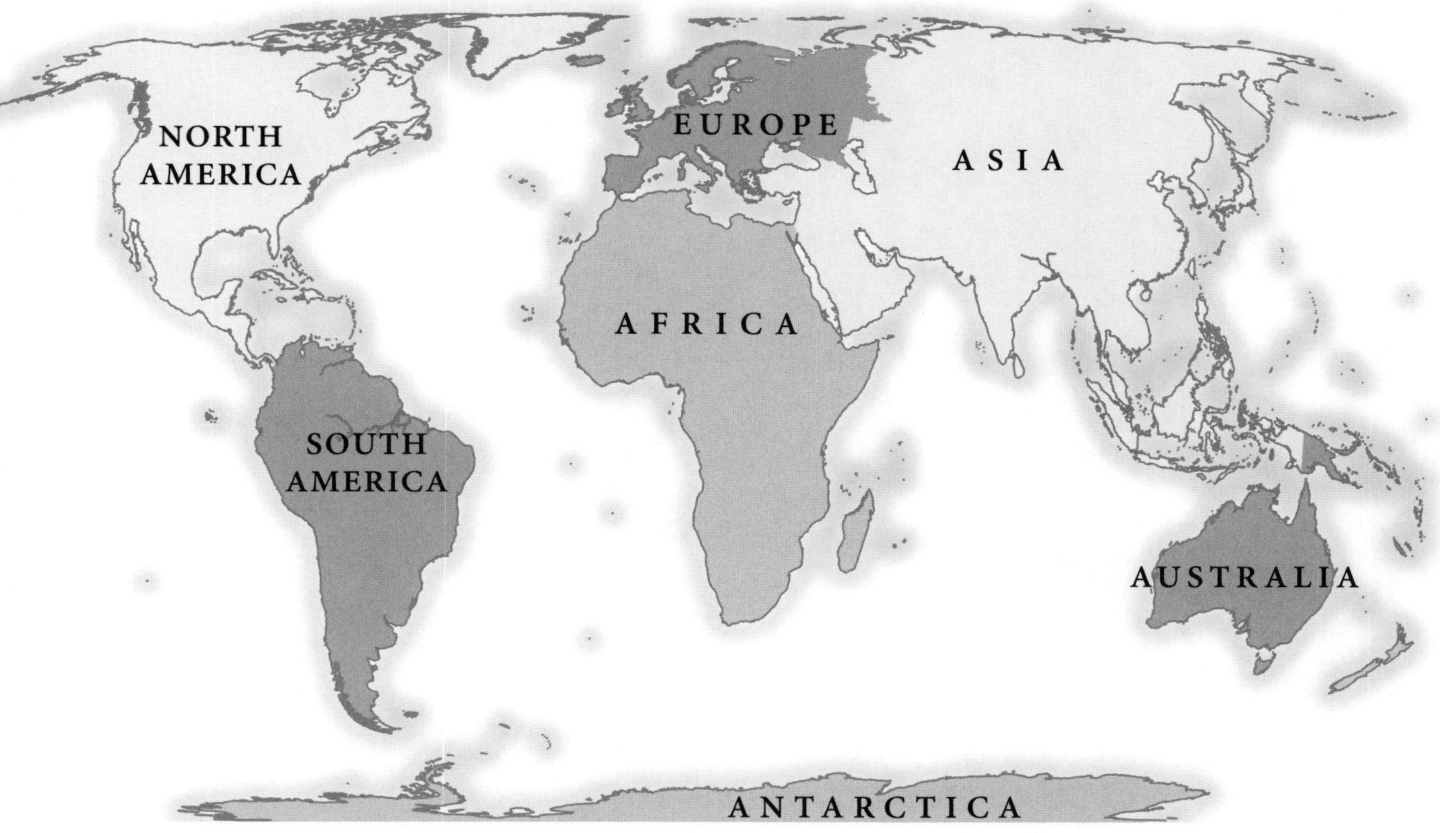

Name the largest continent. ....

Put an **X** on the continent that is the smallest.

Find the continent you live on and circle it.

North America

FACTS

The continent of North America has 23 countries. Of those countries, 12 are islands in the Caribbean Sea. There are seven small countries south of Mexico, which form the region called Central America. The three largest countries in North America are Canada, the United States of America, and Mexico.

Look at the map carefully and follow the instructions given below it.

Color Canada red.

Color the United States blue.

Color Mexico green.

The continent of South America is connected to North America. South America is divided into 12 countries. The largest country in South America is Brazil. The world's second longest river, the Amazon River, begins in the mountains of Peru and flows through northern Brazil.

Look at the map carefully and follow the instructions given below it.

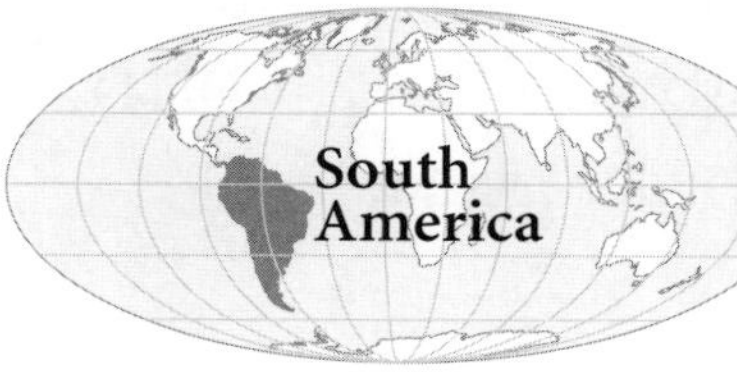

South America

Amazon River

PERU

BRAZIL

Color Brazil green.

Color Peru red.

Find the Amazon River and circle it.

Africa

FACTS

The continent of Africa is divided into 54 countries. Africa has many wild areas. It has the world's hottest desert, the Sahara, and one of the world's biggest waterfalls, Victoria Falls. There is a huge rain forest around the Congo River. Africa's eastern grasslands are home to giraffes, lions, gazelles, and the African elephant, which is the world's largest animal that lives on land.

Use the map and its compass rose to help you complete the sentences below. Write "north," "south," "east," "west," or "center" in each blank space.

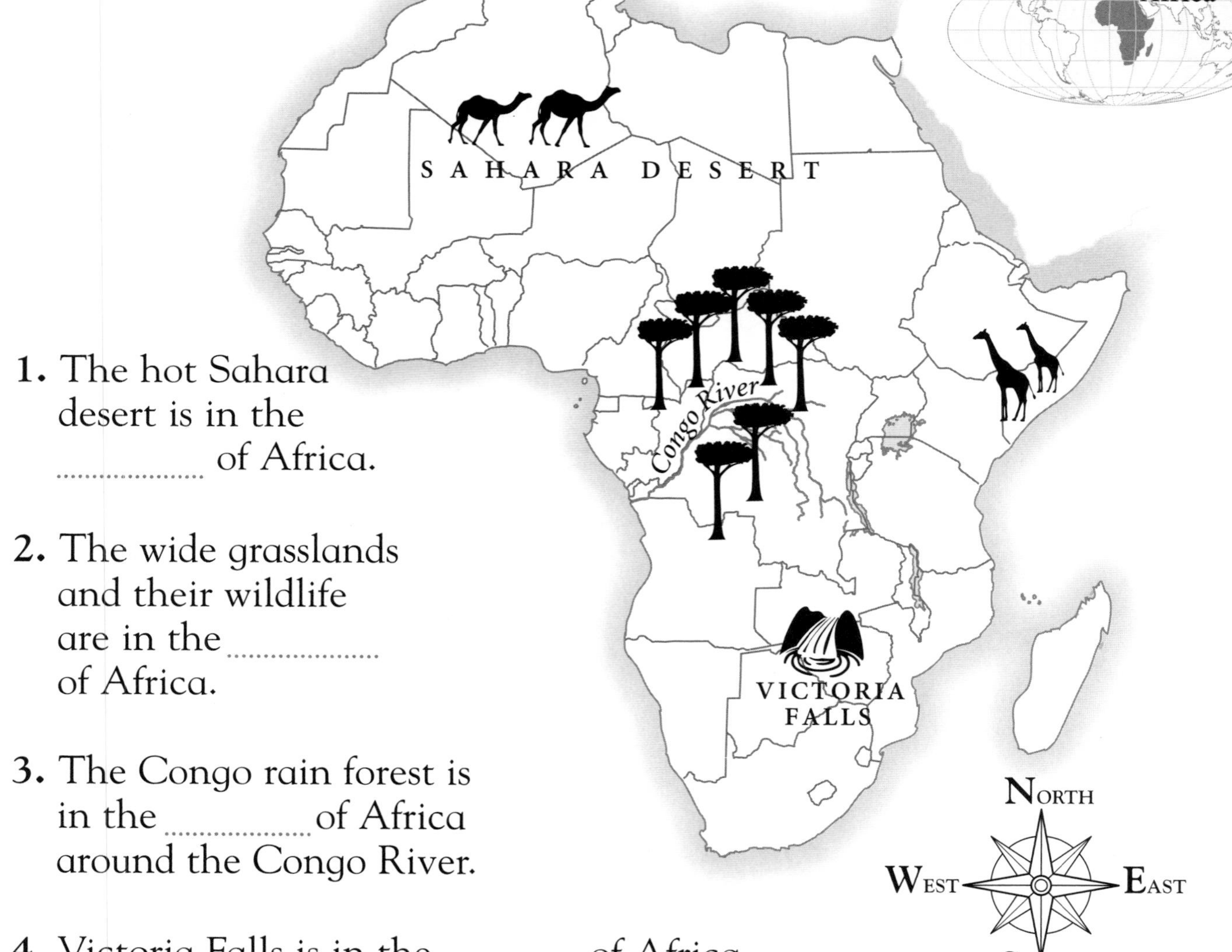

1. The hot Sahara desert is in the .... of Africa.

2. The wide grasslands and their wildlife are in the .... of Africa.

3. The Congo rain forest is in the .... of Africa around the Congo River.

4. Victoria Falls is in the .... of Africa.

Asia is the largest continent in the world. It has 49 countries and includes the world's largest country, Russia, which stretches all the way across the top of Asia. Asia is also home to the world's two most populated countries. They are China and India.

Look at the map of Asia and follow the instructions below it.

Write an **R** in Russia and draw a box around its name.
Write an **I** in India and draw a circle around its name.
Write a **C** in China and draw a triangle around its name.

Europe

FACTS

The continents of Europe and Asia are connected. Europe is divided into 46 countries. Many languages are spoken in the different countries of Europe.

Below is a list of five languages. Draw a line to connect each language to the country on the map where that language is spoken.

Languages

German

Greek

Italian

French

Spanish

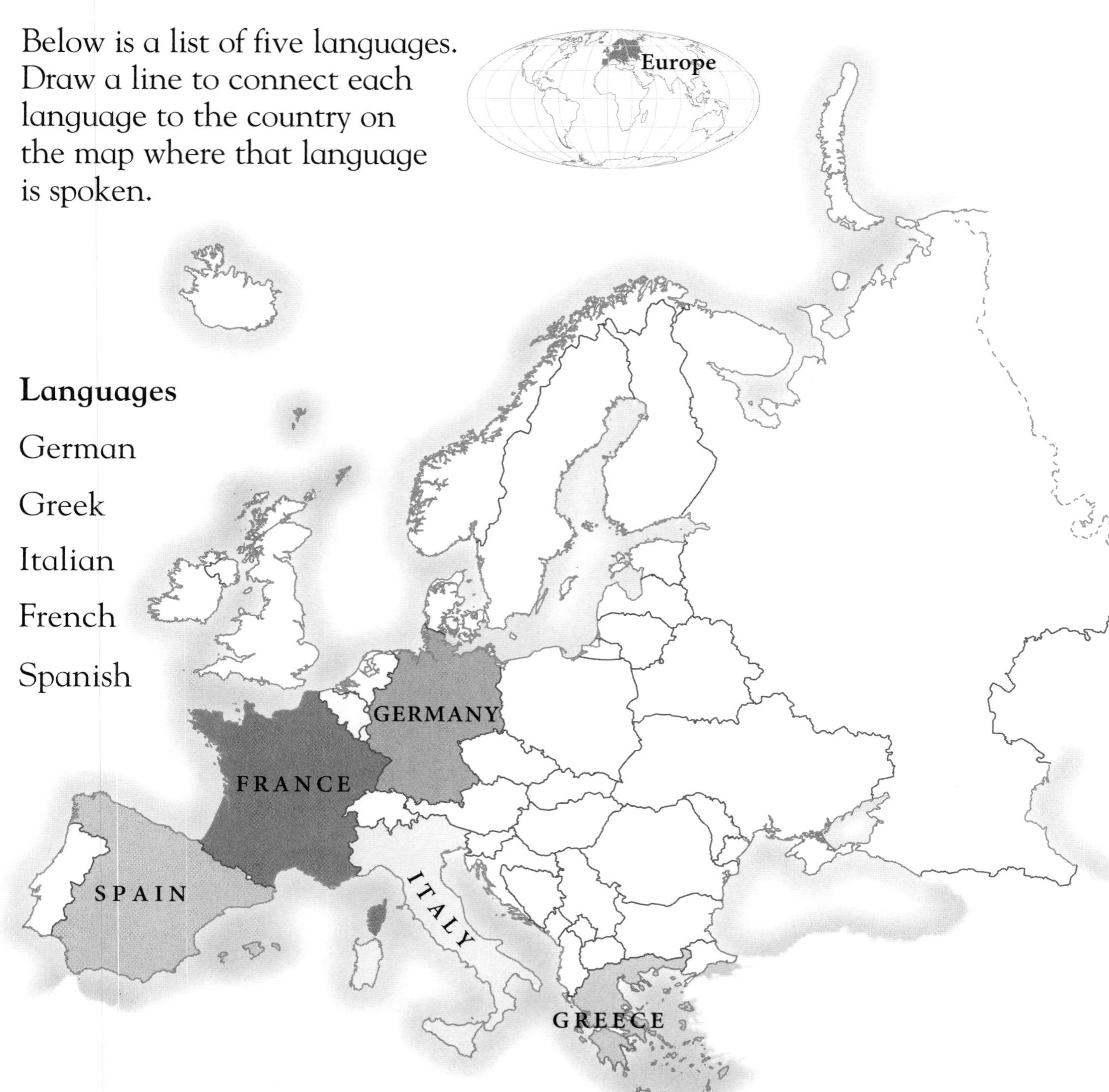

Australia is the smallest continent. It is also one single country. Many of Australia's native animals, such as kangaroos and koalas, do not live in the wild anywhere else on Earth. Australia is near 13 other island countries in the Pacific Ocean. Together, all of those countries are called Oceania.

Read the list of the names of four native Australian animals. Draw a line that connects each name to the picture of the animal on the map of Australia.

Animals

Kangaroo

Wombat

Koala

Squirrel glider

Antarctica

Antarctica is the continent covering the South Pole, the southernmost part of Earth. It is the coldest and windiest continent. It is a land that is always covered in ice and snow. There are no countries in Antarctica. Nobody lives in Antarctica all the time. Most of the people who visit Antarctica are scientists and explorers.

Look at the map of Antarctica below. Then, circle the items that you would need if you were visiting this cold continent.

Antarctica

Equator

The equator is the imaginary line that runs around the middle of Earth, exactly halfway between the North Pole and the South Pole. The equator is at the widest part of Earth. Places on the equator are some of the hottest places on Earth.

Draw a line along the equator on the globe.

Equator

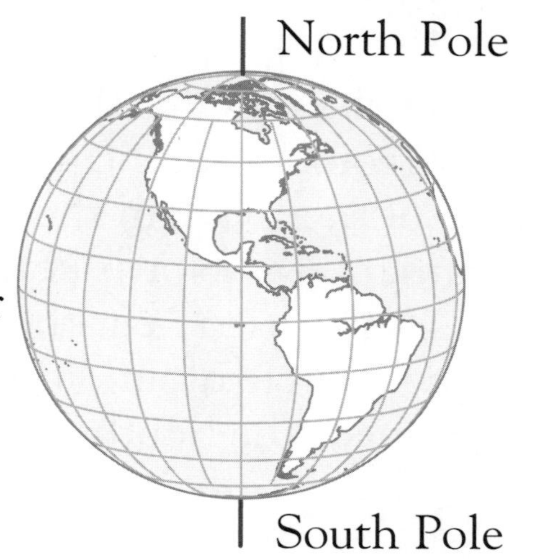

In the map below, color the three continents that the equator goes through.

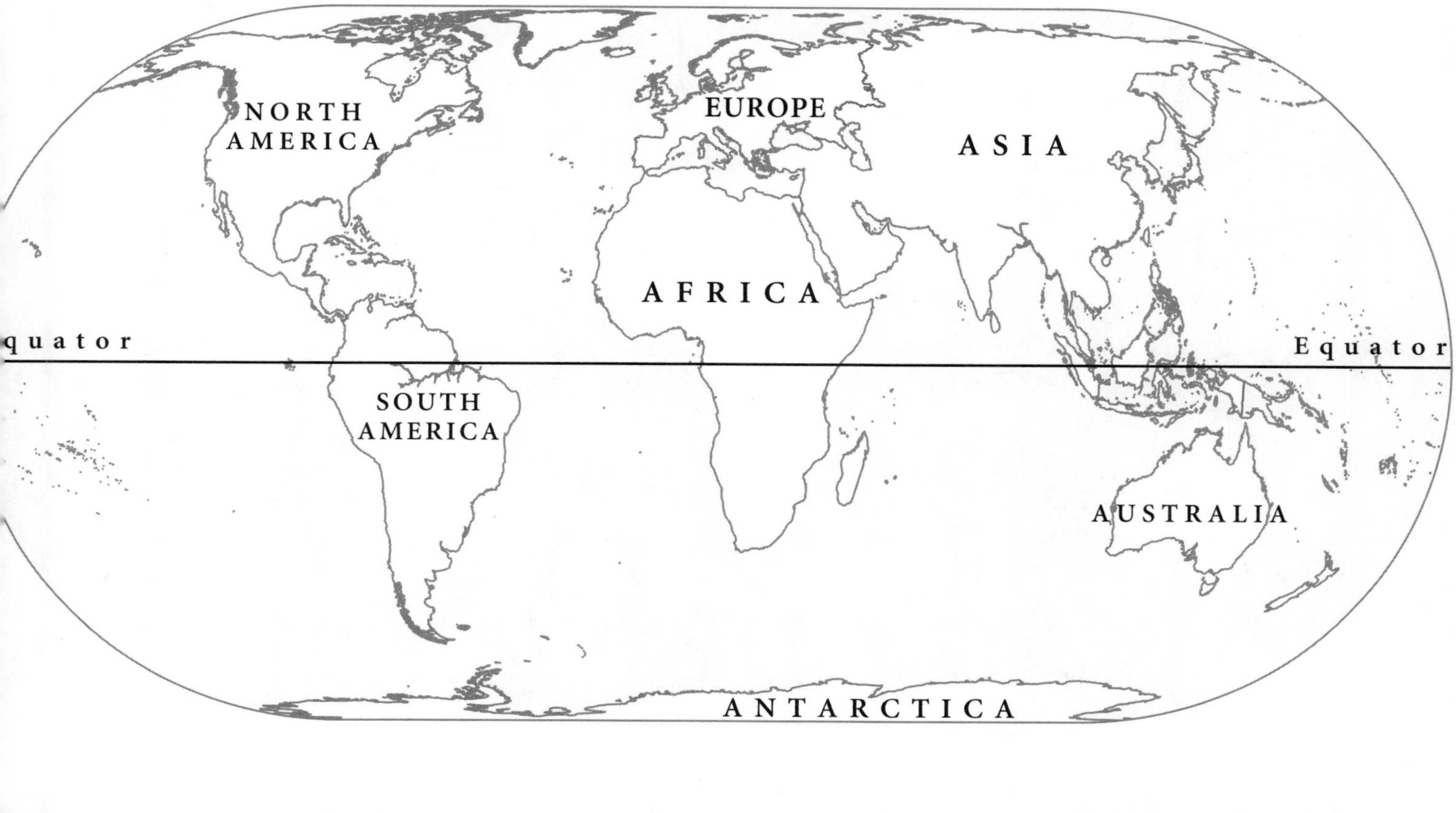

NORTH AMERICA
EUROPE
ASIA
AFRICA
quator
Equator
SOUTH AMERICA
AUSTRALIA
ANTARCTICA

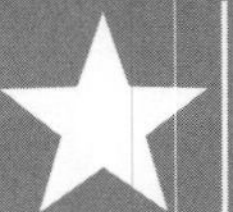

North and South Poles

FACTS

Earth is a sphere, which means it is shaped like a ball. At the very top of Earth is the North Pole, and at the very bottom is the South Pole. The sun does not shine much at the poles. That is why they are very cold and icy. Would you like to live in a freezing place like that?

Below are some of the animals that live in the chilly regions around the poles. Three of them live in the Arctic region, around the North Pole, and one lives in Antarctica near the South Pole. Draw a circle around the animal that lives near the South Pole.

North Pole

South Pole

Polar bear

Penguin

Moose

Arctic fox

FACTS

Most of Earth is covered by water, and most of Earth's water is found in oceans. Oceans are the largest bodies of water in the world. There are five oceans on Earth—the Pacific Ocean, the Atlantic Ocean, the Indian Ocean, the Arctic Ocean, and the Southern Ocean.

Circle the animals that live in the ocean.

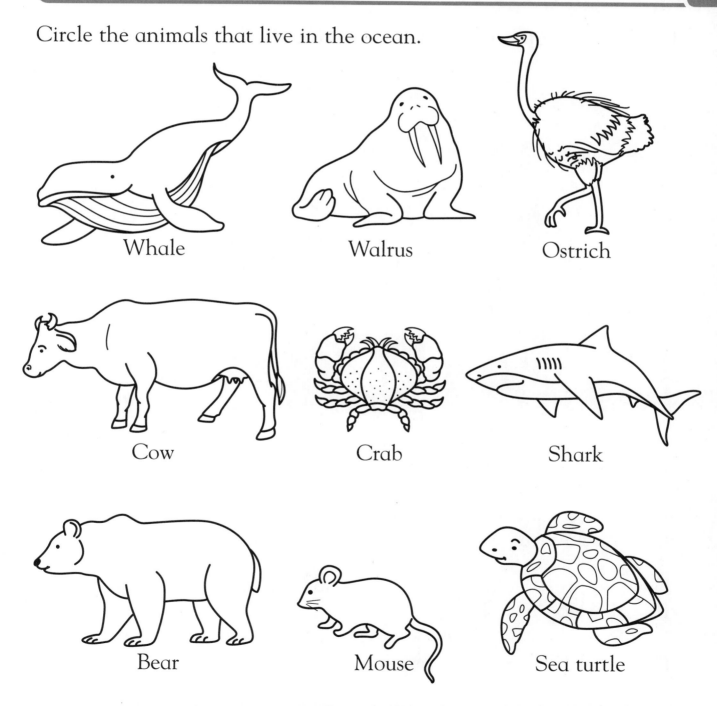

Whale

Walrus

Ostrich

Cow

Crab

Shark

Bear

Mouse

Sea turtle

Pacific Ocean

FACTS

The Pacific Ocean is the world's largest body of water. It lies between four different continents. The Pacific Ocean is so large that it would take you many weeks to cross it in a sailboat. There are more volcanoes around the Pacific Ocean than anywhere else on Earth.

Look at the map below. Color the continents that touch the Pacific Ocean.

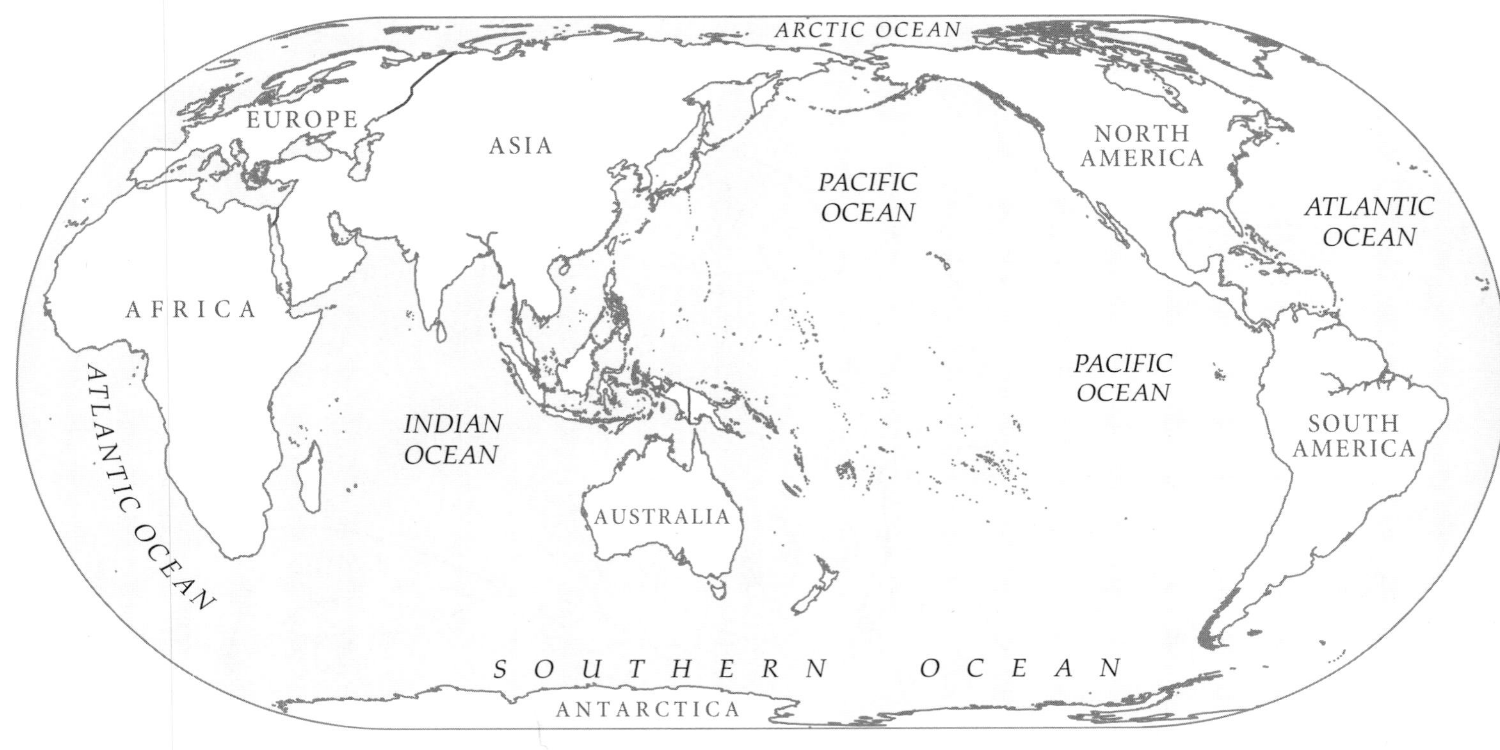

Read the sentences below. Circle the correct option in each sentence.

There are more volcanoes / trees around the Pacific Ocean than any other ocean on Earth.

The Pacific Ocean is the largest / smallest ocean in the world.

Atlantic Ocean

The Atlantic Ocean is the world's second-largest body of water. It lies between four different continents. The first European explorers and settlers to come to the United States sailed across the Atlantic Ocean.

Look at the map below. Color the continents that touch the Atlantic Ocean.

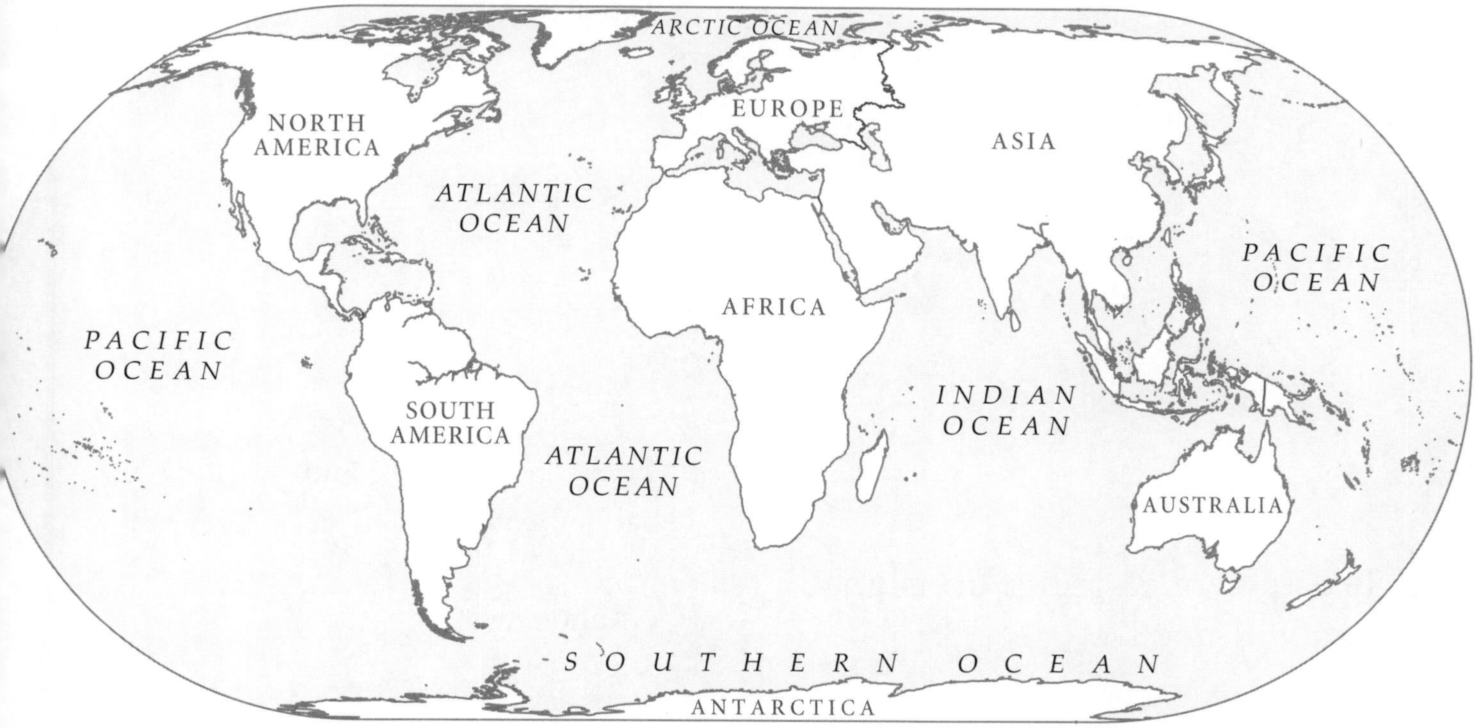

ARCTIC OCEAN
NORTH AMERICA
EUROPE
ASIA
ATLANTIC OCEAN
PACIFIC OCEAN
AFRICA
PACIFIC OCEAN
SOUTH AMERICA
ATLANTIC OCEAN
INDIAN OCEAN
AUSTRALIA
SOUTHERN OCEAN
ANTARCTICA

Read the sentences below. Circle the correct option in each sentence.

The Altantic Ocean is the largest / second-largest ocean in the world.

The first European explorers and settlers to come to the United States sailed across the Atlantic Ocean / Arctic Ocean.

Islands

An island is an area of land that has water all around it. Islands are much smaller than continents. Islands do not float on the water. In fact, islands are like mountains that are mostly underwater. The US state of Hawaii is made up of islands.

Read the words in the box below. Use them to fill in the blanks in the sentences.

float	hot	boat	fish

Kauai

Niihau

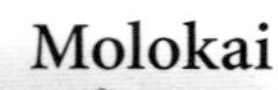

Maui

Lanai

Kahoolawe

1. If you want to reach an island, you will need a ....

2. Islands are connected to Earth. They do not ....

3. If you live on an island, you might eat a lot of ....

4. Some islands are in places where the weather is ....

A lake is a large body of water completely surrounded by land. Lakes come in many sizes. Some lakes are very big. People often build houses, towns, and cities next to lakes. There are many different ways that people use lakes for pleasure and to make their lives easier.

Look at the picture. Circle all the ways that people are using the lake.

Rivers

FACTS

Water always flows from high places to low places. A large amount of running water is called a river. A small amount of running water is called a stream. Some rivers are very long and very wide. Their water can move very quickly, too. Streams are usually much smaller than rivers.

Write an **R** in the box next to the picture of the river, and write an **S** in the box next to the picture of the stream.

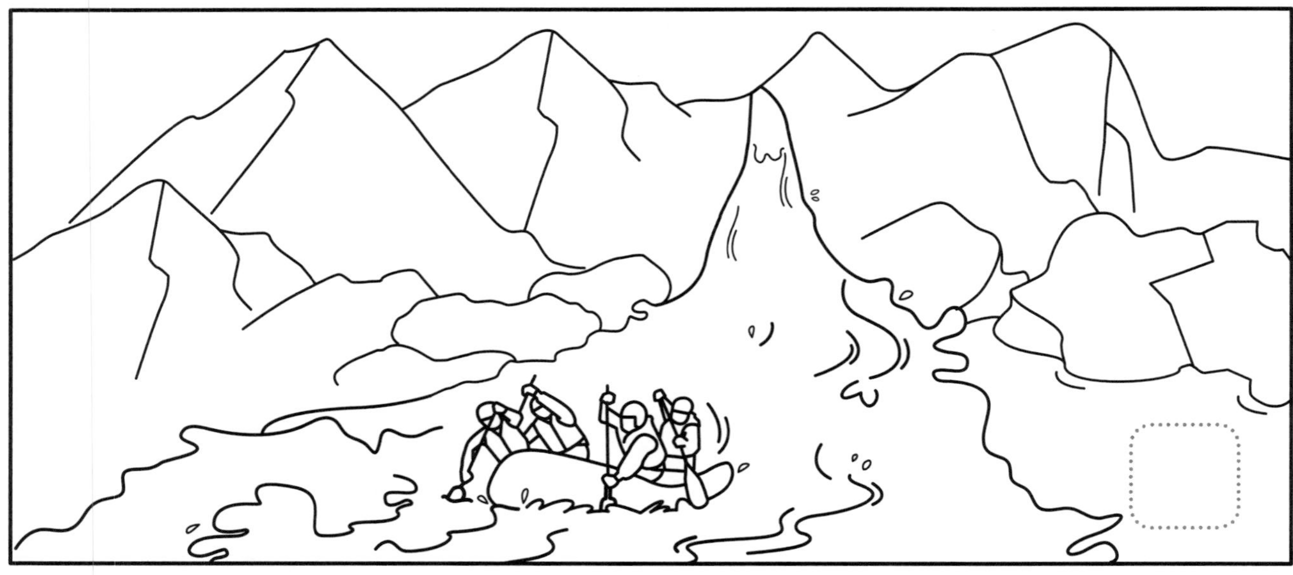

Mountains and hills are areas of land that rise up higher than the land around them. Hills are not as high as mountains. Some mountains are so tall that they touch the cold air high above Earth. That is why some mountains have snow on them, even in warm weather.

Connect the dots in both of the pictures. Then, draw a snowman in the mountain scene and a house in the hill scene.

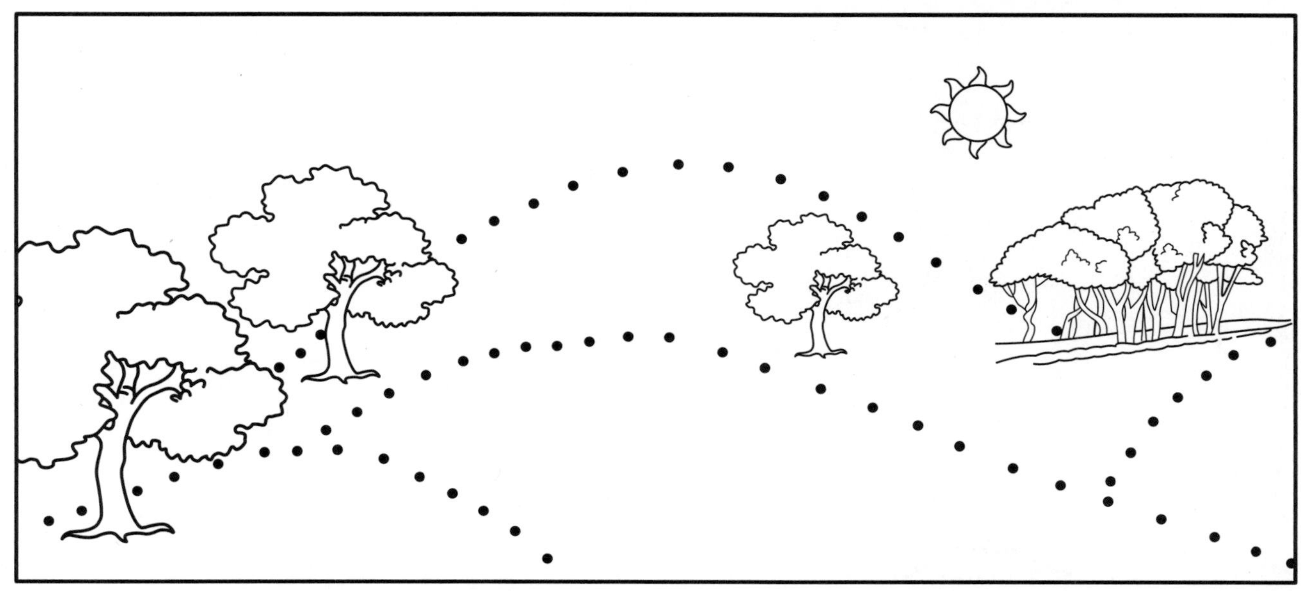

Forests

A forest is a large area of land covered with many trees. Many different kinds of plants grow under the tree cover. Wild animals, all of different sizes, live in forests. Bears, wolves, deer, chipmunks, raccoons, frogs, owls, and many other kinds of animals make their homes in forests. There are many forests on Earth.

Look at the pictures below, and put an **F** next to the things that you might expect to see in a forest.

Jungles are very rainy and wet parts of Earth. Because of all the rain, jungles can support the growth of lots of different kinds of plants. Most of Earth's plants and animals are found in jungles. They are often very hot places. Jungles are usually hard places for people to live in.

Look at the pictures below and put a **J** next to the things that you might expect to see in a jungle.

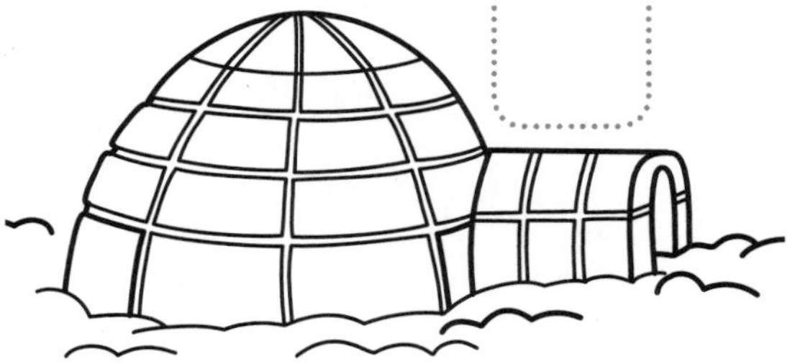

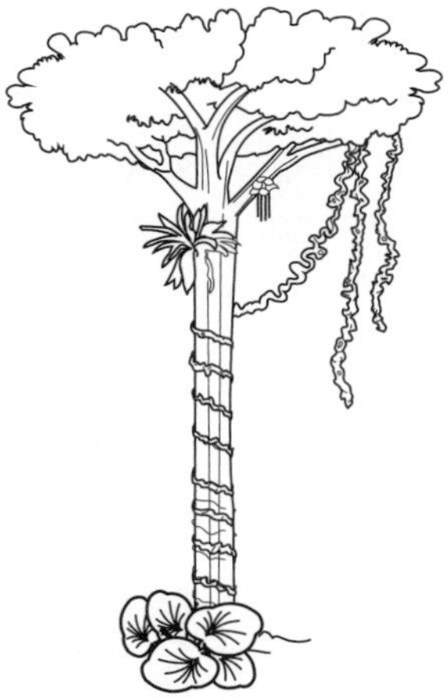

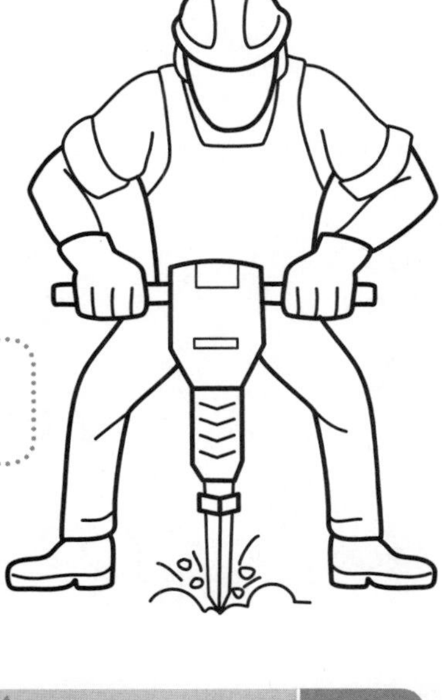

★ Deserts

FACTS

A desert is a very dry part of the world that gets very little rain. Deserts can be very hot in the daytime and very cold at night. Some plants and animals manage to live in the desert, but it is not an easy place for people to live in.

Look at the pictures below, and put a **D** next to the things that you might expect to see in a hot desert.

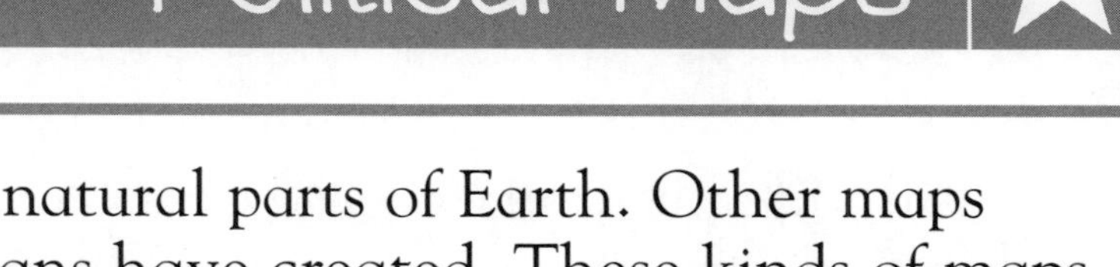

Political Maps

Some maps show just the natural parts of Earth. Other maps show the places that humans have created. These kinds of maps are called political maps. They show countries, cities, and other types of places that are not part of the natural world.

Put a **P** in the box next to the kinds of places that would be on a political map. Put an **N** next to the kinds of places that would be on a map of the natural world.

TEXAS

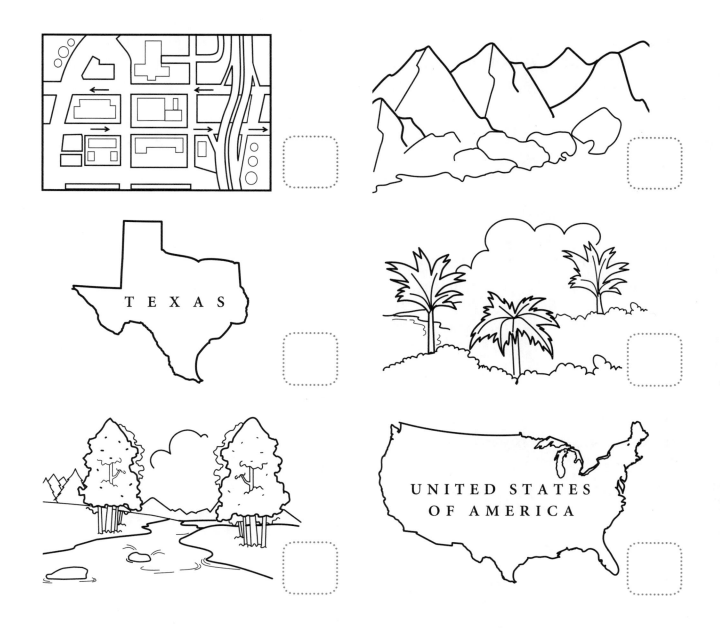

UNITED STATES OF AMERICA

Countries

FACTS

Earth is divided into about 200 countries. Some countries are very big and some are very small. The five largest countries by size are Russia, Canada, the United States, China, and Brazil. The two largest countries by population are China and India.

Look at this map of the world. Then, follow the instructions below. You can ask an adult for help.

Find the country you live in on the map. What is the name of your country?

....

Name the country that is both one of the five largest countries by size and one of the two largest by population.

....

Write the names of the three largest countries in order of their size.

1. ....

2. ....

3. ....

In a country, all the people share the same leaders and government. Generally, most of the people in a country speak the same language and have many things in common.

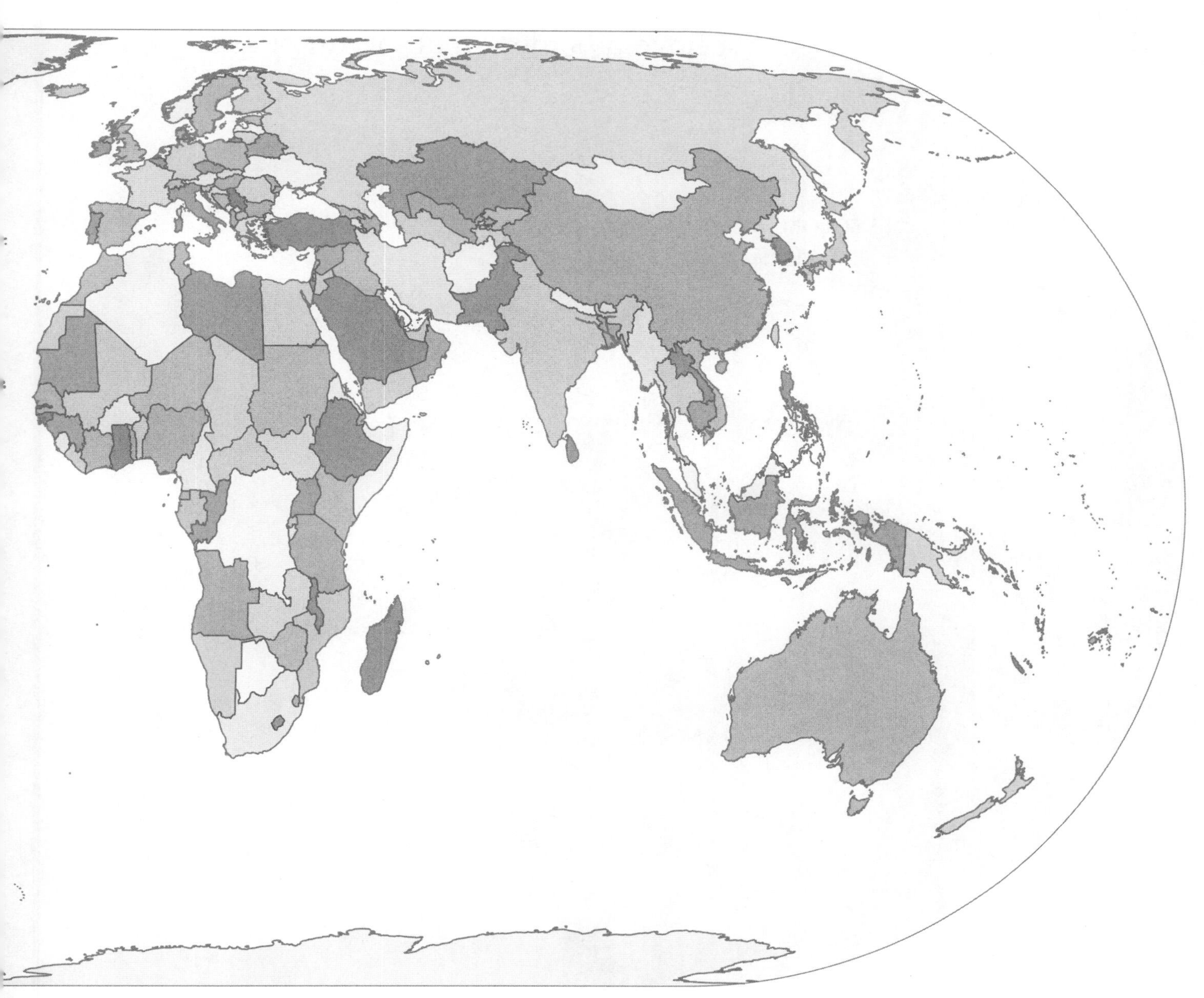

Borders

Sometimes, a country has a natural border that is created by an ocean or sea. Other times, a country's border can be a river or mountains. Sometimes the borders are created by people. Those man-made borders usually look like a straight line on a map.

Here is a map showing the 12 countries of South America. Draw a blue line on the border of every country. In red, color the two countries that do not have a border on an ocean or sea.

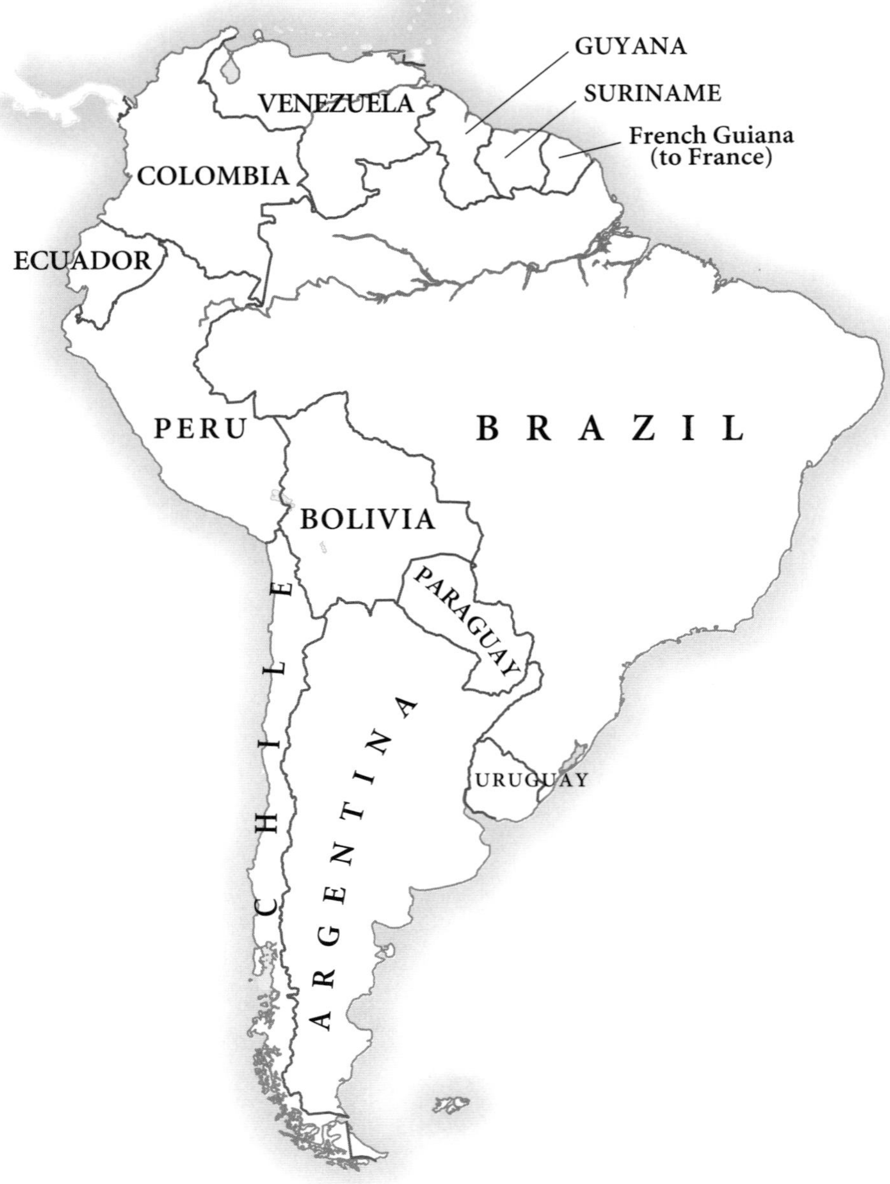

Provinces and Territories

Some countries are divided into areas called provinces. Canada, the world's second-largest country, is divided into 10 provinces. The country also has three large areas called territories, close to the North Pole. The Yukon Territory, the Northwest Territories, and Nunavut are Canada's three territories.

Look at this map of Canada, and then follow the instructions below.

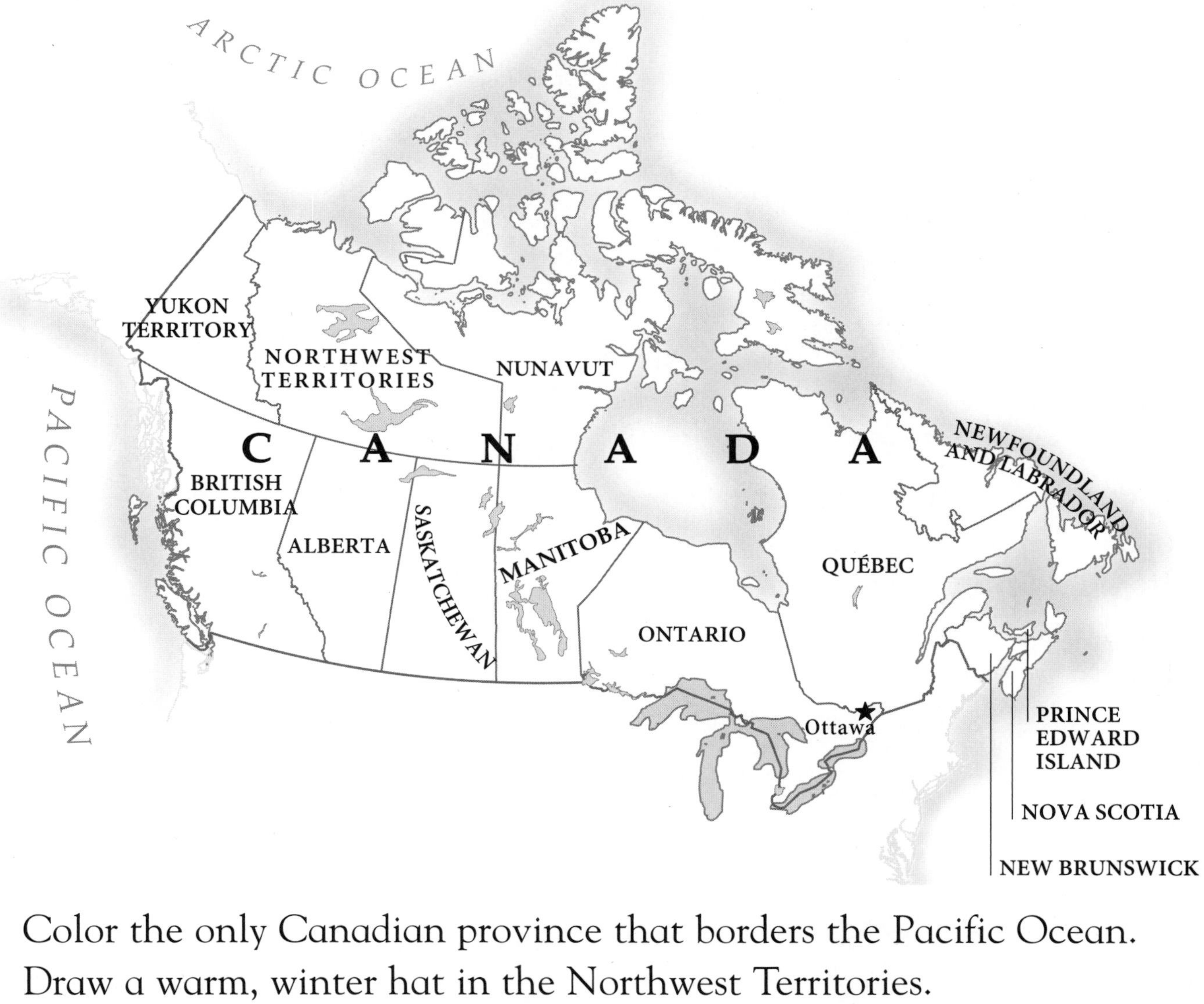

ARCTIC OCEAN
PACIFIC OCEAN
CANADA
YUKON TERRITORY
NORTHWEST TERRITORIES
NUNAVUT
BRITISH COLUMBIA
ALBERTA
SASKATCHEWAN
MANITOBA
ONTARIO
QUÉBEC
NEWFOUNDLAND AND LABRADOR
Ottawa
PRINCE EDWARD ISLAND
NOVA SCOTIA
NEW BRUNSWICK

Color the only Canadian province that borders the Pacific Ocean.
Draw a warm, winter hat in the Northwest Territories.
Draw mittens in the Yukon Territory.
Draw snowflakes in Nunavut.

The 50 States

FACTS

Some large countries, such as the United States of America, are divided into smaller areas called states. Some states, such as California and Texas, are very large. Other states, such as Rhode Island and Delaware, are very small.

Here is a map of the United States.

Color in green the four states whose names start with the word "New."

The names of eight states begin with the letter "M." Color them blue.

The names of four states begin with an "A." Color them red.

If you live in the US, put a check (✓) on your state. If you do not, check (✓) the state you would most like to visit.

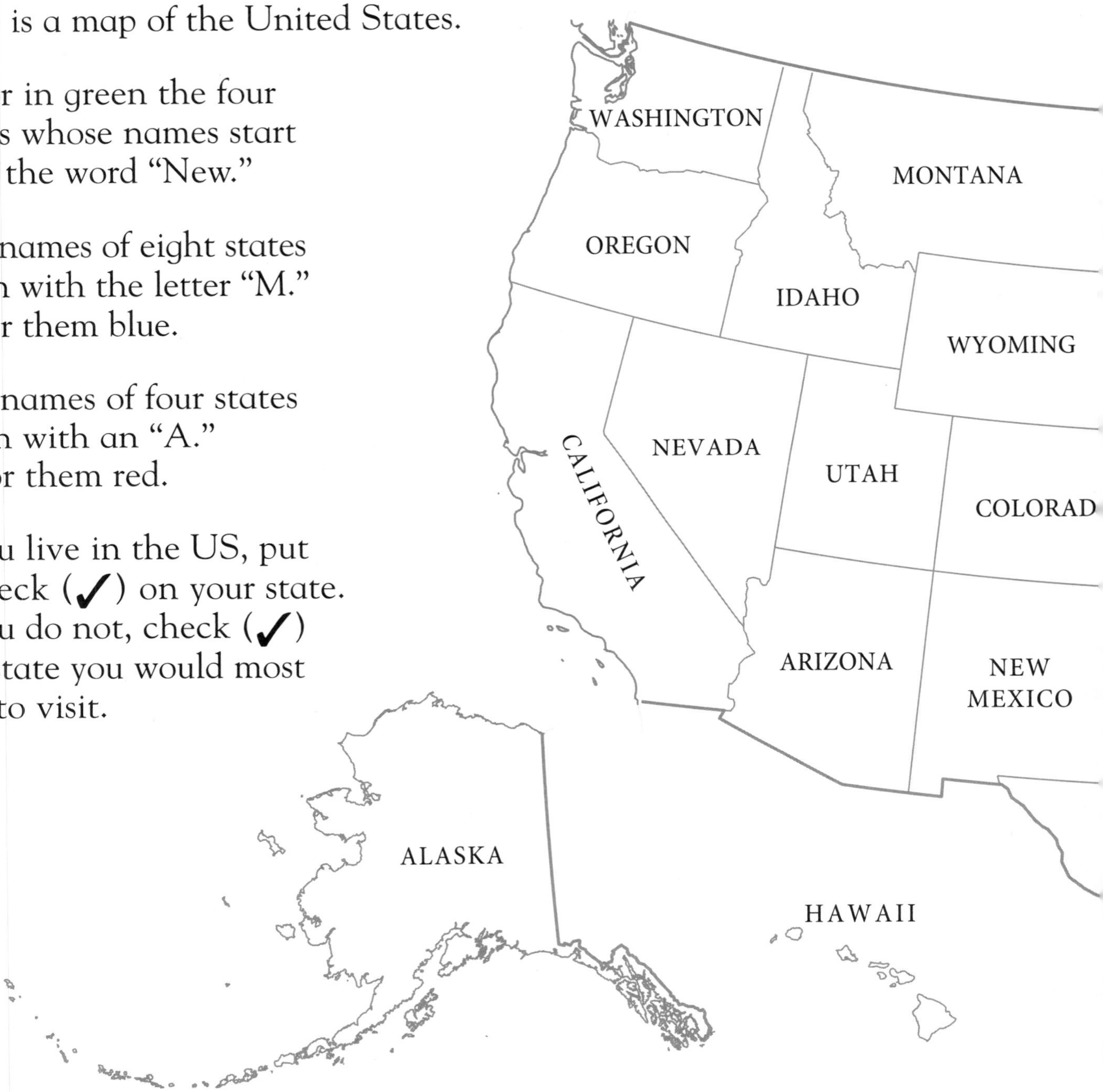

WASHINGTON
MONTANA
OREGON
IDAHO
WYOMING
NEVADA
UTAH
CALIFORNIA
COLORAD
ARIZONA
NEW MEXICO
ALASKA
HAWAII

The United States of America is often called the United States or just the US. It is divided into 50 states. Forty-eight of them share borders with at least one other state on the North American continent. They make up the continental United States. Two states, Alaska and Hawaii, are not connected to the other 48 states.

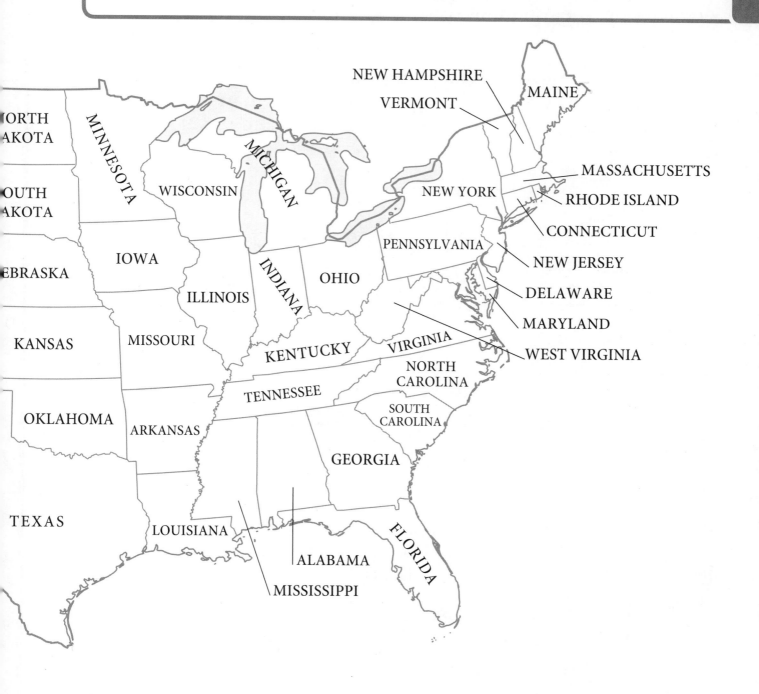

NEW HAMPSHIRE
MAINE
VERMONT
ORTH AKOTA
MINNESOTA
MICHIGAN
MASSACHUSETTS
OUTH AKOTA
WISCONSIN
NEW YORK
RHODE ISLAND
CONNECTICUT
PENNSYLVANIA
IOWA
EBRASKA
INDIANA
OHIO
NEW JERSEY
ILLINOIS
DELAWARE
MARYLAND
KANSAS
MISSOURI
KENTUCKY
VIRGINIA
WEST VIRGINIA
NORTH CAROLINA
TENNESSEE
SOUTH CAROLINA
OKLAHOMA
ARKANSAS
GEORGIA
TEXAS
LOUISIANA
FLORIDA
ALABAMA
MISSISSIPPI

Cities

A city is a place where many people live near each other. In a city, there are many big buildings, houses, schools, parks, and roads. A city has museums, sports teams, theaters, and many things for people to do. Cities are large places, so there are many ways to travel in a city. People living in cities mostly work in offices and factories, not on farms or agricultural land.

Circle the different ways people travel in a city.
Cross out (**X**) the ways people do not usually travel in a city.
Put a check (✓) next to the ways you would like to travel when you are in a city.

Cities come in different sizes. Some cities are very large, with millions of people. Other cities are not as large. A map can show you which cities are large and which cities are small. On a map, the names of the largest cities have the biggest letters.

Here is a map of three states in the US—California, Oregon, and Washington. Circle the names of the large cities in these states.

★ Capital Cities

FACTS

Every country has a capital city. Leaders and the government meet in the capital city to do their work. States and provinces have capital cities, too. Capitals are not always the largest cities in a state or country. They are shown on a map by a dot that is different from the dots showing other cities.

Here is a map of the US showing three states—California, Oregon, and Washington. Circle the capital city of each state.
Hint: In this map, the capitals are marked by stars.

A town is an area where people live near each other. It is smaller than a city and usually has smaller buildings. A town also has fewer people than a city. Many people choose to live in towns because they do not want to live in a big city.

Check (✓) the pictures of places you would find in a town.
Put an X (✗) next to the pictures of places you would find in a city.

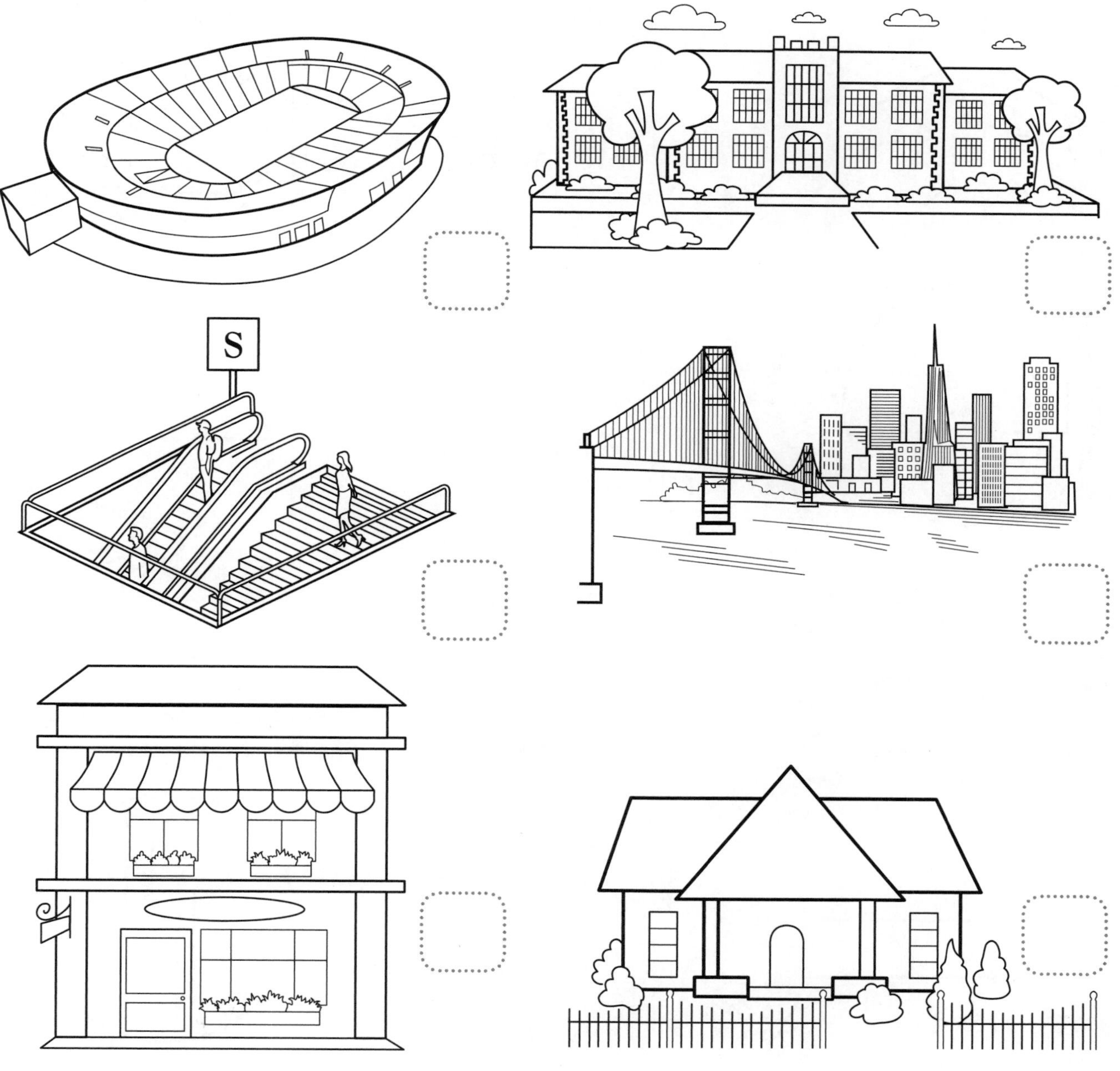

Map Keys and Symbols

FACTS

Maps use symbols to show different kinds of buildings and other features. These symbols are usually pictures that represent the things that they show. All the symbols used on a map, and what they represent, are shown in a map key.

Match each map symbol to the word it is showing.

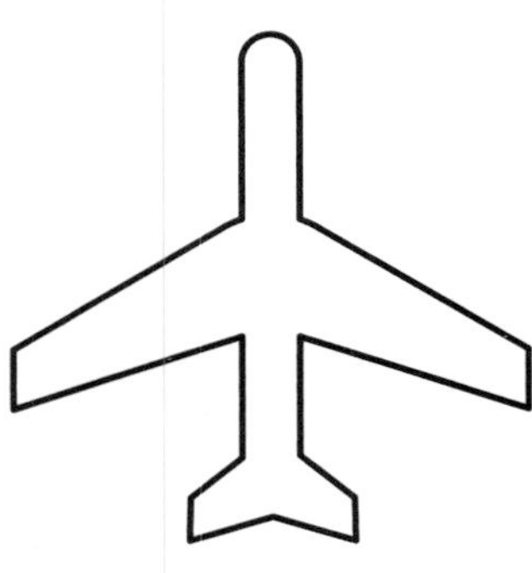

Hospital

Mountain

Bridge

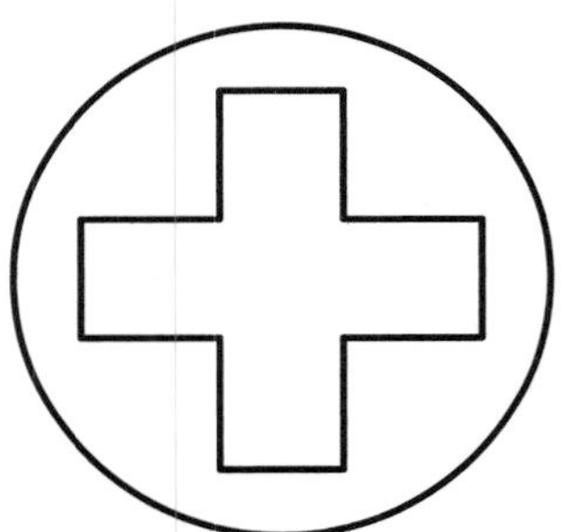

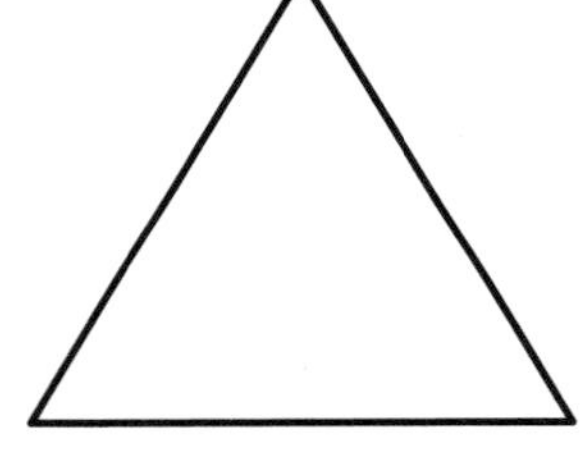

Farm

Airport

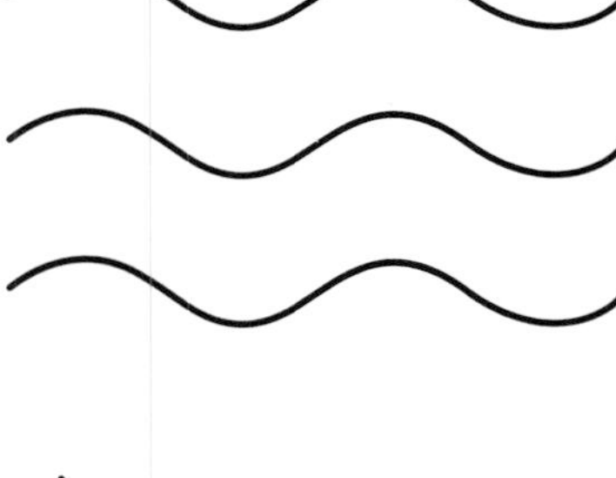

Restaurant

Road

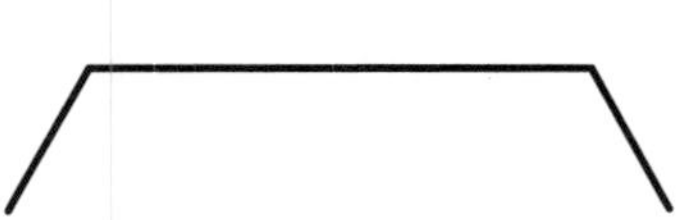

River

A Park Map

A map can help you find your way around a place, such as a park. The park map on this page uses symbols to tell people what activities they can do in the park.

Using the words from the box, label each symbol on the map with what that symbol represents. Then, use the compass rose to help you answer the questions below the map.

Snack bar	Gift shop	Parking lot	Bathroom
Park office	Swimming pool	Playground	

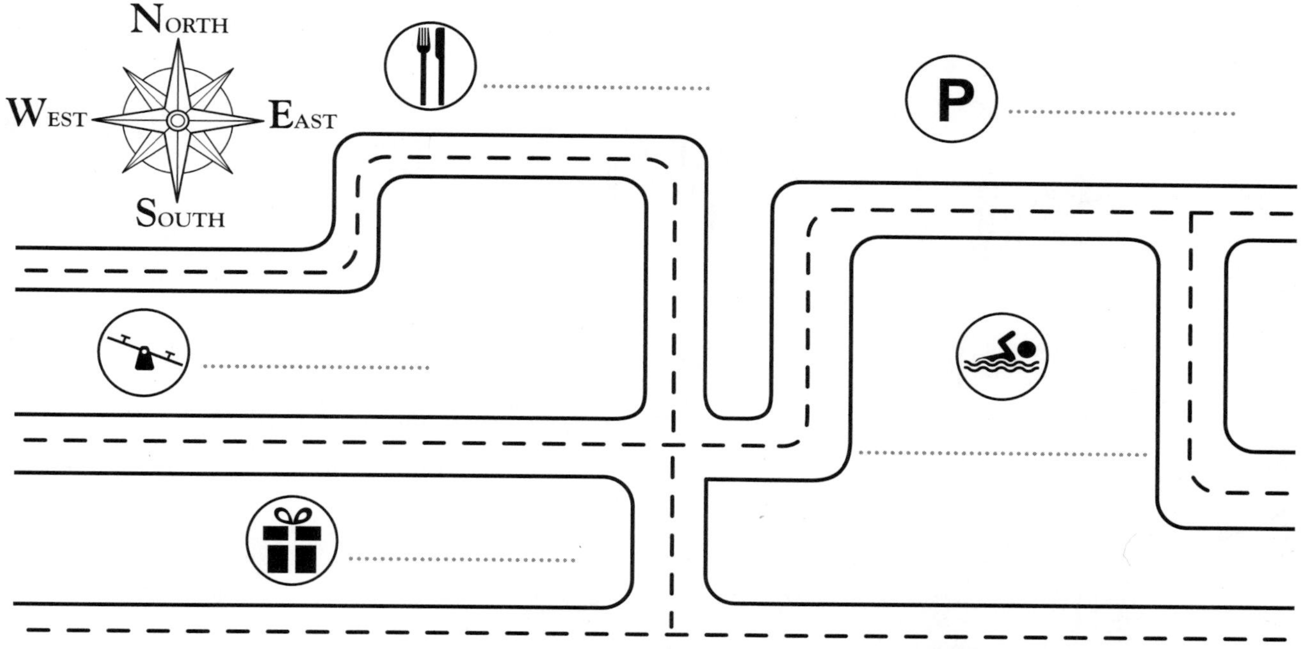

If you are at the playground and you want to go to the swimming pool, what direction will you go?

If you are at the snack bar and you want to go to the bathrooms, what direction will you go?

A Nature Map

FACTS

A nature map tells you about an area of land. Each of the symbols in the key shows a different part of the natural world. The map helps you plan where you want to go.

Using the words from the box, label the different kinds of places from the natural world that are shown on the map. Then, use the compass rose to help you answer the questions below the map.

Beach Waterfall Forest Mountains
Hills Lake River

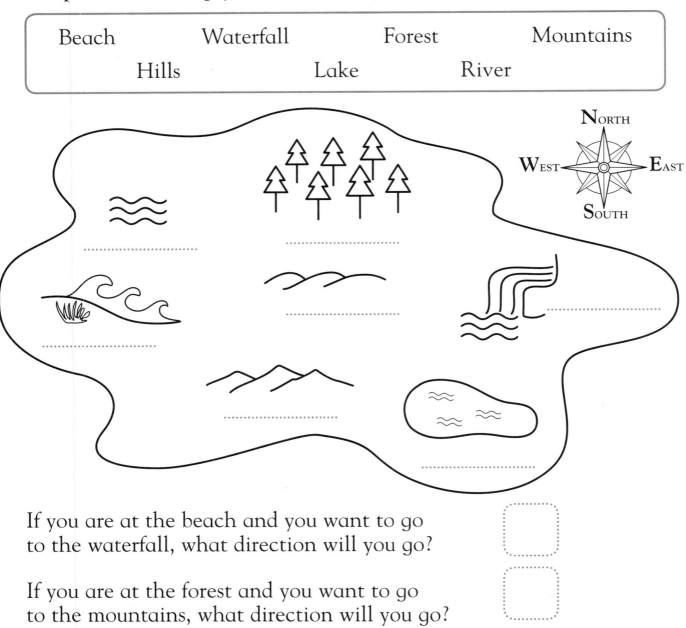

If you are at the beach and you want to go to the waterfall, what direction will you go?

If you are at the forest and you want to go to the mountains, what direction will you go?

A Neighborhood Map

A neighborhood map often uses pictures of buildings as its symbols. This kind of map is helpful for finding the places you want to visit in a town.

Imagine you are traveling from your home to your school. You are going to make a few stops on the way. You are going to stop at these places in the order given in the word box below.

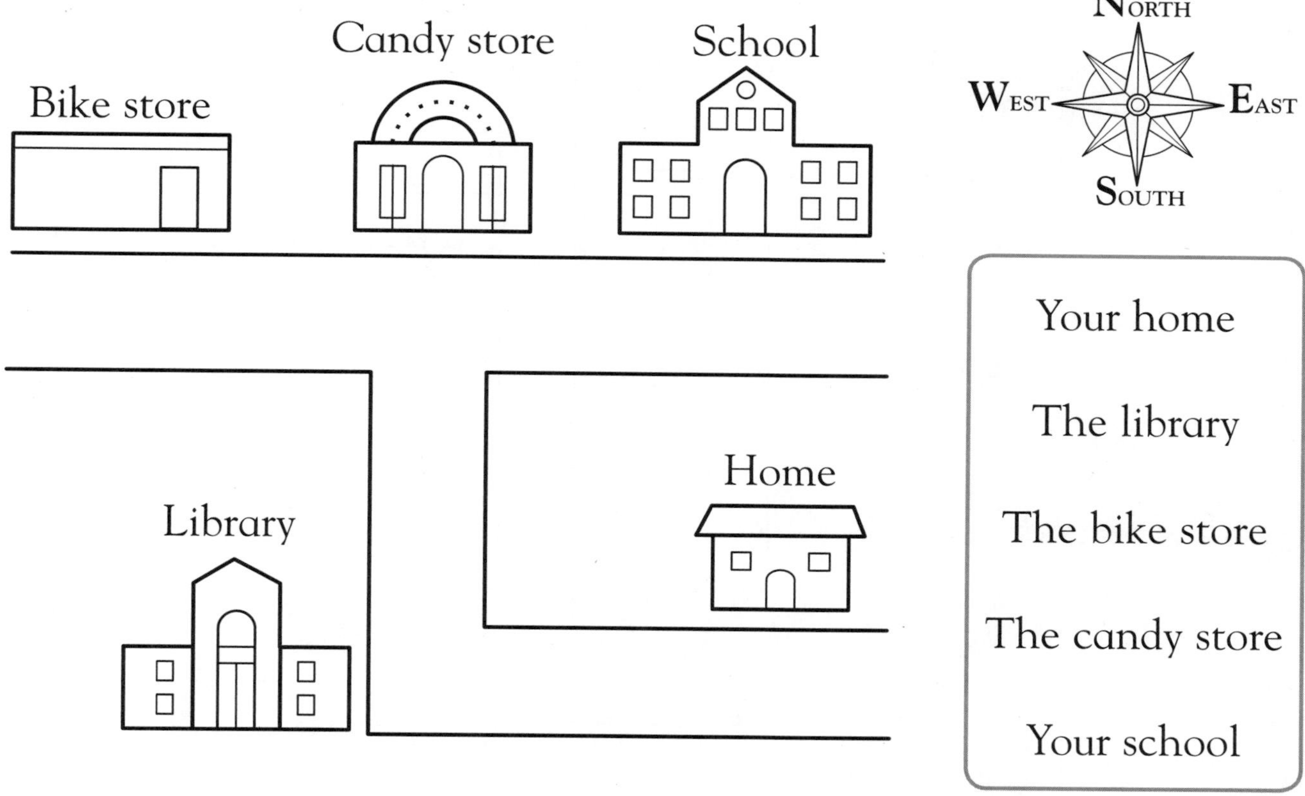

- Your home
- The library
- The bike store
- The candy store
- Your school

Draw a line, along the roads, that connects these places in the order you will visit them.

To go from the bike store to your school, what direction will you go?

To go from the library to the candy store, what direction will you go?

A School Map

FACTS

Not all maps use picture symbols. In this map of a school, each of the different areas uses letters to tell you what you can find there.

Point at each location on the map and say its name aloud, using the key to find its name. Circle the names of your two favorite places. Then, use the compass rose to help you answer the questions below the map.

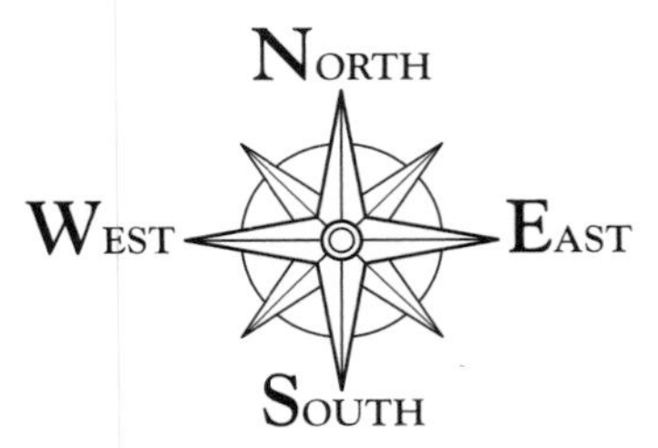

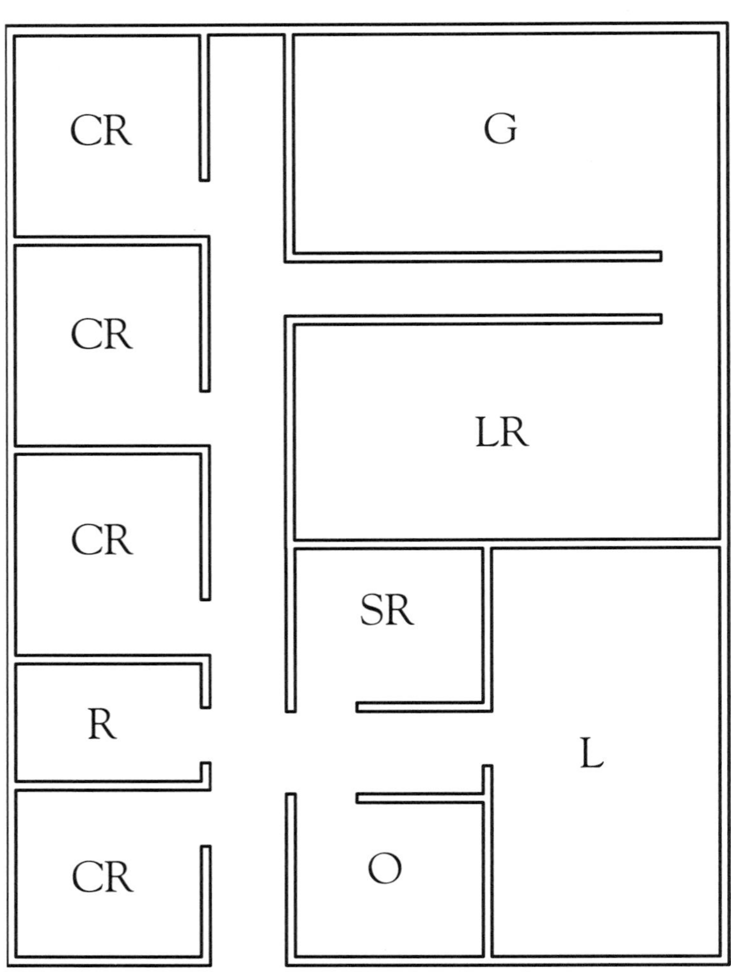

Key	
LR	Lunch room
O	Office
SR	Science room
L	Library
G	Gym
R	Restroom
CR	Classroom

If you are at the library and want to go to the restroom, in what direction will you go?

If you are at the gym and want to go to the lunch room, in what direction will you go?

A map is a plan that can help you describe a place. Everyone can make a map. Look at the world around you. You can use simple symbols or letters to describe a place to other people. You can show the things they will find there.

Make a map of your bedroom by using any of the symbols in the key below. Draw them in the box and label them. You can add your own symbols for anything in your room that is not in the key.

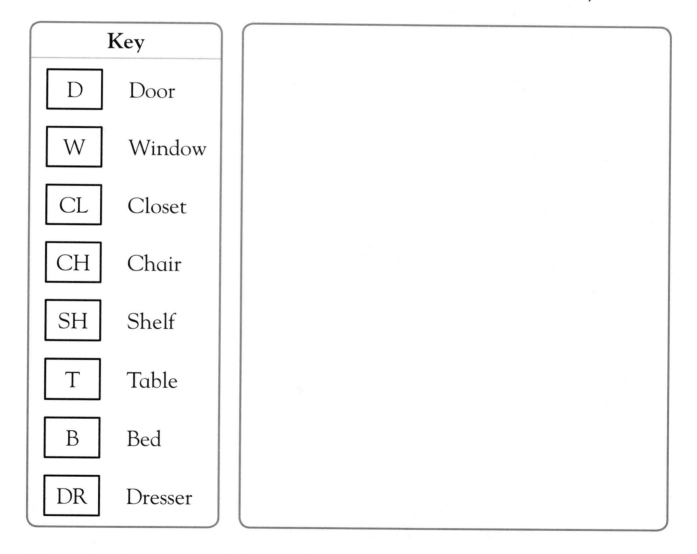

Key

D	Door
W	Window
CL	Closet
CH	Chair
SH	Shelf
T	Table
B	Bed
DR	Dresser

If your bedroom is a different shape from this one, use another piece of paper to draw walls that match the shape of your bedroom.

Mapping Your Classroom

FACTS

A classroom is a place to learn. The objects in a classroom help children learn together.

Make a map of your classroom in the box below, using the symbols in the key. Create your own symbols for anything in your classroom that is missing from the key.

Key	
D	Door
W	Window
CL	Closet
CH	Chair
T	Table
DE	Desk
SH	Shelf
B	Board

If your classroom is a different shape from this one, use another piece of paper to draw walls that match its shape.

Draw a symbol for yourself, to mark the place where you usually sit.

Mapping Your Neighborhood

There are all kinds of neighborhoods. Some neighborhoods have many different kinds of buildings. Others may have very few buildings. A map of your neighborhood can help you understand the things you find there. It can help you describe your neighborhood to a friend.

Imagine the square in the middle of the box below is the home you live in. Draw your neighborhood around where you live. Include squares for buildings like a school or a supermarket.

Your home

What kind of building is your home? Color the middle square the same color as your real home.

On your map, which two buildings are closest to your home? Color those two squares the same color as the real buildings.

Parents' Notes

The geography section of this book is intended to support the concepts that are taught to your child in first grade. The topics covered will test your child's knowledge of the world around him or her. By working through the activities, your child will learn basic geography concepts in a fun and informative way.

Contents

The geography activities are intended to be completed by a child with adult support. The topics covered are as follows:

- the natural and the human (man-made) world;
- bodies of water such as oceans, rivers, and lakes;
- landforms such as mountains, hills, islands, and deserts;
- forests and jungles;
- types of maps and their keys;
- compass directions;
- continents, countries, provinces, and territories;
- cities and towns;
- the United States of America.

How to Help Your Child

As you work through the pages with your child, make sure he or she understands what each activity requires. Read the facts and instructions aloud. Encourage questions and reinforce observations that will build confidence and increase active participation in classes at school.

By working with your child, you will understand how he or she thinks and learns. When appropriate, use props and objects from daily life to help your child make connections with the world outside.

If an activity seems too challenging for your child, encourage him or her to try another page. You can encourage your child by giving praise when he or she completes a page, gives a correct answer, or makes progress. Remember at all times that learning should also be fun!

Language Arts

Author Anne Flounders

Contents

This chart lists all the topics in the Language Arts section.

FACTS

All letters have an uppercase form.

Write the uppercase form of each lowercase letter.

__ a	__ f	__ k	__ p	__ u	__ z
__ b	__ g	__ l	__ q	__ v	
__ c	__ h	__ m	__ r	__ w	
__ d	__ i	__ n	__ s	__ x	
__ e	__ j	__ o	__ t	__ y	

Write a letter to begin each word.
Choose from the letters on the fishing poles.

FACTS

All letters have a lowercase form.

Write the lowercase form of each uppercase letter.

A _	F _	K _	P _	U _	Z _
B _	G _	L _	Q _	V _	
C _	H _	M _	R _	W _	
D _	I _	N _	S _	X _	
E _	J _	O _	T _	Y _	

Write a letter to end each word.
Choose from the letters on the fishing poles.

★ Capital Letters

FACTS

Uppercase letters are also called capital letters.
Use capital letters at the beginning of a sentence.

Read each sentence below. Underline the word that needs a capital letter. Write the word, using correct capitalization, in the space below the sentence.

the girl fed the cat.

....

snow falls in the winter.

....

a monkey eats fruit.

....

rockets zoom through the sky.

....

quiet mice are hard to find.

....

Use a capital letter at the beginning of the name of a person, place, day of the week, or month of the year.

Complete each line below.

My full name is ....

The people in my family are ....

....

The day of the week today is ....

The month is ....

My friend's name is ....

The name of my school is ....

The city or town where I live is ....

Creating a Character

FACTS

A character is a person or an animal in a story.

Pick one word from each column that could describe a character. Combine the three words to create a character!

huge	monkey	cook
tiny	snake	dancer
purple	ant	detective
silly	horse	firefighter
upside-down	elephant	movie star

My character is a ....

Draw your character below. Tell a story about your character.

Describing a Character

Every story is about a character.

Think of your favorite character from a book or movie.
Complete the sentence and answer the questions that follow.

My favorite character is ....

What does your character look like? ....

....

What does your character do? ....

....

What do you like best about your favorite character?

....

Draw your character below.

Short or Long Vowels

FACTS

The letter **a** can sound like the **a** in "at" (short "a") or the **a** in "ape" (long "a").

Read the words aloud. Connect the words with the long "a" sound to get through the maze.

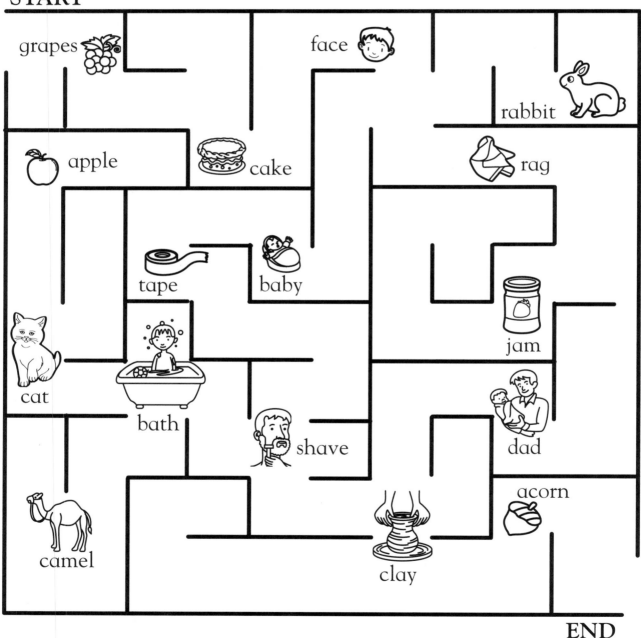

START

grapes

face

rabbit

apple

cake

rag

tape

baby

jam

cat

bath

shave

dad

acorn

camel

clay

END

The letter **e** can sound like the **e** in “bet” (short “e”) or the **e** in “eat” (long “e”).

Read the words aloud. Some of the words in the grid have a short “e” sound. Some have a long “e” sound. Color the spaces with the short “e” sound red. Color the spaces with the long “e” sound green.

end	teach	beach	see	vet
wet	tree	edge	red	yes
send	heat	best	egg	well
bed	sheep	flee	tea	step
them	treat	tent	jet	bell
yet	eat	neck	web	sled
hen	clean	bead	sleep	shell

★ Sentence Fun

FACTS

Sentences always end with punctuation, such as a period (.), a question mark (?), or an exclamation point (!).

Write a sentence for each picture. Make sure your sentence begins with a capital letter and ends with correct punctuation.

1.

2.

3.

4.

A simple sentence ends with a period. A question sentence ends with a question mark. An exclamation point shows excitement.

Each sentence below is missing punctuation at the end. Help end the sentences by deciding which punctuation fits best: a period, a question mark, or an exclamation point.

Mix red and blue to make purple ....

Let's go to the zoo ....

The fox slept under the log ....

Rain helps flowers to grow ....

Where is my dog ....

Grandpa will be so happy to see us ....

How do you build a stool ....

What is that noise ....

Magic E

FACTS

Adding an **e** to the end of some words can turn a short vowel sound into a long vowel sound.

In each pair of words, choose the word that needs a magic **e** to match its picture. Write the **e** to complete the word.

Spelling with Blends

Often two consonants are used together in a word.
Those pairs of letters are called blends.

Each of the following words can be completed with one of the **s**-consonant blends. Write the blend that completes each word.

sk	sp	st

__onge

__is

__ar

__ate

__ore

__ots

__ider

__y

__ick

Setting

FACTS

A setting is where and when a story takes place.

Read the story. Then circle the picture that shows the setting from the story.

Franny Frog looked around the pond. She was tired of the lily pad life. She thought of visiting the moon. A fly buzzed by. Franny stuck out her tongue and caught the fly. "Yum! There are no flies on the moon," she said. "I will stay where I am."

FACTS

A story can have more than one character.

Here are characters from a story. Read the words in the word bank. Write the words that describe the characters in the spaces below the characters.

alone	happy	inside	mean	outside	together

Wolf	**Pigs**
....	....
....	....
....	....

★ Initial and Final Sounds

Knowing how words sound can help you to spell them.

These words are missing letters! Some are missing the first letter. Some are missing the last letter. Fill in the missing letters using the letters in the letter bank.

b	d	h	n	r	t

Some words have short vowel sounds.
Others have long vowel sounds.

Read the words aloud. Circle the two words in each set that have the same long vowel sound.

 rain	 patch	 braid
 hose	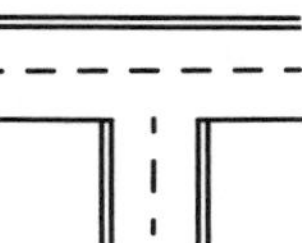 road	 mop
 bee	 bread	 see
 quill	 ice	 dine

★ Pronouns

FACTS

Pronouns are words that can take the place of nouns in a sentence.

Circle the pronoun in each sentence. Then write the pronoun.

My dog is small and fluffy.

Where are you going?

They went to the movies.

Jane gave her a book.

He needs new shoes.

I like to bake cookies.

We sang together.

The most common pronouns are "he," "she," and "it."

Find the pronoun from the word bank to replace the bold word in each sentence. Then write the word.

He	It	She

Jenny got into the car.

.... got into the car.

Mr. Brown told us a story.

.... told us a story.

The star shines brightly.

.... shines brightly.

The frog hopped into the pond.

.... hopped into the pond.

My aunt made pizza.

.... made pizza.

Mixed-up Story

FACTS

Stories have a beginning, a middle, and an end.

Two friends find a heap of junk and decide to build a robot out of it. The pictures tell the story of what happens, but they are out of order. Write a 1 next to the picture that shows what should happen first. Then write 2, 3, and 4 to show the order of the rest of the pictures. When you are done, tell the story!

FACTS

Stories have characters and settings.

Write or tell a story based on what you see in the picture.

Spelling with Blends

A blend is a pair of consonants used together in a word.

Each of the following words can be completed with one of the **b**- or **p**-consonant blends. Write the blend that completes each word.

bl	br	pl	pr

__ane

__ince

__ead

__etend

__ug

__oom

__ueberry

__anket

The vowels are **a**, **e**, **i**, **o**, **u**, and sometimes **y**. All the other letters are consonants. **Y** is sometimes a consonant.

Each of the following words can be completed with a vowel. Fill in the vowels to spell each word.

a e i o u y

f_re  d_g 

tr_ck  fl_ 

h_se  b_ne 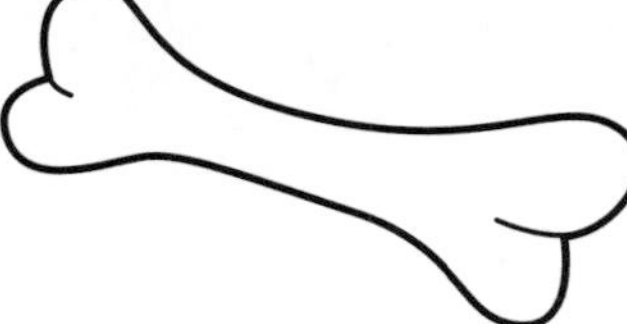

m_n  w_t 

FACTS

A verb is a word that names an action or a state of being.

Read each sentence aloud. Draw a line under the verb.

The skunk plays the horn.

The fox dances.

The moose sings.

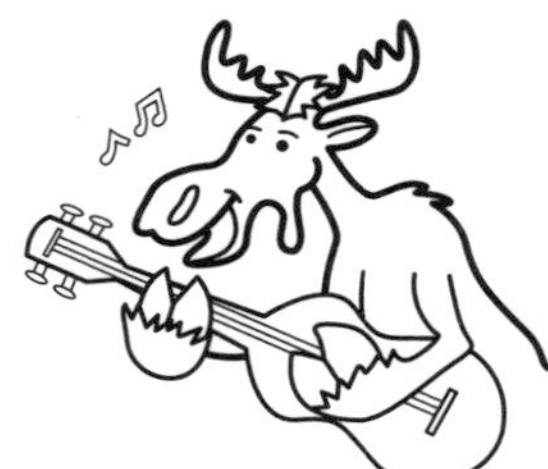

The bear listens.

The raccoon claps.

The owl flies away.

Verbs in the present tense name an action that is happening now.

Read the sentences aloud. Pick the verb from the word bank that completes each sentence.

eat	rests	sinks	wait	whistle

The cat .... on the bed.

I .... my lunch.

I can .... a tune.

We .... for the bus.

The rock .... to the bottom of the pond.

Past Tense

FACTS

Verbs in the past tense name an action that has already happened. Some verbs can be put in the past tense by adding **-ed** to the end.

Read the sentences aloud. Pick the verb from the word bank that completes each sentence.

baked	helped	planted	played	skated

Dear Grandma and Grandpa,

I had a busy day today! My mom and I ______________ a cake. Then my dad and I ______________ seeds in the garden. After that, my friend and I ______________ at an ice-skating rink. I fell on the ice, but my friend ______________ me up. Finally, we ______________ video games until it was time to go home. I am tired now!

Love,

Chris

Future Tense

A verb is a word that names an action. Verbs in the future tense name an action that has not yet happened but will happen later.

Verbs in the future tense are usually paired with "will."
Complete each sentence by writing the verb in the future tense.

Dad .... the car. (wash)

You .... dinner tonight. (cook)

We .... the bus to school tomorrow. (ride)

I .... you at the park at 3:00 p.m. (meet)

James .... his cousins next summer. (visit)

The chef .... salt to the soup if she needs to. (add)

My Favorite Book

FACTS

Books are written by authors. They have titles.

Stories are fiction, or made up. Books that are true are called nonfiction. What is your favorite book to read? Fill in the blanks.

The title of my favorite book is:

....

The author is: ....

The book is about: ....

Check one. My favorite book is:

☐ fiction ☐ nonfiction

A book's cover gives the reader an idea of what the book is about. Design a cover for your favorite book.

FACTS

A diary is a record of what you did or felt during a day.

Fill in the blanks.

My Day

Write today's date: ....

Write the names of three people you saw today.

1. ....

2. ....

3. ....

Write three sentences describing what you did or how you felt today.

1. ....

2. ....

3. ....

Irregular Spellings

FACTS

Some words have spellings that break all the rules.

Circle the correct spelling for each word.

do/doo

wut/what

friend/frend

thay/they

giv/give

Earth/Erth

does/duz

bild/build

mother/muther

sez/says

FACTS

Some words are words that readers need to know by sight.

Choose the correct word from the word bank.
Write it in the space provided.

done	eyes	father	old	one	some	two	young

The first number is ....

The second number is ....

We see with our ....

A parent who is a man is a ....

Babies are ....

Grandparents are ....

Not all, but .... things are true.

If you are finished, you are ....

Singular to Plural Nouns

FACTS

Singular means one. Plural means more than one.

To make some words plural, add an **s** at the end of the word. Add **es** to make a plural of a word that ends in **ch**, **sh**, **s**, or **x**. Make these words plural.

head__

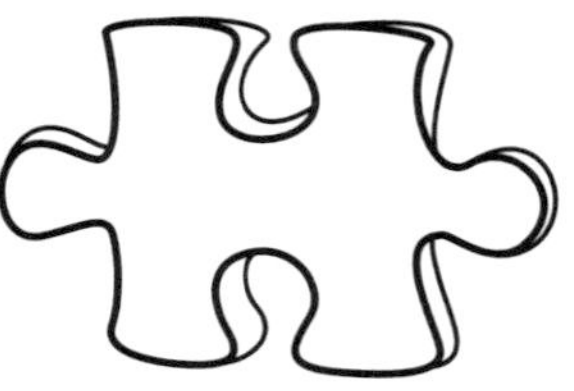

piece__

heart__

watch__

class__

school__

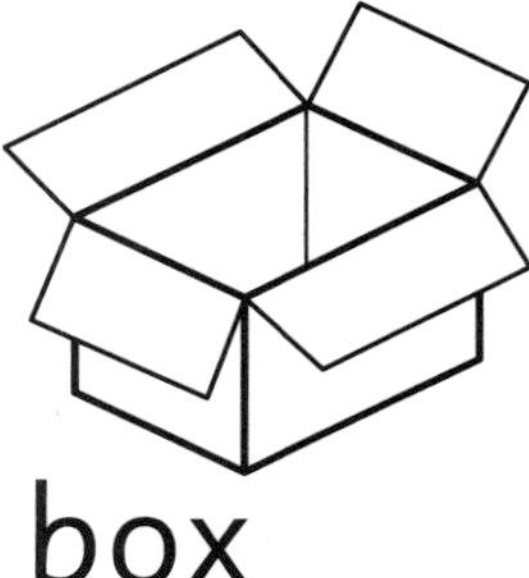

box__

wish__

Nouns and verbs combine to make sentences.

A verb that tells what a single person or thing does usually ends in **s**. Circle the correct verb to complete each sentence.

The rabbit dig digs a deep hole.

The acrobat flip flips through the air.

The wizard turn turns the elephant into a mouse.

Birds lay lays their eggs in a nest.

Authors write writes books.

The Earth spin spins on its axis.

A bagel taste tastes yummy with jelly.

The soccer players practice practices every day.

Instructions

FACTS

Instructions tell us how to do something in a clear, logical order.

Think of something you know how to do well.
Then fill in the instructions below.

How to ....

First, ...

....

Next, ...

....

Then, ...

....

Finally, ...

....

Now you know how to ....

....

Instructions use numbered steps or words like "first," "next," and "last" to help the reader understand the order of the instructions.

Read the instructions. Then underline the words that tell what items you need to complete the activity. Finally, answer the questions that follow.

1. Ask an adult to help you use the toaster.
2. Place a new piece of bread in the toaster. Turn on the toaster.
3. After about a minute, take the bread out of the toaster.
4. Place the toasted bread on a plate.
5. Use a knife to spread butter, jelly, or peanut butter on the toast.
6. Eat.

What do the instructions tell how to do?

....

How many steps are there?

....

Conjunctions

FACTS

Conjunctions are words that join other words together.
Conjunctions include "and," "but," "or," "so," and "because."

Put each pair of sentences into the conjunction mixer!
Add "and" to make one sentence.

1. Owls fly.
2. Dad needs a hammer.
3. We will play tag.
4. I will eat a pear.
5. Mice like cheese.

and

1. Owls hunt.
2. Dad needs nails.
3. We will play hopscotch.
4. I will eat a banana.
5. Mice like crackers.

1. ....
2. ....
3. ....
4. ....
5. ....

Conjunctions combine ideas.
"Because" gives a reason for an action or thought.

Put each pair of sentences into the conjunction mixer!
Add "because" to make one sentence.

1. Mom is napping.
2. Sophie is late.
3. The baby claps.
4. I am in trouble.
5. Take an umbrella.

because

1. She is tired.
2. She missed the bus.
3. He is happy.
4. I broke a window.
5. It is going to rain.

1. ....

2. ....

3. ....

4. ....

5. ....

Folktales

FACTS

Folktales are stories. They often teach a lesson in which those who are kind or clever are successful.

Help the librarian return books to the shelves.
Some of these books are folktales. Some are not.
Circle the books that should be put on the folktale shelf.

One way to learn about a book is to look at the pictures in the book. Pictures give clues about what the book is about.

Look at the pictures. Then complete the sentence.

Dog Food

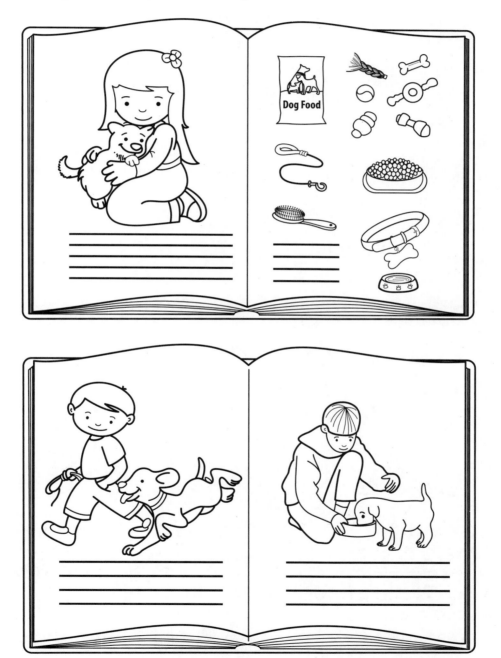

I think this book is about ....

Is and Are

FACTS

The word "is" tells what one person or thing is doing now. The word "are" tells what more than one person or thing is doing now.

Complete each sentence with "is" or "are."

The cats .... having a party.

Joe Cat .... hanging balloons.

Moe Cat .... putting out food.

Zoe Cat and Roe Cat .... playing music.

Loe Cat .... dancing.

They .... having fun!

Verbs can have endings that tell when the action took place. The verb on its own is called a root word.

Read the pairs of sentences. Use **-ing** to complete the root word that describes something happening now. Use **-ed** to complete the root word that describes something that has already happened.

Dad is cook___ dinner.

Mom cook___ dinner last night.

I sew___ a button on my shirt last week.

It fell off, so I am sew___ it again.

We watch___ a movie in school this morning.

Now we are watch___ a movie at home.

Adjectives

FACTS

Adjectives are words that describe people, places, and things.

Pair each noun with an adjective from the word bank.
Then write a complete sentence using both words.
Finally, draw your characters in the woods.

Nouns			
bear	snake	bird	fox

Adjectives			
colorful	huge	silly	sleepy

....

....

....

....

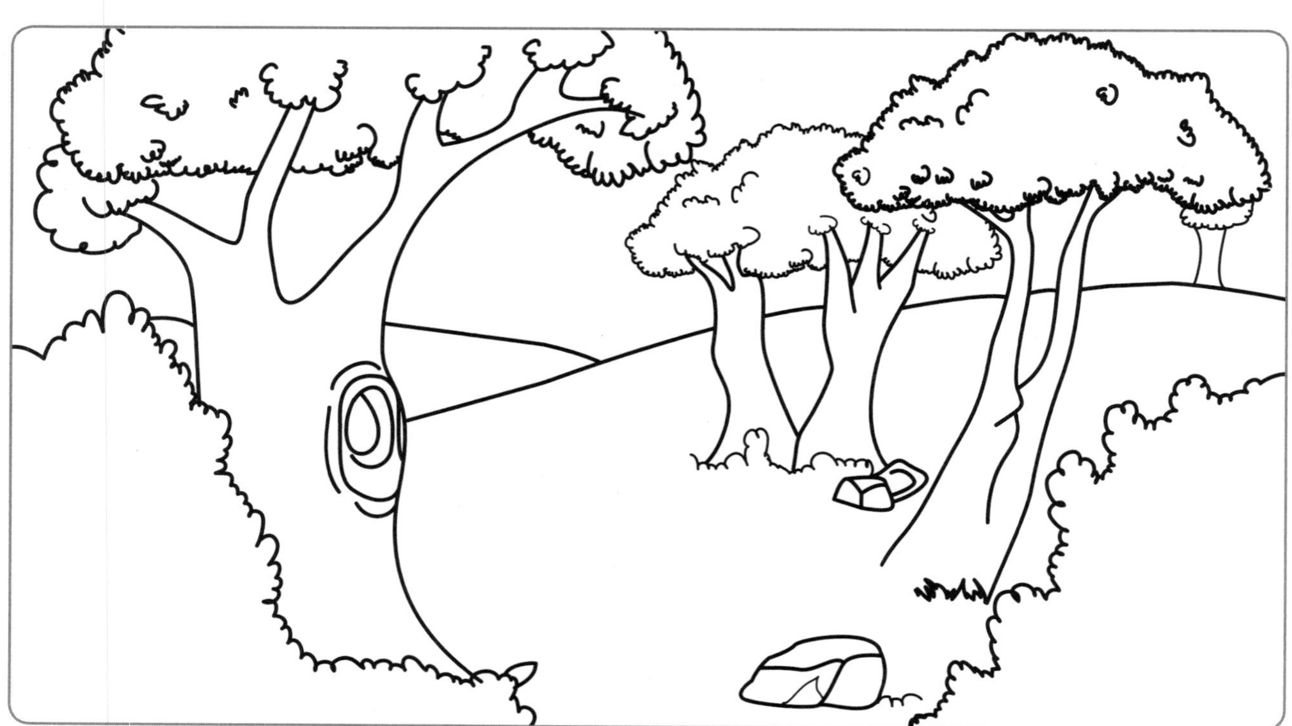

FACTS

A preposition relates a noun or a pronoun to another word in the sentence.

Complete each sentence with a preposition from the word bank.

behind	beside	in	on	over	under

The bird is .... the tree.

The bird is .... the tree.

The bird is .... the tree.

The bird is .... the tree.

The bird is .... the tree.

The bird is .... the tree.

Poetry

FACTS

Poems can paint a picture in our minds.
They can also make us feel a certain way.

This is a poem that has been read by children for many years. Read the poem aloud.

The north wind doth blow,
And we shall have snow,
And what will poor robin do then,
Poor thing?

He'll sit in a barn,
And keep himself warm,
And hide his head under his wing,
Poor thing!

How does the poem make you feel? What does it make you think of?

....

....

Circle the words in the poem that made you feel or think. Draw a picture to go with the poem.

Writing a Diamond Poem

When a diamond poem is written out, it is in the shape of a diamond.

Write a diamond poem! First, think of a noun (person, place, or thing) that you really like. Write it on the top line.
That is the subject of the poem.
Next, think of a noun that means the same thing as your first noun.
Write it on the bottom line. If you can't think of another noun, write the same noun again.
Then fill in the rest of the blanks with words that describe the subject.

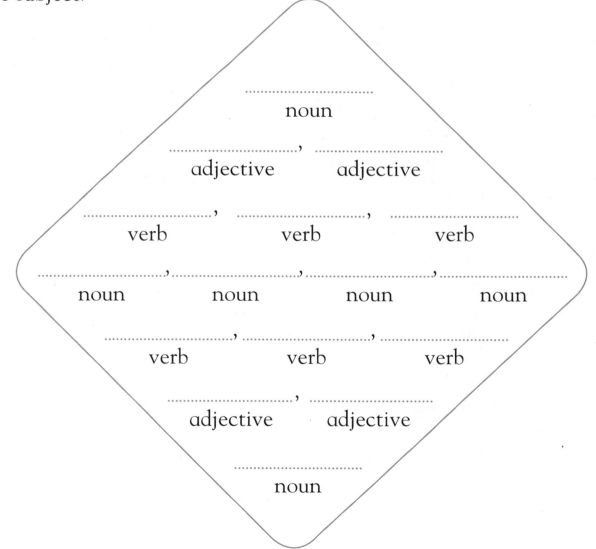

....
noun

.............................., ...
adjective adjective

.............................., ..., ...
verb verb verb

.............................., ..., ..., ...
noun noun noun noun

.............................., ..., ...
verb verb verb

.............................., ...
adjective adjective

....
noun

Parents' Notes

The language arts section of this book provides a fun way to help your child build first-class literacy skills. All of the activities support the language arts work that your child will encounter in first grade.

Contents

The language arts activities in this book are intended for a child to complete with adult support. The topics covered help children understand and make connections to the world of words around them. The topics are:

- writing letters;
- using capital letters;
- long and short vowel sounds;
- parts of speech: nouns, pronouns, verbs, adjectives, prepositions, and conjunctions;
- phonics;
- using punctuation;
- spelling;
- elements of stories: character, setting, sequence of events, and print features;
- literary genres (poetry, folktales, and nonfiction).

How to Help Your Child

On each page, read the facts and instructions aloud. Provide support while your child completes the activity. Encourage questions and reinforce observations to build confidence and increase active participation in classes at school. This type of engagement boosts success in learning.

Keep making connections between the activities and the world around you. Look for common sight words or irregularly spelled words on signs around town. Visit the library together and look through books, trying to predict what they might be about. Invite your child to retell a story in time order. Find instructions for making a craft and follow them together, step-by-step.

Be sure to praise your child as he or she completes a page, gives a correct answer, or makes progress. This will help build the child's confidence and enjoyment in learning. Above all, have fun!

1st Grade

Spelling

Author Linda Ruggieri

Contents

This chart lists all the topics in the Spelling section.

Letters and Sounds

FACTS

Aa Bb Cc Dd Ee Ff Gg Hh Ii Jj Kk Ll Mm
Nn Oo Pp Qq Rr Ss Tt Uu Vv Ww Xx Yy Zz

We spell words using the 26 letters of the alphabet. The alphabet has uppercase and lowercase letters, which are written together above. Letters are either consonants or vowels.

Circle the letter that makes the beginning sound of the name of each picture.

u s

b d

m b

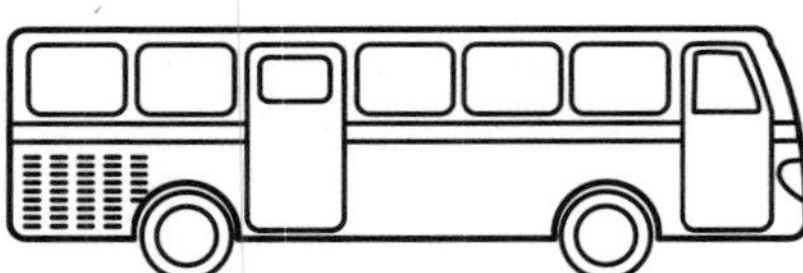

b s

c s

c f

w f

a q

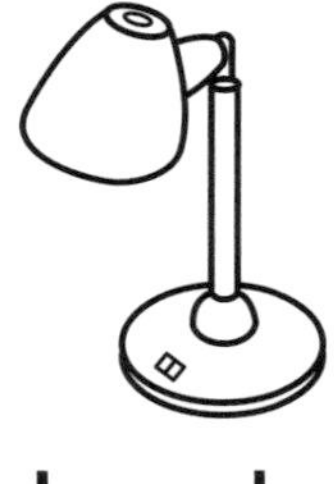

l h

There are 20 consonants in the alphabet. Five letters in the alphabet (**a**, **e**, **i**, **o**, and **u**) are always vowels. The letter **y** is sometimes a consonant and sometimes a vowel. Consonants often come at the beginning of words.

Write the letter that begins the name of each picture.

_an

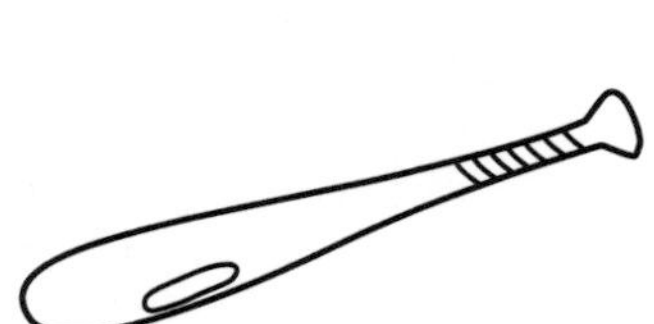

_at

_ig

_at

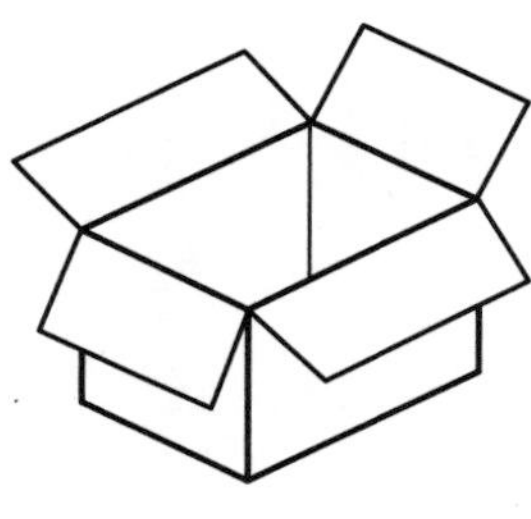

_ox

_ey

Circle the letter that makes the beginning sound of each picture's name.

m s

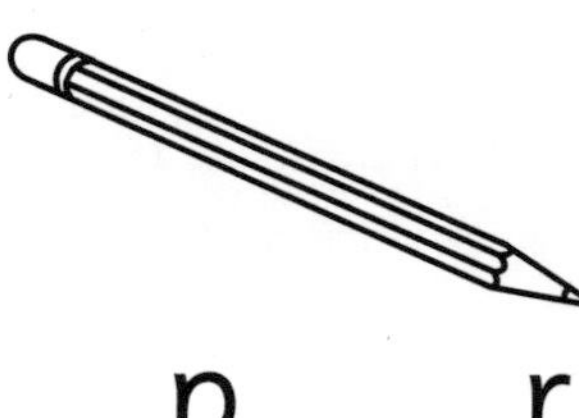

p r

c a

Now write the words in alphabetical order.

....

Ending Consonants

FACTS

Consonants can come at the end of words, too.

Read each word aloud and listen to its ending sound.
Circle the consonant at the end of each word.

bug

sit

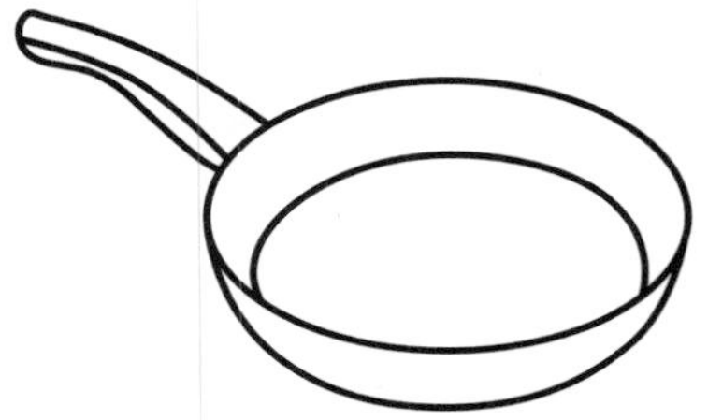

pan

cap

cow

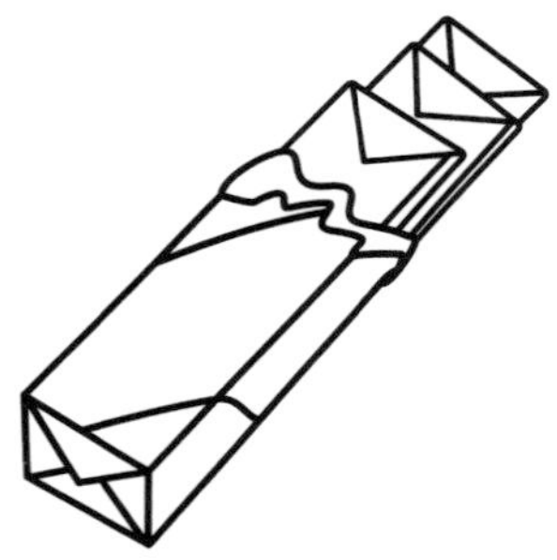

gum

Draw a picture of something whose name ends in the consonant **t**. Then write its name.

Consonant blends are two or more consonants that come together to make one sound. Some consonant blends come at the beginning and others at the end of words. For example, say the word "glove." Listen to the "gl" sound at the beginning.

Read the name of the first picture aloud. Listen to the beginning blend. Then circle the name of the picture with the same beginning sound.

Read the name of the first picture aloud. Listen to the ending blend. Circle the name of the picture with the same ending sound.

The Vowels

FACTS

The vowels in the alphabet are **a**, **e**, **i**, **o**, **u**, and sometimes **y**. We see vowels in the middle of many words.

Write the beginning letter of each picture's name in the box below it. The three letters form a word. Circle the letter in the word that is a vowel. Read the word aloud.

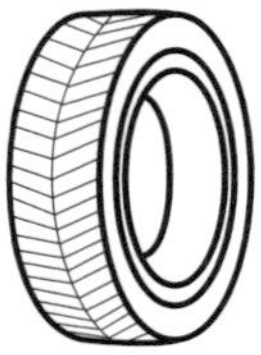

In the words below, move your finger over each letter and make its sound. Read the word aloud.

bag

pen

dog

bib

FACTS

The vowels **a**, **e**, **i**, **o**, and **u** each have a long sound and a short sound. When used as a vowel, **y** makes a long "i" sound or a long "e" sound.

Some vowels in the picture are missing.
Where in the world can they be?
Look at each word in the picture.
Write in its vowel, please!

s_n

sw_ng

n_st

b_ll

b_sh

sl_de

r_ck

r_pe

The Long "a" Sound

FACTS

The vowel **a** can make a long sound. You hear it in the middle of the word "gate."

Write the letter **a** to spell out each word below. Read the word and listen to its long "a" sound. Then complete each sentence by using one of these words.

s_y	A .... is on the tracks.
r_ke	Jon wears a red ....
t_pe	Put some .... on the box.
r_in	It is going to ....
tr_in	We will .... leaves.
c_pe	What did you ....?

Read the words below aloud. Circle the ones with the long "a" sound.

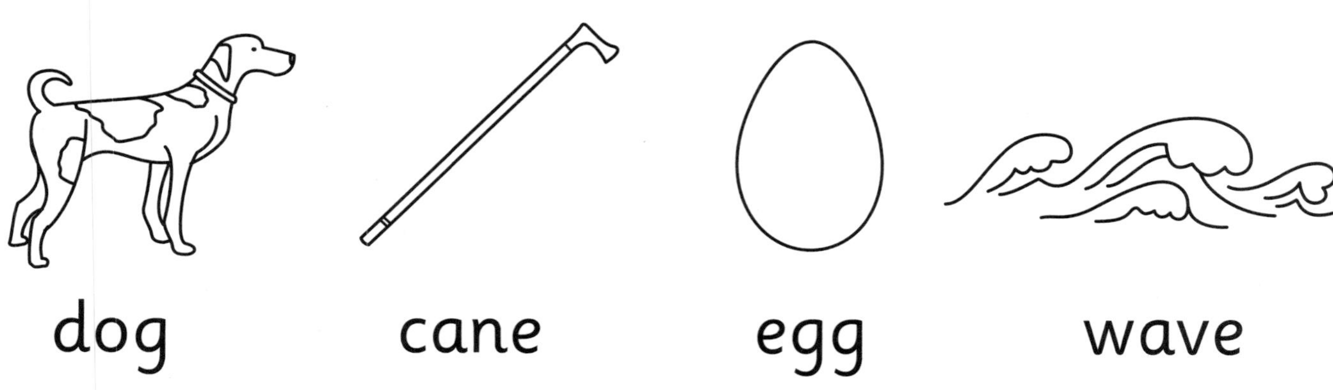

The long "a" sound can be made with the letter groups **ai**, **ay**, or **a** plus a silent **e** (**a_e**), as heard in "train," "pray," and "snake."

Help Jake make his way through the maze and find the cake at the end. Choose a long "a" word from the word box and write it next to the correct picture. Then follow the words to get through the maze.

cake	Jake	jay	cave	cage	rain	vase	rake	tape

START

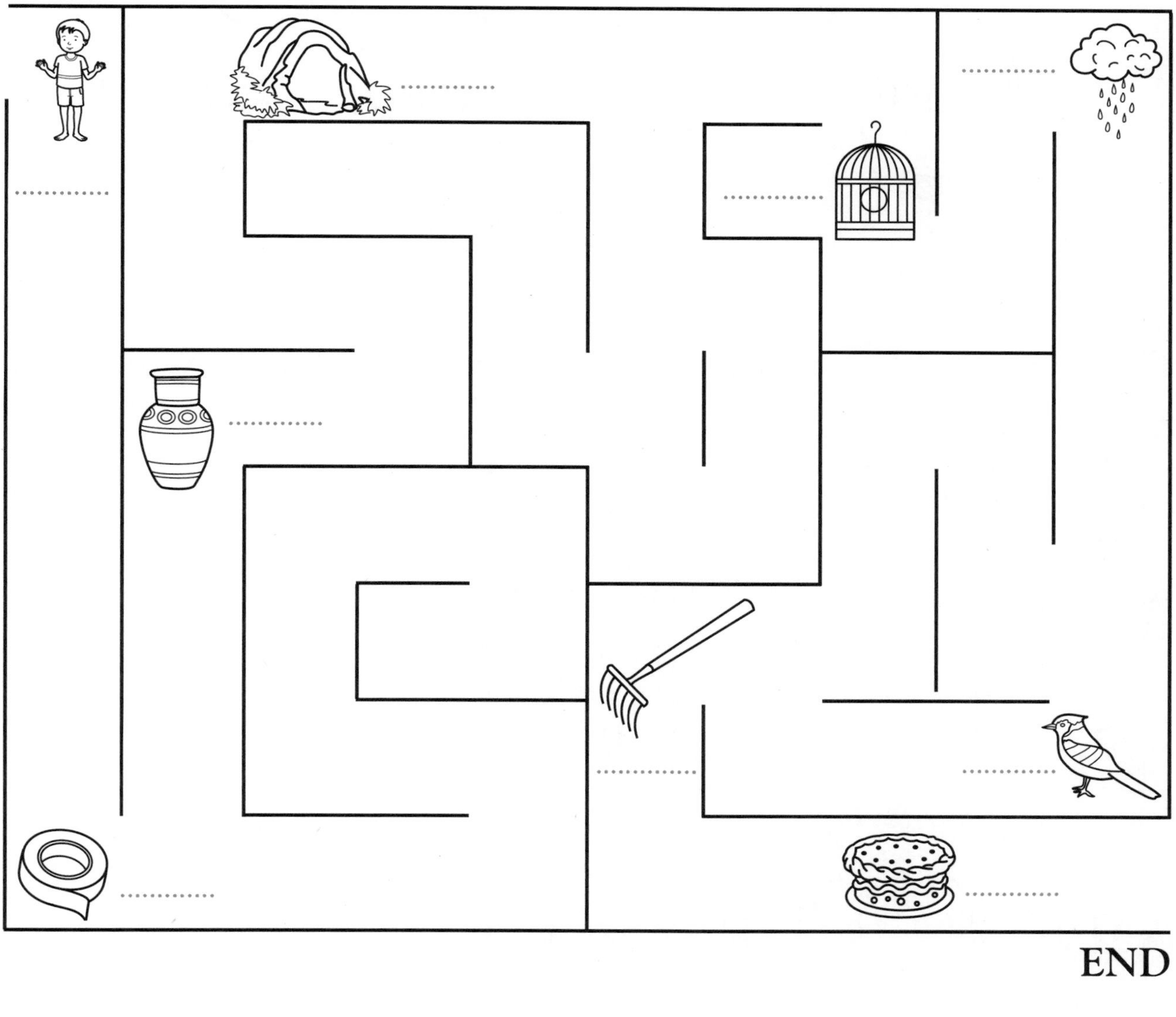

....

....

....

....

....

....

....

....

....

END

The Long "e" Sound

The vowel **e** can make a long sound. You hear it in the word "be."

Read the word on each balloon aloud. Color each balloon that has a word with the long "e" sound on it.

Find the long "e" words in the word search below. Go across or down.

s	e	e	j	t	t
h	t	l	a	r	r
e	h	e	i	u	e
e	r	a	t	e	a
t	e	f	a	k	t
g	e	l	p	q	m

The Long "e" Sound

The long "e" sound can be made by the letter groups **ea**, **ee**, **ey**, **ie**, or a lone **e** at the end of a short word.

Choose the correct long "e" word to finish each sentence. Then read the sentences aloud.

The name of the baseball .... was the Sluggers.	**term**	**team**	**treat**
They were playing in a park near a big	**see**	**tree**	**heel**
The .... baseball field was very smooth.	**feel**	**green**	**treat**
The Sluggers could .... that this would be a hard game.	**sail**	**see**	**she**
.... player took a turn at bat.	**Teach**	**Reach**	**Each**
Brittany threw the ball to	**me**	**we**	**he**
Tom hurt his	**keep**	**peel**	**knee**

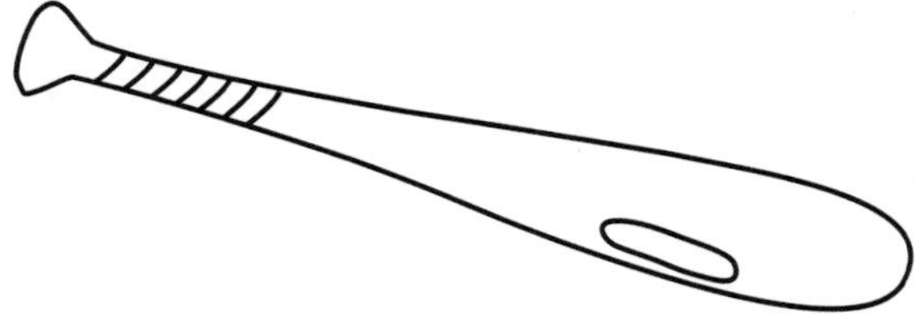

The Long "i" Sound

FACTS

The vowel **i** can make a long sound. You hear it in the middle of the word "hike."

Does each word in the table below have the long "i" sound? Check (✓) **Yes** or **No**.

Word	Yes	No	Word	Yes	No
line			hit		
if			bike		
fire			fix		
find			hide		
kite			side		

Read the clues and pick the correct long "i" word from the word box.

mice	tires	light	bike	smile

It shows you are happy. ....

You ride it. ....

There are four on a car. ....

They are little animals. ....

It helps us to see. ....

The Long "i" Sound

The long "i" sound can be made with the letter **i** plus a silent **e** (**i_e**), as in "shine." Look for the final silent letter **e** as a clue.

Read the words on the kites and follow the directions to color in the kites.

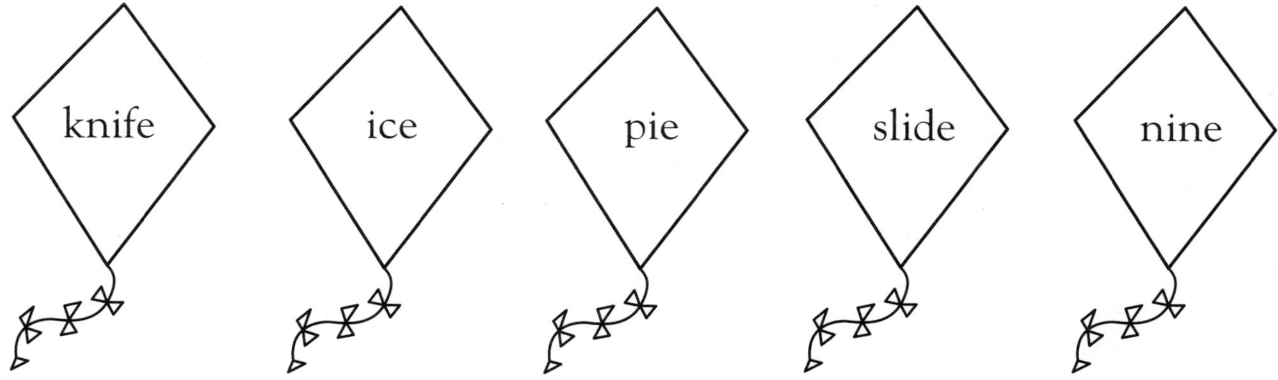

Which word names a number? Color that kite green.

Which word names something you use to cut bread? Color that kite red.

Which word names a food? Color that kite purple.

Which word names something on a playground? Color that kite yellow.

Which word names something that is very cold? Color that kite blue.

Match the words on the left to their meanings on the right.

five	someone who is getting married
side	a number
bride	left or right edge of an object

The Long "o" Sound

FACTS

The vowel **o** can make a long sound. You hear it in the middle of the word "bone."

Write an **o** on each line. Then circle the picture that shows the word. Read the word aloud.

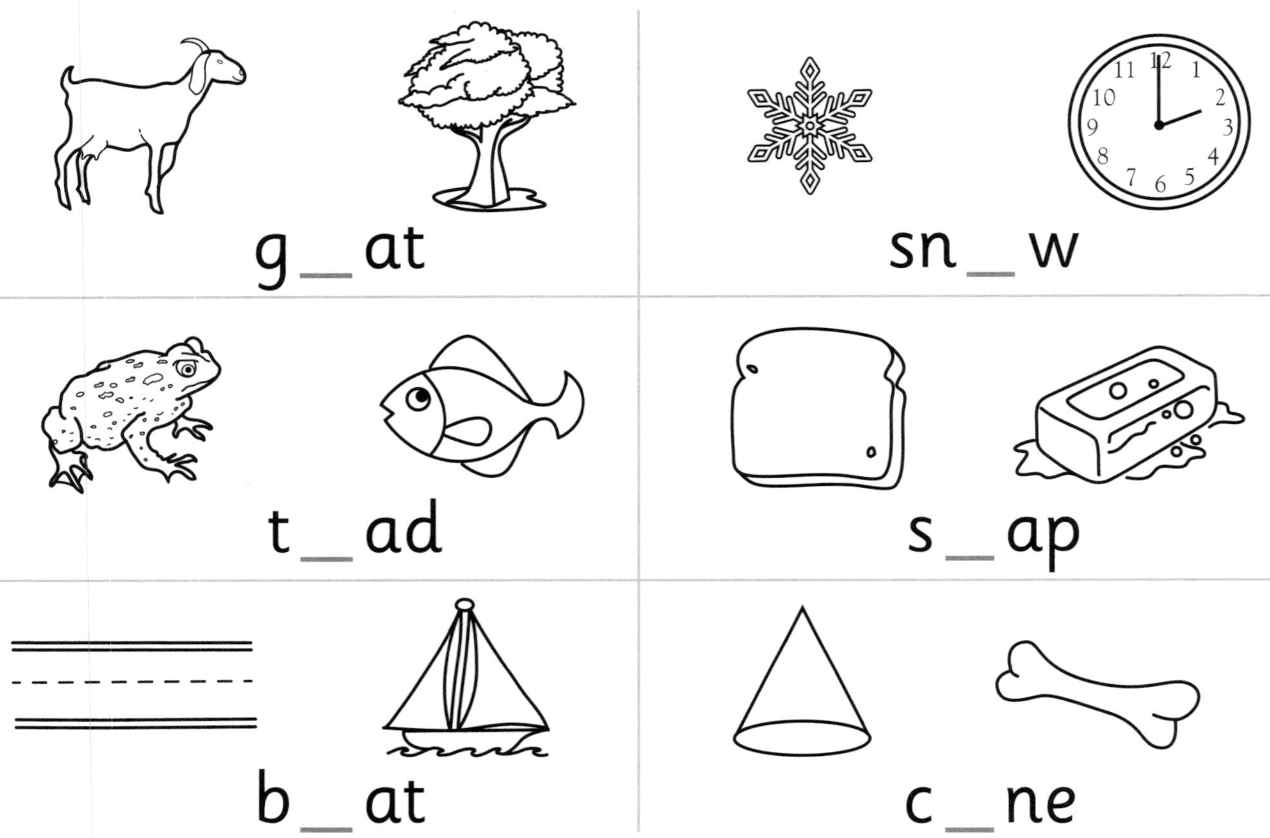

Read each word below. If it has a long "o" sound, color the star red. If it does not, color the star blue.

pole ☆	not ☆	stone ☆
cob ☆	vote ☆	top ☆

The Long "o" Sound

The long "o" sound can be made with the letters **o**, **oa**, **oe**, **ow**, and **o** plus a silent **e (o_e)**, such as "so," "goat," "foe," "sown," and "pole."

Circle the things Sarah should put in her boat.

Sarah has a boat.
In it she will go.
But first she needs to add some things
Whose names have a long "o"!

clock

phone

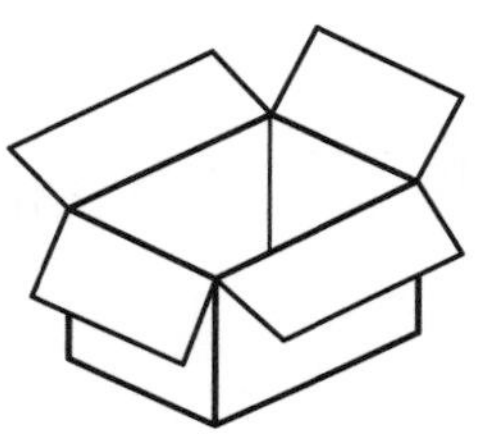

box

soap

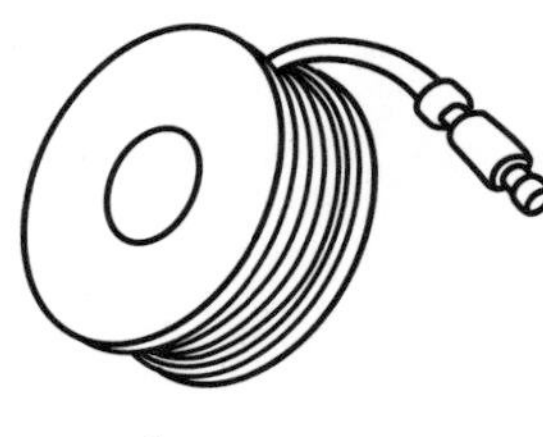

hose

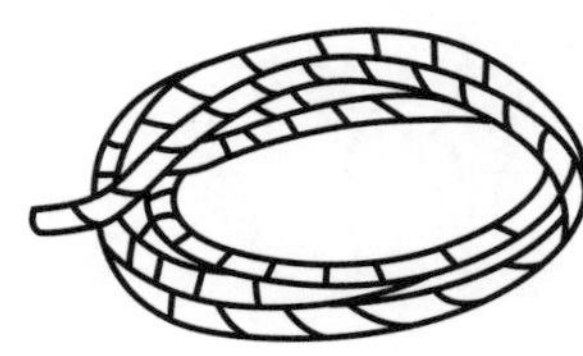

rope

dog

globe

Read the word aloud. Circle the picture that the word names.

oats

hoe

★ The Long "u" Sound

FACTS

The vowel **u** can make a long sound. You hear it in the middle of the word "rule."

Fill in the long "u" word to complete each sentence.

The baby is so .... !

cute **bun**

The .... is filled with toothpaste.

bug **tube**

That dinosaur is .... !

huge **hug**

Read the words below. Circle the words that have the same "u" sound as "rule."

just	tune	gut
June	run	bug
cane	rug	flute
sun	brute	tub

The Long "u" Sound

The long "u" sound can be made with the letters **u**, **ue**, **ui**, **ew**, **oo**, and **u** plus a silent **e** (**u_e**), such as "flu," "glue," "suit," "crew," "boot," and "rude."

Read the words in the box. Which words have the same long "u" sound, as in "fruit"? Write the words inside the circles.

cute proof crew suit mutt root true glue run blue

 The Short "a" Sound

The vowel **a** can make a short sound. You hear it in the middle of the word "sat."

Look at the scrambled letters and the pictures next to them. Unscramble the letters to write a word with the short "a" sound.

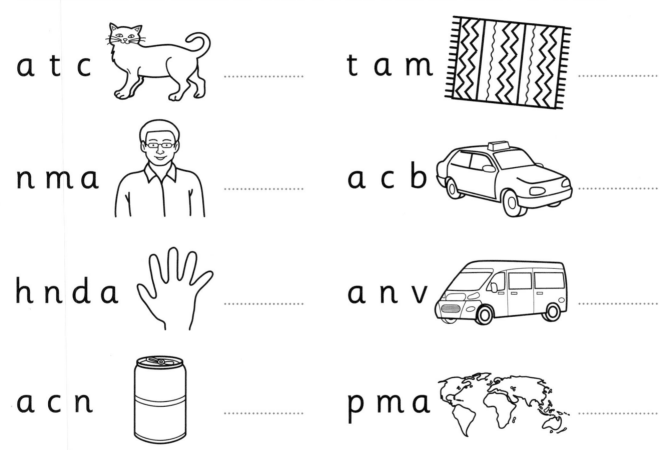

a t c .... t a m ....

n m a  .... a c b ....

h n d a  .... a n v ....

a c n 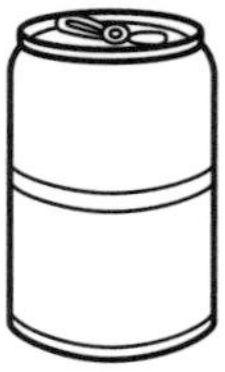 .... p m a ....

The word for each picture below contains the short "a" sound. Name each picture.

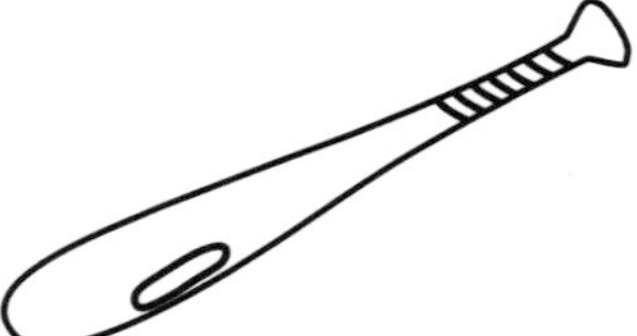

....

FACTS

More words with the short "a" sound are "sat" and "cap."

Help Chloe the Cat get to her kittens. Draw a line that follows the pictures with names that contain the short "a" sound.

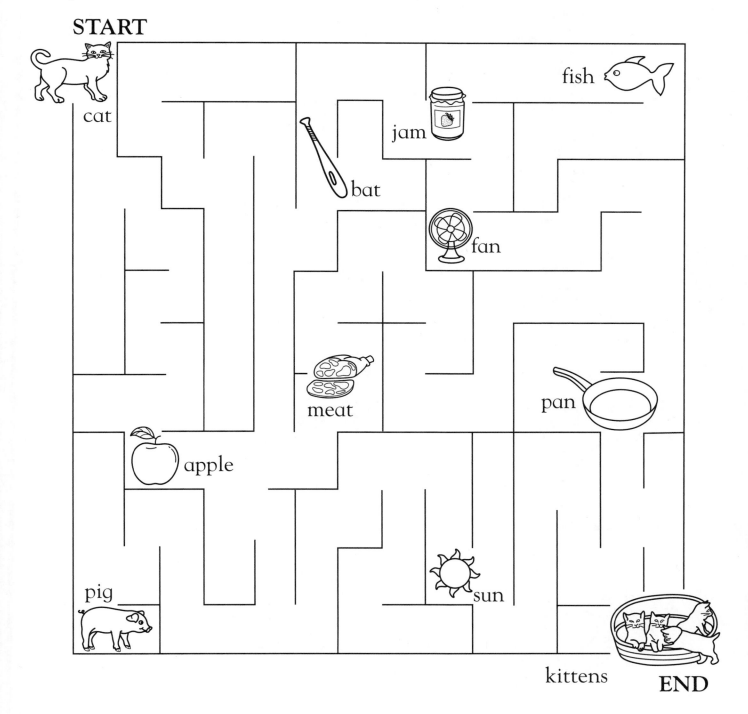

START

cat

jam

fish

bat

fan

meat

pan

apple

pig

sun

kittens

END

 The Short "e" Sound

FACTS

The vowel **e** can make a short sound. You hear it in the middle of the word "get."

Choose a word from the box to match each picture.

jet	net	pen	tent	bed	hen	ten	bell

....

....

....

....

....

....

10 ....

....

More words with the short "e" sound are "pet," "let," and "went."

Hettie the Hen has lots of eggs! Look at the pictures and the words on each egg. If the word has the short "e" sound, color it yellow.

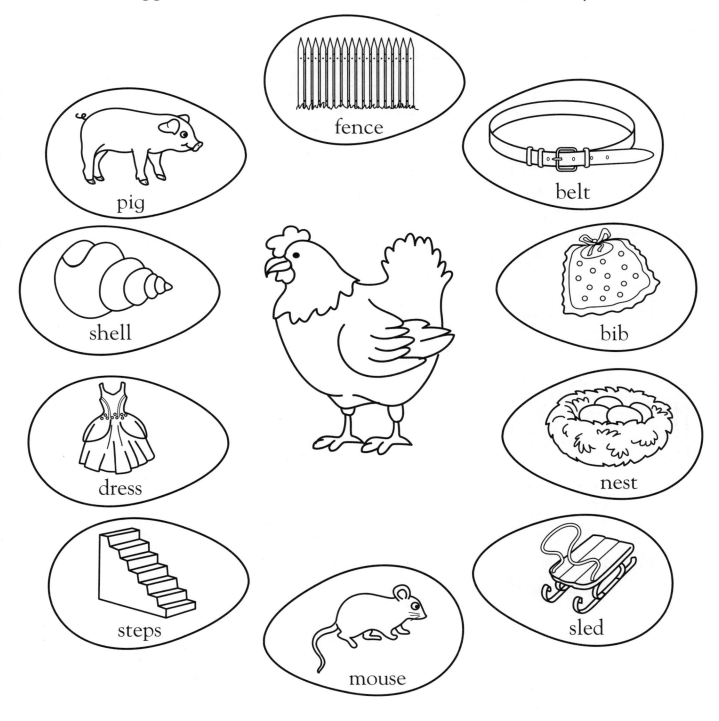

fence

pig

belt

shell

bib

dress

nest

steps

sled

mouse

The Short "i" Sound

FACTS

The vowel **i** can make a short sound. You hear it in the middle of the word "big."

Using the letters above each bag and the ending shown under the bag, write three words on each bag.

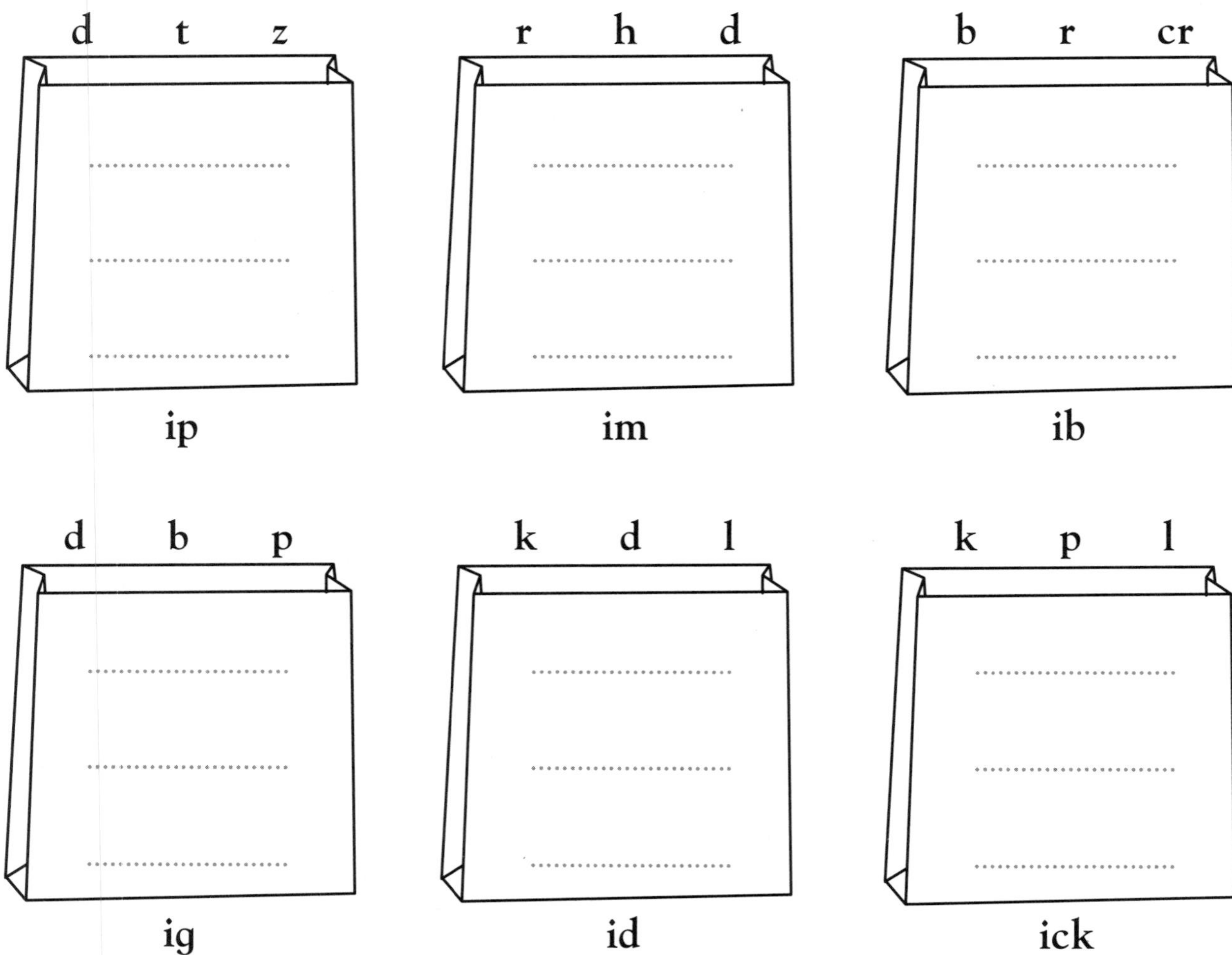

Unscramble these letters to make words. Write each word in the same order on the dotted line. Then read the silly sentence aloud!

heT gip dha a igw nda idd a jgi

....

FACTS

More words with the short "i" sound are "pit," "mill," and "trip."

Read the words on the balloons aloud. Put a check (✓) in the box if the word has a short "i" sound. Put an **X** (✗) if it does not.

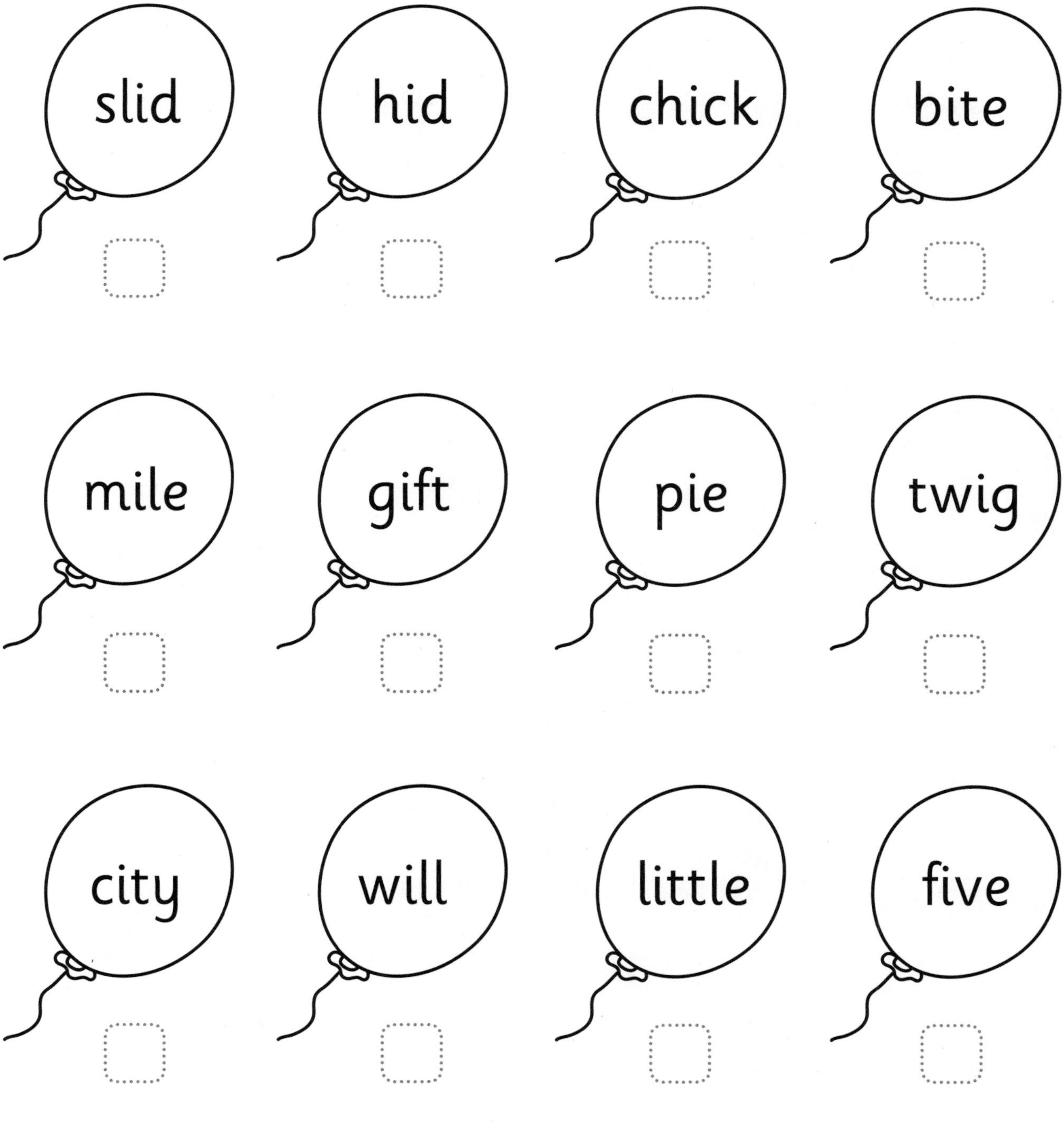

slid ☐ hid ☐ chick ☐ bite ☐

mile ☐ gift ☐ pie ☐ twig ☐

city ☐ will ☐ little ☐ five ☐

The Short "o" Sound

FACTS

The vowel **o** can make a short sound. You hear it in the middle of the word "got."

Unscrambled the letters in each box to make short "o" words. Then write the words.

d r o ....

x b o ....

p m o ....

o g h ....

t o h ....

o g l ....

k o c r ....

g f o r ....

Choosing from the unscrambled short "o" words above, write the answer to each question.

Which word names an animal that croaks? ....

Which word means the opposite of cold? ....

Which word names something you use when fishing? ....

More words with the short "o" sound are "pot," "fox," and "job."

FACTS

Read each word aloud. Draw a line from the word to the picture it matches.

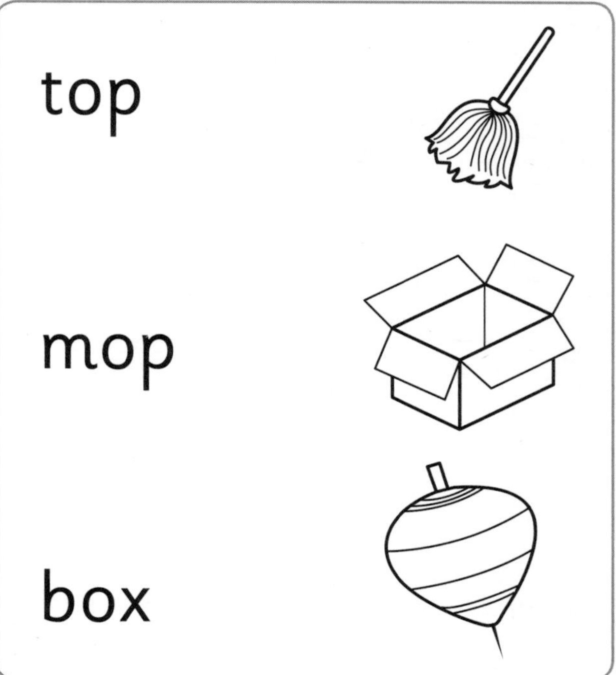

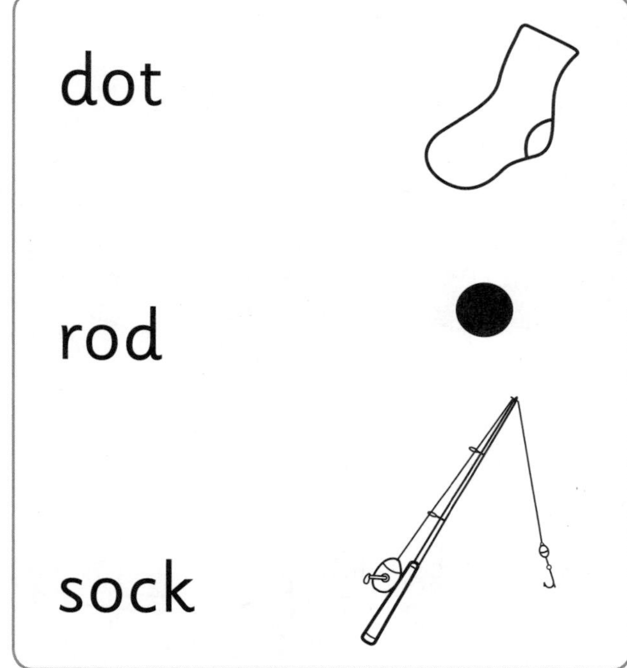

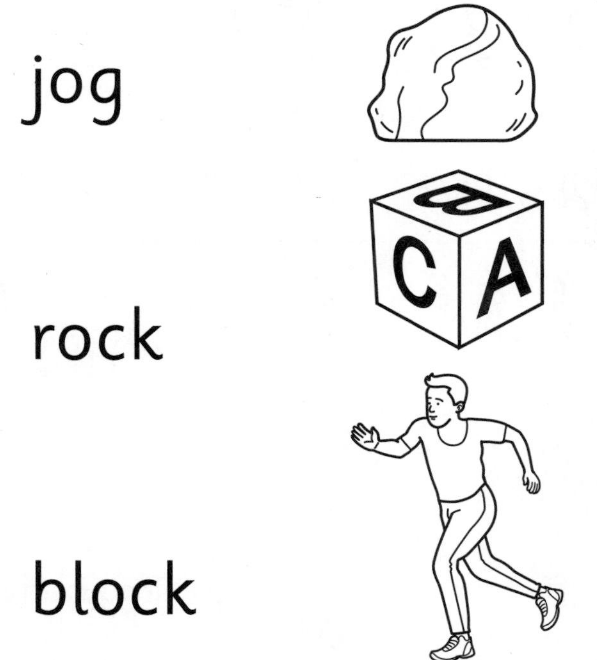

The Short "u" Sound

FACTS

The vowel **u** can make a short sound. You hear it in the middle of the word "nut."

Write the missing **u** to complete the word on each nut. Then draw a line from the word to the picture it matches.

Find the short "u" words in the word search below. Go across or down.

a	s	c	t	y	h
v	t	o	r	q	u
m	u	d	u	b	n
g	f	p	c	u	t
l	f	w	k	g	c

More words with the short "u" sound are "bug," "run," and "stuff."

Help the school bus reach the school by following the short "u" sound. Look at each picture and write its name.

★ The Letter y

FACTS

The letter **y** can be used as a consonant, as in "you." The letter **y** can also be used as a vowel. It can have the sound of the long "i," as in "my," or the sound of the long "e," as in "baby."

Circle the word in which the letter **y** makes the vowel sound of "i" or "e." **Hint:** Two words use **y** as a consonant.

fly

fry

bunny

cry

yogurt

yawn

baby

pony

happy

Every word has a number of beats. Each beat is called a syllable. For example, the word "dog" has one beat, the word "donkey" has two beats, and the word "Saturday" has three beats.

Circle the correct number of beats in the name of each picture.

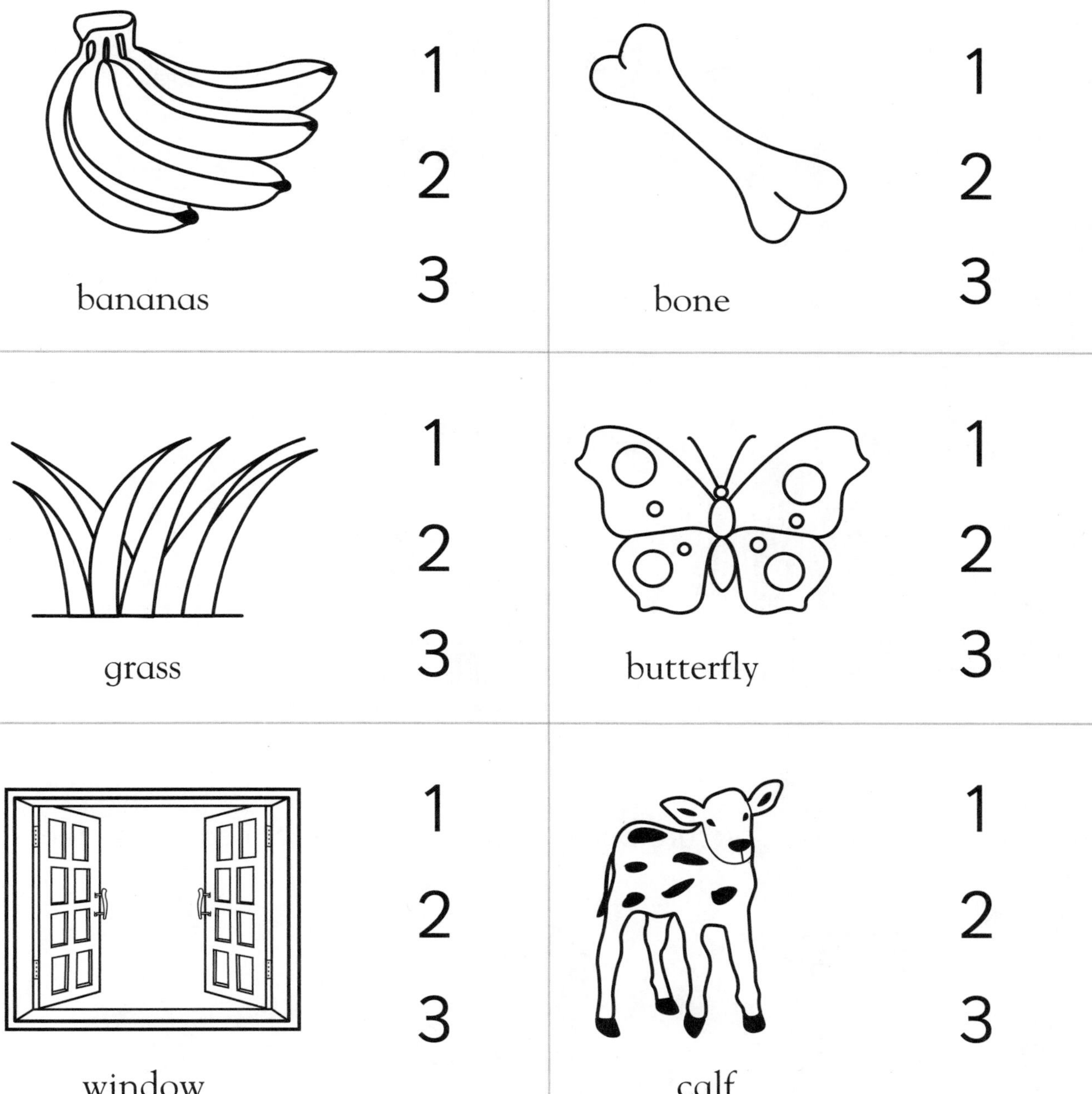

Beginning Consonant Blends

FACTS

A blend is two or more consonant sounds used together. Some blends come at the beginning of words. For example, say the word "frog" and listen to the sound of the "fr" blend.

Say the name of the first picture. Listen to the beginning blend. Circle the pictures that have names that begin with the same blend sound.

glove

goat

globe

glue

crib

crayon

cat

crown

skate

skirt

smoke

skull

Say the name of each picture below. Circle the correct beginning blend.

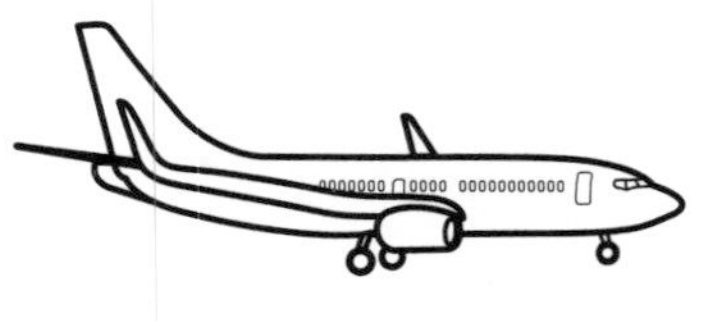

gl pl fl

gr pr br

sq sk st

Ending Consonant Blends

FACTS

Some consonant blends come at the end of words, such as in the word "jump." Listen to the ending "mp" sound.

Write the correct consonant blend to finish each word.

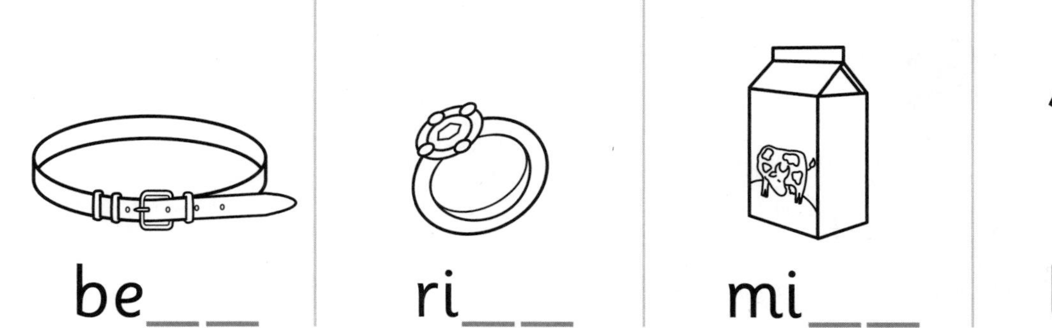

be__ __ ri__ __ mi__ __ la__ __

Use a word from above to complete each sentence.

I have a .... in my bedroom.

He wore a brown .... with his pants.

I like to drink ....

I have a .... on my finger.

Draw a line from the ending consonant blend to the picture it matches.

ng lf nk

shelf sink string

Reading Words

FACTS

Words are made of letters. Each letter has a sound.
Blending the sounds of letters will help you read the word.

Say the sound in each letter aloud. Then read out the word.

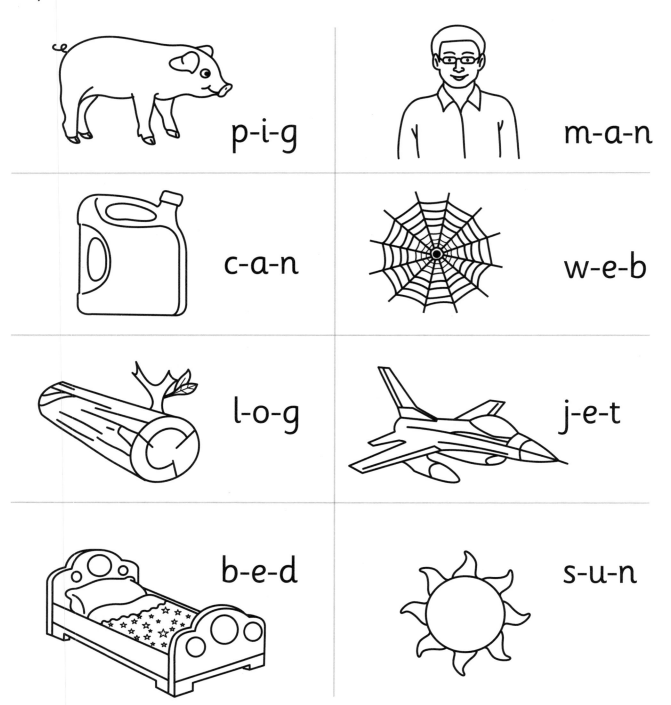

p-i-g

m-a-n

c-a-n

w-e-b

l-o-g

j-e-t

b-e-d

s-u-n

Knowing the letter sounds will help you read and write words, and spell them correctly.

Look at the picture clues. Write the first letter of each picture in the box below it. The letters spell a new word. Write the word.

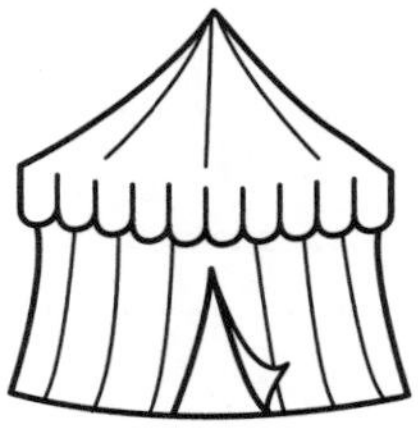

Digraphs at the Beginning

FACTS

Consonant digraphs are two letters that join to make one sound. For example, words like "**ch**ick," "**th**irty," "**sh**ip," and "**wh**eel" have the consonant digraphs **ch**, **th**, **sh**, and **wh** at the beginning.

Look at each picture. Choose the correct beginning sound from the box to write under each picture.

ch	th	sh	wh

__ __　__ __　__ __　__ __

__ __　__ __　__ __　__ __

__ __　__ __　__ __　__ __

Digraphs at the End

Consonant digraphs can sometimes come at the end of words. For example, words like "so**ck**," "ea**ch**," "wi**sh**," and "ma**th**" have the consonant digraphs **ck**, **ch**, **sh**, and **th** at the end.

Look at the pictures below. Choose the correct ending sound from the box to write under each picture.

sh	ch	ck	th

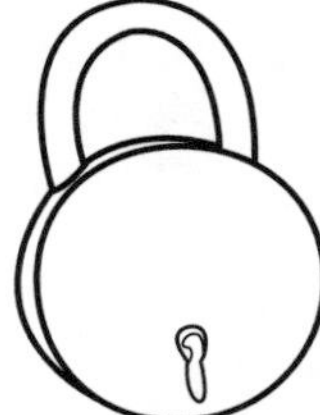

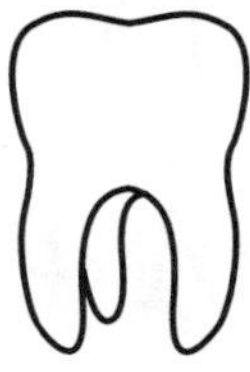

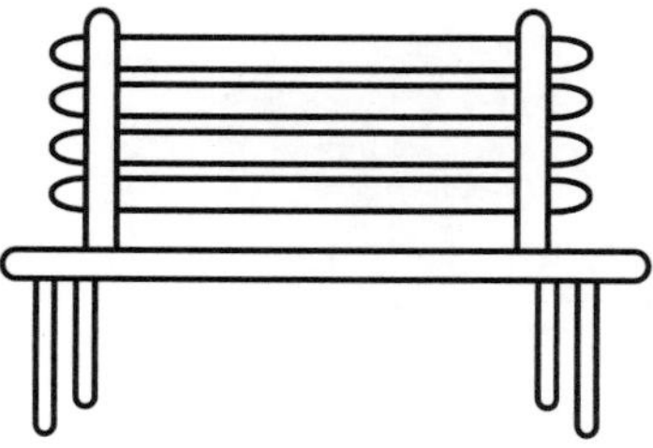

The Silent Letter e

FACTS

When you add an **e** to the end of some words, the short vowel sound becomes long and the **e** is silent.

Read the first word aloud. Add an **e** to it. Write the new word.

pin + e = ...

cub + e = ...

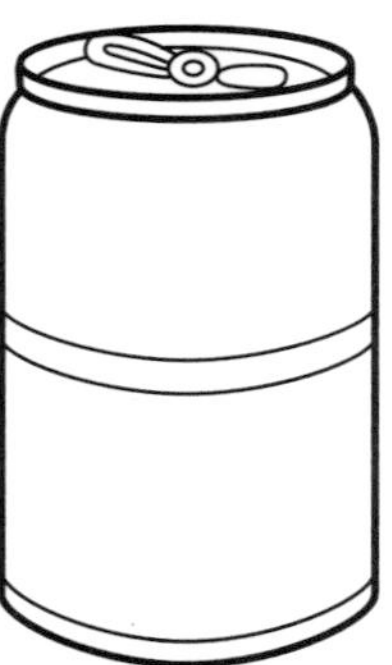

man + e = ...

can + e = ...

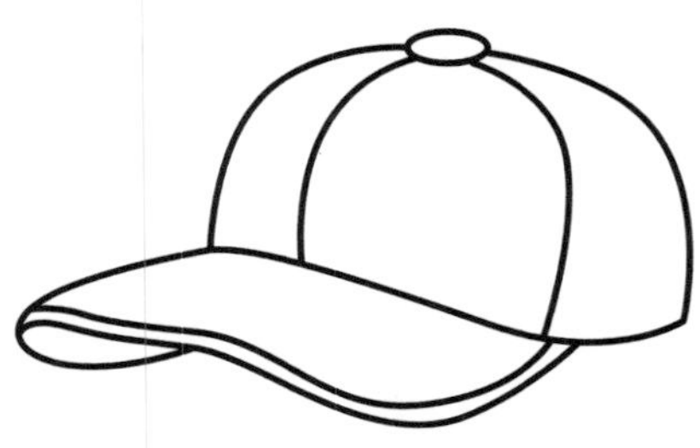

cap + e = ...

pan + e = ...

FACTS

You may have already noticed that two vowels often come together to make one long vowel sound. For example, **ai** in "pain," **ay** in "day," **ee** in "see," **ea** in "bead," **ie** in "lie," **oe** in "woe," and **oa** in "boat."

Circle the word that names each picture.

leak lean

pie tie

wear wheel

ray rain

pay jay

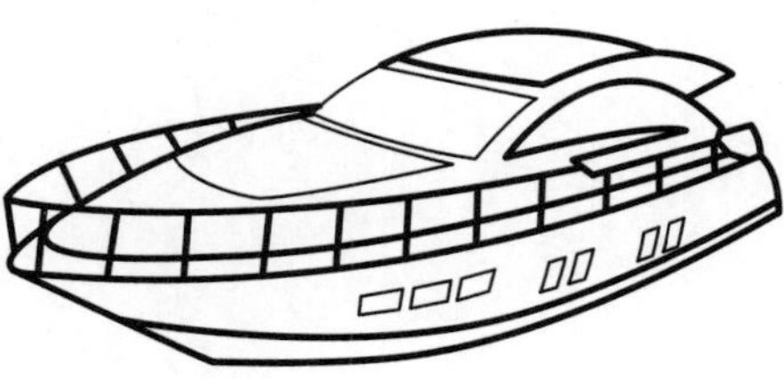

boat moat

sheep seal

hoe foe

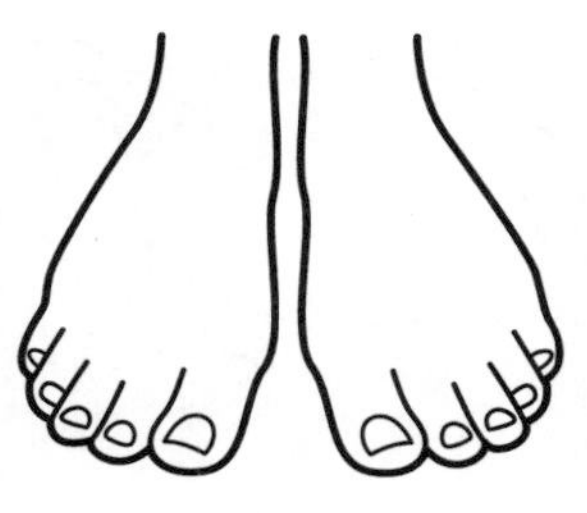

goes toes

Adding the Letter s

FACTS

We add an **s** to some naming words to make them plural, which shows that there is more than one item. For example, we would say "one egg," but "two eggs."

Write the letter **s** to make these words plural.

hat_

dog_

ball_

tree_

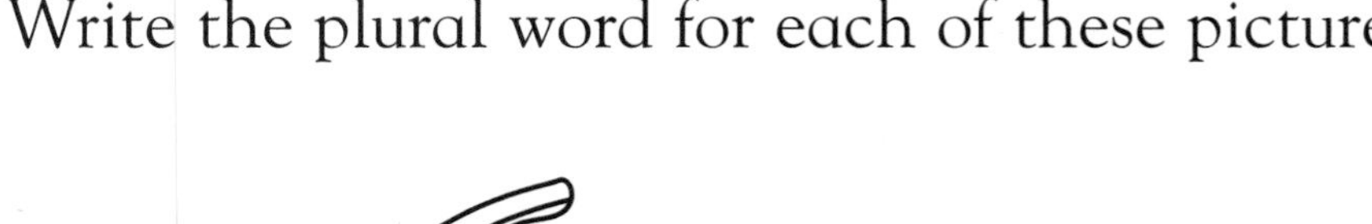

Write the plural word for each of these pictures.

....

....

FACTS

Some action words and naming words can have endings, such as **-ed** and **-ing**, that change their meanings.

Write an **-ed** at the end of each action word and fill in the blanks.

She (play) .... outdoors.

She (laugh) .... at the joke.

Use **-ing** to complete each action word.

They are eat ____ pizza.

She is push ____ the cart.

Maddie is go ____ to the store.

The man is laugh ____ .

Emma is play ____ with a doll.

Sight Words

FACTS

Some words are so common that you will soon begin to recognize them instantly. These are called sight words. Many of them are not sounded out as they are spelled.

Look at the scrambled letters. Unscramble them to form a word from the box. Write each word and read it aloud.

most	of	are	the
put	one	been	two

eth ....   neo ....

owt ....   rea ....

tup ....   fo ....

nebe ....   msto ....

From the word box below, write the correct word for each word meaning.

different	great	four

the word for 4 ....

the opposite of same ....

a word for wonderful ....

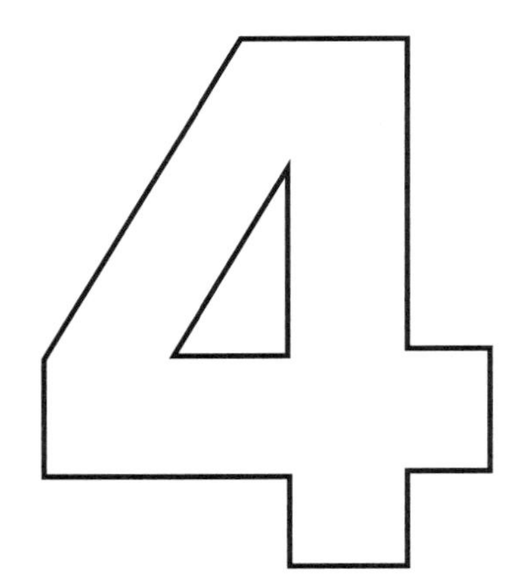

FACTS

Sight words are also known as high-frequency words. Some more high-frequency words are "after," "again," "from," "once," and "thank."

Read each word aloud. Write each word on the basket that shows its beginning letter.

some	what	do	often	they
would	old	where	does	their
should	school	thought	different	only

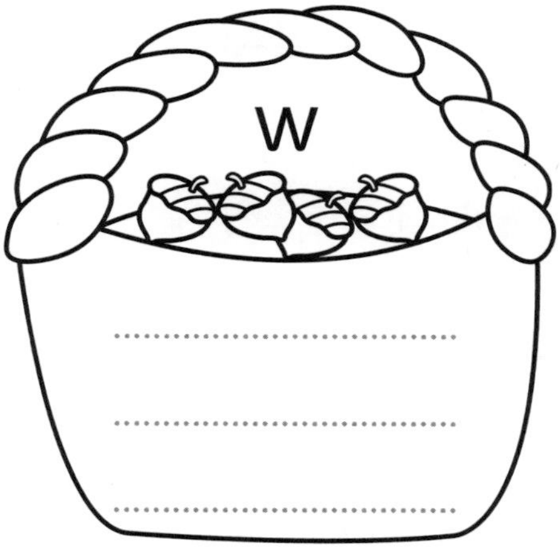

w

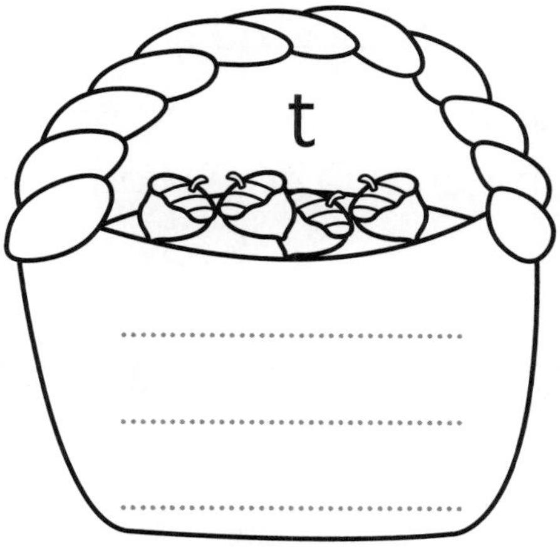

t

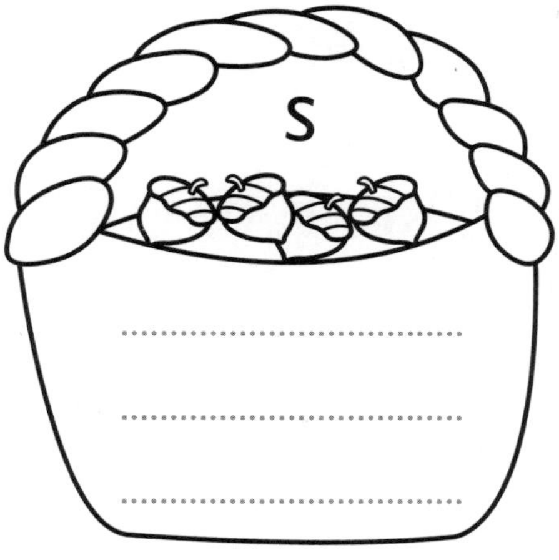

s

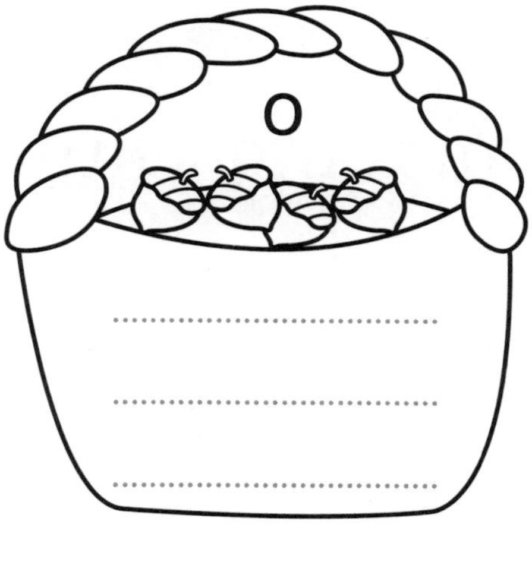

o

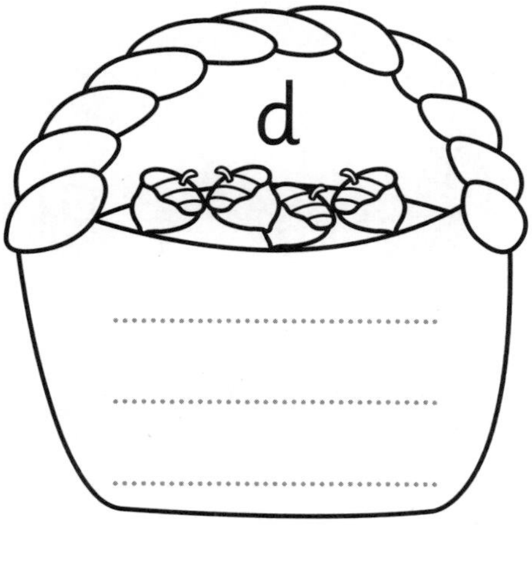

d

What is a Sentence?

FACTS

A sentence is a group of words that expresses a complete thought. For example, "I like toast." is a complete sentence, but "The toy train" is not. Remember that a sentence always begins with a capital letter and ends with punctuation, which is very often a period (.).

Circle the words below that are complete sentences.

The girl is nice.

Mows the lawn

No one else

I know a secret.

Read each sentence below aloud. Underline the capital letter and circle the period at the end of each sentence.

I am six years old.

The puppy is cute.

We are playing with a ball.

This is a big and leafy tree.

FACTS

A sentence can also ask a question. Then the sentence begins with a capital letter and ends with a question mark (?).

Sentences that show excitement, surprise, or a strong feeling begin with a capital letter and end with an exclamation point (!).

Put a question mark at the end of the sentences that ask a question and an exclamation point at the end of the sentences that show excitement, surprise, or a strong feeling.

Do you like hot dogs _

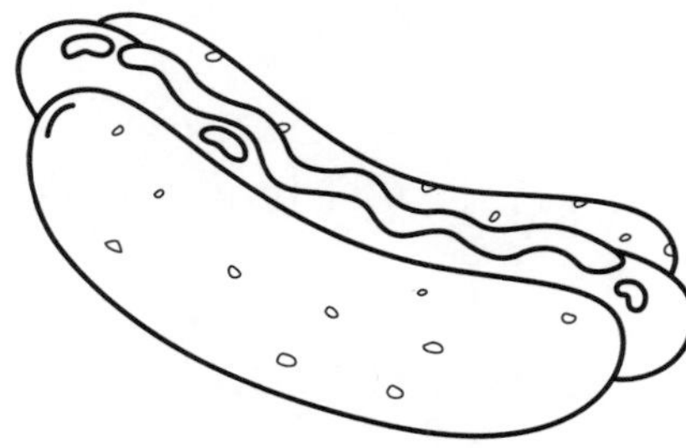

I am starving _

Wow, here comes the parade _

What is your name _

Look, here come the clowns _

Where are we going _

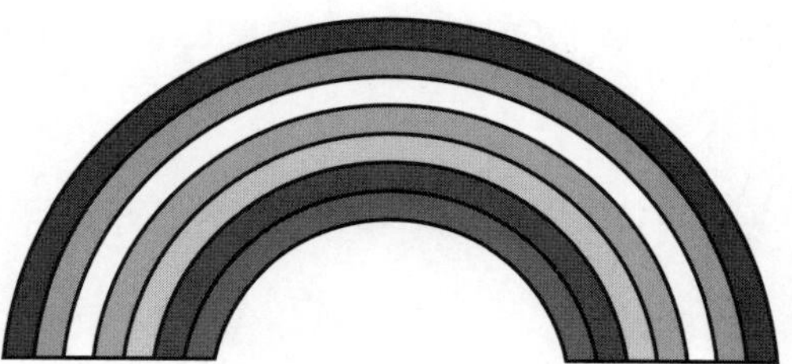

I just saw a rainbow _

Do you know how to swim _

Tongue Twisters and Rhymes

FACTS

Reading words smoothly and with understanding makes us better readers.

Read the words aloud. Follow each direction.

six silly sheep sing sad songs

Read the words a second time quickly.

Now read the words quietly.

Count each **s**. How many did you count? 

Have a friend read the words to you.

Read the poem. Then write answers to the questions.

Ice-cream Treat

Ice cream, ice cream,
cool and sweet.
Which kind is
the best to eat?

In the poem, what is cool and sweet? ....

Which word rhymes with "sweet"? ....

In this poem, what does "kind" mean? ....

Which word in the poem is the opposite of warm? ....

Using expression is important when reading. Expression can change as you read about different characters or feelings.

Read the story once. Read it again out loud. Answer each question.

Sparky's Stuck!

Kim has a white cat.
Its name is Sparky.
Sparky climbs trees.
Sparky will not come down.
Kim holds out food for Sparky.
"Sparky is stuck in the tree,"
calls Kim.
Kim's father gets a ladder.
He climbs up.
Father brings Sparky down.

In the story, who is Sparky? ....

In the story, where is Sparky? ....

In the story, what does Kim hold out to Sparky? ....

What did Kim's father use to get to Sparky? ....

At the end of the story, how do you think Kim felt?

....

Parents' Notes

The work covered by the spelling section of this book is similar to that taught to children in first grade. Working through the activities will help your child to develop strong spelling skills, which are vital to his or her understanding of letters, words, and sentences.

Contents

The spelling activities in this book are intended to be completed by a child with adult support. The topics covered are:

- letters, their sounds, and words;
- vowels and consonants;
- long vowel sounds in single-syllable words;
- short vowel sounds in single-syllable words;
- consonant blends;
- syllables;
- common consonant digraphs;
- silent **e** and common vowel teams in words with long vowel sounds;
- inflectional endings, such as **-s**, **-ed**, and **-ing**;
- sight words, including irregularly spelled common words;
- features of a sentence such as capitalization and end punctuation;
- reading grade-level text orally with accuracy, purpose, and understanding to support comprehension.

How to Help Your Child

As you work through the pages with your child, make sure he or she understands what each activity requires. Read the facts and instructions aloud. Encourage questions and reinforce observations that will build confidence and increase active participation in classes at school.

By working with your child, you will understand how he or she thinks and learns. This workbook is designed to help your child understand the concept of letters and words. When appropriate, use props such as pictures or flash cards to help your child visualize letters and words.

If an activity seems too challenging, encourage your child to try another page. Remember to have fun!

Certificate

1st
Grade

Congratulations to

....

for successfully finishing this book.

GOOD JOB!

You're a star.

Date

....

Answer Section

1st Grade JUMBO Workbook

10

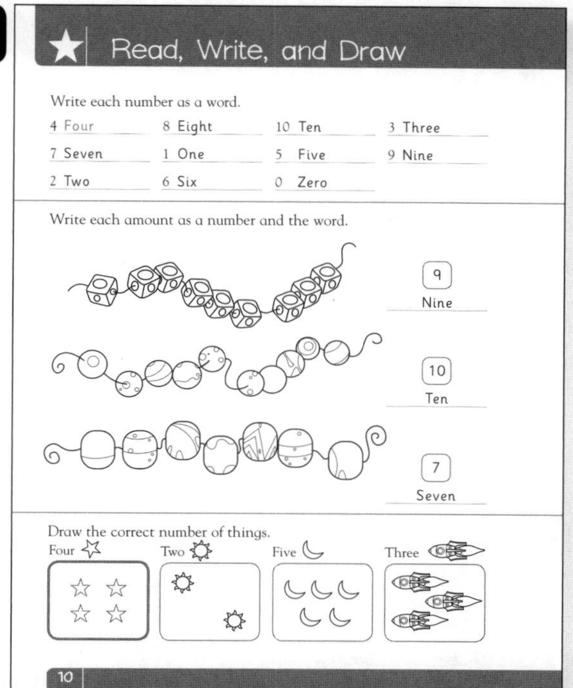

Read, Write, and Draw
Write each number as a word.
4 Four
8 Eight
10 Ten
3 Three
7 Seven
1 One
5 Five
9 Nine
2 Two
6 Six
0 Zero
Write each amount as a number and the word.
9
Nine
10
Ten
7
Seven
Draw the correct number of things.
Four
Two
Five
Three
10

This page provides lots of practice to recognize the number words and being able to correctly write the numbers themselves. It is most important that children see a correspondence between the number of objects and the number that represents that amount.

11

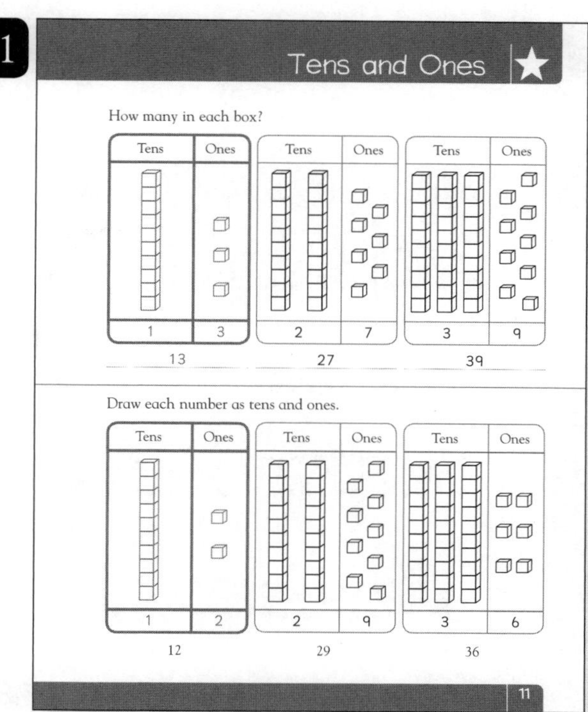

Children will probably use wooden or plastic tens and ones equipment at school and should be familiar with them. Recognizing that a number such as 15 is composed of one "ten" and five "ones" is fundamental.

12

Counting in equal steps helps children reinforce the smaller numbers, and is also an early introduction to times tables.

13

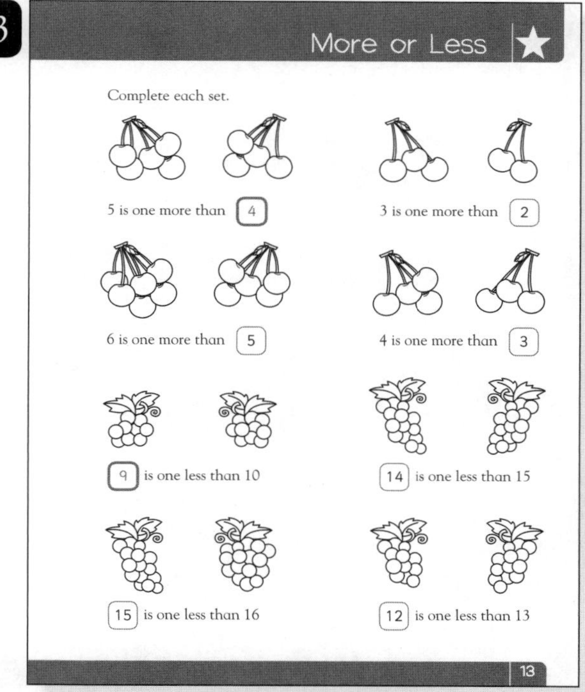

More or Less
Complete each set.
5 is one more than 4
3 is one more than 2
6 is one more than 5
4 is one more than 3
9 is one less than 10
14 is one less than 15
15 is one less than 16
12 is one less than 13
13

At this very early stage it is important for children to learn some of the words that will indicate an operation later on, in this case "more than" representing addition and "less than" representing subtraction.

14

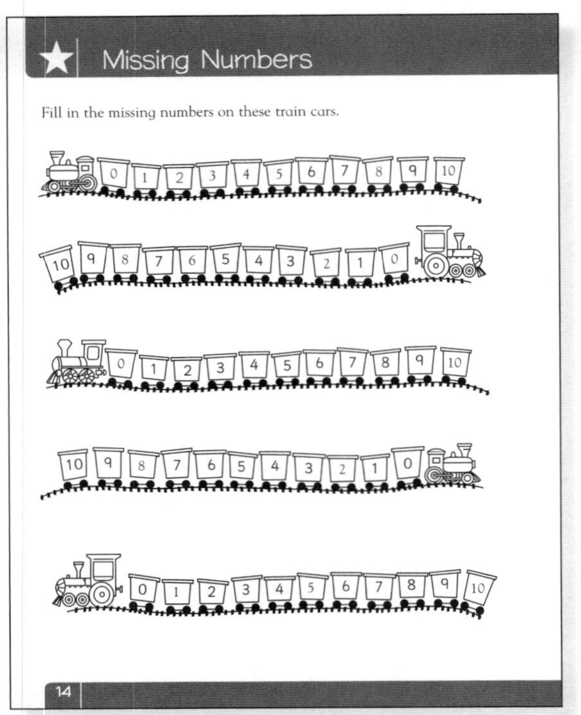

Missing Numbers
Fill in the missing numbers on these train cars.
14

This work helps to reinforce the idea of numbers being in an order and to recognize simple sequences.

15

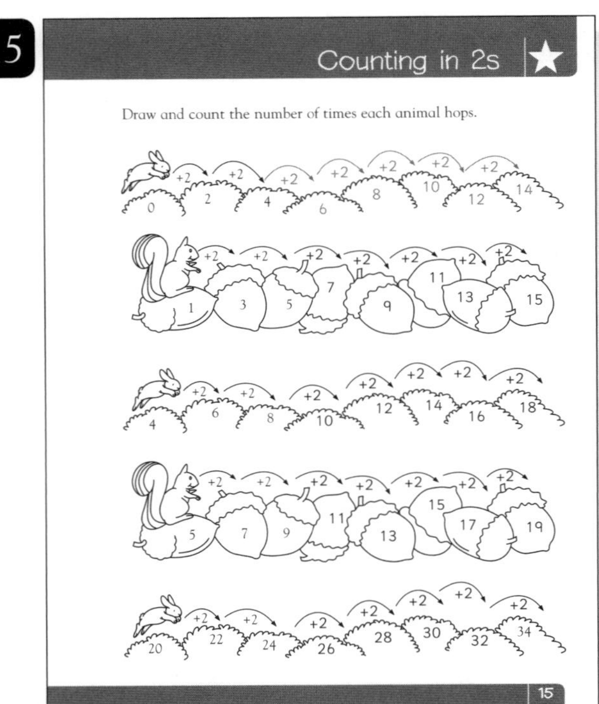

Counting in 2s
Draw and count the number of times each animal hops.
15

This page reinforces number sequences and counting forward and backward.

16

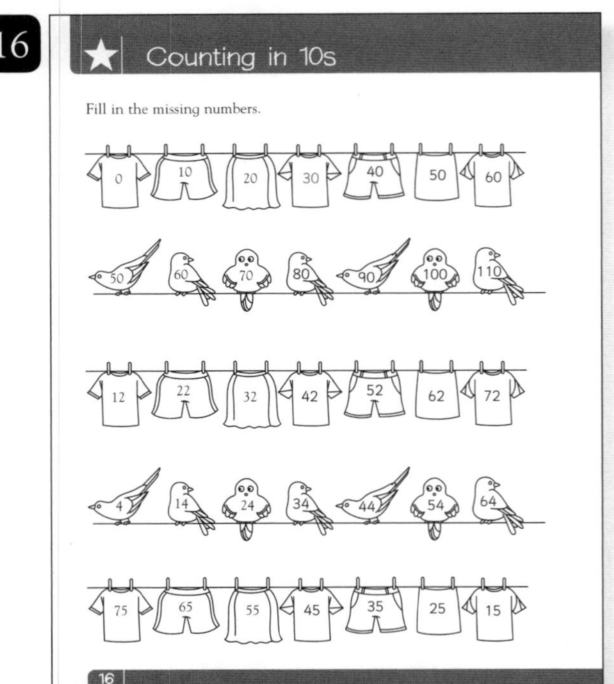

The sequences on this page are a bit more difficult than those before. Children may need some support.

17

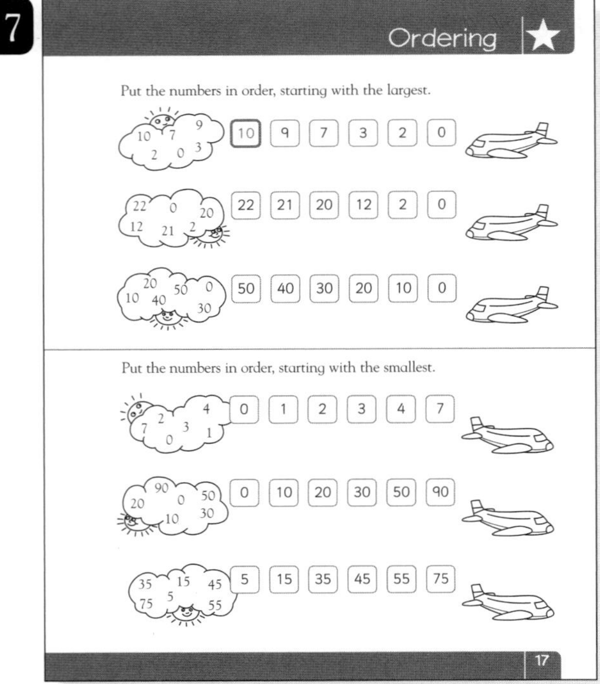

Ordering
Put the numbers in order, starting with the largest.
Put the numbers in order, starting with the smallest.
17

Make sure children notice that sometimes the order is smallest first and sometimes largest first. Reading the question carefully is very important even from this early age!

18

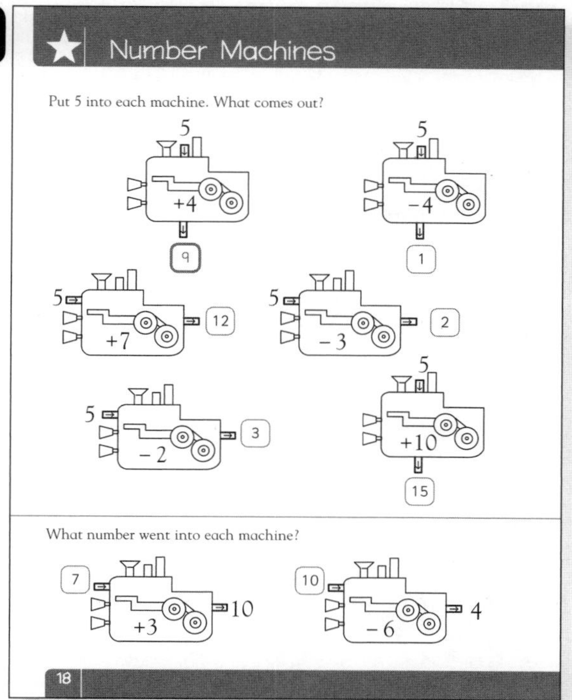

Number Machines

Put 5 into each machine. What comes out?

5 → +4 → 9

5 → −4 → 1

5 → +7 → 12

5 → −3 → 2

5 → −2 → 3

5 → +10 → 15

What number went into each machine?

7 → +3 → 10

10 → −6 → 4

18

These "number machines" are another way to help children understand that problems can be presented in different ways. The use of "+" and "–" signs are intentional and by now children should be aware of them.

19

Patterns

Continue these patterns.

□ ☆ □ ☆ □ ☆ □ ☆ □

△ ○ ○ △ ○ ○ △ ○ ○

□ ▯ □ ▯ □ ▯ □ ▯ □

○ ◇ ○ ◇ ○ ◇ ○ ◇ ○

Continue these number patterns.

2	1	1	2	1	1	2	1	1
3	2	1	3	2	1	3	2	1
4	5	6	4	5	6	4	5	6
6	6	3	6	6	3	6	6	3

19

These questions are not based on simple sequences of numbers but show patterns that children should be able to spot and then continue.

20

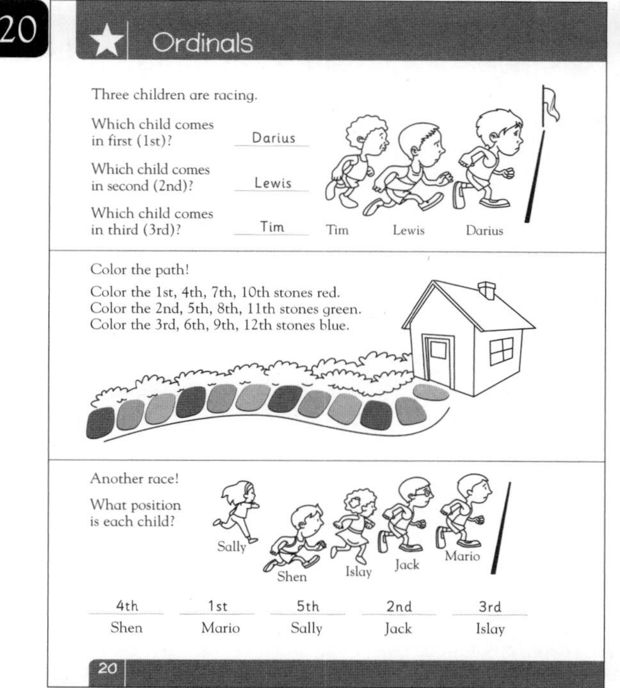

Ordinals

Three children are racing.

Which child comes in first (1st)? Darius

Which child comes in second (2nd)? Lewis

Which child comes in third (3rd)? Tim

Tim Lewis Darius

Color the path!

Color the 1st, 4th, 7th, 10th stones red.
Color the 2nd, 5th, 8th, 11th stones green.
Color the 3rd, 6th, 9th, 12th stones blue.

Another race!

What position is each child?

Sally Shen Islay Jack Mario

4th	1st	5th	2nd	3rd
Shen	Mario	Sally	Jack	Islay

20

The ordinals are a practical way we use numbers in everyday life. Being able to convert from a number in a position to its ordinal is a simple but important skill.

21

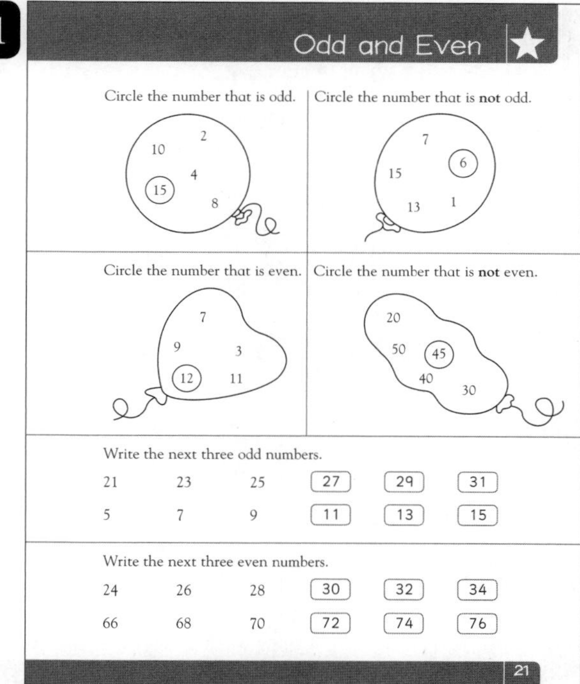

Odd and Even

Circle the number that is odd. (10, 2, 4, 15, 8) — 15

Circle the number that is **not** odd. (7, 6, 15, 13, 1) — 6

Circle the number that is even. (7, 9, 3, 12, 11) — 12

Circle the number that is **not** even. (20, 50, 45, 40, 30) — 45

Write the next three odd numbers.

21	23	25	27	29	31
5	7	9	11	13	15

Write the next three even numbers.

24	26	28	30	32	34
66	68	70	72	74	76

21

The idea of odd and even numbers is usually picked up quickly by children and will be helpful in later work such as division. You may also wish to explain that even numbers can be equally shared by two whereas odd numbers cannot.

22

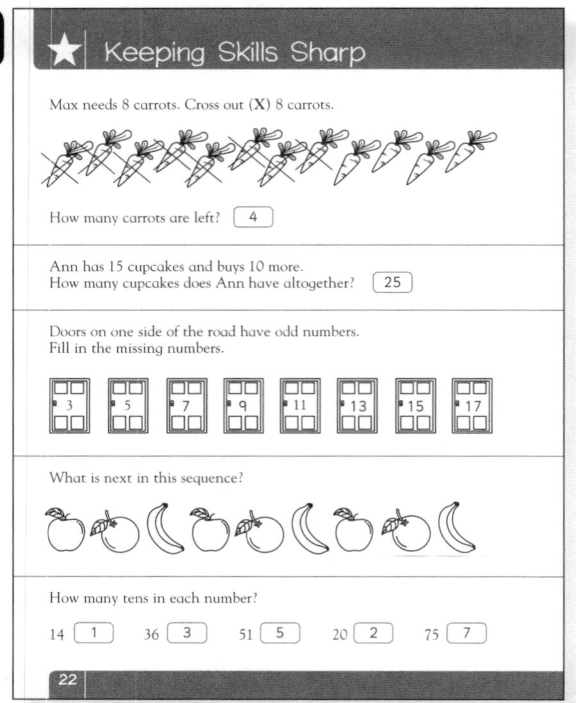

Keeping Skills Sharp
Max needs 8 carrots. Cross out (X) 8 carrots.
How many carrots are left? 4
Ann has 15 cupcakes and buys 10 more.
How many cupcakes does Ann have altogether? 25
Doors on one side of the road have odd numbers.
Fill in the missing numbers.
3 5 7 9 11 13 15 17
What is next in this sequence?
How many tens in each number?
14 1 36 3 51 5 20 2 75 7
22

The test on this page and the following page should be treated as both review and a chance to see how well your child is learning.

23

Keeping Skills Sharp

The race!

Smithy Bonnie Dan Sanji

Who is 1st? Smithy Who is 3rd? Dan

Who is 2nd? Bonnie Who is 4th? Sanji

Write the numbers in order, with the smallest number first.

5 10 1 7 3 6 8 4 2 9

1 2 3 4 5 6 7 8 9 10

Write the amounts in order with the largest first.

2¢ 1¢ 5¢ 10¢ 20¢ 50¢

50¢ 20¢ 10¢ 5¢ 2¢ 1¢

Each group has three chicks.
How many chicks are there in three groups? 9

23

24

Fractions of Shapes

Color half ($\frac{1}{2}$) of each shape.

Now color half ($\frac{1}{2}$) of each shape in a different way.

Color a quarter ($\frac{1}{4}$) of each shape.

Now color a quarter ($\frac{1}{4}$) of each shape in a different way. **Answers may vary**

What fraction of each shape is shaded?

$\frac{1}{2}$ $\frac{1}{4}$ $\frac{1}{4}$

24

This page invites children to think more imaginatively in the way they divide the shapes. Encourage them to look for the diagonal possibilities and not just the horizontal and vertical lines.

25

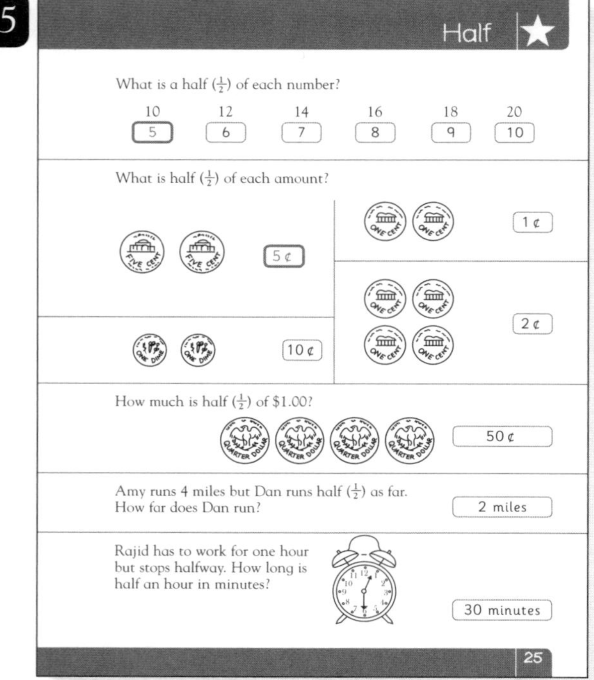

Half
What is a half (1/2) of each number?
10 12 14 16 18 20
5 6 7 8 9 10
What is half (1/2) of each amount?
5¢
1¢
2¢
10¢
How much is half (1/2) of $1.00?
50¢
Amy runs 4 miles but Dan runs half (1/2) as far.
How far does Dan run?
2 miles
Rajid has to work for one hour but stops halfway. How long is half an hour in minutes?
30 minutes
25

This page provides practice of finding halves of numbers and amounts. Using actual coins will help a great deal. The last question relates to time and might be new to your child.

26

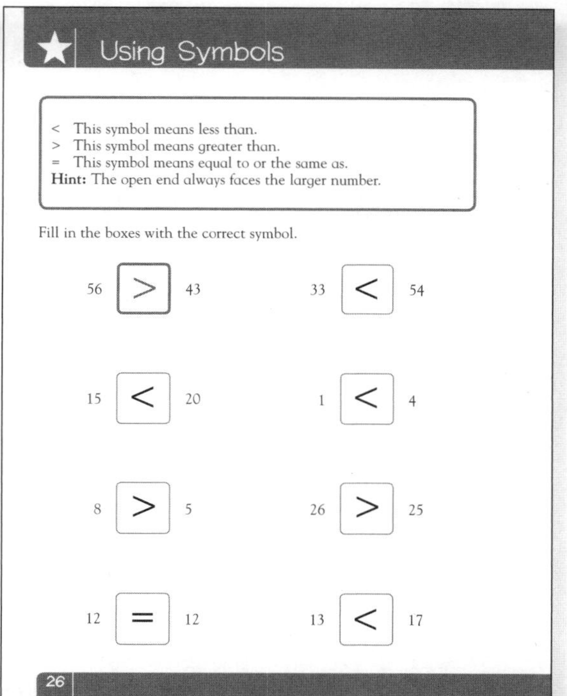

Using Symbols

< This symbol means less than.
> This symbol means greater than.
= This symbol means equal to or the same as.
Hint: The open end always faces the larger number.

Fill in the boxes with the correct symbol.

56	>	43	33	<	54
15	<	20	1	<	4
8	>	5	26	>	25
12	=	12	13	<	17

26

At this early stage, children are being introduced to many math symbols, such as "+," "–," "=," "<," and ">," so plenty of practice in their appropriate use is essential.

27

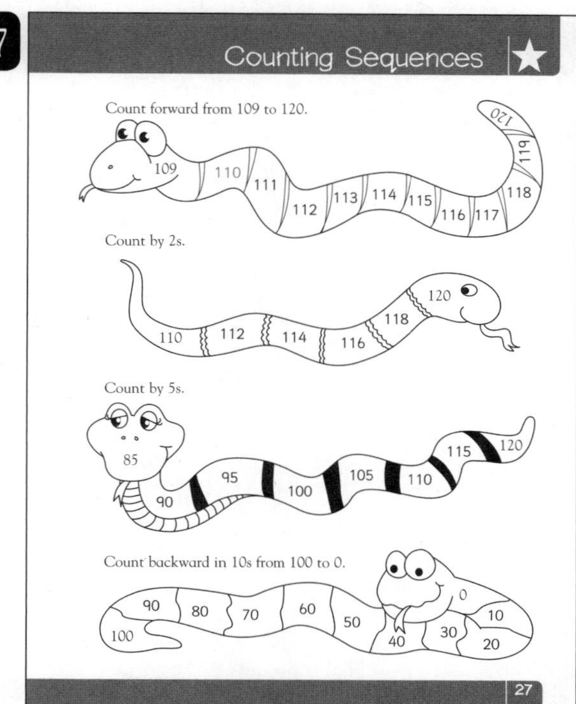

Counting Sequences

Count forward from 109 to 120.

Count by 2s.

Count by 5s.

Count backward in 10s from 100 to 0.

27

Counting forward and backward in 2s, 5s, and 10s are great ways for children to become familiar with the sequence of numbers. Encourage them to enjoy and get plenty of practice counting with numbers just below and above 100.

28

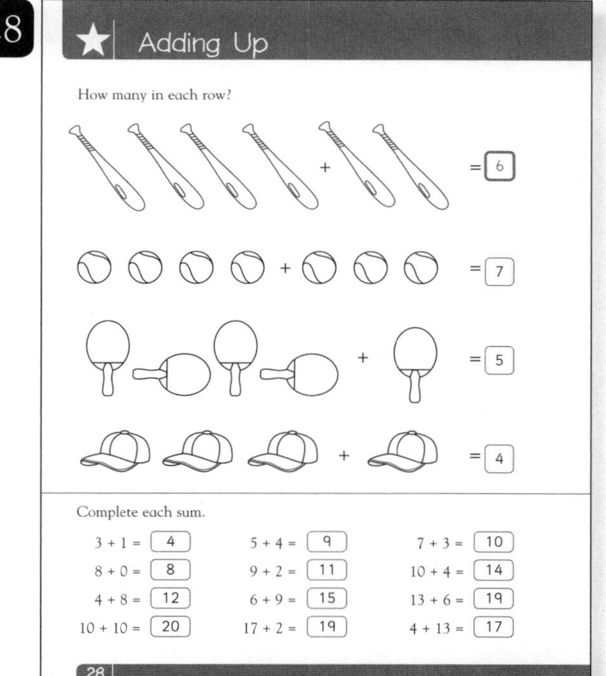

Adding Up

How many in each row?

Complete each sum.

3 + 1 = 4	5 + 4 = 9	7 + 3 = 10
8 + 0 = 8	9 + 2 = 11	10 + 4 = 14
4 + 8 = 12	6 + 9 = 15	13 + 6 = 19
10 + 10 = 20	17 + 2 = 19	4 + 13 = 17

28

Children will have already done addition work at school, but this page helps to show how addition is a process of putting groups together. It is important for children to go through the 9 to 10 barrier to understand place values.

29

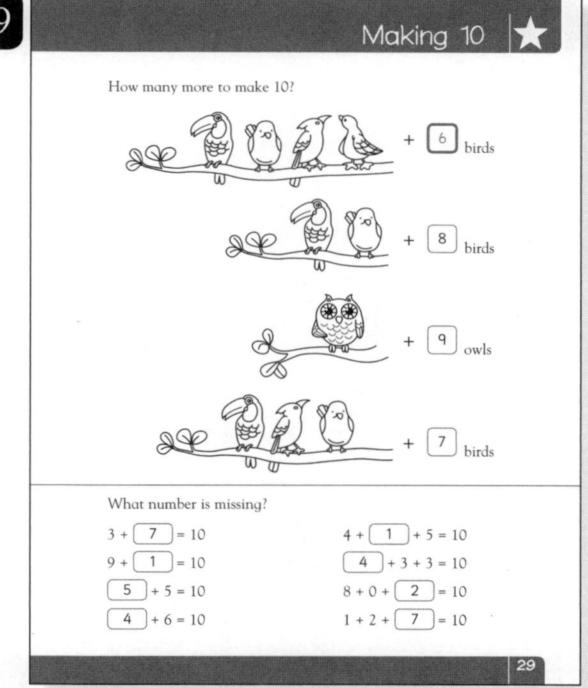

Making 10

How many more to make 10?

What number is missing?

3 + 7 = 10	4 + 1 + 5 = 10
9 + 1 = 10	4 + 3 + 3 = 10
5 + 5 = 10	8 + 0 + 2 = 10
4 + 6 = 10	1 + 2 + 7 = 10

29

Children are encouraged to think about combinations of numbers that add up to 10. The process can be seen as either an addition or subtraction problem making children see the solution by asking "how many more do I need."

30

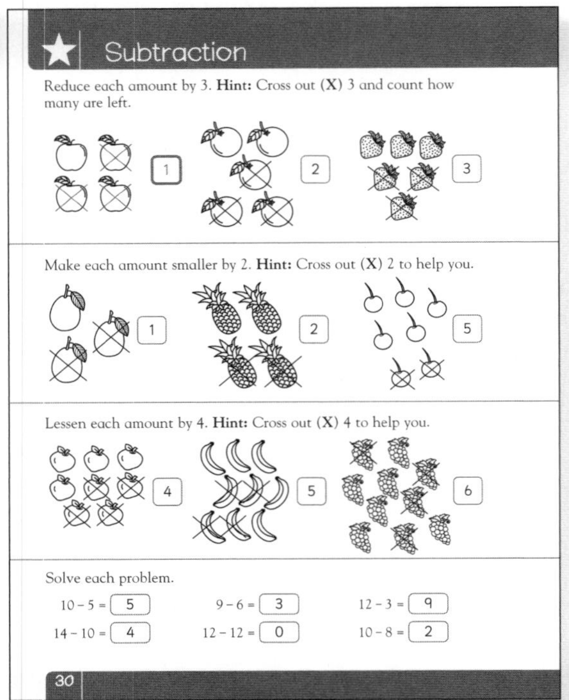

Subtraction

Reduce each amount by 3. **Hint:** Cross out **(X)** 3 and count how many are left.

1 | 2 | 3

Make each amount smaller by 2. **Hint:** Cross out **(X)** 2 to help you.

1 | 2 | 5

Lessen each amount by 4. **Hint:** Cross out **(X)** 4 to help you.

4 | 5 | 6

Solve each problem.

10 – 5 = 5	9 – 6 = 3	12 – 3 = 9
14 – 10 = 4	12 – 12 = 0	10 – 8 = 2

30

These simple subtraction problems use terms such as “reduce” and “lessen.” The formal subtraction problems are laid out horizontally at this early age.

31

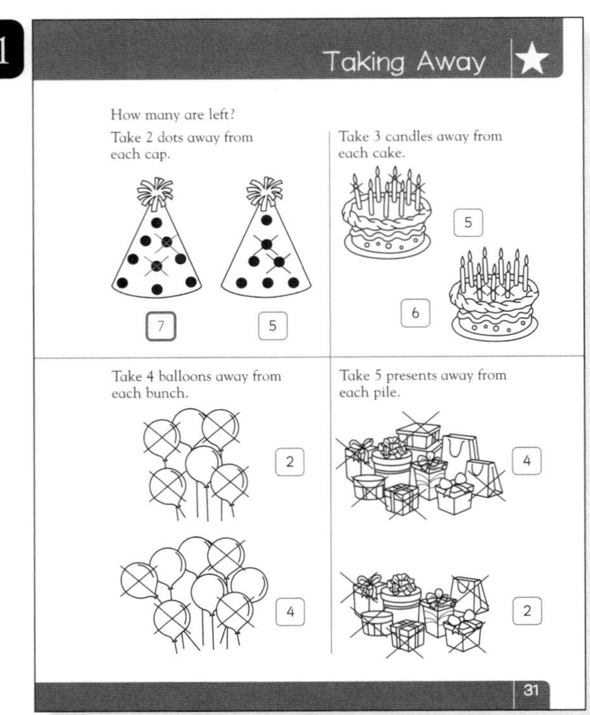

Taking Away

How many are left?

Take 2 dots away from each cap.

7 | 5

Take 3 candles away from each cake.

5 | 6

Take 4 balloons away from each bunch.

2 | 4

Take 5 presents away from each pile.

4 | 2

31

This page combines informal wording and everyday objects. Provide children with solid objects such as beads or buttons to help reinforce the concept of subtraction.

32

Doubles

What is double each number?

2 4	3 6	4 8	5 10
1 2	6 12	7 14	8 16

Double each amount.

5¢ 10¢	2¢ 4¢	10¢ 20¢	20¢ 40¢
1¢ 2¢	4¢ 8¢	6¢ 12¢	11¢ 22¢

What were these numbers before they were doubled?

12 6	10 5	8 4	6 3
10¢ 5¢	20¢ 10¢	12¢ 6¢	14¢ 7¢

Try and double these larger numbers.

30 60	40 80	50 100	100 200
15¢ 30¢	25¢ 50¢	60¢ 120¢	$6.00 $12

32

“Double” and “doubling” are typical mathematical terms that children will encounter over the years. You may also want to point out that doubling a whole number will always produce an even number.

33

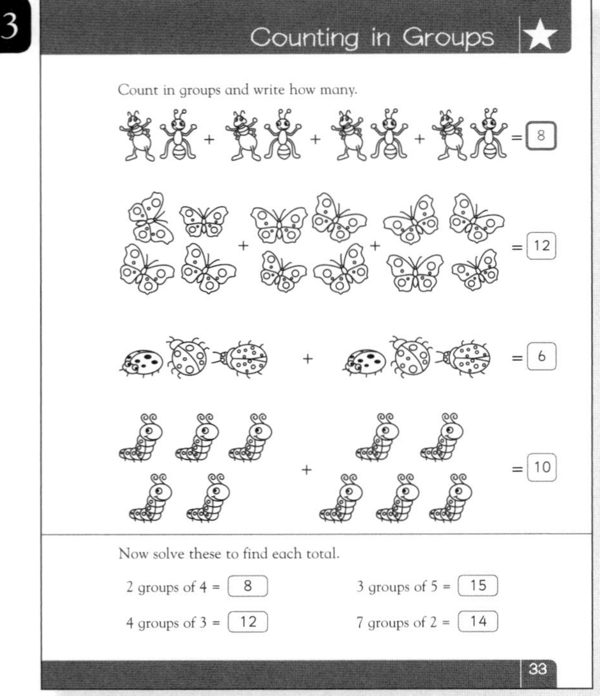

Counting in Groups

Count in groups and write how many.

+ + + = 8

+ + = 12

+ = 6

+ = 10

Now solve these to find each total.

2 groups of 4 = 8	3 groups of 5 = 15
4 groups of 3 = 12	7 groups of 2 = 14

33

The use of “groups of” is a common way to introduce multiplication and times tables although children need to know that these things are the same as repeated addition, just a lot quicker!

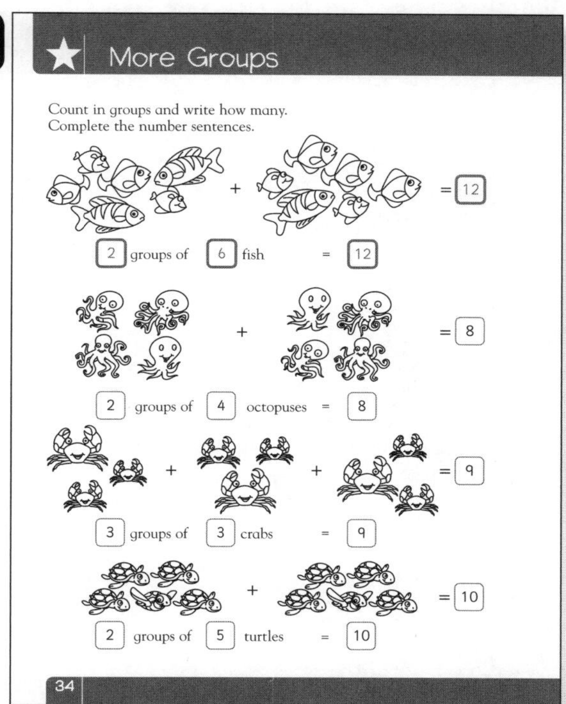

34
More Groups
Count in groups and write how many.
Complete the number sentences.
+ = 12
2 groups of 6 fish = 12
+ = 8
2 groups of 4 octopuses = 8
+ + = 9
3 groups of 3 crabs = 9
+ = 10
2 groups of 5 turtles = 10
34

These exercises reinforce more "groups of" using larger numbers.

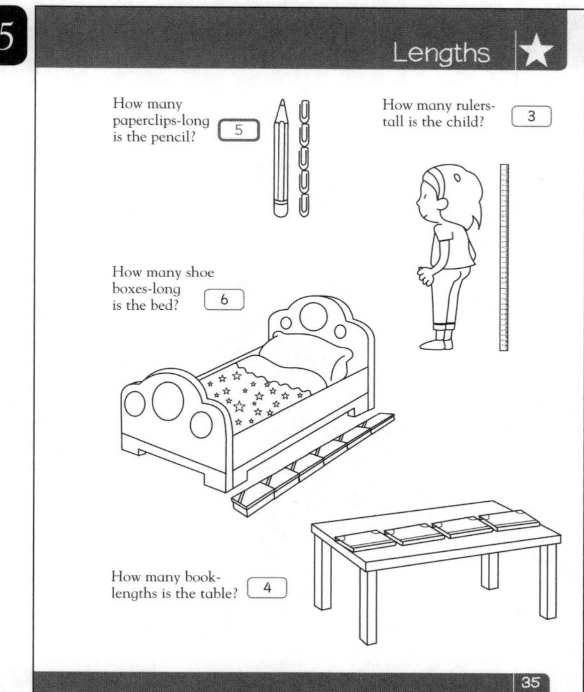

35
Lengths
How many paperclips-long is the pencil? 5
How many rulers-tall is the child? 3
How many shoe boxes-long is the bed? 6
How many book-lengths is the table? 4
35

The first stage of measuring length is to use familiar objects to compare and estimate the length of other objects. This shows the importance of a standard unit of measure, so that comparisons can be made accurately.

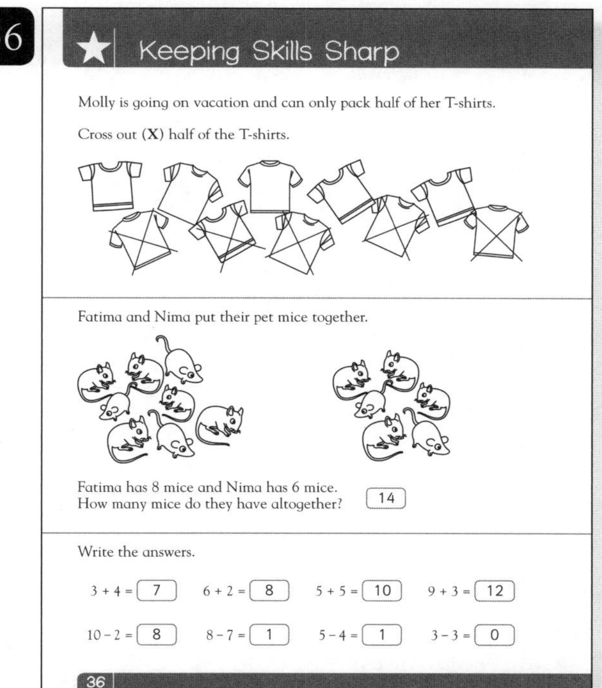

36
Keeping Skills Sharp
Molly is going on vacation and can only pack half of her T-shirts.
Cross out (X) half of the T-shirts.
Fatima and Nima put their pet mice together.
Fatima has 8 mice and Nima has 6 mice.
How many mice do they have altogether? 14
Write the answers.
3 + 4 = 7
6 + 2 = 8
5 + 5 = 10
9 + 3 = 12
10 – 2 = 8
8 – 7 = 1
5 – 4 = 1
3 – 3 = 0
36

As with the previous test, this one reviews some of the topics already covered. Sometimes your child has to work out what is the best operation to use to solve the problem.

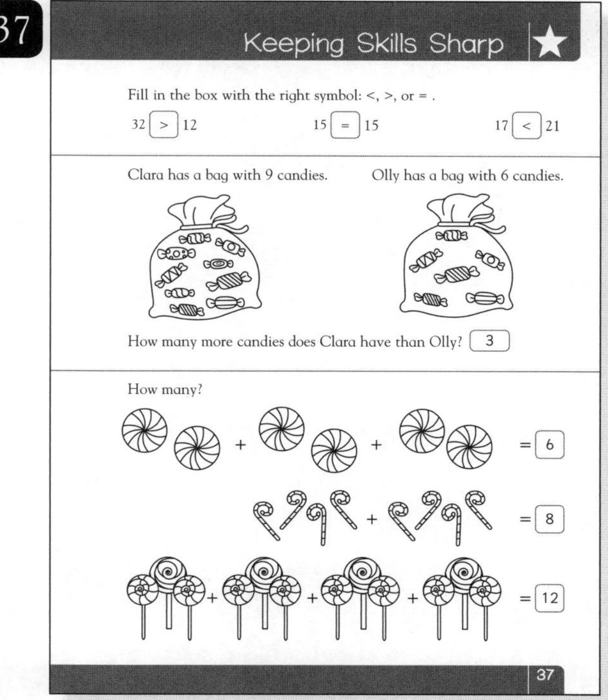

37
Keeping Skills Sharp
Fill in the box with the right symbol: <, >, or = .
32 > 12
15 = 15
17 < 21
Clara has a bag with 9 candies.
Olly has a bag with 6 candies.
How many more candies does Clara have than Olly? 3
How many?
+ + = 6
+ = 8
+ + + = 12
37

38

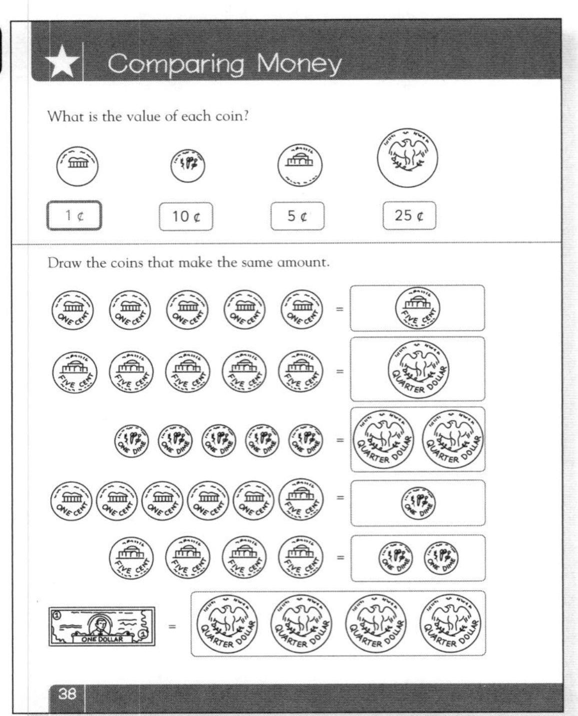

Comparing Money
What is the value of each coin?
1 ¢
10 ¢
5 ¢
25 ¢
Draw the coins that make the same amount.
ONE DOLLAR
38

This work quickly progresses from helping children recognize the coins to working out what combinations make other amounts. For example, five pennies are equivalent to one nickel. The more practical help the better.

39

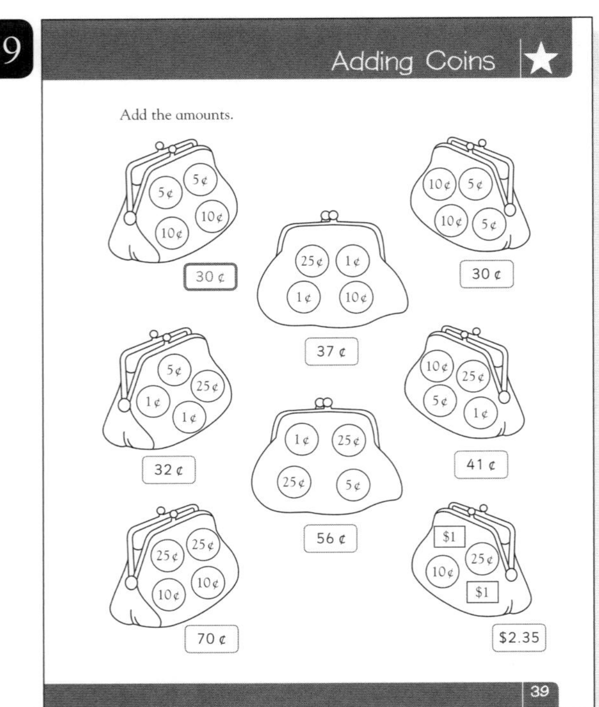

This activity involves simple addition using coins. The exercise uses a mix of smaller and larger coins.

40

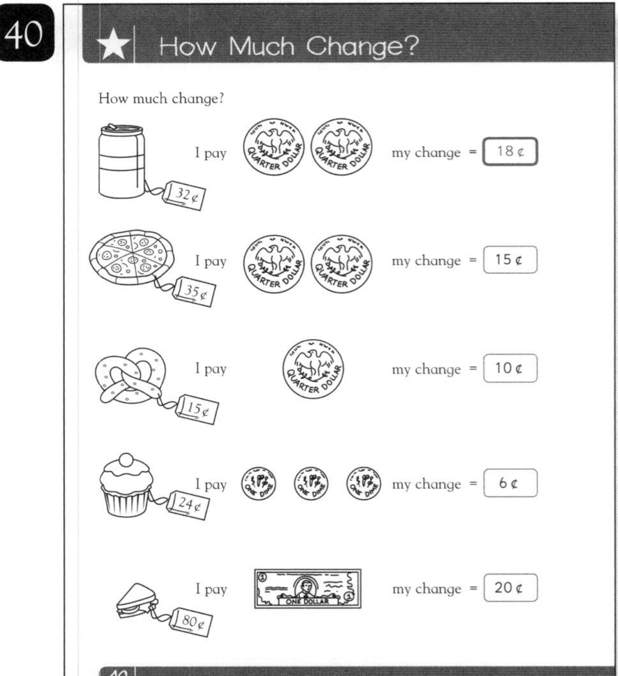

Figuring out what change is needed is a useful skill for children to learn. Giving them some pocket money and then going to the store to spend some of it would be a helpful way to reinforce the concept.

41

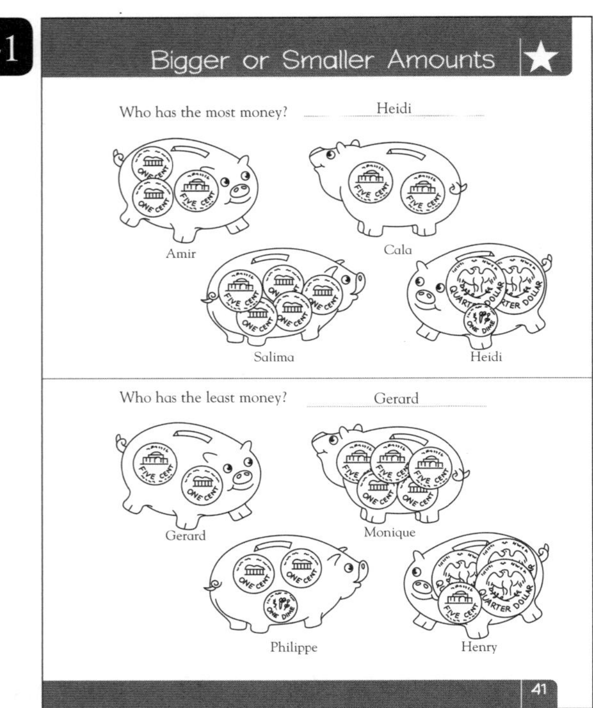

This page requires children to figure out simple amounts, and then make comparisons. Make sure your child reads the questions carefully.

42

Comparing Sizes
Circle the largest animal in each group.
Circle the smallest animal in each group.
Circle the animal that is the tallest.
Circle the caterpillar that is the longest.
42

To an adult, these problems and words can seem very simplistic but it is surprising how often children become confused. To be sure they really are getting the hang of it, throw them a few extra "homemade" questions as and when appropriate.

43

These exercises give children a clear understanding of how to put things in order, from the earliest to the last stage.

44

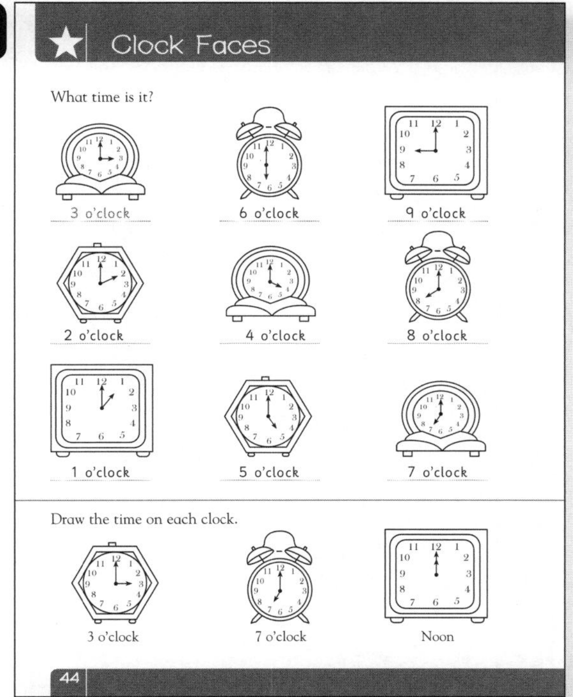

Children should be able to read the whole hours fairly well by now and draw them on blank clock faces. Many children are more used to digital displays and not so confident with analog faces.

45

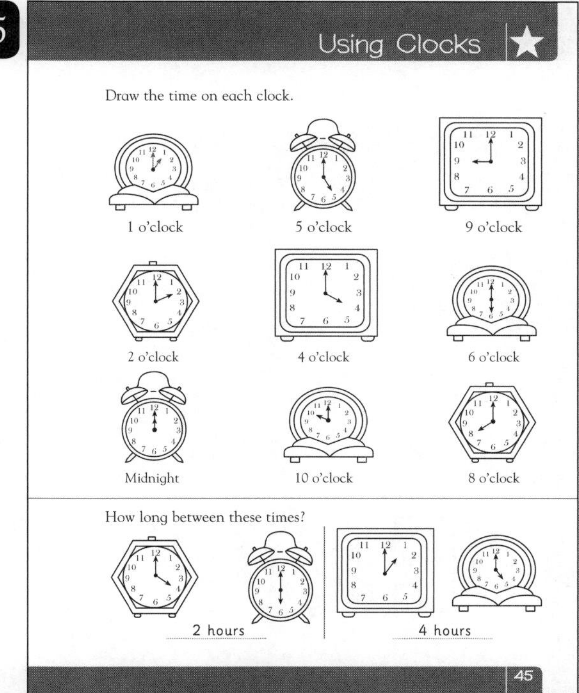

This page provides more practice with whole hours. Note that the final two questions are a little more difficult.

46

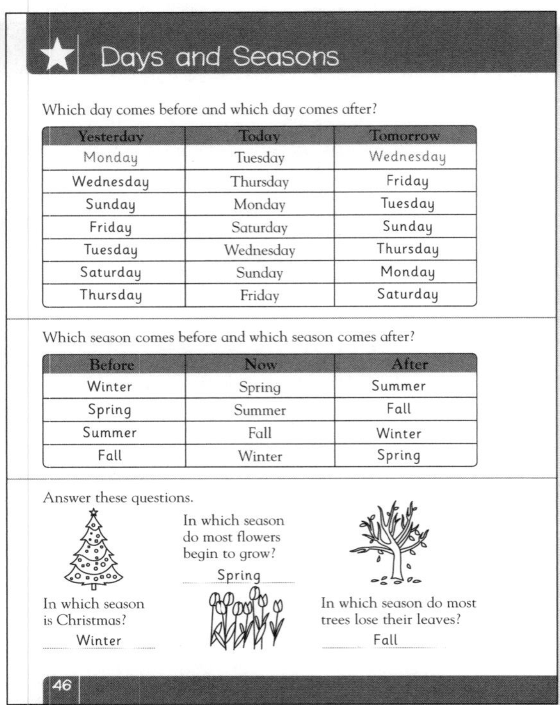

Days and Seasons

Which day comes before and which day comes after?

Yesterday	Today	Tomorrow
Monday	Tuesday	Wednesday
Wednesday	Thursday	Friday
Sunday	Monday	Tuesday
Friday	Saturday	Sunday
Tuesday	Wednesday	Thursday
Saturday	Sunday	Monday
Thursday	Friday	Saturday

Which season comes before and which season comes after?

Before	Now	After
Winter	Spring	Summer
Spring	Summer	Fall
Summer	Fall	Winter
Fall	Winter	Spring

Answer these questions.

In which season is Christmas? Winter

In which season do most flowers begin to grow? Spring

In which season do most trees lose their leaves? Fall

46

Young children need constant practice with days and seasons.

47

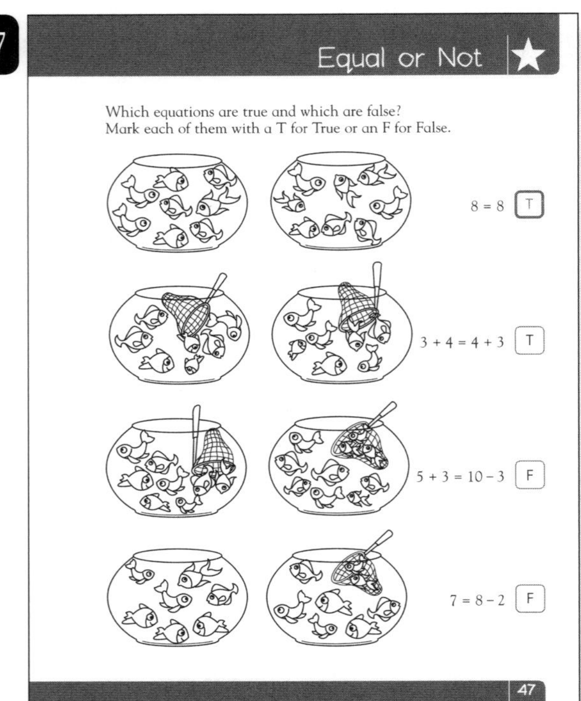

Equal or Not

Which equations are true and which are false?
Mark each of them with a T for True or an F for False.

8 = 8 T

3 + 4 = 4 + 3 T

5 + 3 = 10 − 3 F

7 = 8 − 2 F

47

This page reinforces the meaning of the equal sign, and will help children understand that each side of an equation must have the same value.

48

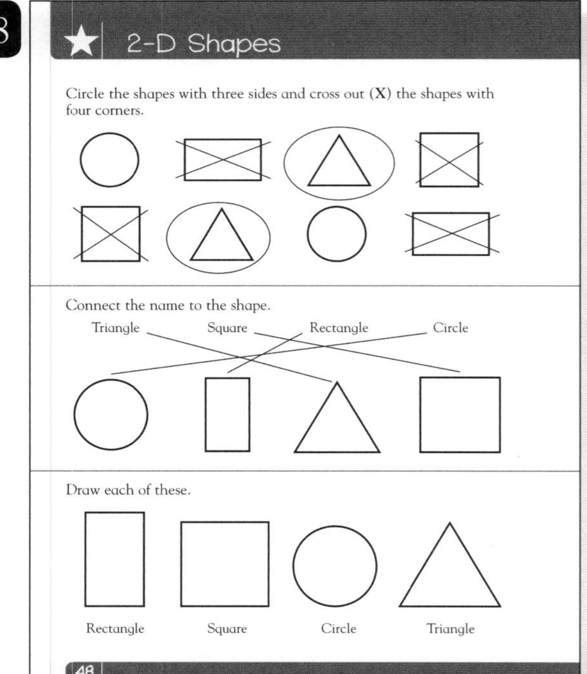

2-D Shapes

Circle the shapes with three sides and cross out (**X**) the shapes with four corners.

Connect the name to the shape.

Draw each of these.

48

Children will probably know the names of most simple shapes but may not be aware of attributes such as "side," "surface," or "corner."

49

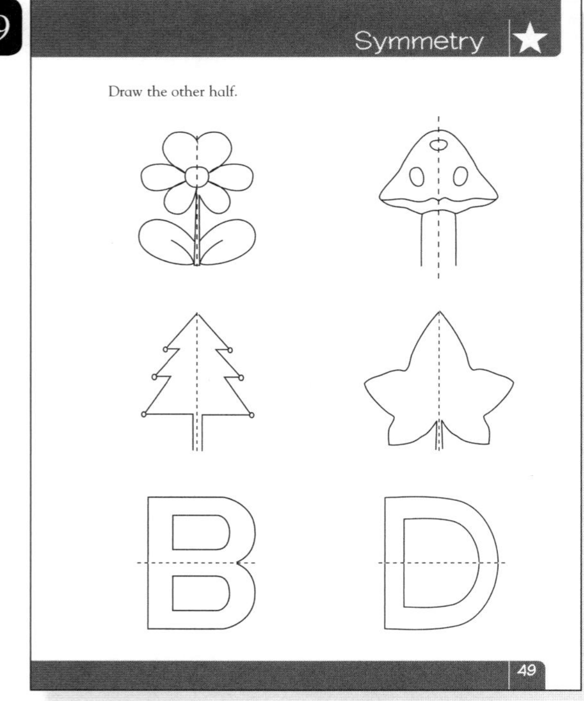

Symmetry

Draw the other half.

49

Symmetry is usually enjoyable and easily picked up by children. A small mirror can be very helpful and a line of symmetry is often referred to as a mirror line.

50

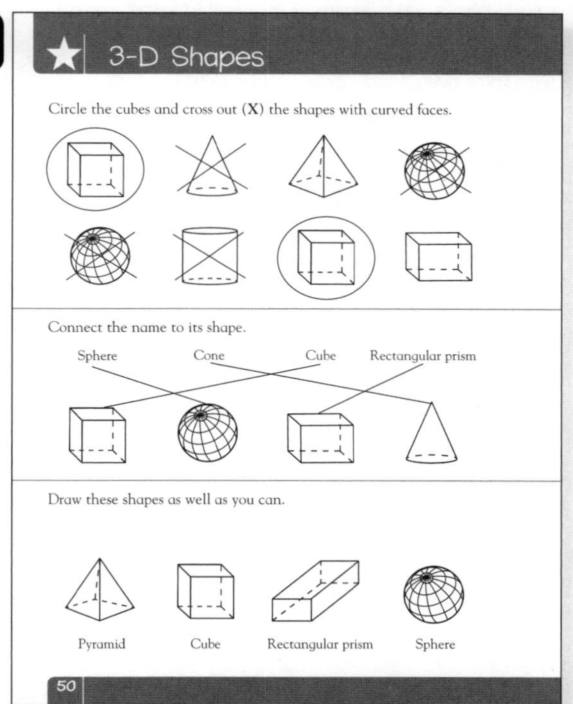

★ 3-D Shapes

Circle the cubes and cross out (**X**) the shapes with curved faces.

Connect the name to its shape.

Sphere Cone Cube Rectangular prism

Draw these shapes as well as you can.

Pyramid Cube Rectangular prism Sphere

50

While children pick up names of 2-D shapes fairly readily through everyday experiences, the 3-D names are less well known. "Spheres," "cubes," "rectangular prisms," "cylinders," and "cones" may need to be explained with actual examples from around the house.

51

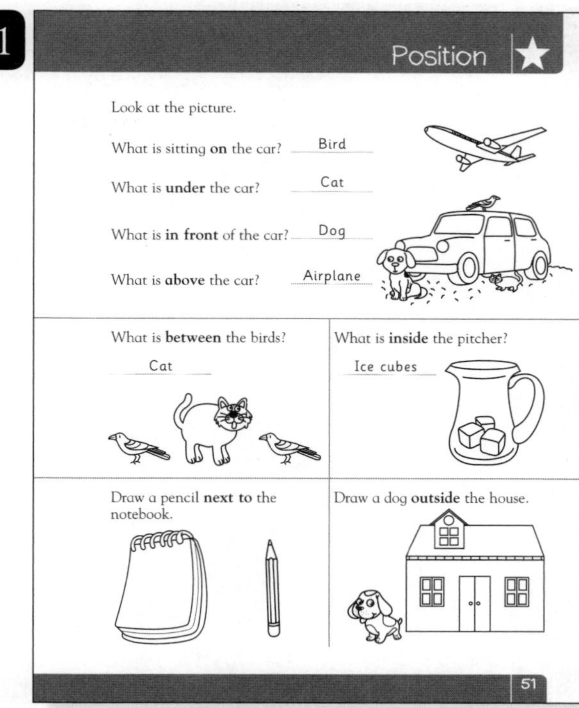

Position ★

Look at the picture.

What is sitting **on** the car? Bird

What is **under** the car? Cat

What is **in front** of the car? Dog

What is **above** the car? Airplane

What is **between** the birds? Cat

What is **inside** the pitcher? Ice cubes

Draw a pencil **next to** the notebook.

Draw a dog **outside** the house.

51

This page provides more examples of common words of comparison that children will need to practice and learn.

52

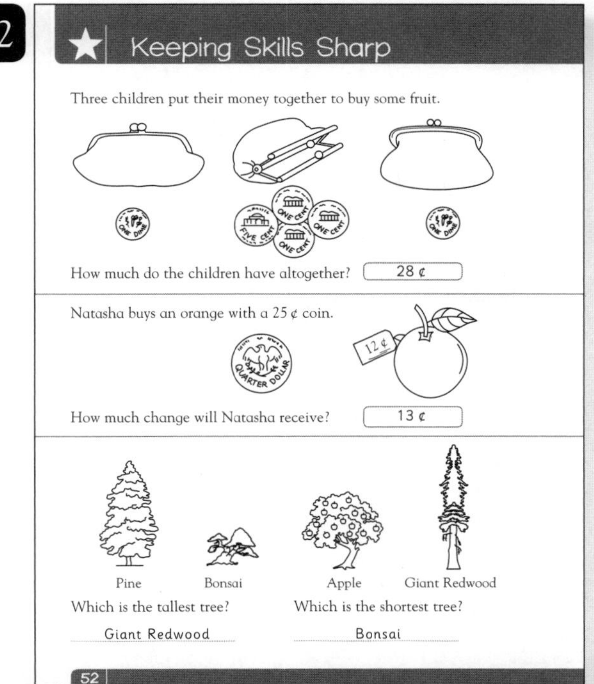

★ Keeping Skills Sharp

Three children put their money together to buy some fruit.

How much do the children have altogether? 28 ¢

Natasha buys an orange with a 25 ¢ coin.

How much change will Natasha receive? 13 ¢

Pine Bonsai Apple Giant Redwood

Which is the tallest tree? Giant Redwood

Which is the shortest tree? Bonsai

52

These two revision pages provide a good indication of the success children have had with the math activities completed so far.

53

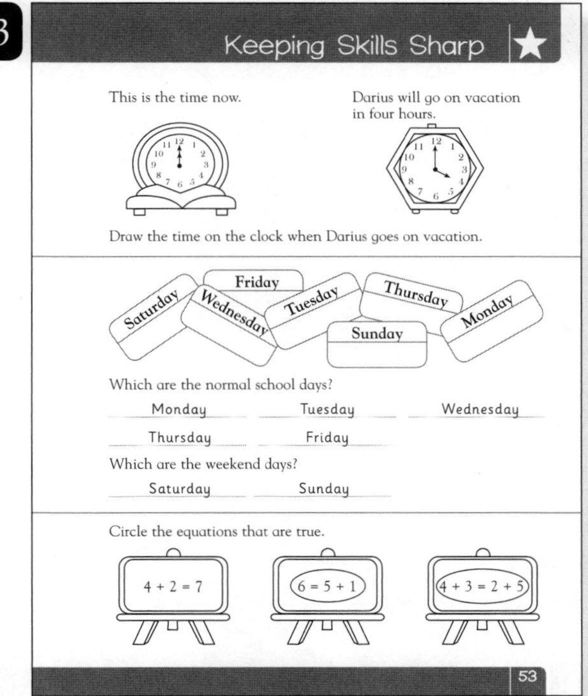

Keeping Skills Sharp ★

This is the time now.

Darius will go on vacation in four hours.

Draw the time on the clock when Darius goes on vacation.

Friday Saturday Wednesday Tuesday Thursday Sunday Monday

Which are the normal school days?

Monday Tuesday Wednesday Thursday Friday

Which are the weekend days?

Saturday Sunday

Circle the equations that are true.

4 + 2 = 7 6 = 5 + 1 4 + 3 = 2 + 5

53

54

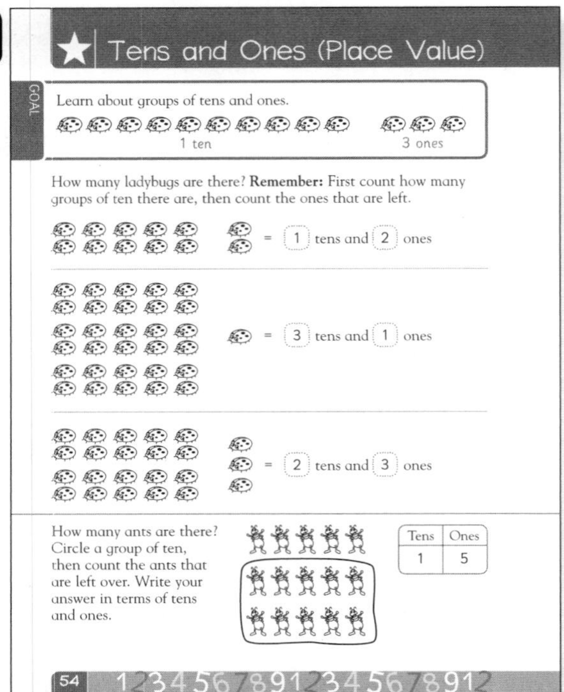

Tens and Ones (Place Value)

GOAL

Learn about groups of tens and ones.

1 ten 3 ones

How many ladybugs are there? **Remember:** First count how many groups of ten there are, then count the ones that are left.

= 1 tens and 2 ones

= 3 tens and 1 ones

= 2 tens and 3 ones

How many ants are there? Circle a group of ten, then count the ants that are left over. Write your answer in terms of tens and ones.

Tens	Ones
1	5

54 123456789123456789l2

Be sure children count groups of ten carefully. If they miscount a group of ten, they will reach an incorrect answer. You may want to have children practice counting tens and ones using groups of buttons.

55

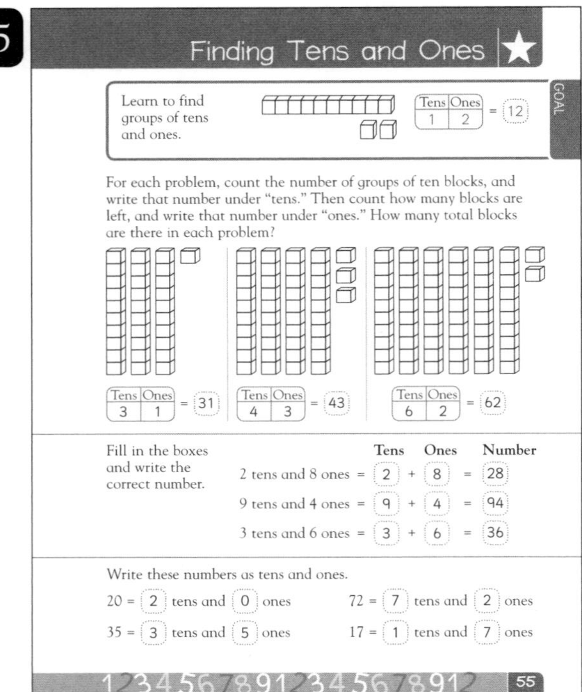

Finding Tens and Ones

GOAL

Learn to find groups of tens and ones.

Tens 1 Ones 2 = 12

For each problem, count the number of groups of ten blocks, and write that number under "tens." Then count how many blocks are left, and write that number under "ones." How many total blocks are there in each problem?

Tens 3 Ones 1 = 31

Tens 4 Ones 3 = 43

Tens 6 Ones 2 = 62

Fill in the boxes and write the correct number.

	Tens		Ones		Number
2 tens and 8 ones =	2	+	8	=	28
9 tens and 4 ones =	9	+	4	=	94
3 tens and 6 ones =	3	+	6	=	36

Write these numbers as tens and ones.

20 = 2 tens and 0 ones 72 = 7 tens and 2 ones

35 = 3 tens and 5 ones 17 = 1 tens and 7 ones

123456789123456789l2 55

Be sure children understand that in two-digit numbers, the second digit stands for the number of units in the ones column, and the first digit stands for the number of units in the tens column.

56

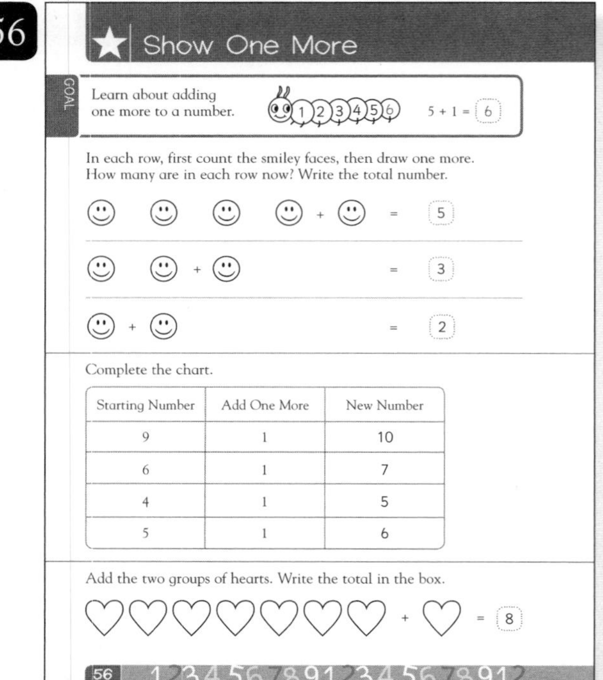

Show One More

GOAL

Learn about adding one more to a number.

5 + 1 = 6

In each row, first count the smiley faces, then draw one more. How many are in each row now? Write the total number.

+ = 5

+ = 3

+ = 2

Complete the chart.

Starting Number	Add One More	New Number
9	1	10
6	1	7
4	1	5
5	1	6

Add the two groups of hearts. Write the total in the box.

+ = 8

56 123456789123456789l2

Use groups of clothespins to show a number. Ask children to count them aloud. Then add one more clothespin to the group of clothespins, and have children count aloud again. Clarify that the new total number of clothespins is larger because you added one more.

57

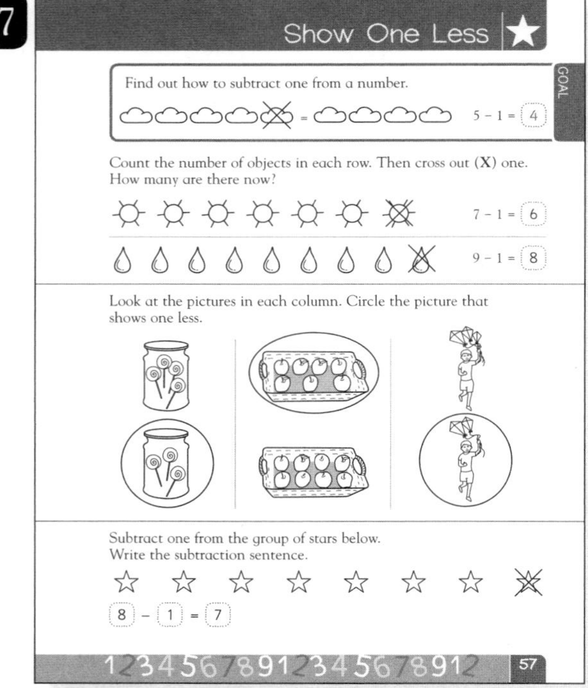

Show One Less

GOAL

Find out how to subtract one from a number.

= 5 − 1 = 4

Count the number of objects in each row. Then cross out (**X**) one. How many are there now?

7 − 1 = 6

9 − 1 = 8

Look at the pictures in each column. Circle the picture that shows one less.

Subtract one from the group of stars below. Write the subtraction sentence.

8 − 1 = 7

123456789123456789l2 57

Show children a group of small toys. Let children count them. Then take one toy away, and ask them to count the toys again. Help them figure out and recite the subtraction sentence, such as, "five minus one equals four."

58

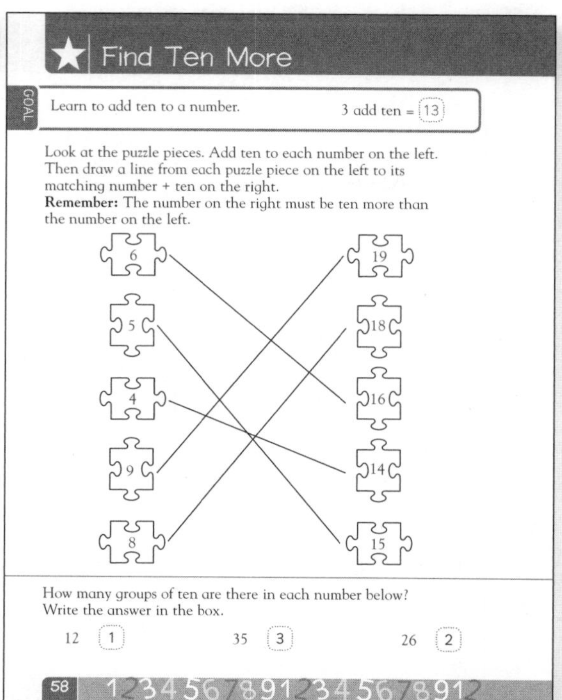

Find Ten More

GOAL: Learn to add ten to a number. 3 add ten = 13

Look at the puzzle pieces. Add ten to each number on the left. Then draw a line from each puzzle piece on the left to its matching number + ten on the right.
Remember: The number on the right must be ten more than the number on the left.

6, 5, 4, 9, 8 — 19, 18, 16, 14, 15

How many groups of ten are there in each number below? Write the answer in the box.

12 [1] 35 [3] 26 [2]

58

Help children understand that ten more have been added to the number in the first column to come up with its match in the second column. You can demonstrate the concept by using blocks.

59

Find Ten Less

GOAL: Learn to subtract ten from a number. 15 subtract ten = 5

Subtract ten from each number in the left column. Then write the subtraction sentence and the answer in the right column.

32 subtract ten	32 – 10 = 22
28 subtract ten	28 – 10 = 18
25 subtract ten	25 – 10 = 15
56 subtract ten	56 – 10 = 46
21 subtract ten	21 – 10 = 11
36 subtract ten	36 – 10 = 26
44 subtract ten	44 – 10 = 34
18 subtract ten	18 – 10 = 8
68 subtract ten	68 – 10 = 58
95 subtract ten	95 – 10 = 85

Finish the pattern. Write the number that is ten less each time.

50 40 [30] [20] 10 [0]

59

Use a set of dominoes to help children understand subtraction: have them count the dots on a domino, then cover up one or more dots and ask them to count again. Help children write the corresponding subtraction sentence each time.

60

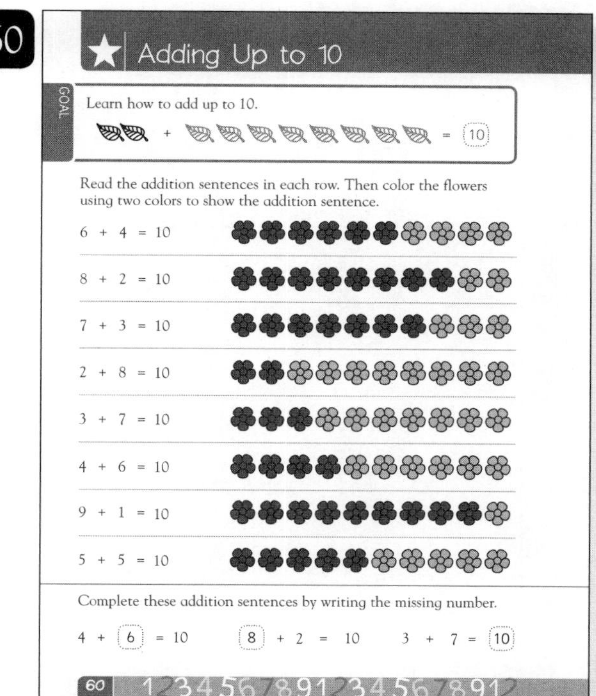

Adding Up to 10

GOAL: Learn how to add up to 10. 2 + 8 = 10

Read the addition sentences in each row. Then color the flowers using two colors to show the addition sentence.

6 + 4 = 10
8 + 2 = 10
7 + 3 = 10
2 + 8 = 10
3 + 7 = 10
4 + 6 = 10
9 + 1 = 10
5 + 5 = 10

Complete these addition sentences by writing the missing number.

4 + [6] = 10 [8] + 2 = 10 3 + 7 = [10]

60

Have children first say the number sentence, then count out the corresponding groups of flowers to color. Create more number and coloring sentences for children to complete using other objects, like stars, suns, or balls.

61

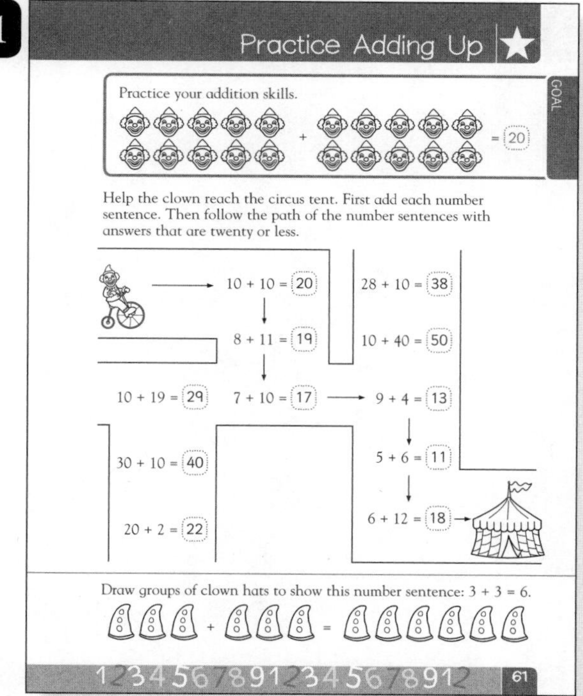

Practice Adding Up

GOAL: Practice your addition skills. 10 + 10 = 20

Help the clown reach the circus tent. First add each number sentence. Then follow the path of the number sentences with answers that are twenty or less.

10 + 10 = 20
28 + 10 = 38
8 + 11 = 19
10 + 40 = 50
10 + 19 = 29
7 + 10 = 17
9 + 4 = 13
30 + 10 = 40
5 + 6 = 11
20 + 2 = 22
6 + 12 = 18

Draw groups of clown hats to show this number sentence: 3 + 3 = 6.

61

You may want to ask children to rewrite each number sentence on another piece of paper, to practice and reinforce adding up to twenty.

62

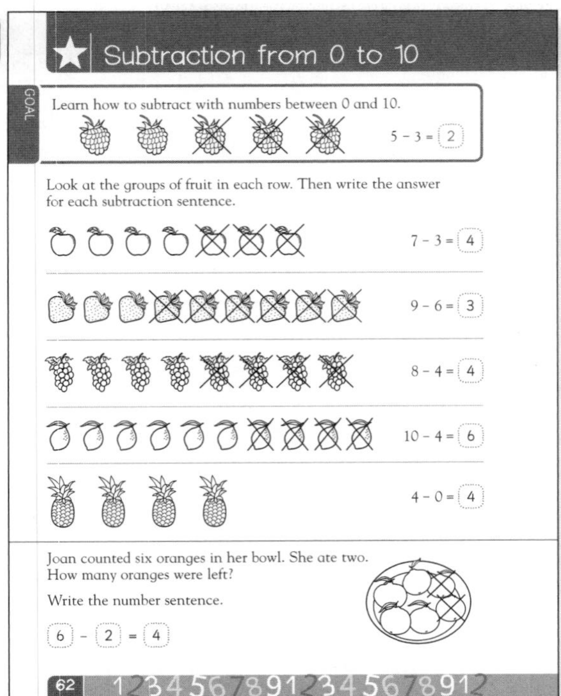

Subtraction from 0 to 10

GOAL

Learn how to subtract with numbers between 0 and 10.

5 − 3 = 2

Look at the groups of fruit in each row. Then write the answer for each subtraction sentence.

7 − 3 = 4

9 − 6 = 3

8 − 4 = 4

10 − 4 = 6

4 − 0 = 4

Joan counted six oranges in her bowl. She ate two. How many oranges were left?

Write the number sentence.

6 − 2 = 4

62 12345678912345678912

Place ten or fewer marbles in a jar. Have children count them. Then ask them to close their eyes as you remove a number of the marbles. Let them recount the marbles and write the corresponding subtraction sentence.

63

Practice Subtraction

GOAL

Practice your subtraction skills.

16 − 6 = 10

Subtract and write the answers in each row.

15 − 4 = 11	29 − 6 = 23	18 − 5 = 13	16 − 4 = 12	12 − 2 = 10	19 − 3 = 16
10 − 7 = 3	9 − 5 = 4	39 − 4 = 35	20 − 10 = 10	16 − 8 = 8	56 − 6 = 50
14 − 7 = 7	9 − 6 = 3	60 − 30 = 30	89 − 9 = 80	18 − 15 = 3	58 − 8 = 50

Read each story. Then write the answer for each subtraction problem.

Juan had thirteen crayons. He broke two crayons. How many of his crayons were not broken? 13 − 2 = 11

We saw twenty-five bunnies. Four bunnies ran away. How many bunnies were left? 25 − 4 = 21

Jen made nineteen cupcakes. She gave away six cupcakes. How many cupcakes were left? 19 − 6 = 13

12345678912345678912 63

Write subtraction problems up to twenty on index cards. Write an answer for each problem on another index card. Place all cards on a table faceup. Let children match a problem card with the correct answer card.

64

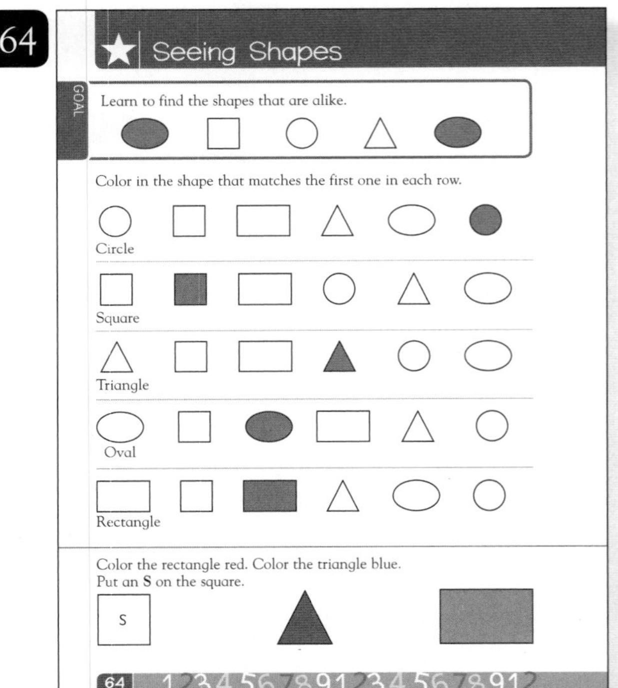

Seeing Shapes

GOAL

Learn to find the shapes that are alike.

Color in the shape that matches the first one in each row.

Circle

Square

Triangle

Oval

Rectangle

Color the rectangle red. Color the triangle blue. Put an S on the square.

S

64 12345678912345678912

Go on a "Looking for Shapes" hunt around your home or neighborhood. Encourage children to find objects or lines that represent known shapes (circles, triangles, rectangles, ovals, and squares) and to call them by the correct shape name.

65

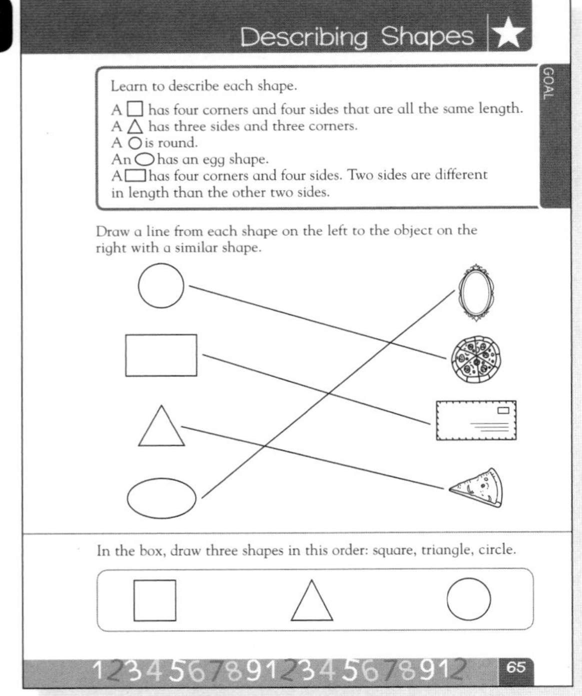

Describing Shapes

GOAL

Learn to describe each shape.

A □ has four corners and four sides that are all the same length.
A △ has three sides and three corners.
A ○ is round.
An ⬭ has an egg shape.
A ▭ has four corners and four sides. Two sides are different in length than the other two sides.

Draw a line from each shape on the left to the object on the right with a similar shape.

In the box, draw three shapes in this order: square, triangle, circle.

12345678912345678912 65

Encourage children to use the shapes they have worked with on this page to create pictures. Invite them to draw neighborhoods, playgrounds, shopping areas, and so on.

66

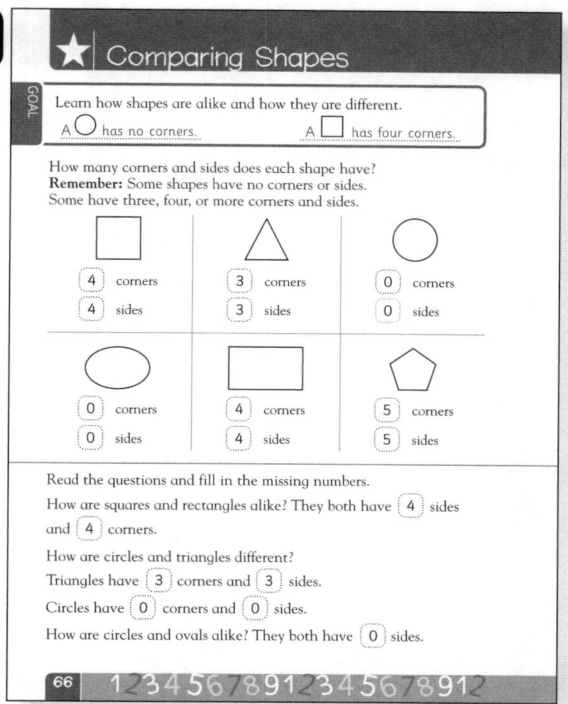
Comparing Shapes

GOAL

Learn how shapes are alike and how they are different.

A ○ has no corners. A □ has four corners.

How many corners and sides does each shape have?
Remember: Some shapes have no corners or sides.
Some have three, four, or more corners and sides.

Shape	Corners	Sides
Square	4	4
Triangle	3	3
Circle	0	0
Oval	0	0
Rectangle	4	4
Pentagon	5	5

Read the questions and fill in the missing numbers.

How are squares and rectangles alike? They both have 4 sides and 4 corners.

How are circles and triangles different?

Triangles have 3 corners and 3 sides.

Circles have 0 corners and 0 sides.

How are circles and ovals alike? They both have 0 sides.

Let children create flat shapes from modeling clay. Ask them to make at least three of each shape on the page, each one a different size. Then have children order the three clay versions of each shape by size, either from largest to smallest or from smallest to largest.

67

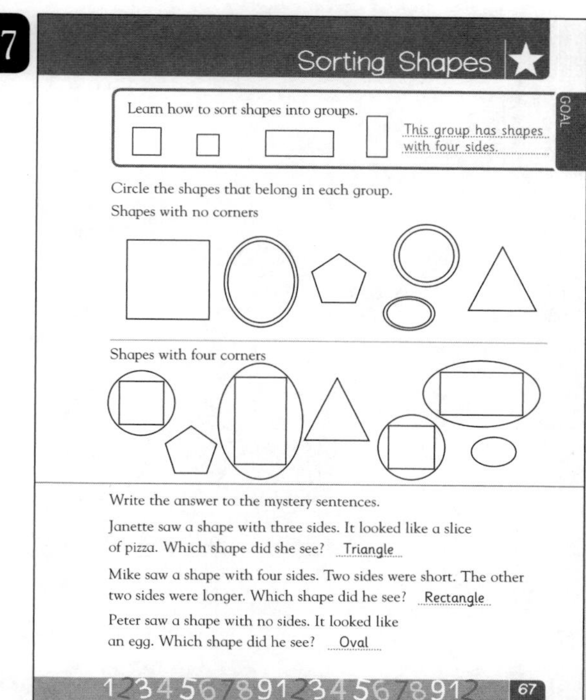
Sorting Shapes

GOAL

Learn how to sort shapes into groups.

This group has shapes with four sides.

Circle the shapes that belong in each group.

Shapes with no corners

Shapes with four corners

Write the answer to the mystery sentences.

Janette saw a shape with three sides. It looked like a slice of pizza. Which shape did she see? Triangle

Mike saw a shape with four sides. Two sides were short. The other two sides were longer. Which shape did he see? Rectangle

Peter saw a shape with no sides. It looked like an egg. Which shape did he see? Oval

Help children find pictures of objects with the shape of a circle, rectangle, square, oval, and triangle in a magazine. Assist them with cutting out several pictures of each shape. Then let children sort the pictures into groups by shape and create a shape poster.

68

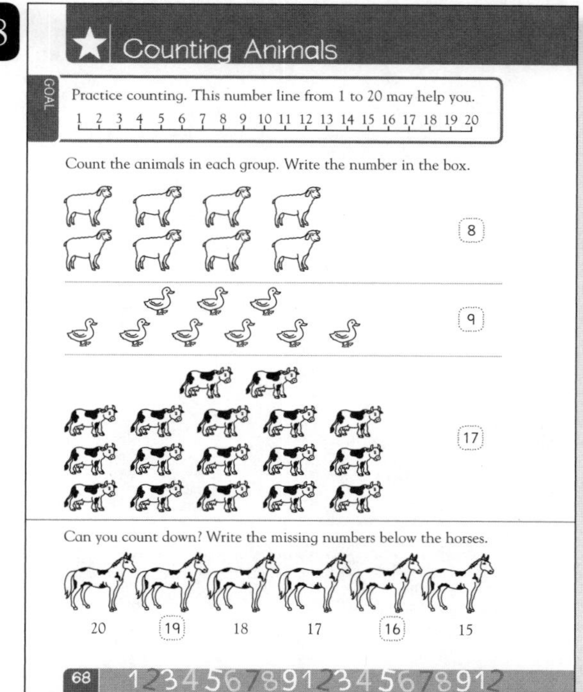
Counting Animals

GOAL

Practice counting. This number line from 1 to 20 may help you.

1 2 3 4 5 6 7 8 9 10 11 12 13 14 15 16 17 18 19 20

Count the animals in each group. Write the number in the box.

8

9

17

Can you count down? Write the missing numbers below the horses.

20 19 18 17 16 15

Provide additional counting practice by placing a row of uncooked beans on a table. Remove several beans from their position in the row, leaving a space. Let children count aloud, saying the number of each missing bean.

69

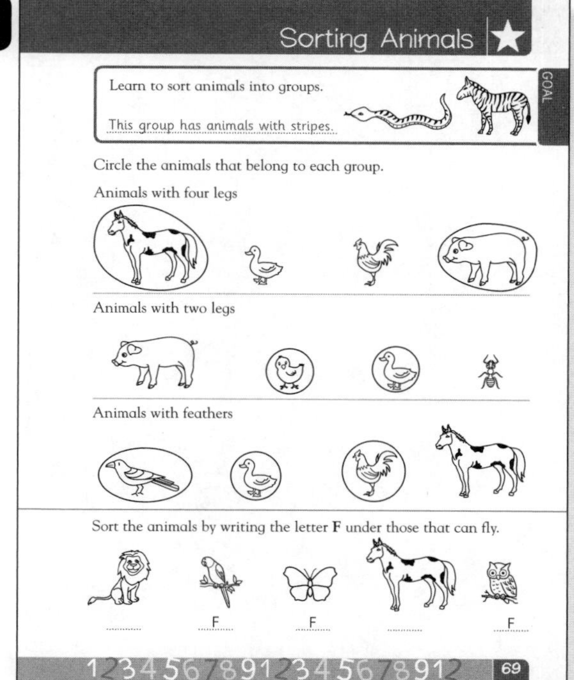
Sorting Animals

GOAL

Learn to sort animals into groups.

This group has animals with stripes.

Circle the animals that belong to each group.

Animals with four legs

Animals with two legs

Animals with feathers

Sort the animals by writing the letter **F** under those that can fly.

F F F

Provide children with small plastic animals. Invite them to sort the animals into groups by various characteristics (by color, with four legs, with two legs, with tails, and so on). For each group, have children explain the characteristic that they are using.

70

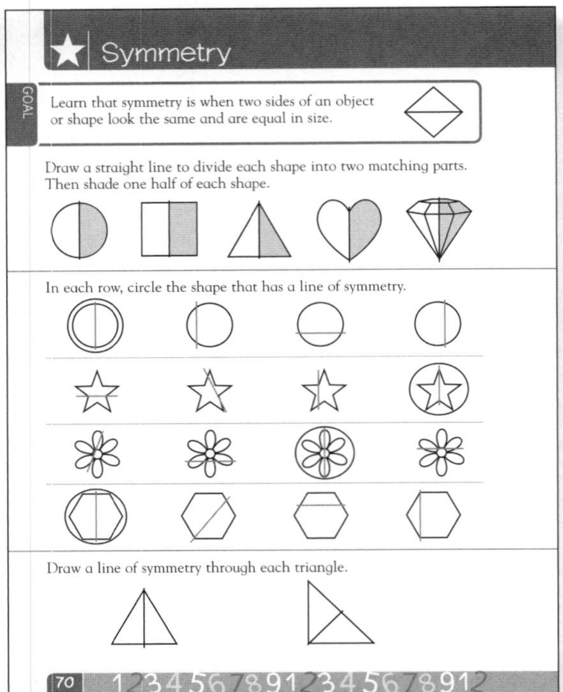

Symmetry

GOAL: Learn that symmetry is when two sides of an object or shape look the same and are equal in size.

Draw a straight line to divide each shape into two matching parts. Then shade one half of each shape.

In each row, circle the shape that has a line of symmetry.

Draw a line of symmetry through each triangle.

70 1234567891234567891 2

Draw various shapes on index cards. Then cut the cards so that the shapes on them are divided in half equally. Mix up the cards. Invite children to find the matching halves and place them together.

71

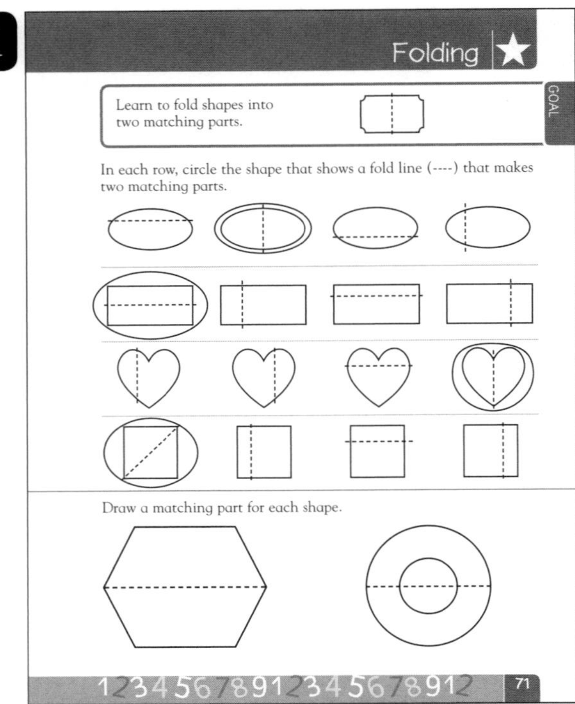

Folding

GOAL: Learn to fold shapes into two matching parts.

In each row, circle the shape that shows a fold line (----) that makes two matching parts.

Draw a matching part for each shape.

1234567891234567891 2 71

Let children practice folding pieces of paper into equal halves. Explain that each side of the fold is a half. Have children color one of the halves, and help them understand that the fold is a dividing line, or a line of symmetry.

72

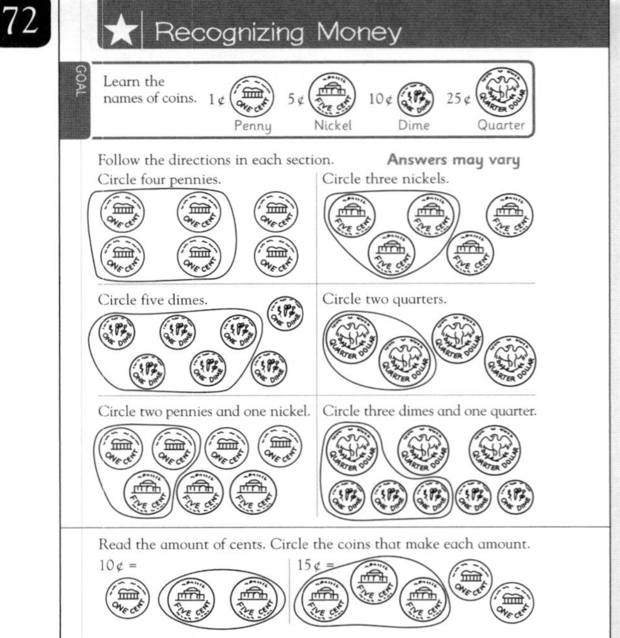

Recognizing Money

GOAL: Learn the names of coins. 1¢ Penny 5¢ Nickel 10¢ Dime 25¢ Quarter

Follow the directions in each section. **Answers may vary**

Circle four pennies. | Circle three nickels.

Circle five dimes. | Circle two quarters.

Circle two pennies and one nickel. | Circle three dimes and one quarter.

Read the amount of cents. Circle the coins that make each amount.

10¢ = | 15¢ =

72 1234567891234567891 2

Engage children in coin riddles: give clues to a coin you are thinking of, such as, "two of this coin makes two cents," (penny) or "two of this coin makes ten cents" (nickel). Let them work out what the mystery coin is.

73

Adding Money

GOAL: Practice adding money.

$$25¢ + 12¢ = 37¢$$

Add the amounts of money in each row.

30¢ + 12¢ = 42¢	17¢ + 22¢ = 39¢	33¢ + 25¢ = 58¢	37¢ + 30¢ = 67¢	14¢ + 10¢ = 24¢
50¢ + 30¢ = 80¢	27¢ + 61¢ = 88¢	17¢ + 21¢ = 38¢	35¢ + 13¢ = 48¢	32¢ + 17¢ = 49¢
21¢ + 50¢ = 71¢	16¢ + 11¢ = 27¢	30¢ + 24¢ = 54¢	23¢ + 22¢ = 45¢	18¢ + 20¢ = 38¢
33¢ + 12¢ = 45¢	25¢ + 22¢ = 47¢	40¢ + 23¢ = 63¢	23¢ + 60¢ = 83¢	16¢ + 12¢ = 28¢

Look at each group of coins. Circle the one with the most money.

1234567891234567891 2 73

Write simple addition money problems for children to mirror using coins. For example, if you write "4¢ + 10¢," they could mirror the sentence by showing four pennies plus one dime, or four pennies plus two nickels. Let them count the coins to find the sum.

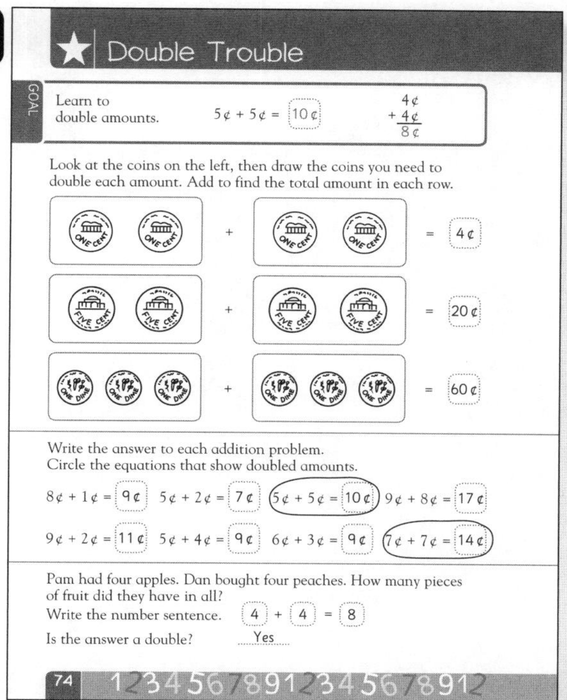

74

Double Trouble

GOAL

Learn to double amounts. 5¢ + 5¢ = 10¢   4¢ + 4¢ = 8¢

Look at the coins on the left, then draw the coins you need to double each amount. Add to find the total amount in each row.

+ = 4¢

+ = 20¢

+ = 60¢

Write the answer to each addition problem.
Circle the equations that show doubled amounts.

8¢ + 1¢ = 9¢   5¢ + 2¢ = 7¢   5¢ + 5¢ = 10¢   9¢ + 8¢ = 17¢

9¢ + 2¢ = 11¢   5¢ + 4¢ = 9¢   6¢ + 3¢ = 9¢   7¢ + 7¢ = 14¢

Pam had four apples. Dan bought four peaches. How many pieces of fruit did they have in all?

Write the number sentence. 4 + 4 = 8

Is the answer a double? Yes

74

Let children practice adding doubles by creating doubles number sentences using buttons or paper clips. Help them add the doubles to reach the correct sum.

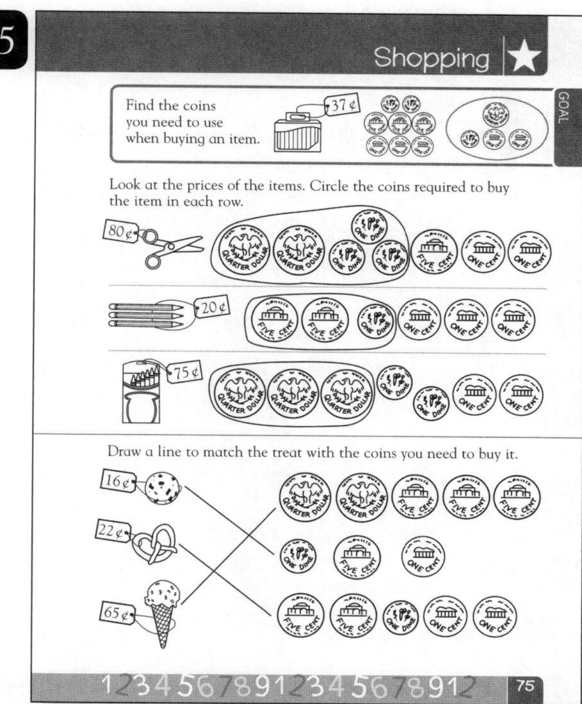

75

Shopping

GOAL

Find the coins you need to use when buying an item. 37¢

Look at the prices of the items. Circle the coins required to buy the item in each row.

80¢

20¢

75¢

Draw a line to match the treat with the coins you need to buy it.

16¢

22¢

65¢

75

Place pennies, nickels, dimes, and quarters on a table. Hold up an object, such as a box of crayons or a small toy, and tell the children what it costs to buy. Let them find the correct coins from the money on the table to "buy" the object.

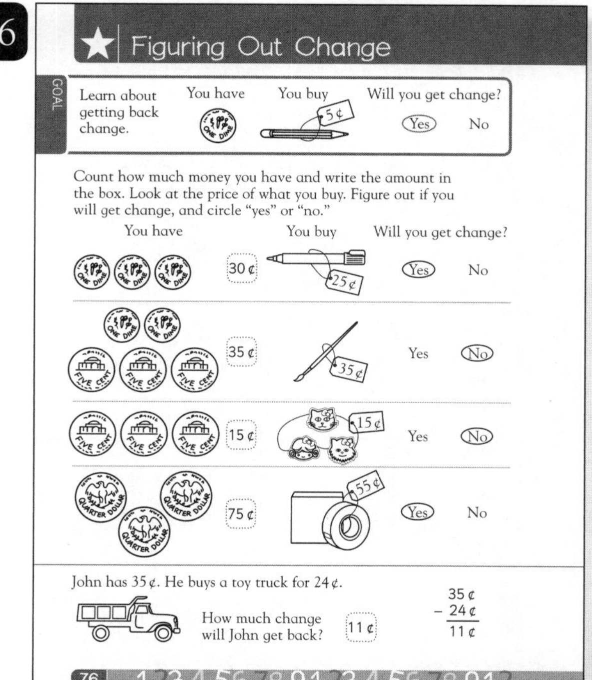

76

Figuring Out Change

GOAL

Learn about getting back change. You have / You buy 5¢ / Will you get change? Yes No

Count how much money you have and write the amount in the box. Look at the price of what you buy. Figure out if you will get change, and circle "yes" or "no."

You have	You buy	Will you get change?
30¢	25¢	Yes No
35¢	35¢	Yes No
15¢	15¢	Yes No
75¢	55¢	Yes No

John has 35¢. He buys a toy truck for 24¢.

How much change will John get back? 11¢   35¢ − 24¢ = 11¢

76

Remind children that they will receive change if the amount of money they have is greater than the cost of the item they are buying. Also have them practice writing amounts of money using the cents (¢) sign.

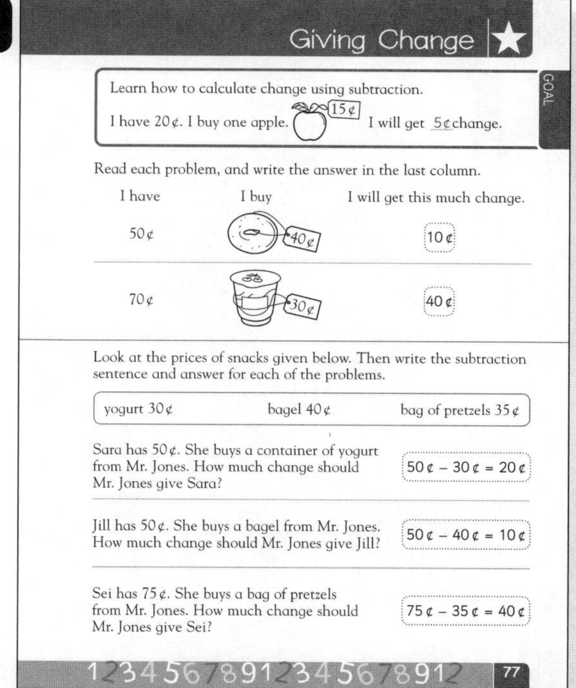

77

Giving Change

GOAL

Learn how to calculate change using subtraction.

I have 20¢. I buy one apple. 15¢ I will get 5¢ change.

Read each problem, and write the answer in the last column.

I have	I buy	I will get this much change.
50¢	40¢	10¢
70¢	30¢	40¢

Look at the prices of snacks given below. Then write the subtraction sentence and answer for each of the problems.

yogurt 30¢   bagel 40¢   bag of pretzels 35¢

Sara has 50¢. She buys a container of yogurt from Mr. Jones. How much change should Mr. Jones give Sara? 50¢ − 30¢ = 20¢

Jill has 50¢. She buys a bagel from Mr. Jones. How much change should Mr. Jones give Jill? 50¢ − 40¢ = 10¢

Sei has 75¢. She buys a bag of pretzels from Mr. Jones. How much change should Mr. Jones give Sei? 75¢ − 35¢ = 40¢

77

Ask children to pretend they have 99¢.
Cut pictures of toys from magazines, and give each toy a price of less than 99¢. Children can select a toy to "buy," then subtract its price from 99¢ to find the change they would receive.

78

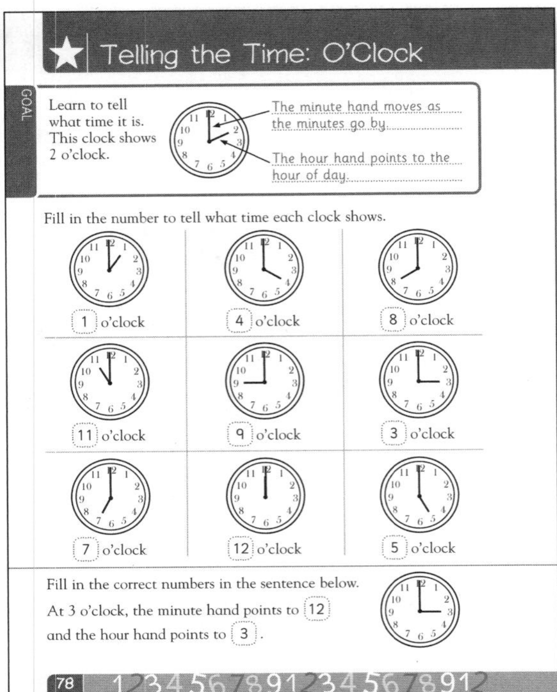

Telling the Time: O'Clock

GOAL

Learn to tell what time it is. This clock shows 2 o'clock.

The minute hand moves as the minutes go by.

The hour hand points to the hour of day.

Fill in the number to tell what time each clock shows.

1 o'clock | 4 o'clock | 8 o'clock
11 o'clock | 9 o'clock | 3 o'clock
7 o'clock | 12 o'clock | 5 o'clock

Fill in the correct numbers in the sentence below.

At 3 o'clock, the minute hand points to 12 and the hour hand points to 3 .

78

Use a toy clock to help children tell the time. Say a time, and let them move the hands to the correct hour. Then have children say the hour and name an activity that might take place at that time.

79

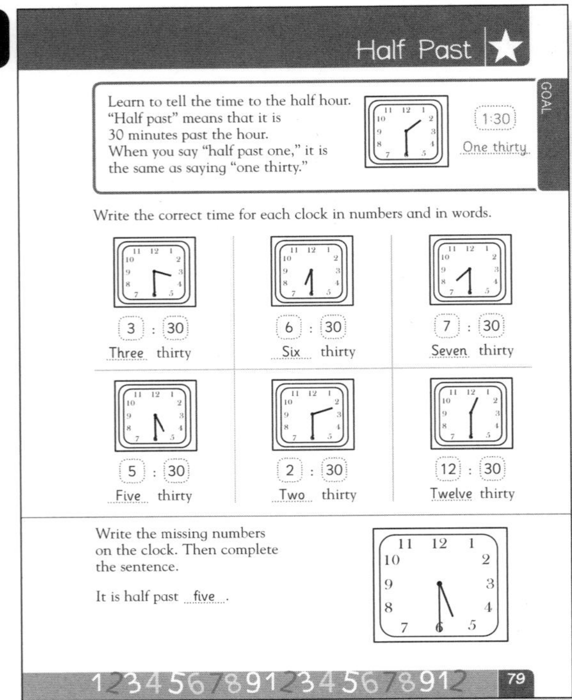

Half Past

GOAL

Learn to tell the time to the half hour. "Half past" means that it is 30 minutes past the hour. When you say "half past one," it is the same as saying "one thirty."

1:30

One thirty

Write the correct time for each clock in numbers and in words.

3 : 30 Three thirty | 6 : 30 Six thirty | 7 : 30 Seven thirty
5 : 30 Five thirty | 2 : 30 Two thirty | 12 : 30 Twelve thirty

Write the missing numbers on the clock. Then complete the sentence.

It is half past five.

79

On index cards, write times to the hour and half hour. Place them facedown. Let children pick up cards and place them in the correct order from the time they wake up in the morning to the time they go to bed.

80

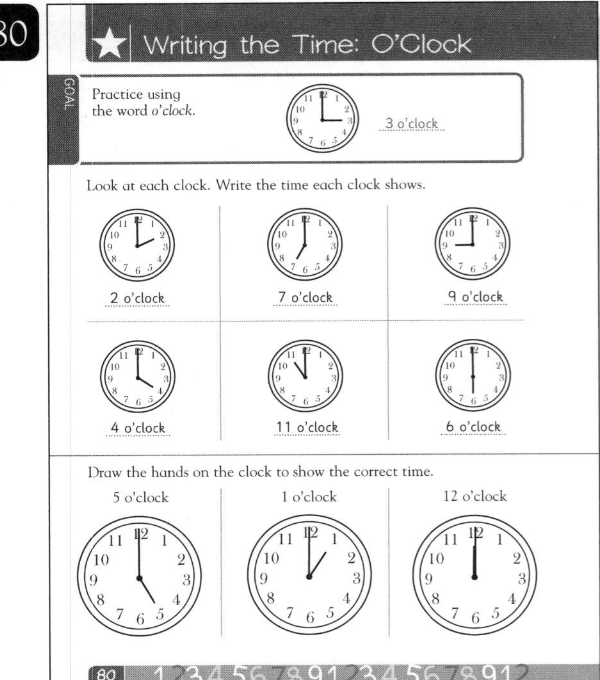

Writing the Time: O'Clock

GOAL

Practice using the word *o'clock*.

3 o'clock

Look at each clock. Write the time each clock shows.

2 o'clock | 7 o'clock | 9 o'clock
4 o'clock | 11 o'clock | 6 o'clock

Draw the hands on the clock to show the correct time.

5 o'clock | 1 o'clock | 12 o'clock

80

On a toy clock, let children show times that are on the hour and on the half hour. Let them practice writing in numbers and words the time they are showing.

81

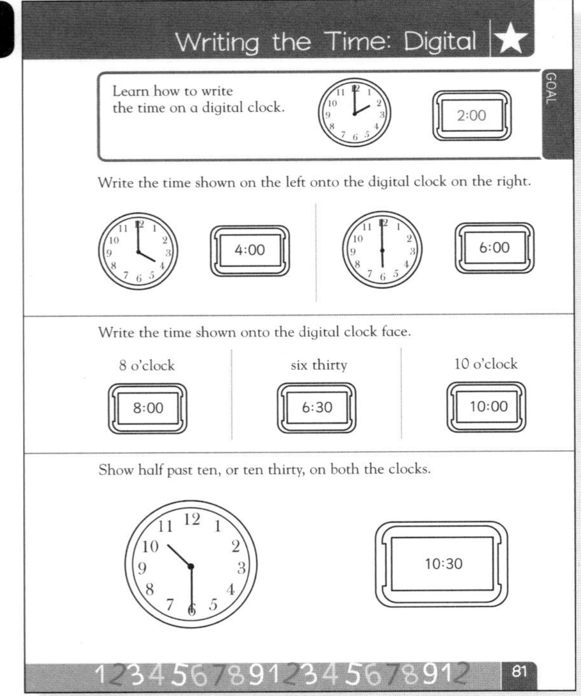

Writing the Time: Digital

GOAL

Learn how to write the time on a digital clock.

2:00

Write the time shown on the left onto the digital clock on the right.

4:00 | 6:00

Write the time shown onto the digital clock face.

8 o'clock 8:00 | six thirty 6:30 | 10 o'clock 10:00

Show half past ten, or ten thirty, on both the clocks.

10:30

81

Write times on index cards, using a colon between hours and minutes. Cut the cards in half, using puzzle-piece lines. Mix the cards, and have children find and put together the matching pieces. Ask them to write the time revealed on each matching pair in words.

82

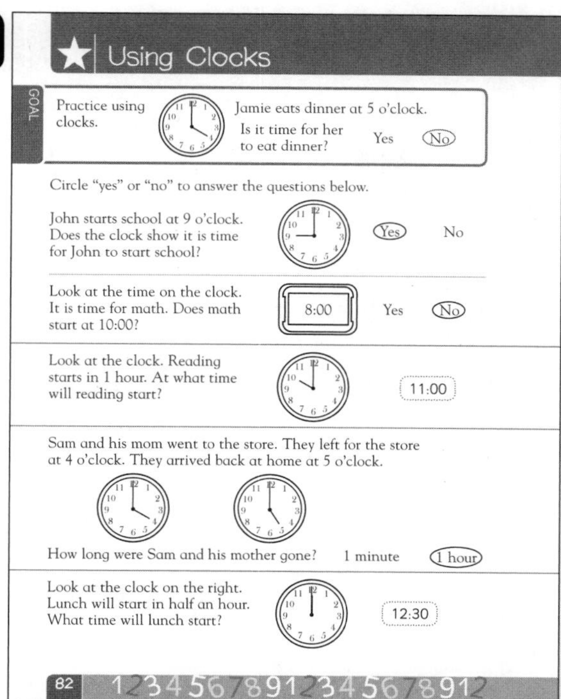

Using Clocks

GOAL

Practice using clocks.

Jamie eats dinner at 5 o'clock. Is it time for her to eat dinner? Yes (No)

Circle "yes" or "no" to answer the questions below.

John starts school at 9 o'clock. Does the clock show it is time for John to start school? (Yes) No

Look at the time on the clock. It is time for math. Does math start at 10:00? 8:00 Yes (No)

Look at the clock. Reading starts in 1 hour. At what time will reading start? 11:00

Sam and his mom went to the store. They left for the store at 4 o'clock. They arrived back at home at 5 o'clock.

How long were Sam and his mother gone? 1 minute (1 hour)

Look at the clock on the right. Lunch will start in half an hour. What time will lunch start? 12:30

82

Draw analog and digital clock faces, showing times on the hour and on the half hour, on index cards. Mix the cards, and let children sort the cards to match the analog clock time with its corresponding digital time.

83

Differences in Time

GOAL

Learn about how long it takes to do some activities.

The activity circled here takes more time than the other.

Circle the activity in each group below that takes more time.

Circle the activity in each group below that takes less time.

About how long does each activity take? Circle the best answer.

1 minute (1 hour) | (1 minute) 1 hour | (1 minute) 1 hour

83

Discuss various other activities with children, and let them give an approximate time it might take to perform each one. As children practice assessing differences in time duration, they will become increasingly competent at judging lengths of time.

84

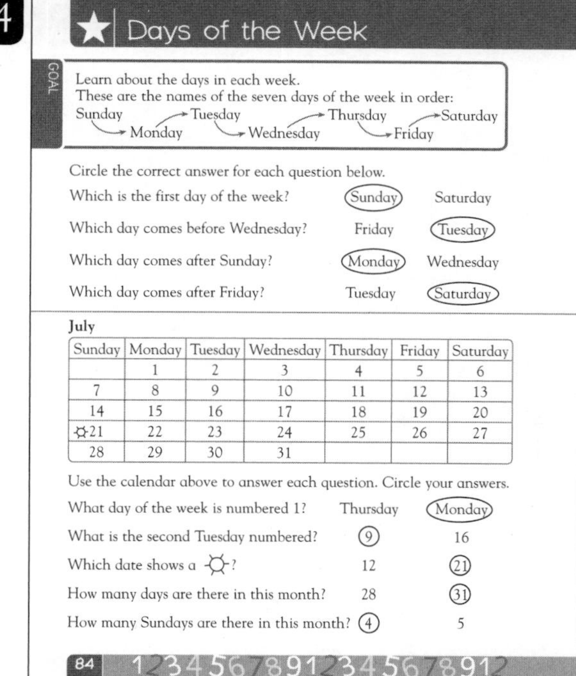

Days of the Week

GOAL

Learn about the days in each week.
These are the names of the seven days of the week in order:
Sunday → Monday → Tuesday → Wednesday → Thursday → Friday → Saturday

Circle the correct answer for each question below.

Which is the first day of the week? (Sunday) Saturday

Which day comes before Wednesday? Friday (Tuesday)

Which day comes after Sunday? (Monday) Wednesday

Which day comes after Friday? Tuesday (Saturday)

July

Sunday	Monday	Tuesday	Wednesday	Thursday	Friday	Saturday
	1	2	3	4	5	6
7	8	9	10	11	12	13
14	15	16	17	18	19	20
☼21	22	23	24	25	26	27
28	29	30	31			

Use the calendar above to answer each question. Circle your answers.

What day of the week is numbered 1? Thursday (Monday)

What is the second Tuesday numbered? (9) 16

Which date shows a ☼? 12 (21)

How many days are there in this month? 28 (31)

How many Sundays are there in this month? (4) 5

84

For additional practice, say the name of a day of the week, then ask children to name the day that comes either before it or after it. Let children check their answers by looking at a calendar.

85

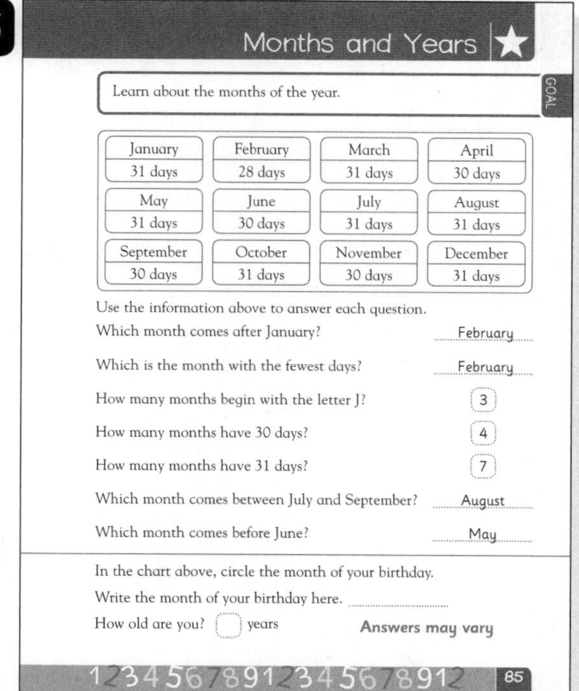

Months and Years

GOAL

Learn about the months of the year.

January 31 days	February 28 days	March 31 days	April 30 days
May 31 days	June 30 days	July 31 days	August 31 days
September 30 days	October 31 days	November 30 days	December 31 days

Use the information above to answer each question.

Which month comes after January? February

Which is the month with the fewest days? February

How many months begin with the letter J? 3

How many months have 30 days? 4

How many months have 31 days? 7

Which month comes between July and September? August

Which month comes before June? May

In the chart above, circle the month of your birthday.

Write the month of your birthday here.

How old are you? years **Answers may vary**

85

Have children repeat after you the names of the months of the year. Then talk about the weather where you live; let them choose different months and draw pictures to show what the weather is typically like during each of those months.

86

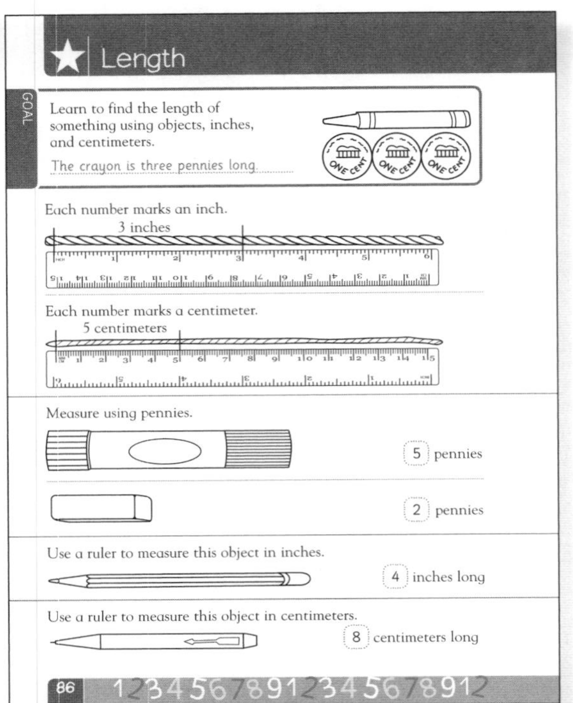

Length

GOAL

Learn to find the length of something using objects, inches, and centimeters.

The crayon is three pennies long.

Each number marks an inch.

3 inches

Each number marks a centimeter.

5 centimeters

Measure using pennies.

5 pennies

2 pennies

Use a ruler to measure this object in inches.

4 inches long

Use a ruler to measure this object in centimeters.

8 centimeters long

86 1234567891234567891 2

Let children practice measuring straight objects using a ruler. Help them understand where each inch and centimeter mark appears on the ruler. Have children write down the measurements, using the words "inches" or "centimeters."

87

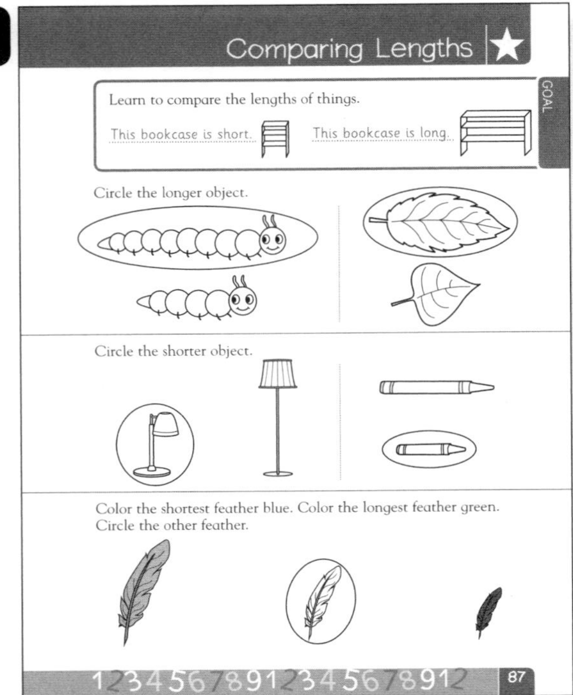

Comparing Lengths

GOAL

Learn to compare the lengths of things.

This bookcase is short. This bookcase is long.

Circle the longer object.

Circle the shorter object.

Color the shortest feather blue. Color the longest feather green. Circle the other feather.

1234567891234567891 2 87

Give children pieces of colored paper. Invite them to cut strips of different lengths that they can then label "long," "longer," and "longest." Children can then do the same activity, labeling the strips "short," "shorter," and "shortest."

88

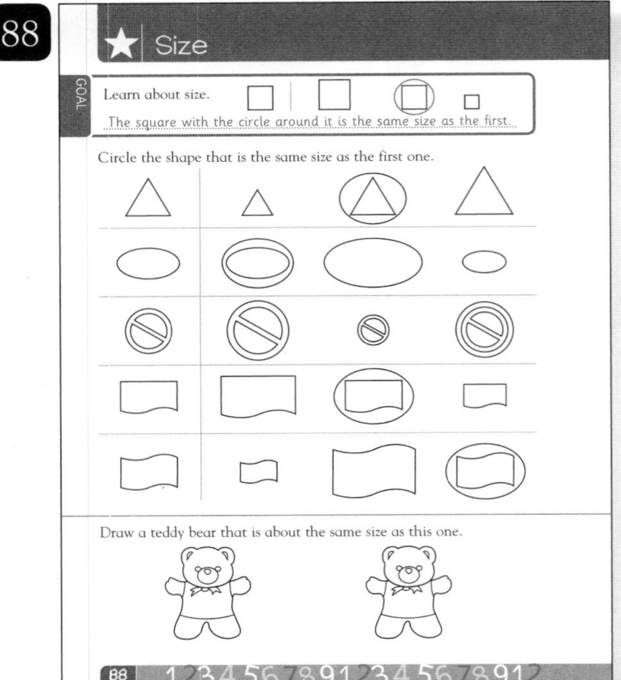

Size

GOAL

Learn about size.

The square with the circle around it is the same size as the first.

Circle the shape that is the same size as the first one.

Draw a teddy bear that is about the same size as this one.

88 1234567891234567891 2

Make sure that children carefully examine the shapes and their sizes. Explain that shapes can sometimes appear to be a different size because they are turned a different way.

89

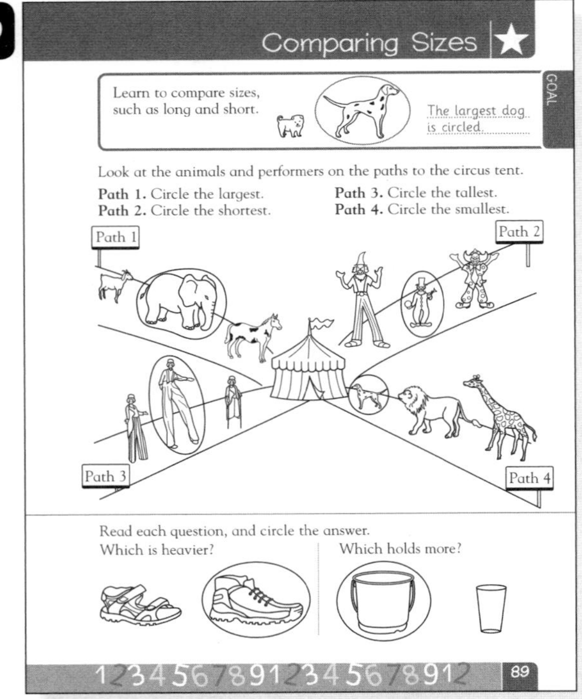

Comparing Sizes

GOAL

Learn to compare sizes, such as long and short.

The largest dog is circled.

Look at the animals and performers on the paths to the circus tent.

Path 1. Circle the largest.
Path 2. Circle the shortest.
Path 3. Circle the tallest.
Path 4. Circle the smallest.

Read each question, and circle the answer.

Which is heavier?

Which holds more?

1234567891234567891 2 89

Show children hats, mittens, or boxes of different sizes. Let them indicate which is biggest or smallest, widest, thinnest, and so on. Do the same with other objects, letting children order them from smallest to largest.

90

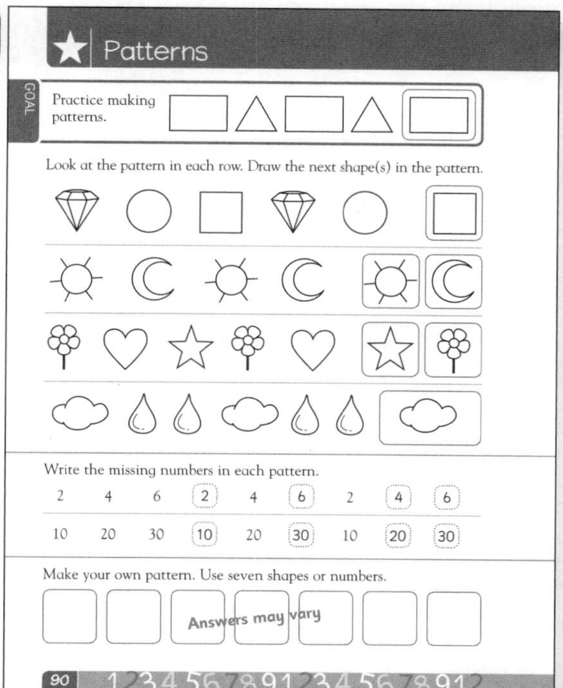

Patterns

GOAL: Practice making patterns.

Look at the pattern in each row. Draw the next shape(s) in the pattern.

Write the missing numbers in each pattern.

2 4 6 2 4 6 2 4 6

10 20 30 10 20 30 10 20 30

Make your own pattern. Use seven shapes or numbers.

Answers may vary

90

Cut different shapes from a piece of paper. Arrange them in any pattern you wish. Let children add the next shape or shapes to extend the pattern. You can also draw objects in a pattern and let them complete the pattern by drawing the next object.

91

Sequences

GOAL: A sequence shows the order in which something happens. 1 2 3

Write 1, 2, 3, and 4 to put each story in the correct order.

1 3 2 4

3 4 1 2

2 3 4 1

Write the missing numbers in each squence.

20 19 18 17 16 15

5 10 15 20 25 30

91

Explain to children that if someone is No. 3 in line, then he or she is in the 3rd position; No. 4 in line is in the 4th position; and so on. Then place a row of buttons in front of children, and have them say the names of each position from left to right.

92

Picture Graphs

GOAL: Learn to read and use picture graphs to find the answers.

Frogs Tom and Matt Saw at the Pond

Tom	🐸 🐸 🐸
Matt	🐸 🐸 🐸 🐸

Matt saw the most frogs.

Use this picture graph to answer each question.

Dogs in Need of Homes

Black Dogs	🐕 🐕 🐕 🐕
White Dogs	🐕 🐕 🐕
Spotted Dogs	🐕 🐕 🐕
Gray Dogs	🐕 🐕 🐕 🐕 🐕

How many black dogs need homes? 4

How many spotted dogs need homes? 3

Which two kinds of dog are the same in number? White dogs and spotted dogs

Of which kind of dog is there the most? Gray dogs

How many more gray dogs are there than spotted dogs? 2

How many black and white dogs need homes? 7

How many dogs are there in all? 15

Write the subtraction problem and the answer. There are 15 dogs in all. People take 4 black dogs home. How many other dogs still need homes? 15 – 4 = 11

92

Help children understand that each picture on the picture graph stands for one object. Show them how to count each object in each row. When children understand this concept, ask questions like, “How many more black dogs than white dogs are there?”

93

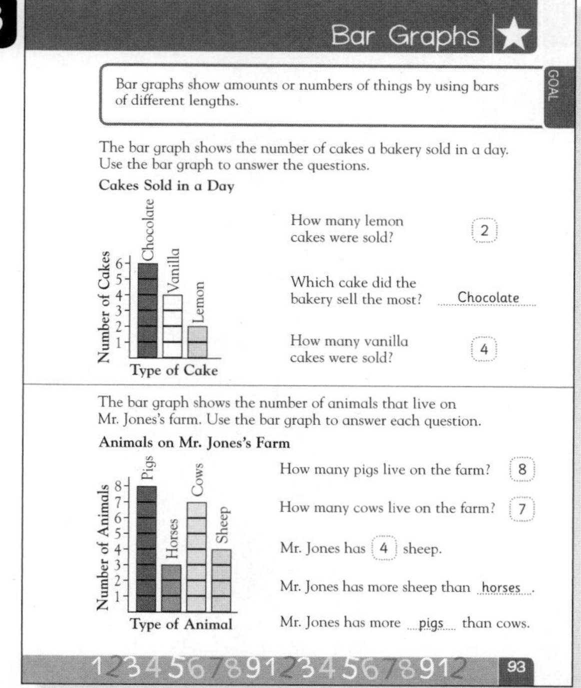

Bar Graphs

GOAL: Bar graphs show amounts or numbers of things by using bars of different lengths.

The bar graph shows the number of cakes a bakery sold in a day. Use the bar graph to answer the questions.

Cakes Sold in a Day

How many lemon cakes were sold? 2

Which cake did the bakery sell the most? Chocolate

How many vanilla cakes were sold? 4

The bar graph shows the number of animals that live on Mr. Jones's farm. Use the bar graph to answer each question.

Animals on Mr. Jones's Farm

How many pigs live on the farm? 8

How many cows live on the farm? 7

Mr. Jones has 4 sheep.

Mr. Jones has more sheep than horses.

Mr. Jones has more pigs than cows.

93

Explain to children that each box on the bar graph stands for one object. They can count the boxes in each bar to find the answers to the questions on this page.

94

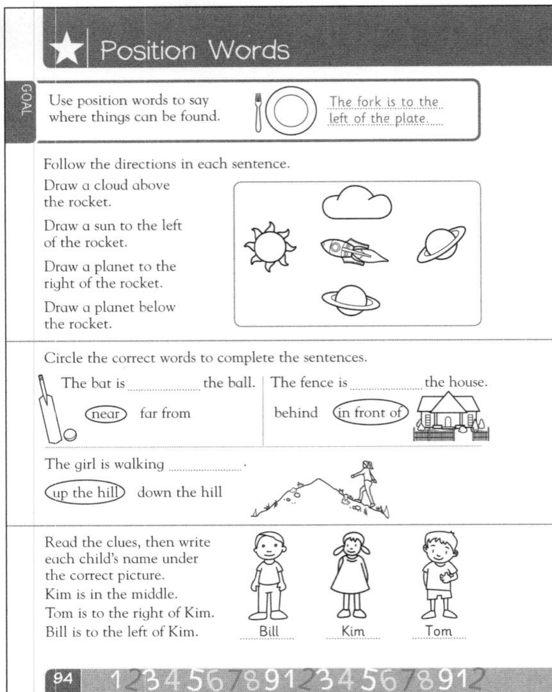

Position Words

GOAL: Use position words to say where things can be found. The fork is to the left of the plate.

Follow the directions in each sentence.

Draw a cloud above the rocket.

Draw a sun to the left of the rocket.

Draw a planet to the right of the rocket.

Draw a planet below the rocket.

Circle the correct words to complete the sentences.

The bat is .... the ball. near far from

The fence is .... the house. behind in front of

The girl is walking .... up the hill down the hill

Read the clues, then write each child's name under the correct picture.
Kim is in the middle.
Tom is to the right of Kim.
Bill is to the left of Kim.

Bill Kim Tom

94 12345678912345678912

Write position words—such as "behind," "near," "next to," "to the left of," and so on—on index cards. Let children choose a card and use its word or phrase to describe where objects in the home are located in relation to other objects. For example, "The stove is *near* the sink," or "The mirror is *above* the dresser."

95

Following

GOAL: Use direction words to find your way. *Behind, right, left, in front of, between, up, down, above,* and *below* are some direction words.

Pam's dog has run off into the maze. Can you help her find him? Read the clues and draw a line to show her the way.

Clues
1. At the gate turn right.
2. At the ice cream stand turn left and pass between two apple trees.
3. Turn right and follow the path until you get to a bench.
4. Turn left, then right, and follow the path. Go up the steps.
5. Look behind the goldfish pond.

Start

12345678912345678912 95

Invite children to draw a house. When the drawing is complete, give them directions, using position words, on what to add to the picture. For example: "Draw a tree *next to* the house." Later, have children describe their pictures using position words.

96

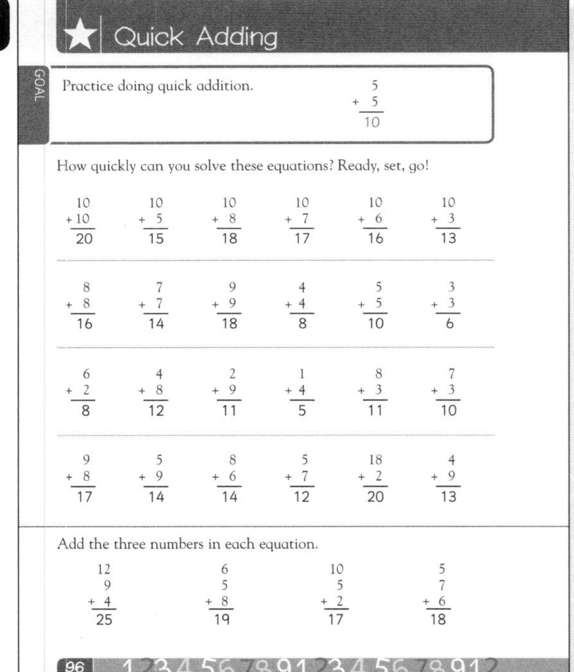

Quick Adding

GOAL: Practice doing quick addition. 5 + 5 = 10

How quickly can you solve these equations? Ready, set, go!

10 + 10 = 20	10 + 5 = 15	10 + 8 = 18	10 + 7 = 17	10 + 6 = 16	10 + 3 = 13
8 + 8 = 16	7 + 7 = 14	9 + 9 = 18	4 + 4 = 8	5 + 5 = 10	3 + 3 = 6
6 + 2 = 8	4 + 8 = 12	2 + 9 = 11	1 + 4 = 5	8 + 3 = 11	7 + 3 = 10
9 + 8 = 17	5 + 9 = 14	8 + 6 = 14	5 + 7 = 12	18 + 2 = 20	4 + 9 = 13

Add the three numbers in each equation.

12 + 9 + 4 = 25	6 + 5 + 8 = 19	10 + 5 + 2 = 17	5 + 7 + 6 = 18

96 12345678912345678912

Try covering all the rows, except the one children are currently working on, with paper to help them avoid losing their place. Also help them learn quick addition facts through frequent practice, using flash cards or manipulative items such as marbles, paper clips, and blocks.

97

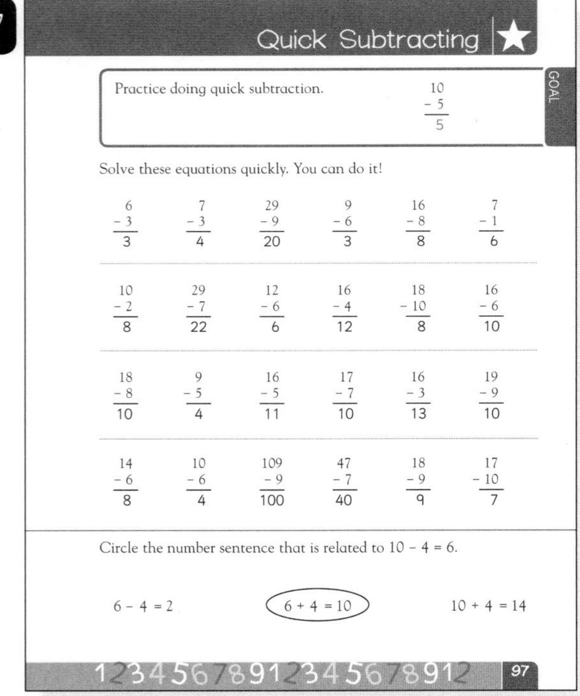

Quick Subtracting

GOAL: Practice doing quick subtraction. 10 − 5 = 5

Solve these equations quickly. You can do it!

6 − 3 = 3	7 − 3 = 4	29 − 9 = 20	9 − 6 = 3	16 − 8 = 8	7 − 1 = 6
10 − 2 = 8	29 − 7 = 22	12 − 6 = 6	16 − 4 = 12	18 − 10 = 8	16 − 6 = 10
18 − 8 = 10	9 − 5 = 4	16 − 5 = 11	17 − 7 = 10	16 − 3 = 13	19 − 9 = 10
14 − 6 = 8	10 − 6 = 4	109 − 9 = 100	47 − 7 = 40	18 − 9 = 9	17 − 10 = 7

Circle the number sentence that is related to 10 − 4 = 6.

6 − 4 = 2 6 + 4 = 10 10 + 4 = 14

12345678912345678912 97

Again, cover all the rows children are not currently working on, to help them keep their concentration. Frequent practice, using flash cards or manipulative items, is important for them to become quick at working out subtraction equations.

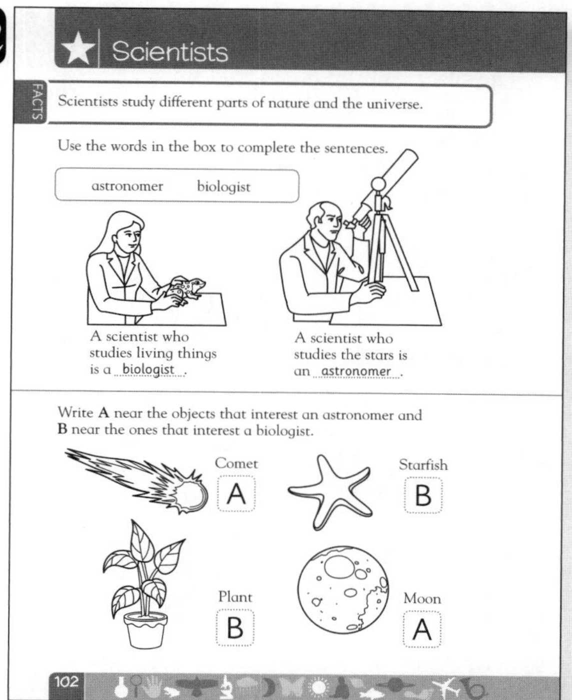

Scientists

FACTS

Scientists study different parts of nature and the universe.

Use the words in the box to complete the sentences.

astronomer biologist

A scientist who studies living things is a biologist.

A scientist who studies the stars is an astronomer.

Write **A** near the objects that interest an astronomer and **B** near the ones that interest a biologist.

Comet A

Starfish B

Plant B

Moon A

102

Do scientists work or live in your community? What types of scientists are they? Ask your child: "If you were going to be a scientist, what kind of scientist would you be? What would you study? Why?"

103

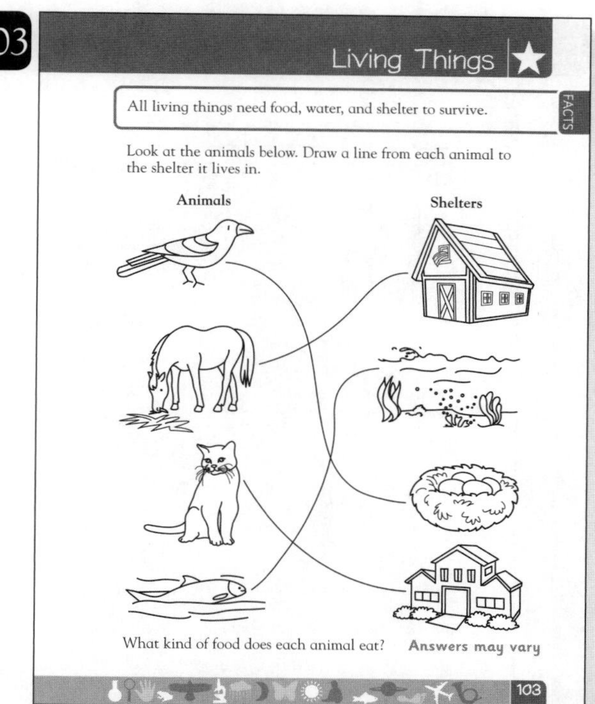

Living Things

FACTS

All living things need food, water, and shelter to survive.

Look at the animals below. Draw a line from each animal to the shelter it lives in.

Animals

Shelters

What kind of food does each animal eat? **Answers may vary**

103

All animals need food, water, and shelter to survive. Discuss with your child that people are animals, too, and also need food, water, and shelter to survive. With your help, have your child draw the foods that they eat every day, and where they make their shelter.

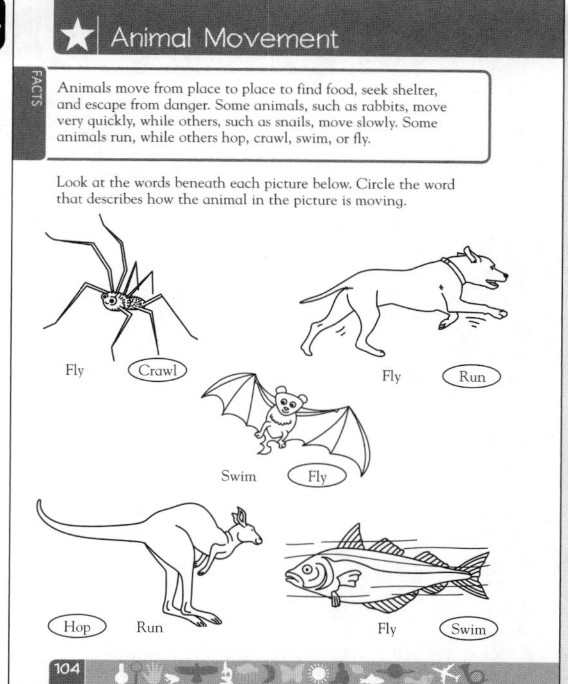

Animal Movement

FACTS

Animals move from place to place to find food, seek shelter, and escape from danger. Some animals, such as rabbits, move very quickly, while others, such as snails, move slowly. Some animals run, while others hop, crawl, swim, or fly.

Look at the words beneath each picture below. Circle the word that describes how the animal in the picture is moving.

Fly Crawl

Fly Run

Swim Fly

Hop Run

Fly Swim

104

Ask your child how they move around every day. Do they walk? Run? Hop? Swim? Fly? If so, when? How? Have them list other animals that walk, run, swim, and fly. Can they think of any other ways animals can move. (Possible answers are snakes slither, worms inch or burrow, etc.)

105

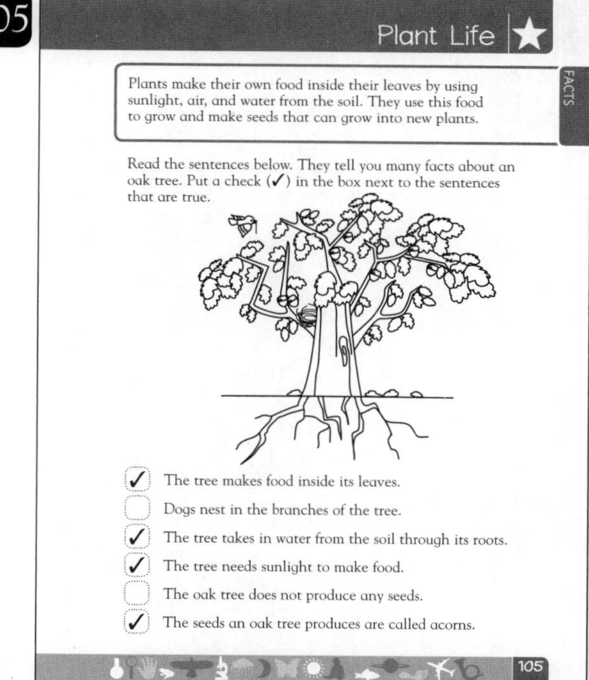

Plant Life

FACTS

Plants make their own food inside their leaves by using sunlight, air, and water from the soil. They use this food to grow and make seeds that can grow into new plants.

Read the sentences below. They tell you many facts about an oak tree. Put a check (✓) in the box next to the sentences that are true.

- [x] The tree makes food inside its leaves.
- [ ] Dogs nest in the branches of the tree.
- [x] The tree takes in water from the soil through its roots.
- [x] The tree needs sunlight to make food.
- [ ] The oak tree does not produce any seeds.
- [x] The seeds an oak tree produces are called acorns.

105

Discuss with your child that the oak tree is a deciduous tree, meaning it has broad leaves that grow in spring, make food for the tree in summer, and fall off in autumn. Even without its leaves, the oak tree survives winter. During winter, deciduous trees conserve food and energy (like hibernation) until it is time to grow new leaves again.

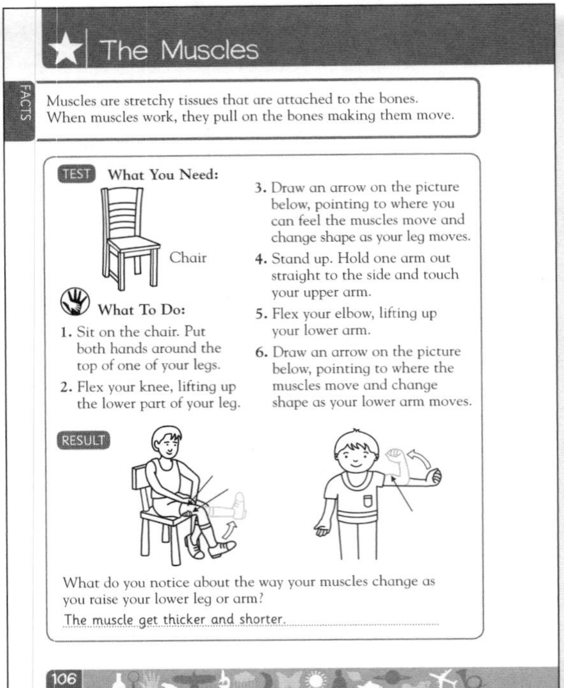

The Muscles

FACTS

Muscles are stretchy tissues that are attached to the bones. When muscles work, they pull on the bones making them move.

TEST **What You Need:**

Chair

What To Do:

1. Sit on the chair. Put both hands around the top of one of your legs.
2. Flex your knee, lifting up the lower part of your leg.
3. Draw an arrow on the picture below, pointing to where you can feel the muscles move and change shape as your leg moves.
4. Stand up. Hold one arm out straight to the side and touch your upper arm.
5. Flex your elbow, lifting up your lower arm.
6. Draw an arrow on the picture below, pointing to where the muscles move and change shape as your lower arm moves.

RESULT

What do you notice about the way your muscles change as you raise your lower leg or arm?

The muscle get thicker and shorter.

106

There are lots of muscles in the body. Help your child identify some of the more obvious ones in his or her body. Knowing the proper names can be a source of pride for first graders. Start with pointing out the biceps, triceps, abdominals, calves, quadriceps, and the gluteal muscles.

107

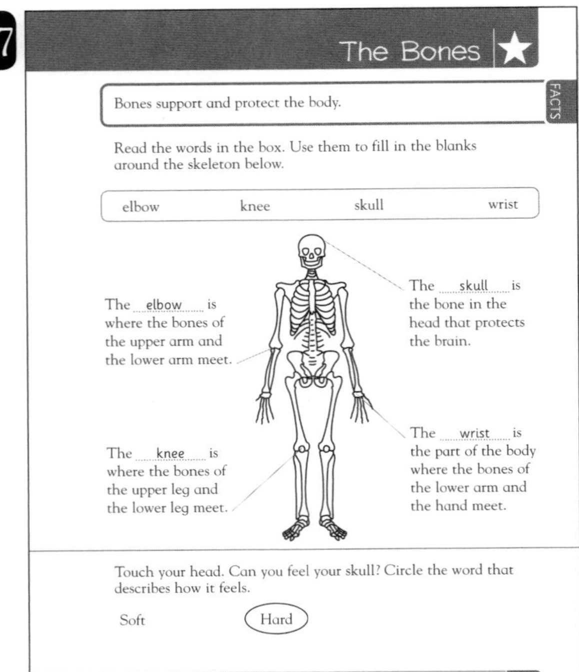

The Bones

FACTS

Bones support and protect the body.

Read the words in the box. Use them to fill in the blanks around the skeleton below.

elbow	knee	skull	wrist

The elbow is where the bones of the upper arm and the lower arm meet.

The skull is the bone in the head that protects the brain.

The knee is where the bones of the upper leg and the lower leg meet.

The wrist is the part of the body where the bones of the lower arm and the hand meet.

Touch your head. Can you feel your skull? Circle the word that describes how it feels.

Soft (Hard)

107

Like the muscles, the bones have proper names. Show your child the skull, jaw, collar bone, and ribs. Tell your child that his or her arm has three main bones: humerus (upper arm) and radius and ulna (lower arm). And three main bones in the leg: femur (thigh) and tibia and fibula (lower leg).

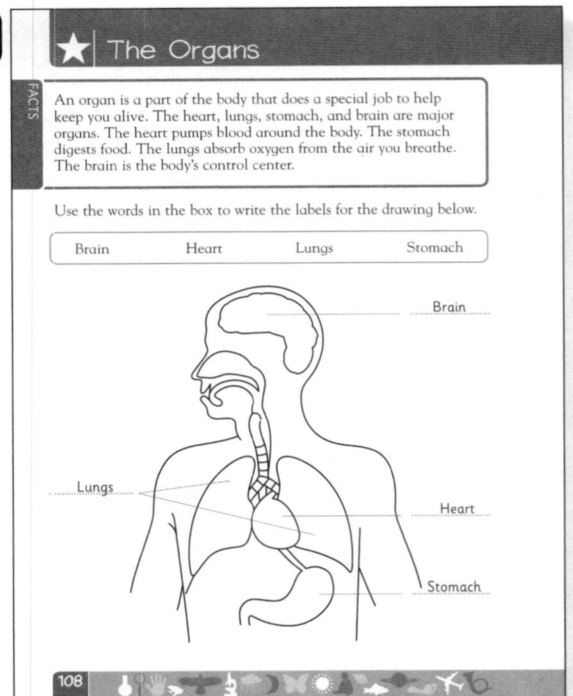

The Organs

FACTS

An organ is a part of the body that does a special job to help keep you alive. The heart, lungs, stomach, and brain are major organs. The heart pumps blood around the body. The stomach digests food. The lungs absorb oxygen from the air you breathe. The brain is the body's control center.

Use the words in the box to write the labels for the drawing below.

Brain	Heart	Lungs	Stomach

108

This activity does not mention the largest organs in the body. The largest internal organ is the liver, which, among other things, stores fat and sugar. It also helps clean toxins from the body. The largest organ of all is the skin, which covers and protects the entire body.

109

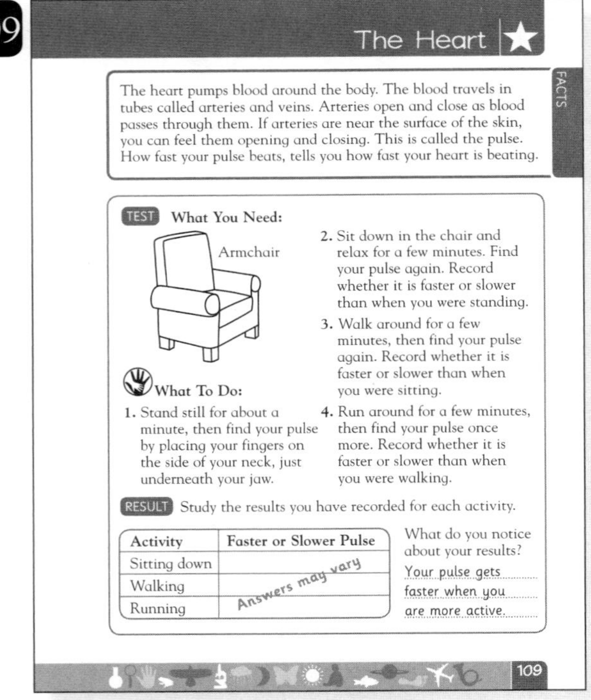

The Heart

FACTS

The heart pumps blood around the body. The blood travels in tubes called arteries and veins. Arteries open and close as blood passes through them. If arteries are near the surface of the skin, you can feel them opening and closing. This is called the pulse. How fast your pulse beats, tells you how fast your heart is beating.

TEST **What You Need:**

Armchair

What To Do:

1. Stand still for about a minute, then find your pulse by placing your fingers on the side of your neck, just underneath your jaw.
2. Sit down in the chair and relax for a few minutes. Find your pulse again. Record whether it is faster or slower than when you were standing.
3. Walk around for a few minutes, then find your pulse again. Record whether it is faster or slower than when you were sitting.
4. Run around for a few minutes, then find your pulse once more. Record whether it is faster or slower than when you were walking.

RESULT Study the results you have recorded for each activity.

Activity	Faster or Slower Pulse
Sitting down	Answers may vary
Walking	
Running	

What do you notice about your results?

Your pulse gets faster when you are more active.

109

Discuss with your child that the heart is made of a special kind of muscle that never gets tired. So even when they're tired, their heart just keeps pumping and pumping. By moving the blood around the body, the heart helps deliver oxygen and nutrients to the muscles and organs. It also helps remove waste products.

110

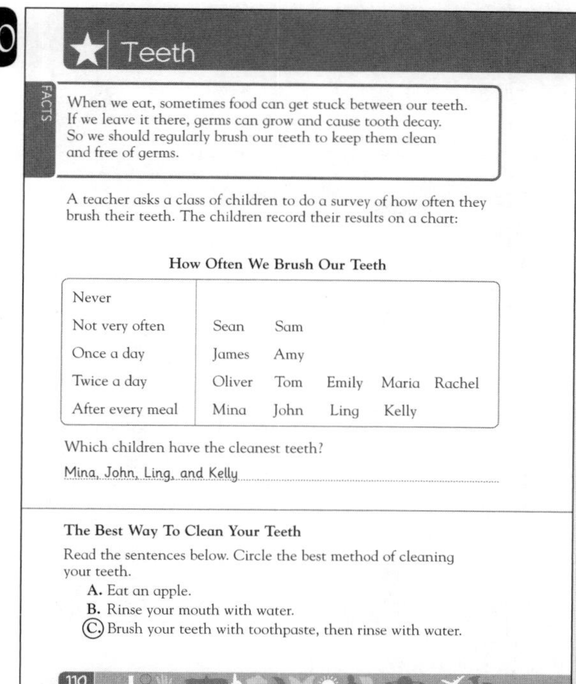

Teeth

FACTS

When we eat, sometimes food can get stuck between our teeth. If we leave it there, germs can grow and cause tooth decay. So we should regularly brush our teeth to keep them clean and free of germs.

A teacher asks a class of children to do a survey of how often they brush their teeth. The children record their results on a chart:

How Often We Brush Our Teeth

Never					
Not very often	Sean	Sam			
Once a day	James	Amy			
Twice a day	Oliver	Tom	Emily	Maria	Rachel
After every meal	Mina	John	Ling	Kelly	

Which children have the cleanest teeth?

Mina, John, Ling, and Kelly

The Best Way To Clean Your Teeth

Read the sentences below. Circle the best method of cleaning your teeth.

A. Eat an apple.
B. Rinse your mouth with water.
(C.) Brush your teeth with toothpaste, then rinse with water.

By now, your child has learned the importance of good oral hygiene. But it is always good to review the basics: brushing twice a day (or after meals) is key, using toothpaste and small, circular motions. Discuss that this will keep their teeth and mouth healthy and enable them to eat their favorite foods.

111

Eating Well

FACTS

We get our energy and nutrients from the foods we eat. It is important to eat fresh foods from different food groups to be fit and healthy.

Look at the food groups above. Do you eat foods from each of those groups every day? Which are your favorites? Which are your least favorites? Color in the food groups, and add any of your favorite foods that we left out. **Answers may vary**

Ask your child to list their favorite foods. From which food groups do those foods come? Are there important food groups missing from your child's list? If so, discuss the importance of that food group with your child. Ask them to think of a favorite food from that group and eat it a few times a week.

112

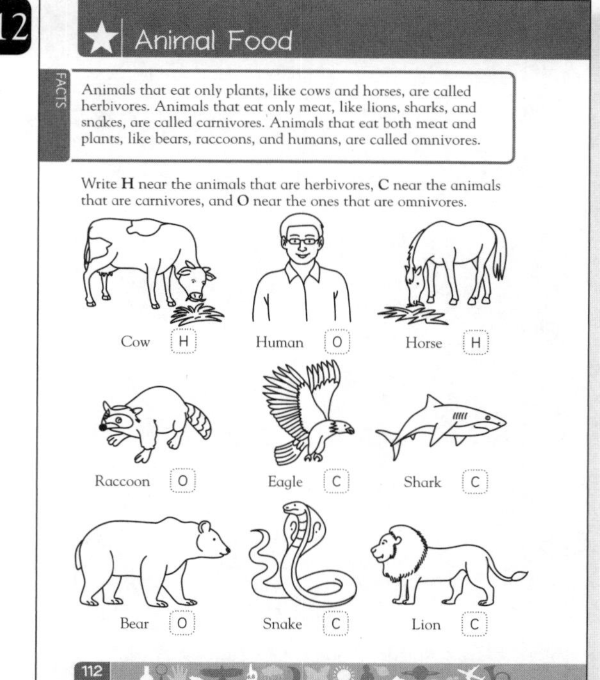

Animal Food

FACTS

Animals that eat only plants, like cows and horses, are called herbivores. Animals that eat only meat, like lions, sharks, and snakes, are called carnivores. Animals that eat both meat and plants, like bears, raccoons, and humans, are called omnivores.

Write **H** near the animals that are herbivores, **C** near the animals that are carnivores, and **O** near the ones that are omnivores.

Ask your child if they think they are a carnivore, herbivore, or omnivore, and why. Have them name their favorite foods, and discuss if those foods are meat or plants. If your child could choose to be a carnivore, herbivore, or omnivore, which one would they choose?

113

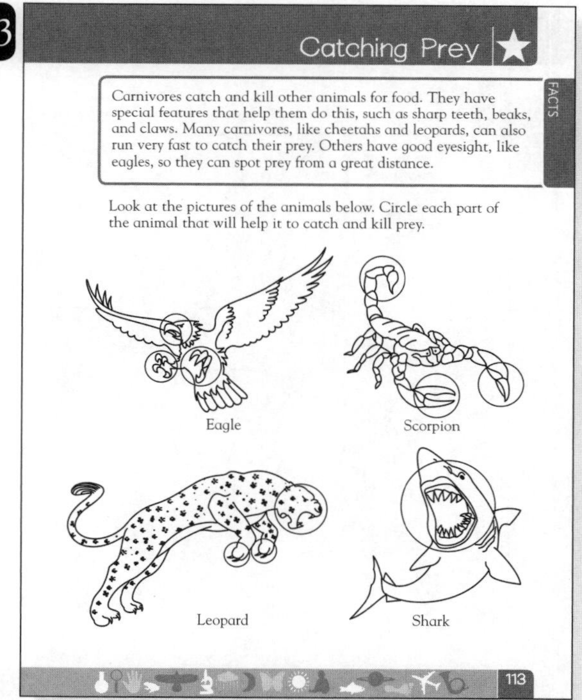

Catching Prey

FACTS

Carnivores catch and kill other animals for food. They have special features that help them do this, such as sharp teeth, beaks, and claws. Many carnivores, like cheetahs and leopards, can also run very fast to catch their prey. Others have good eyesight, like eagles, so they can spot prey from a great distance.

Look at the pictures of the animals below. Circle each part of the animal that will help it to catch and kill prey.

Ask your child the special features they have to help them "catch" and eat their food. (Possible answers are hands, to pick up food and use utensils; strong teeth for tearing and chewing food; good senses to see, smell, and taste delicious things (and avoid poisonous things).

114

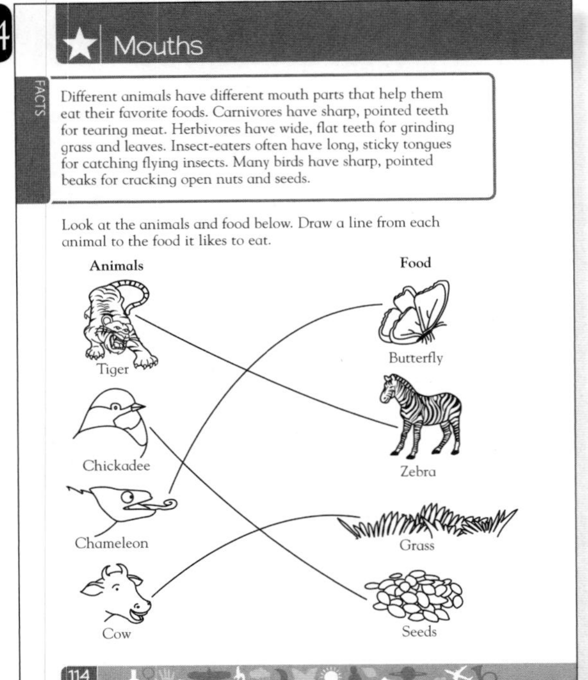

Mouths

FACTS

Different animals have different mouth parts that help them eat their favorite foods. Carnivores have sharp, pointed teeth for tearing meat. Herbivores have wide, flat teeth for grinding grass and leaves. Insect-eaters often have long, sticky tongues for catching flying insects. Many birds have sharp, pointed beaks for cracking open nuts and seeds.

Look at the animals and food below. Draw a line from each animal to the food it likes to eat.

114

Ask your child what features their mouth has to eat food. Point out that because we are omnivores, we have some sharp teeth like carnivores (incisors and canines) and some flat teeth like herbivores (molars). We also have a tongue and lips and saliva to help us eat the foods we need to survive.

115

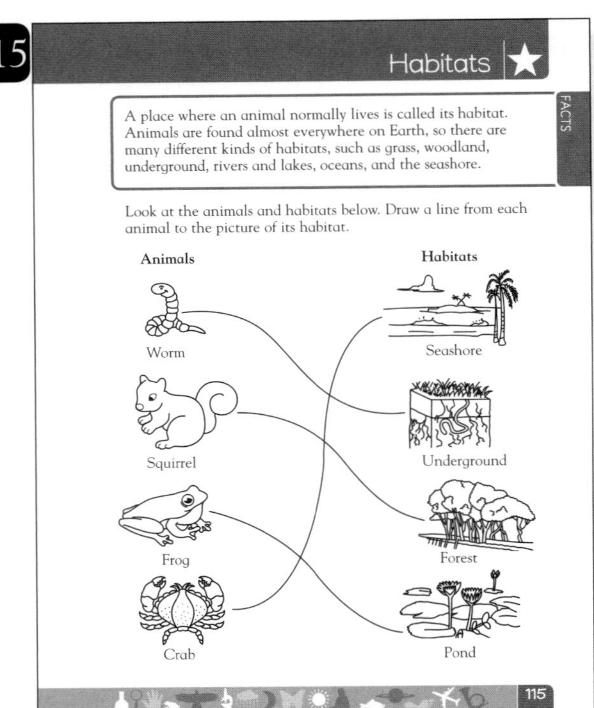

Habitats

FACTS

A place where an animal normally lives is called its habitat. Animals are found almost everywhere on Earth, so there are many different kinds of habitats, such as grass, woodland, underground, rivers and lakes, oceans, and the seashore.

Look at the animals and habitats below. Draw a line from each animal to the picture of its habitat.

115

This page discusses four common habitats: seashore, underground, forest, and pond. Discuss a few more habitats with your child, and have them name the plants and animals that live there. Suggestions include ocean (kelp, fish, sharks, etc.), desert (cactus, scorpions), and mountain (eagles).

116

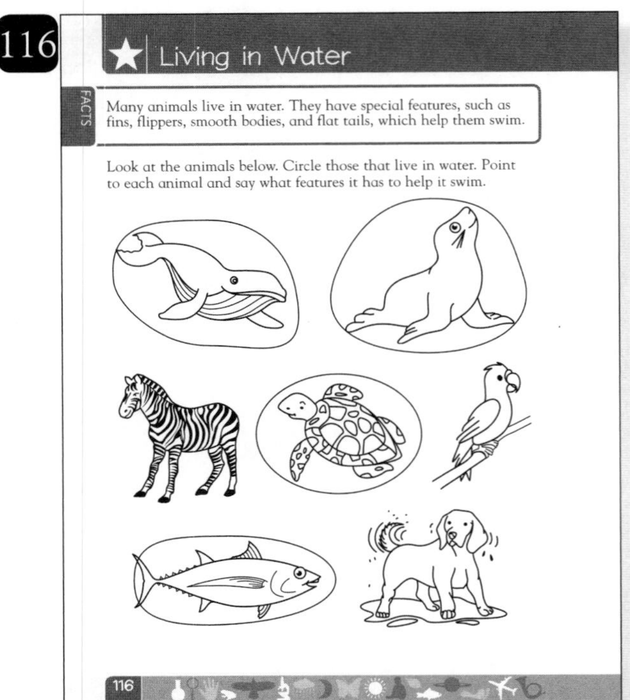

Living in Water

FACTS

Many animals live in water. They have special features, such as fins, flippers, smooth bodies, and flat tails, which help them swim.

Look at the animals below. Circle those that live in water. Point to each animal and say what features it has to help it swim.

116

People don't have flippers or fins but can swim. Ask your child what people do to swim like fish and other water animals. Possible answers are we move our arms and legs (like flippers), close our fingers (so our hands are like fins), and blow bubbles (so water stays out of our nose and mouth).

117

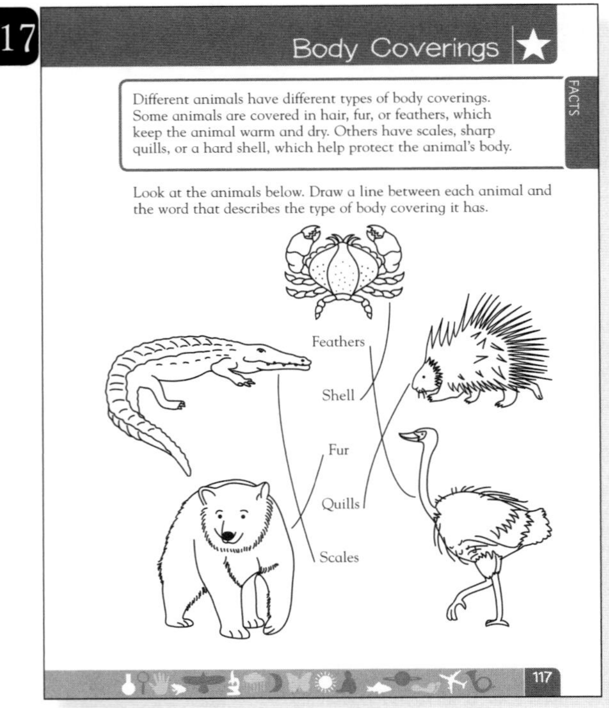

Body Coverings

FACTS

Different animals have different types of body coverings. Some animals are covered in hair, fur, or feathers, which keep the animal warm and dry. Others have scales, sharp quills, or a hard shell, which help protect the animal's body.

Look at the animals below. Draw a line between each animal and the word that describes the type of body covering it has.

117

Ask your child to describe the body coverings they see on themselves. Help point out the fine hairs that grow on the skin and that they trap heat to keep us warm. Sometimes that is not enough, though. People wear clothes to further protect themselves. Ask your child what they wear during each season to help protect their body.

118

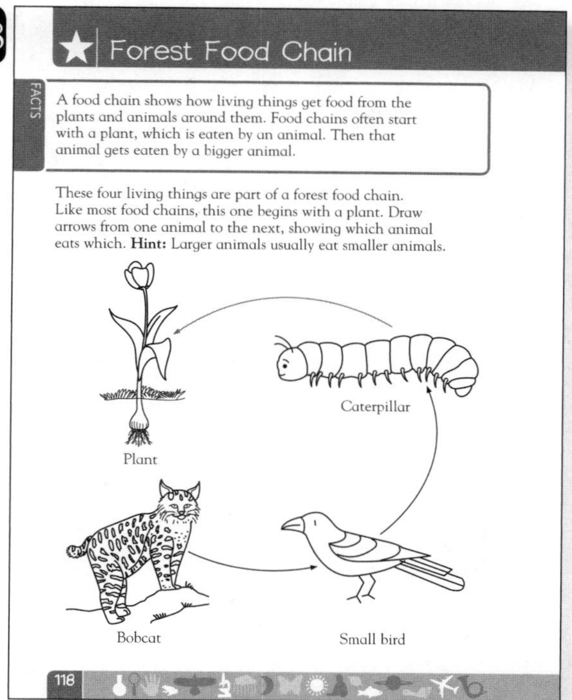

Forest Food Chain

FACTS

A food chain shows how living things get food from the plants and animals around them. Food chains often start with a plant, which is eaten by an animal. Then that animal gets eaten by a bigger animal.

These four living things are part of a forest food chain. Like most food chains, this one begins with a plant. Draw arrows from one animal to the next, showing which animal eats which. **Hint:** Larger animals usually eat smaller animals.

Plant

Caterpillar

Bobcat

Small bird

118

There is one last link on the food chain not mentioned in this activity: decomposers. Discuss with your child that dead plant and animal matter is broken down by the decomposers (fungi and bacteria). This enriches the soil for new plants to grow, starting the chain again.

119

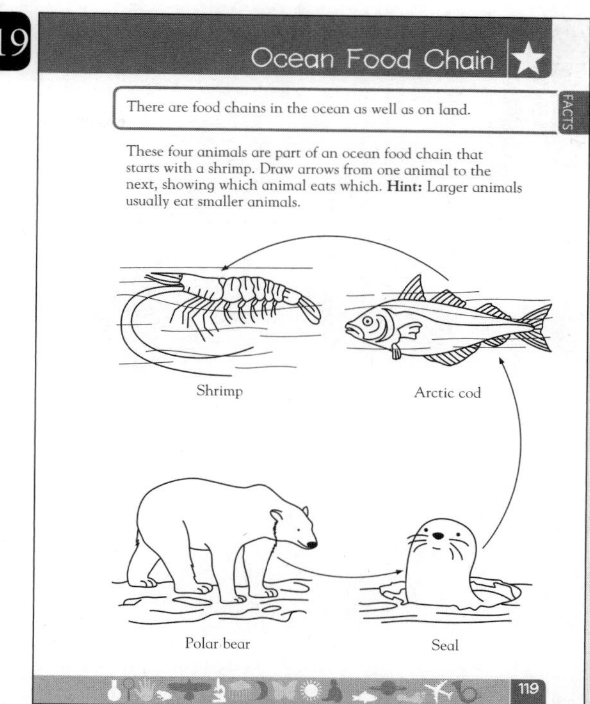

Ocean Food Chain

FACTS

There are food chains in the ocean as well as on land.

These four animals are part of an ocean food chain that starts with a shrimp. Draw arrows from one animal to the next, showing which animal eats which. **Hint:** Larger animals usually eat smaller animals.

Shrimp

Arctic cod

Polar bear

Seal

119

The ocean food chain starts with a small shrimp. However, shrimp feed on something even smaller. In the ocean's top layer—called the sunlit zone—the sun shines into the water and supports the growth of tiny plants known as phytoplankton. Many tiny sea creatures, including shrimp, feed on the phytoplankton.

120

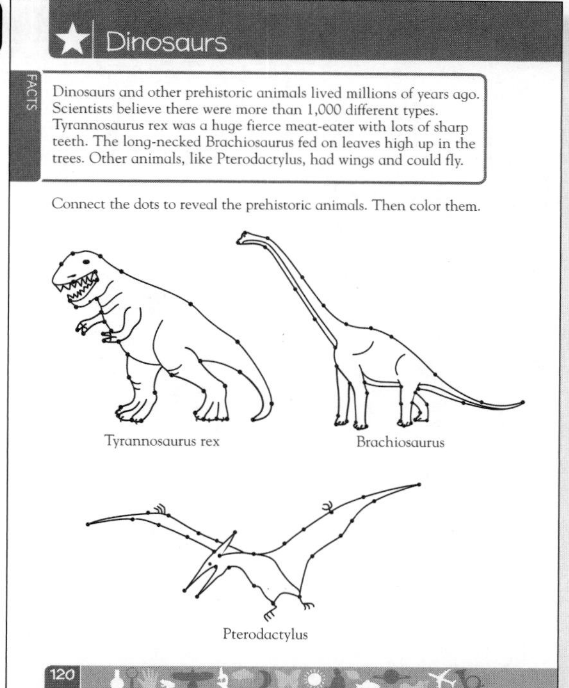

Dinosaurs

FACTS

Dinosaurs and other prehistoric animals lived millions of years ago. Scientists believe there were more than 1,000 different types. Tyrannosaurus rex was a huge fierce meat-eater with lots of sharp teeth. The long-necked Brachiosaurus fed on leaves high up in the trees. Other animals, like Pterodactylus, had wings and could fly.

Connect the dots to reveal the prehistoric animals. Then color them.

Tyrannosaurus rex

Brachiosaurus

Pterodactylus

120

There were thousands of species of dinosaur and other prehistoric creatures alive millions of years ago. Ask your child which dinosaurs they know of. Do they know Triceratops? Stegosaurus? Apatosaurus? Velociraptor? Together, find images of these dinosaurs online.

121

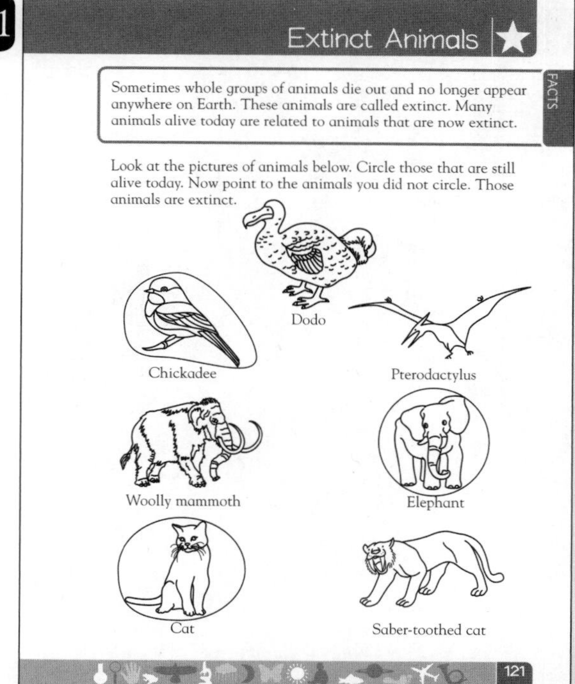

Extinct Animals

FACTS

Sometimes whole groups of animals die out and no longer appear anywhere on Earth. These animals are called extinct. Many animals alive today are related to animals that are now extinct.

Look at the pictures of animals below. Circle those that are still alive today. Now point to the animals you did not circle. Those animals are extinct.

Dodo

Chickadee

Pterodactylus

Woolly mammoth

Elephant

Cat

Saber-toothed cat

121

When animals, such as the dinosaurs, go extinct, they disappear from Earth forever. Ask your child what he or she thinks can make an animal go extinct. (Possible answers are habitat destruction, lack of safe food and water, and increase of predators.)

122

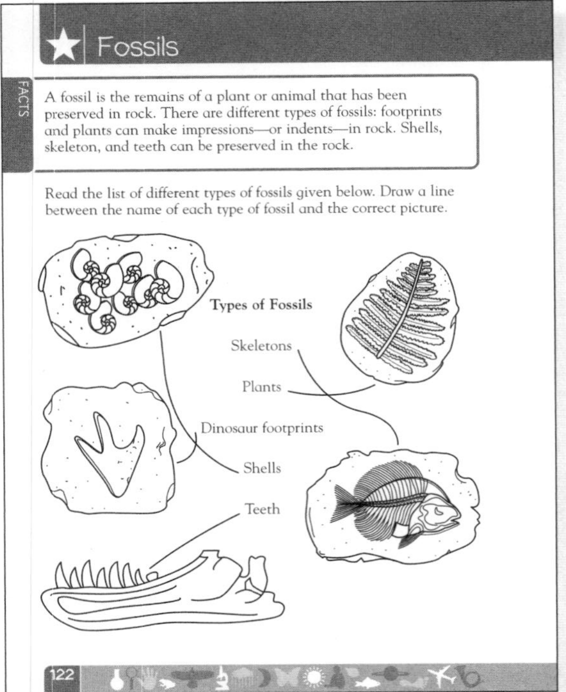

Fossils

FACTS

A fossil is the remains of a plant or animal that has been preserved in rock. There are different types of fossils: footprints and plants can make impressions—or indents—in rock. Shells, skeleton, and teeth can be preserved in the rock.

Read the list of different types of fossils given below. Draw a line between the name of each type of fossil and the correct picture.

Types of Fossils

Skeletons

Plants

Dinosaur footprints

Shells

Teeth

122

Discuss with your child what a scientist might learn from a fossil of a footprint. We can guess how big or small the animal was, or how old or young it was. We can guess by the shape of the footprint if the animal was a fast runner, a slow walker, or a swimmer.

123

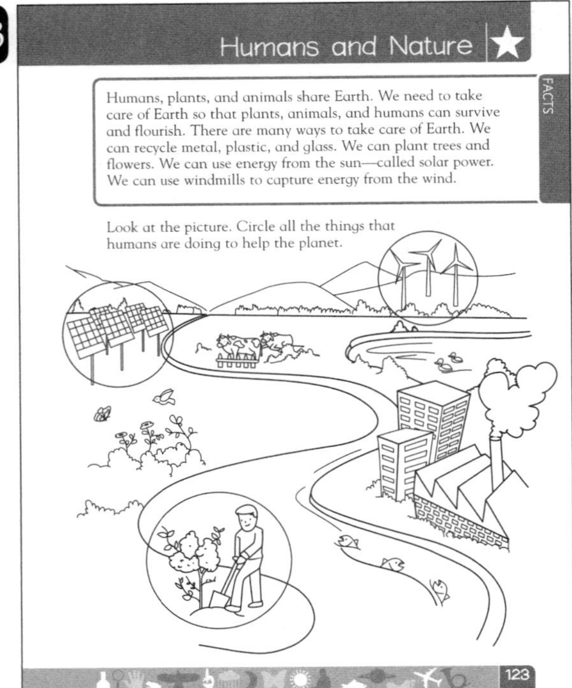

Humans and Nature

FACTS

Humans, plants, and animals share Earth. We need to take care of Earth so that plants, animals, and humans can survive and flourish. There are many ways to take care of Earth. We can recycle metal, plastic, and glass. We can plant trees and flowers. We can use energy from the sun—called solar power. We can use windmills to capture energy from the wind.

Look at the picture. Circle all the things that humans are doing to help the planet.

123

Ask your child how they can help the planet. Do they recycle metal, plastic, glass, and paper? Do they give away old toys and clothes so other people can use them? Do they reuse materials? For example, they can take old bottles, ribbons, bubble wrap, etc., and use them in craft projects.

124

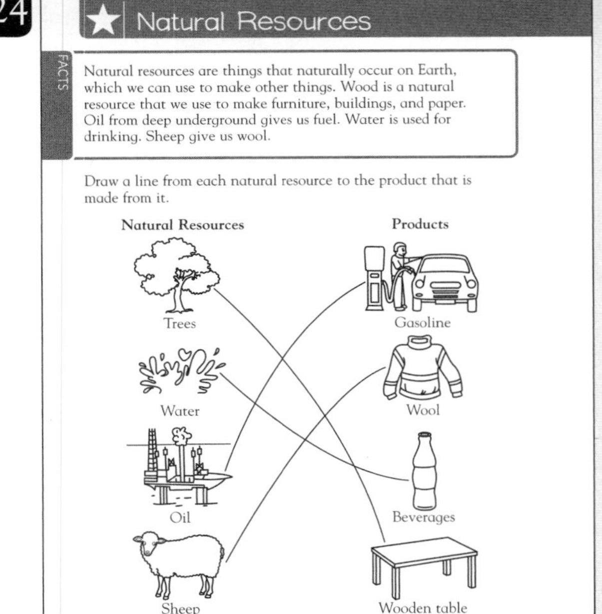

Natural Resources

FACTS

Natural resources are things that naturally occur on Earth, which we can use to make other things. Wood is a natural resource that we use to make furniture, buildings, and paper. Oil from deep underground gives us fuel. Water is used for drinking. Sheep give us wool.

Draw a line from each natural resource to the product that is made from it.

Natural Resources	Products
Trees	Gasoline
Water	Wool
Oil	Beverages
Sheep	Wooden table

124

Have children look around their home or their room. Ask them to identify things made from natural resources. Remind them that books and wooden furniture and some toys come from trees; wool comes from sheep; cotton comes from plants; etc.

125

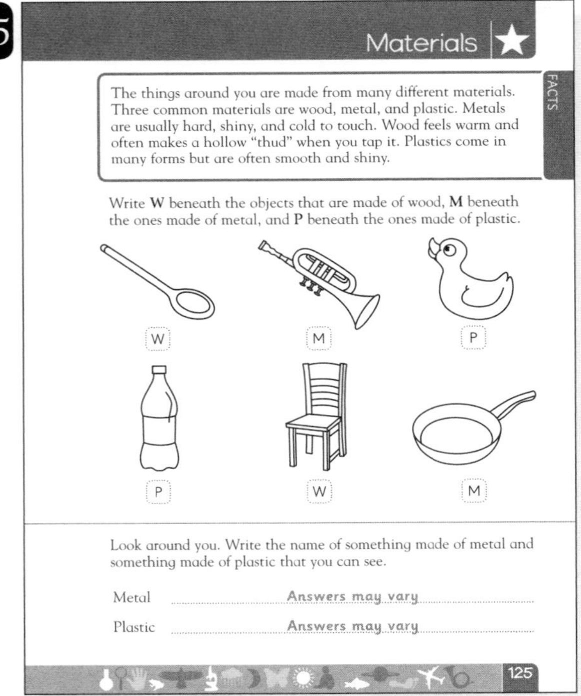

Materials

FACTS

The things around you are made from many different materials. Three common materials are wood, metal, and plastic. Metals are usually hard, shiny, and cold to touch. Wood feels warm and often makes a hollow "thud" when you tap it. Plastics come in many forms but are often smooth and shiny.

Write **W** beneath the objects that are made of wood, **M** beneath the ones made of metal, and **P** beneath the ones made of plastic.

W M P

P W M

Look around you. Write the name of something made of metal and something made of plastic that you can see.

Metal Answers may vary

Plastic Answers may vary

125

Continue this activity with your child. Have them pick out five to ten of their favorite items, and together, categorize them by material.

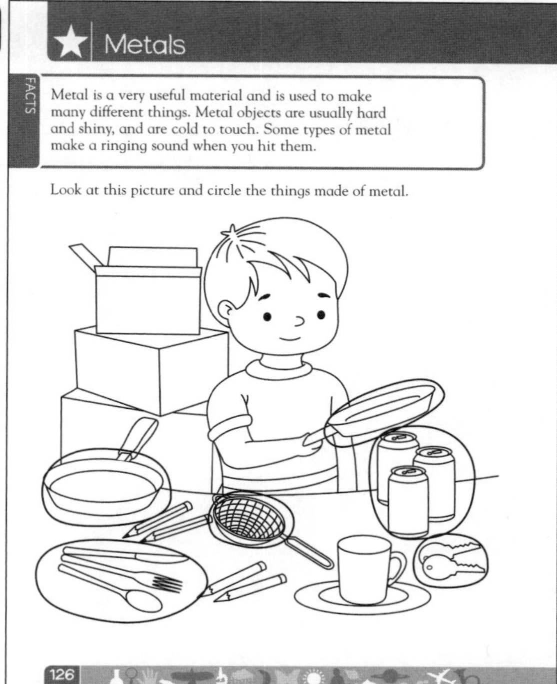

Metals

FACTS

Metal is a very useful material and is used to make many different things. Metal objects are usually hard and shiny, and are cold to touch. Some types of metal make a ringing sound when you hit them.

Look at this picture and circle the things made of metal.

126

Again, having your child find items that they know and use every day brings these concepts to life. Have your child find five to ten metal items from their home or room. Ask them why they think those items are made of metal, instead of another material.

127

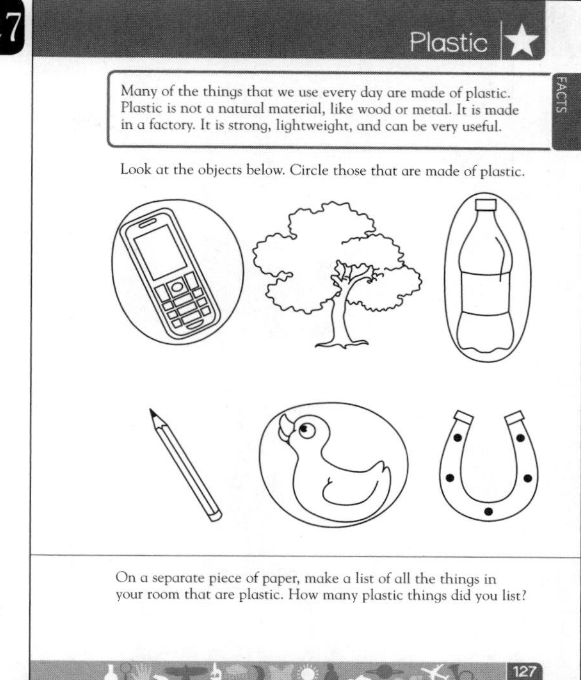

Plastic

FACTS

Many of the things that we use every day are made of plastic. Plastic is not a natural material, like wood or metal. It is made in a factory. It is strong, lightweight, and can be very useful.

Look at the objects below. Circle those that are made of plastic.

On a separate piece of paper, make a list of all the things in your room that are plastic. How many plastic things did you list?

127

Plastic is a material that people make. It does not come from nature. But it provides us with lots of useful things. Have your child point out five to ten items from your home that are very useful and made from plastic. Ask them if those items would be as useful if they were made from glass or metal.

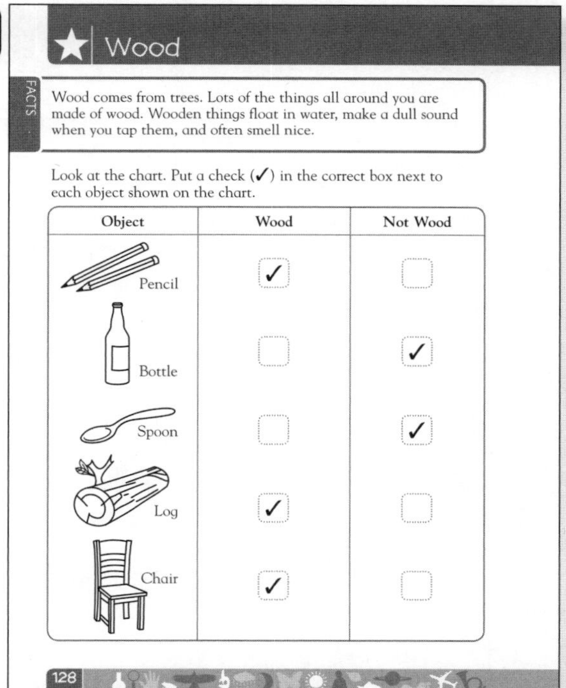

Wood

FACTS

Wood comes from trees. Lots of the things all around you are made of wood. Wooden things float in water, make a dull sound when you tap them, and often smell nice.

Look at the chart. Put a check (✓) in the correct box next to each object shown on the chart.

Object	Wood	Not Wood
Pencil	✓	
Bottle		✓
Spoon		✓
Log	✓	
Chair	✓	

128

Discuss the properties of wood with your child, and discuss that wood is used to build not only toys and furniture but also houses. Tell them that it is strong and can resist weather and wind, so it makes a good building material. Ask your child what other materials are needed to build a house.

Paper

FACTS

Paper is also made from wood. You use paper objects every day at home and at school. Books, newspapers, cardboard, notebooks, and tissues are some of the paper things that people use every day.

Look at the objects shown below. Circle the objects that are made of paper.

129

There are many types of paper. Collect different types of paper and discuss them with your child. Have your child point out the differences and similarities. For example, tissue paper and construction paper both crease when folded. But construction paper is heavier and thicker.

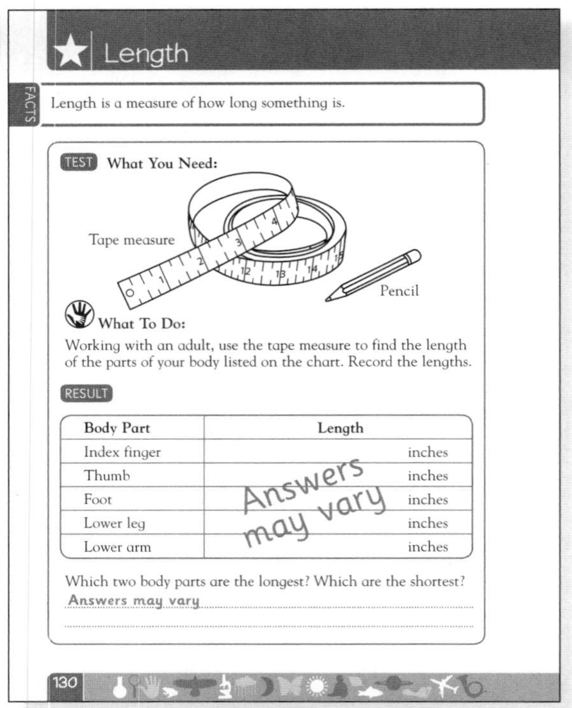
130

Length

FACTS

Length is a measure of how long something is.

TEST **What You Need:**

Tape measure

Pencil

What To Do:

Working with an adult, use the tape measure to find the length of the parts of your body listed on the chart. Record the lengths.

RESULT

Body Part	Length
Index finger	inches
Thumb	inches
Foot	inches
Lower leg	inches
Lower arm	inches

Answers may vary

Which two body parts are the longest? Which are the shortest?

Answers may vary

130

Discuss with your child how inches can be put into larger groups, such as feet and yards. Explain that there are 12 inches in a foot, and three feet in a yard. Then ask which unit (inch, foot, yard) is best when measuring their fingers, their bed, the front door, and the playground.

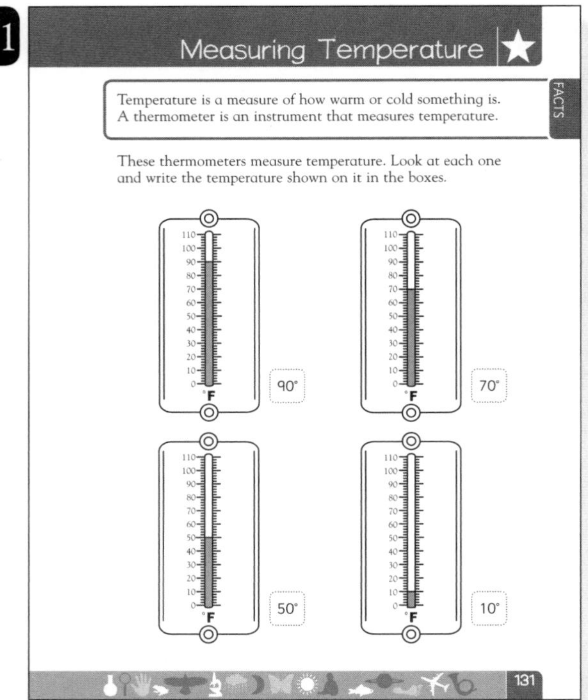
131

Measuring Temperature

FACTS

Temperature is a measure of how warm or cold something is. A thermometer is an instrument that measures temperature.

These thermometers measure temperature. Look at each one and write the temperature shown on it in the boxes.

90°

70°

50°

10°

131

If you have an outdoor thermometer, read it every day with your child, and explain that the mercury goes up when it is warm, and down when it is cold. If possible, put it in different locations each day to show the differences in temperature. You can also check daily temperatures online.

132

Height

FACTS

Height is a measure of how high or tall something is.

The heights of the four animals shown below are measured using a ruler. The seahorse is 4 in. tall. Write down the height of the other three animals.

4 in.

6 in.

3 in.

5 in.

132

Using a tape measure, have your child measure the height of each person in the household. Have each person take off his or her shoes and socks, and stand against the wall. Using a pencil, mark each family member's height on the wall and help your child measure from the mark to the ground.

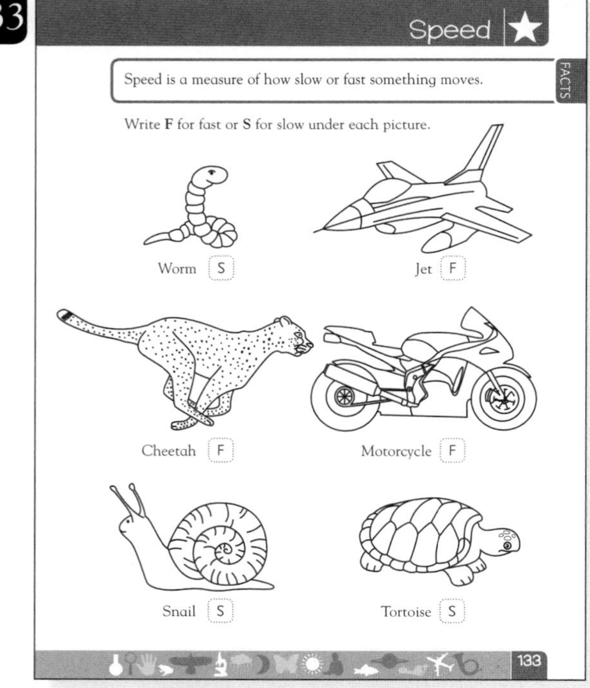
133

Speed

FACTS

Speed is a measure of how slow or fast something moves.

Write **F** for fast or **S** for slow under each picture.

Worm S

Jet F

Cheetah F

Motorcycle F

Snail S

Tortoise S

133

Get your child to pick four of their favorite wheeled toys. Line them up on the floor, and push! See which toy goes the fastest. Repeat two or three times, and record the fastest toy each time. Discuss with your child why that toy might be going fastest. Is it very light? Very heavy?

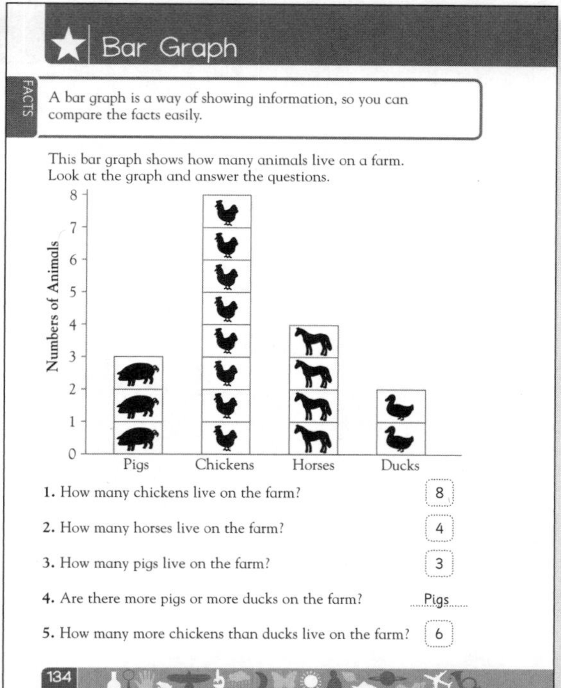
134

Bar Graph

FACTS

A bar graph is a way of showing information, so you can compare the facts easily.

This bar graph shows how many animals live on a farm. Look at the graph and answer the questions.

1. How many chickens live on the farm? 8
2. How many horses live on the farm? 4
3. How many pigs live on the farm? 3
4. Are there more pigs or more ducks on the farm? Pigs
5. How many more chickens than ducks live on the farm? 6

134

Have your child create a brand new bar graph. Choose 10 books and help your child categorize them. For example, how many books are about animals? How many are about sports? How many feature people? How many include insects? Help your child record this information on a bar graph.

135

My Day

FACTS

There are 24 hours in every day, and 60 minutes in each hour.

How do you spend the hours and minutes in your day? Write your name at the top of the chart.

For one day, ask your mom, dad, or other adult to time how long it takes you to do the activities shown on the chart below. Ask the person timing you to write on the chart the number of hours or minutes you spent on each activity.

My Day:	
Activities	**Time**
Eat breakfast	
Brush teeth	
Play	Answers may vary
Eat lunch	
Eat dinner	
Watch television	
Read	
Brush teeth/ Get ready for bed	

135

Discuss with your child that sleep is very important for learning. They cannot learn well if they have not had enough sleep the night before. A good night's sleep helps them remember what they have learned. Add "Sleep" to the chart on this page, and have your child fill in how long they sleep.

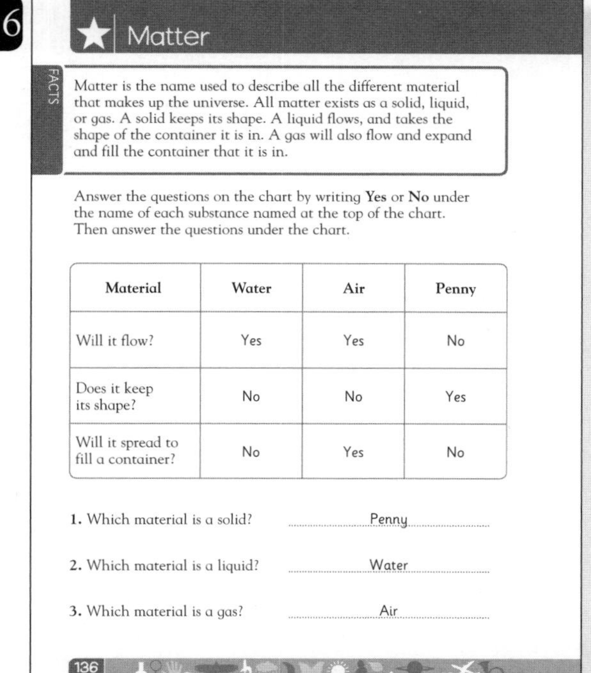
136

Matter

FACTS

Matter is the name used to describe all the different material that makes up the universe. All matter exists as a solid, liquid, or gas. A solid keeps its shape. A liquid flows, and takes the shape of the container it is in. A gas will also flow and expand and fill the container that it is in.

Answer the questions on the chart by writing **Yes** or **No** under the name of each substance named at the top of the chart. Then answer the questions under the chart.

Material	Water	Air	Penny
Will it flow?	Yes	Yes	No
Does it keep its shape?	No	No	Yes
Will it spread to fill a container?	No	Yes	No

1. Which material is a solid? Penny
2. Which material is a liquid? Water
3. Which material is a gas? Air

136

Have your child list their five favorite treats. Ask them if those treats are a solid, liquid, or gas. Discuss the crossover between states: chocolate is a solid that melts into a liquid, as are ice cream and ice pops. Discuss that those liquids will then become solid again when put back in the freezer.

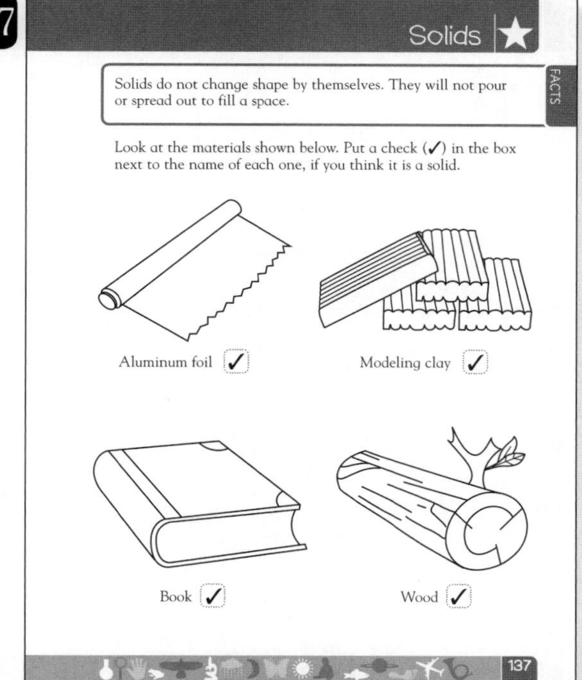
137

Solids

FACTS

Solids do not change shape by themselves. They will not pour or spread out to fill a space.

Look at the materials shown below. Put a check (✓) in the box next to the name of each one, if you think it is a solid.

Aluminum foil ✓

Modeling clay ✓

Book ✓

Wood ✓

137

Continue the exercise on this page, and have your child walk around the house naming the solids that they see. Have them record the solids they see on a chart.

138

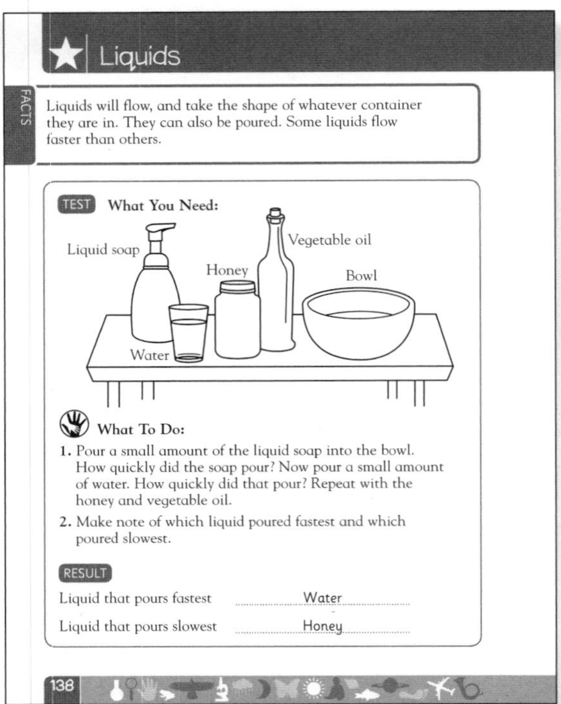

Liquids

FACTS

Liquids will flow, and take the shape of whatever container they are in. They can also be poured. Some liquids flow faster than others.

TEST **What You Need:**

What To Do:

1. Pour a small amount of the liquid soap into the bowl. How quickly did the soap pour? Now pour a small amount of water. How quickly did that pour? Repeat with the honey and vegetable oil.
2. Make note of which liquid poured fastest and which poured slowest.

RESULT

Liquid that pours fastest .... Water

Liquid that pours slowest .... Honey

138

Pour some water into a pitcher. Show your child that the water is now in the shape of the pitcher. Then pour the water into a bowl. What shape is the water now? Pour the water into a glass and then into a rectangular container. Reiterate that liquid changes its shape according to the vessel.

139

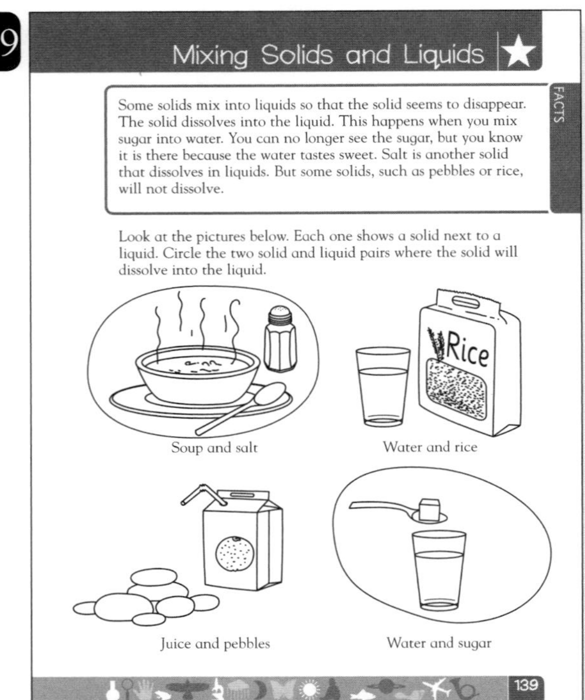

Mixing Solids and Liquids

FACTS

Some solids mix into liquids so that the solid seems to disappear. The solid dissolves into the liquid. This happens when you mix sugar into water. You can no longer see the sugar, but you know it is there because the water tastes sweet. Salt is another solid that dissolves in liquids. But some solids, such as pebbles or rice, will not dissolve.

Look at the pictures below. Each one shows a solid next to a liquid. Circle the two solid and liquid pairs where the solid will dissolve into the liquid.

Soup and salt

Water and rice

Juice and pebbles

Water and sugar

139

Have your child identify three solids that they would like to try to dissolve in water (such as sand, toys, pasta, cocoa powder, flour, dirt, etc.). One at a time, put the solid into a bowl of water and stir. Record the results on a chart.

140

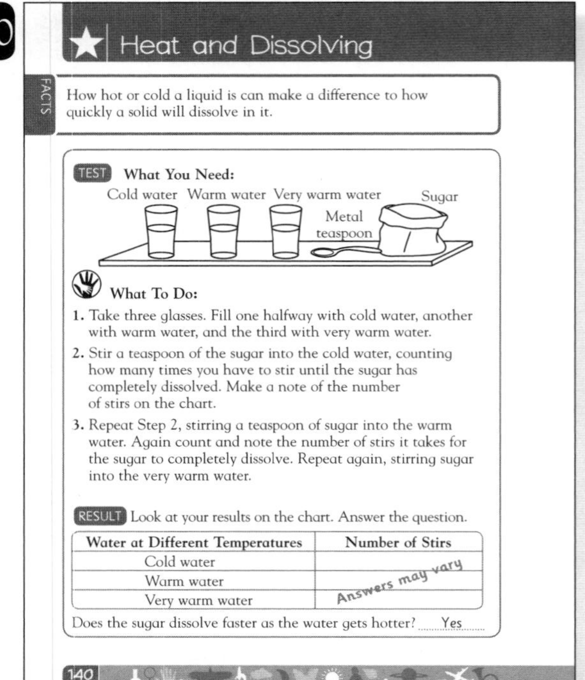

Heat and Dissolving

FACTS

How hot or cold a liquid is can make a difference to how quickly a solid will dissolve in it.

TEST **What You Need:**

What To Do:

1. Take three glasses. Fill one halfway with cold water, another with warm water, and the third with very warm water.
2. Stir a teaspoon of the sugar into the cold water, counting how many times you have to stir until the sugar has completely dissolved. Make a note of the number of stirs on the chart.
3. Repeat Step 2, stirring a teaspoon of sugar into the warm water. Again count and note the number of stirs it takes for the sugar to completely dissolve. Repeat again, stirring sugar into the very warm water.

RESULT Look at your results on the chart. Answer the question.

Water at Different Temperatures	Number of Stirs
Cold water	
Warm water	Answers may vary
Very warm water	

Does the sugar dissolve faster as the water gets hotter? ...... Yes

140

Reward your little scientist by repeating this activity using powdered hot cocoa or soup or other dissolvable treat. Discuss at which temperature the items dissolve best, and then help your child prepare their treat.

141

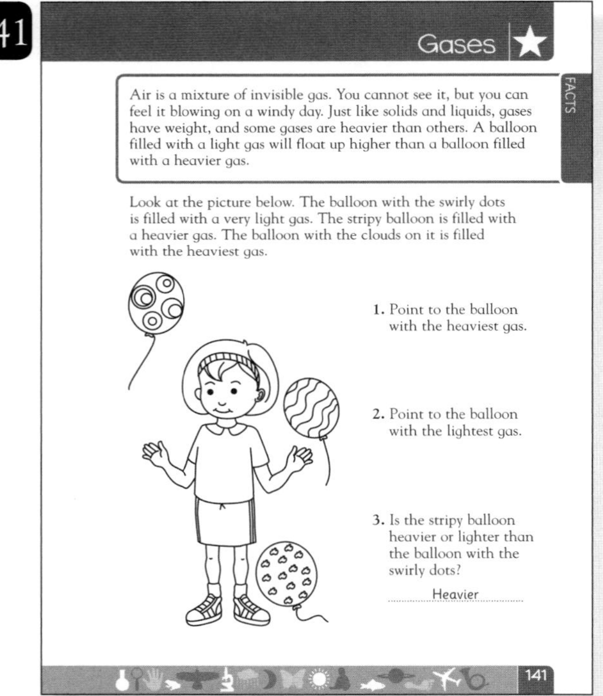

Gases

FACTS

Air is a mixture of invisible gas. You cannot see it, but you can feel it blowing on a windy day. Just like solids and liquids, gases have weight, and some gases are heavier than others. A balloon filled with a light gas will float up higher than a balloon filled with a heavier gas.

Look at the picture below. The balloon with the swirly dots is filled with a very light gas. The stripy balloon is filled with a heavier gas. The balloon with the clouds on it is filled with the heaviest gas.

1. Point to the balloon with the heaviest gas.
2. Point to the balloon with the lightest gas.
3. Is the stripy balloon heavier or lighter than the balloon with the swirly dots?

   .... Heavier

141

The concept of gas can be abstract for a first grader. Blowing up balloons is a helpful way of showing your child how gas (the air from your lungs) will fill a balloon, not just pool at the bottom, the way a liquid would (as with water balloons). Bubbles are also a good example.

142

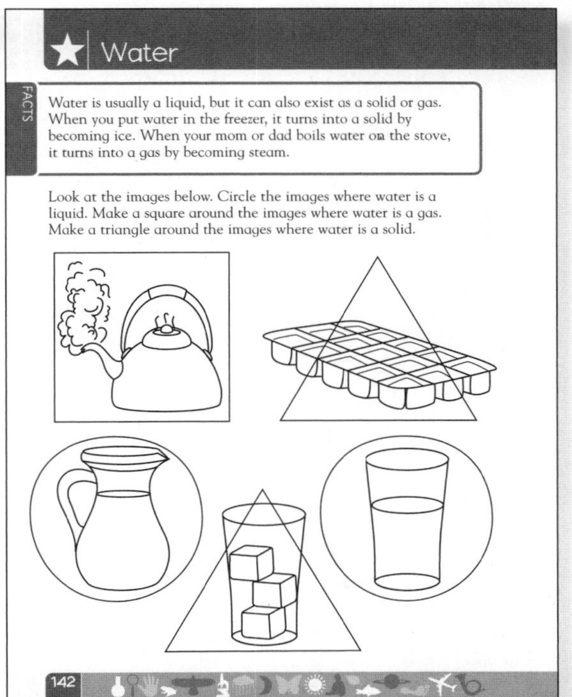

Water

FACTS

Water is usually a liquid, but it can also exist as a solid or gas. When you put water in the freezer, it turns into a solid by becoming ice. When your mom or dad boils water on the stove, it turns into a gas by becoming steam.

Look at the images below. Circle the images where water is a liquid. Make a square around the images where water is a gas. Make a triangle around the images where water is a solid.

142

To illustrate water becoming a solid, have your child choose a few small freezer-safe containers. Help them pour some water into each one, and place them in the freezer. After three or four hours, pull the containers out, and discuss what happened to the water.

143

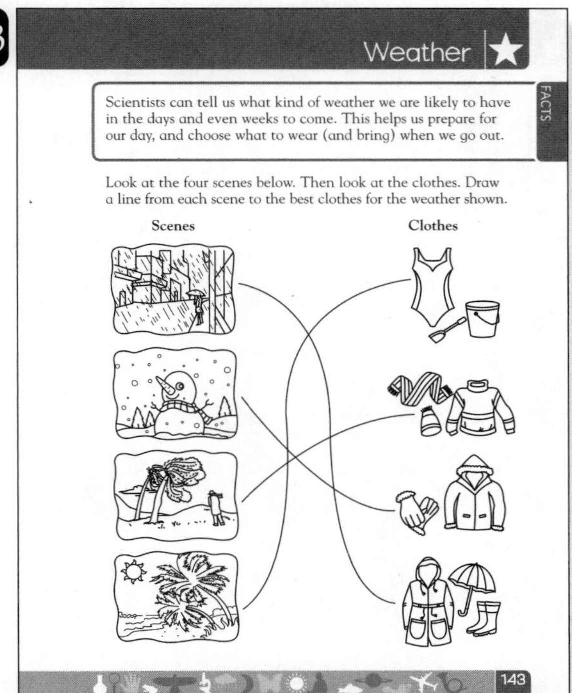

Weather

FACTS

Scientists can tell us what kind of weather we are likely to have in the days and even weeks to come. This helps us prepare for our day, and choose what to wear (and bring) when we go out.

Look at the four scenes below. Then look at the clothes. Draw a line from each scene to the best clothes for the weather shown.

Scenes **Clothes**

143

Weather changes daily around the world. With your child look in the newspaper or online to find out the weather in five cities around the world. Discuss what preparations people in each city will need to make for the day's weather. Will anyone need an umbrella? Snow boots? Sunglasses?

144

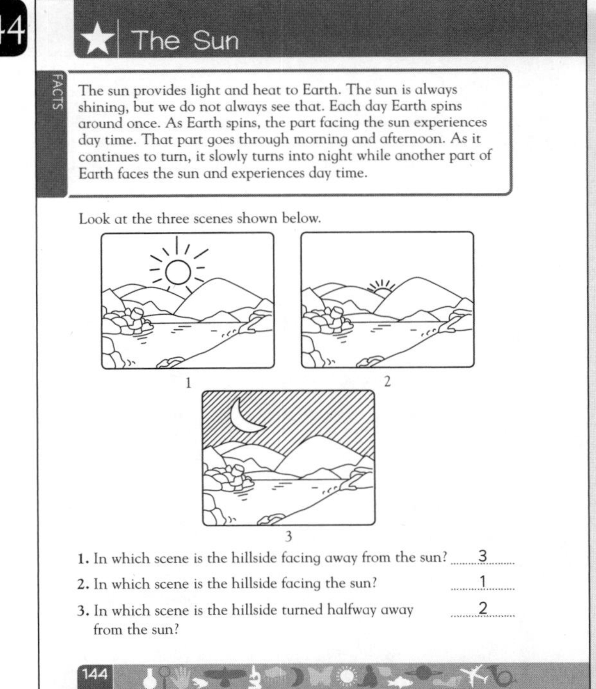

The Sun

FACTS

The sun provides light and heat to Earth. The sun is always shining, but we do not always see that. Each day Earth spins around once. As Earth spins, the part facing the sun experiences day time. That part goes through morning and afternoon. As it continues to turn, it slowly turns into night while another part of Earth faces the sun and experiences day time.

Look at the three scenes shown below.

1 2

3

1. In which scene is the hillside facing away from the sun? 3
2. In which scene is the hillside facing the sun? 1
3. In which scene is the hillside turned halfway away from the sun? 2

144

Discuss with your child that the sun is always shining, and when it is daytime at home, it's night in other parts of the world. Pick five cities around the world (perhaps one or two on each continent), and research what time it is in each place and what activities people there are doing.

145

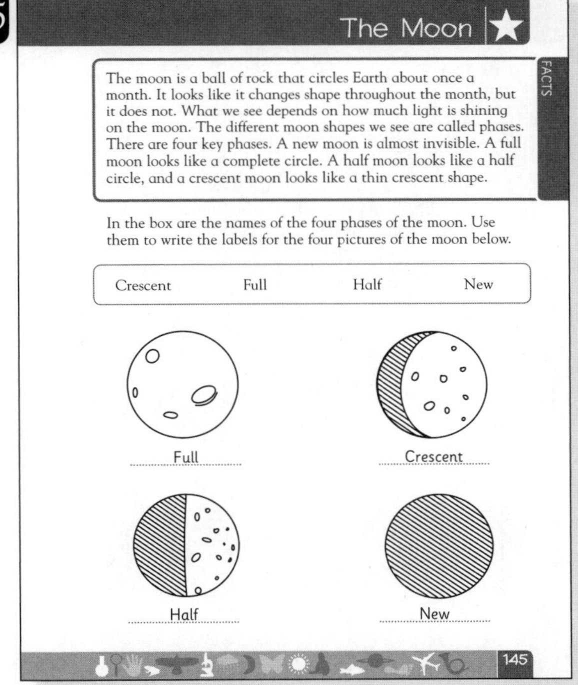

The Moon

FACTS

The moon is a ball of rock that circles Earth about once a month. It looks like it changes shape throughout the month, but it does not. What we see depends on how much light is shining on the moon. The different moon shapes we see are called phases. There are four key phases. A new moon is almost invisible. A full moon looks like a complete circle. A half moon looks like a half circle, and a crescent moon looks like a thin crescent shape.

In the box are the names of the four phases of the moon. Use them to write the labels for the four pictures of the moon below.

Crescent Full Half New

Full Crescent

Half New

145

The light we see from the moon is actually light from the sun reflecting off the moon's surface. When part of the moon is dark, the Earth is getting in the way of the sun's light reaching the moon. Earth is casting a shadow on the moon. Discuss this with your child.

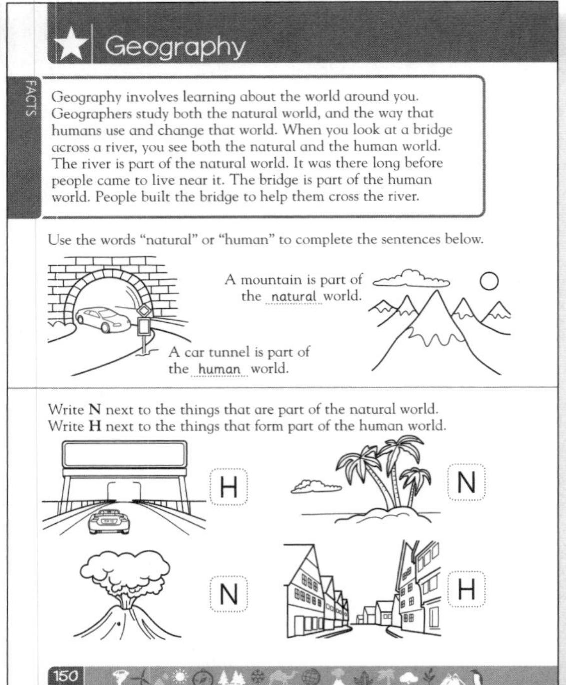

★ Geography

FACTS

Geography involves learning about the world around you. Geographers study both the natural world, and the way that humans use and change that world. When you look at a bridge across a river, you see both the natural and the human world. The river is part of the natural world. It was there long before people came to live near it. The bridge is part of the human world. People built the bridge to help them cross the river.

Use the words "natural" or "human" to complete the sentences below.

A mountain is part of the natural world.

A car tunnel is part of the human world.

Write **N** next to the things that are part of the natural world.
Write **H** next to the things that form part of the human world.

H N N H

150

As an extension to this activity, look at pictures in books, magazines, or on the internet with your child. Point to objects and ask him or her whether each one is part of the natural world or has been made by humans.

151

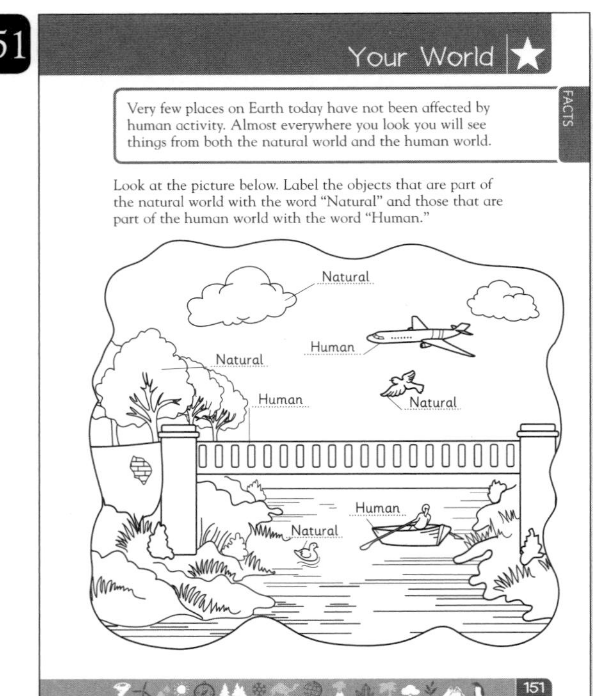

Your World ★

FACTS

Very few places on Earth today have not been affected by human activity. Almost everywhere you look you will see things from both the natural world and the human world.

Look at the picture below. Label the objects that are part of the natural world with the word "Natural" and those that are part of the human world with the word "Human."

151

You can continue this activity next time you go outside with your child. Point at buildings, cars, trees, or birds and ask whether they are part of the natural or the human world.

152

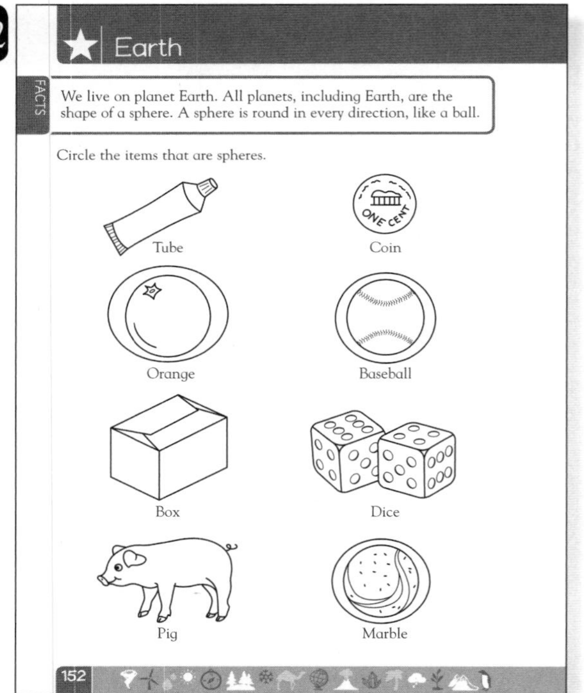

★ Earth

FACTS

We live on planet Earth. All planets, including Earth, are the shape of a sphere. A sphere is round in every direction, like a ball.

Circle the items that are spheres.

152

Combine this exercise with that on the previous page by asking your child whether the spherical objects mentioned on this page—Earth, orange, baseball, and marble—are natural or man-made.

153

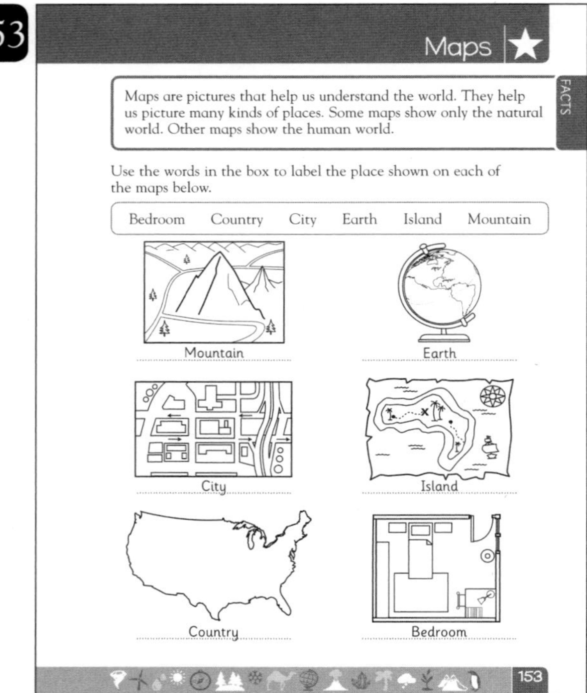

Maps ★

FACTS

Maps are pictures that help us understand the world. They help us picture many kinds of places. Some maps show only the natural world. Other maps show the human world.

Use the words in the box to label the place shown on each of the maps below.

Bedroom Country City Earth Island Mountain

153

You could reinforce the idea of maps by sketching a "treasure map" of your home, drawing crosses on places where you have hidden objects for your child to find.

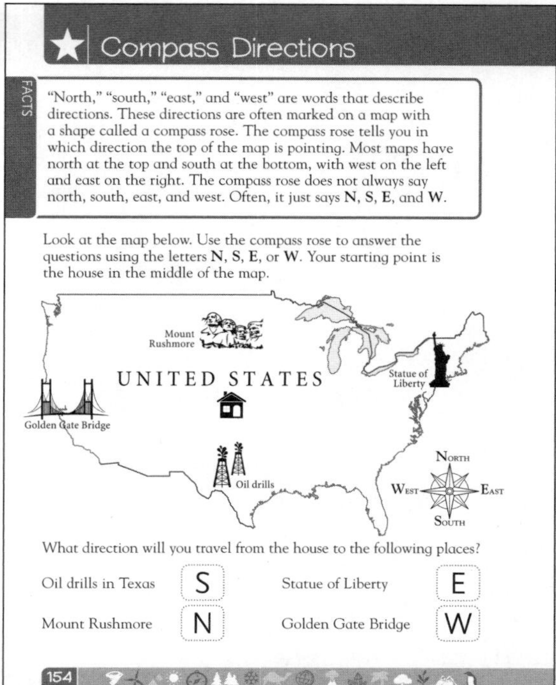

Compass Directions

FACTS

"North," "south," "east," and "west" are words that describe directions. These directions are often marked on a map with a shape called a compass rose. The compass rose tells you in which direction the top of the map is pointing. Most maps have north at the top and south at the bottom, with west on the left and east on the right. The compass rose does not always say north, south, east, and west. Often, it just says **N**, **S**, **E**, and **W**.

Look at the map below. Use the compass rose to answer the questions using the letters **N**, **S**, **E**, or **W**. Your starting point is the house in the middle of the map.

What direction will you travel from the house to the following places?

Oil drills in Texas S

Statue of Liberty E

Mount Rushmore N

Golden Gate Bridge W

154

Sketch a compass rose and ask your child to complete it by adding the directions, using **N** for "north," **S** for "south," and so on. Look outside a window together and tell your child which direction you are looking at, if you know. Having a compass with you will be handy!

155

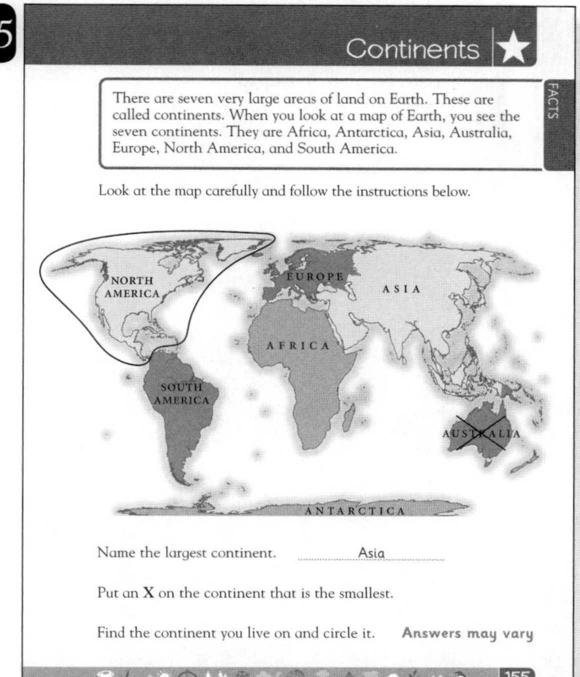

Continents

FACTS

There are seven very large areas of land on Earth. These are called continents. When you look at a map of Earth, you see the seven continents. They are Africa, Antarctica, Asia, Australia, Europe, North America, and South America.

Look at the map carefully and follow the instructions below.

Name the largest continent. Asia

Put an **X** on the continent that is the smallest.

Find the continent you live on and circle it. **Answers may vary**

155

As an extra activity after completing this page, ask your child if he or she can recall the names of any of the seven continents. If this is too difficult, offer clues such as, "Kangaroos and koalas come from this continent."

156

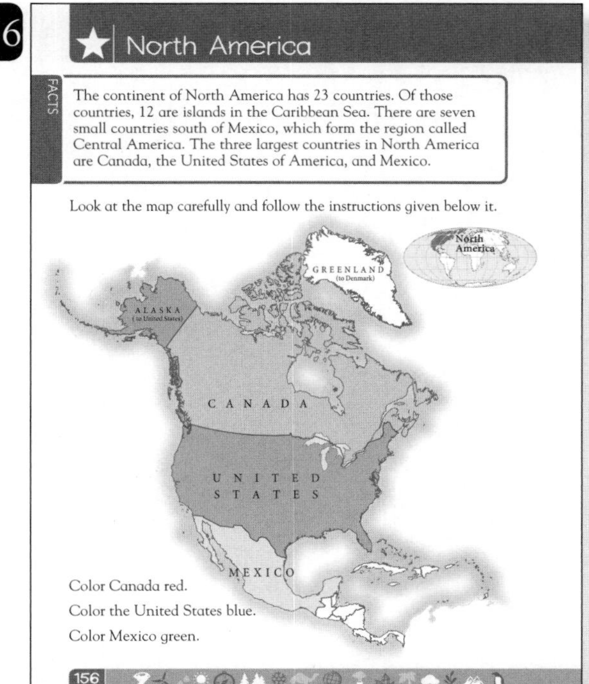

North America

FACTS

The continent of North America has 23 countries. Of those countries, 12 are islands in the Caribbean Sea. There are seven small countries south of Mexico, which form the region called Central America. The three largest countries in North America are Canada, the United States of America, and Mexico.

Look at the map carefully and follow the instructions given below it.

Color Canada red.

Color the United States blue.

Color Mexico green.

156

After this exercise, talk about some of the other countries in North America, mentioning well-known natural or man-made landmarks you may know about, such as the Panama Canal, or the Rio Grande River.

157

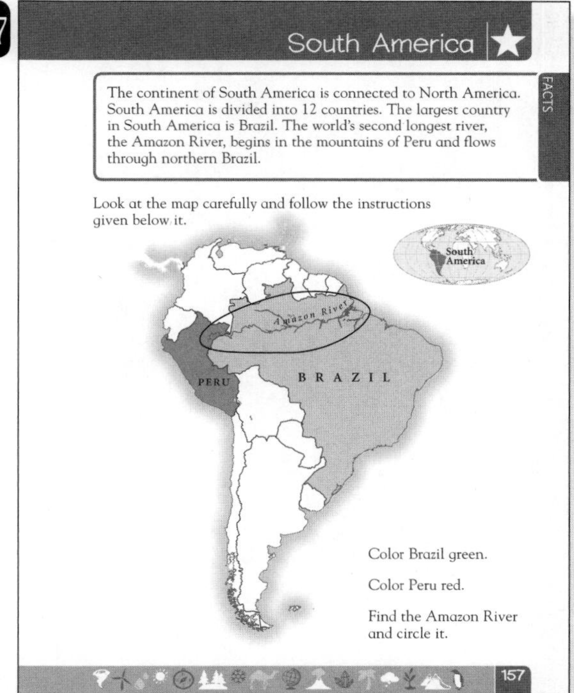

South America

FACTS

The continent of South America is connected to North America. South America is divided into 12 countries. The largest country in South America is Brazil. The world's second longest river, the Amazon River, begins in the mountains of Peru and flows through northern Brazil.

Look at the map carefully and follow the instructions given below it.

Color Brazil green.

Color Peru red.

Find the Amazon River and circle it.

157

You could also tell your child about the Amazon rain forest and how it is home to a great many animals and plants. You could also mention other countries in South America, such as Argentina and Chile, not labeled on the page.

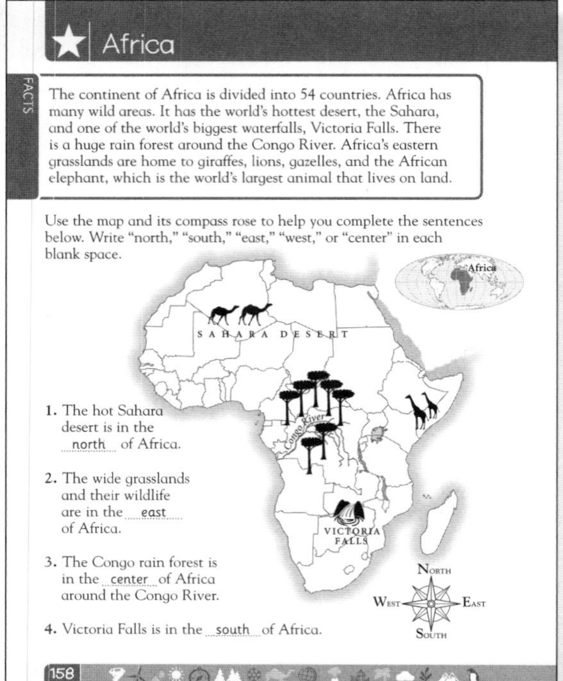

Africa

FACTS

The continent of Africa is divided into 54 countries. Africa has many wild areas. It has the world's hottest desert, the Sahara, and one of the world's biggest waterfalls, Victoria Falls. There is a huge rain forest around the Congo River. Africa's eastern grasslands are home to giraffes, lions, gazelles, and the African elephant, which is the world's largest animal that lives on land.

Use the map and its compass rose to help you complete the sentences below. Write "north," "south," "east," "west," or "center" in each blank space.

1. The hot Sahara desert is in the north of Africa.
2. The wide grasslands and their wildlife are in the east of Africa.
3. The Congo rain forest is in the center of Africa around the Congo River.
4. Victoria Falls is in the south of Africa.

158

It will be interesting to share with your child that some of the most famous animals come from Africa, including rhinoceroses, lions, giraffes, African elephants, and more. Do you have friends or family from Africa? Discuss with your child.

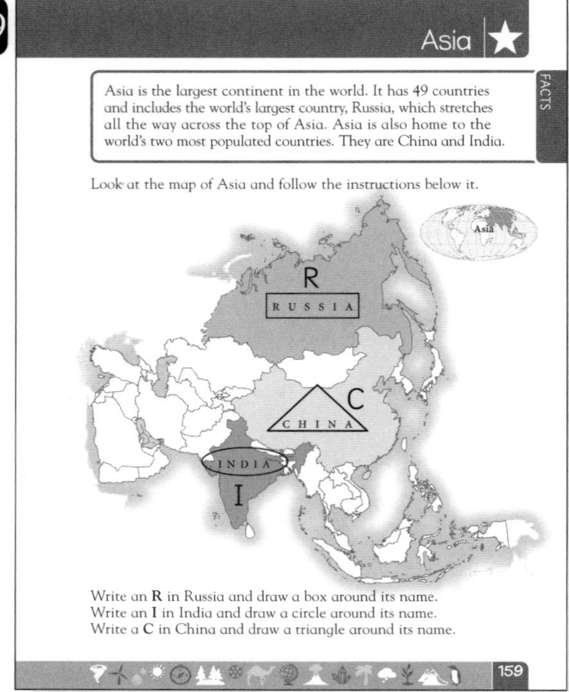

Asia

FACTS

Asia is the largest continent in the world. It has 49 countries and includes the world's largest country, Russia, which stretches all the way across the top of Asia. Asia is also home to the world's two most populated countries. They are China and India.

Look at the map of Asia and follow the instructions below it.

Write an **R** in Russia and draw a box around its name.
Write an **I** in India and draw a circle around its name.
Write a **C** in China and draw a triangle around its name.

159

Point out to your child that Russia is a country that spans both Europe and Asia. You could also point out other regions of Asia, such as the Middle East, Central Asia, and Southeast Asia. Do you have friends or family from Asia? Discuss with your child.

160

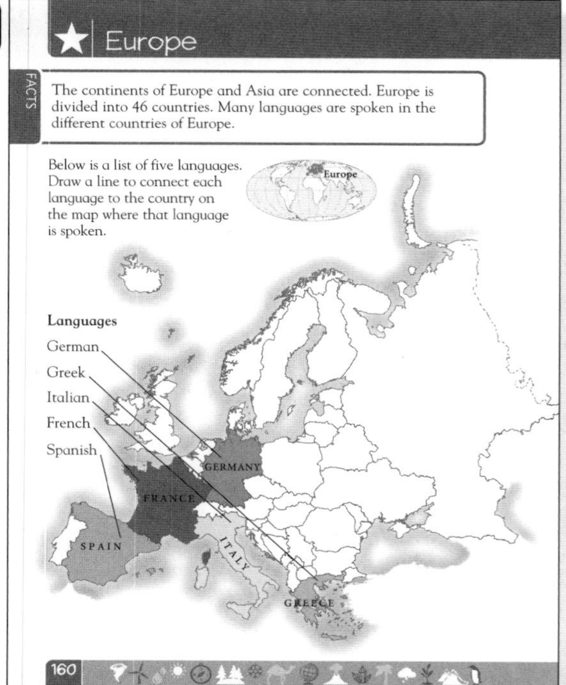

Europe

FACTS

The continents of Europe and Asia are connected. Europe is divided into 46 countries. Many languages are spoken in the different countries of Europe.

Below is a list of five languages. Draw a line to connect each language to the country on the map where that language is spoken.

160

Do you have family or friends from Europe? Discuss with your child that many people from Europe came to settle in the United States.

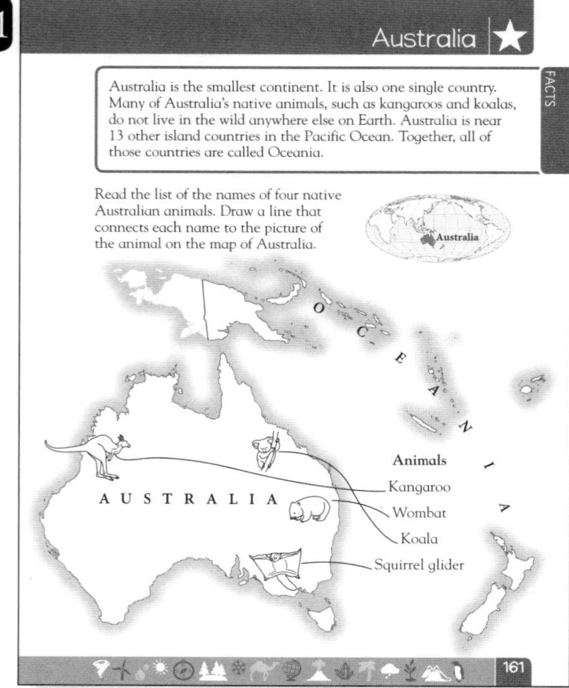

Australia

FACTS

Australia is the smallest continent. It is also one single country. Many of Australia's native animals, such as kangaroos and koalas, do not live in the wild anywhere else on Earth. Australia is near 13 other island countries in the Pacific Ocean. Together, all of those countries are called Oceania.

Read the list of the names of four native Australian animals. Draw a line that connects each name to the picture of the animal on the map of Australia.

161

You could mention to your child that marsupials, such as wombats, kangaroos, and koalas, carry and protect their young in a pouch of skin, unlike the more familiar mammals, such as cats, dogs, and horses, he or she may know.

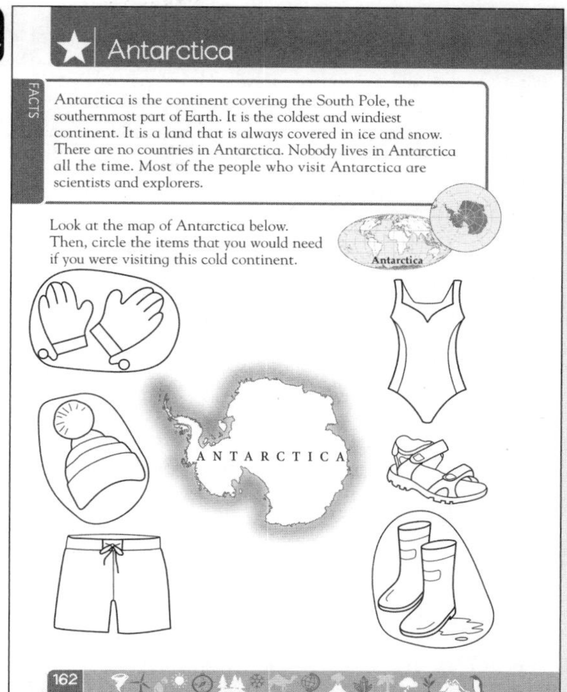

Antarctica

FACTS

Antarctica is the continent covering the South Pole, the southernmost part of Earth. It is the coldest and windiest continent. It is a land that is always covered in ice and snow. There are no countries in Antarctica. Nobody lives in Antarctica all the time. Most of the people who visit Antarctica are scientists and explorers.

Look at the map of Antarctica below. Then, circle the items that you would need if you were visiting this cold continent.

Your child may know very little about Antarctica. Explain that it was discovered by explorers less than 200 years ago, and that scientists from around the world travel there each year to do research.

163

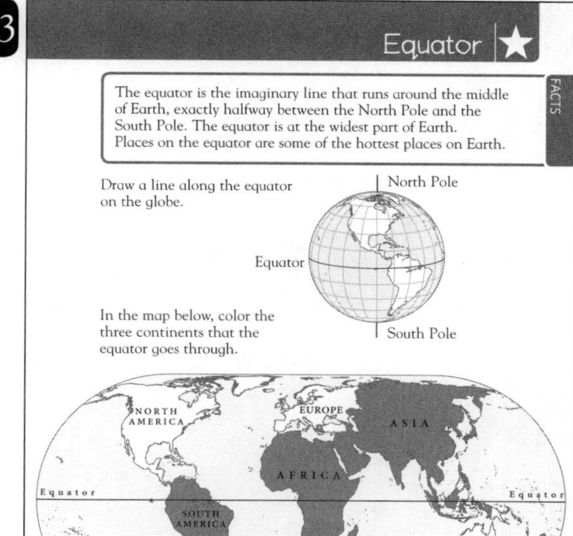

Equator

FACTS

The equator is the imaginary line that runs around the middle of Earth, exactly halfway between the North Pole and the South Pole. The equator is at the widest part of Earth. Places on the equator are some of the hottest places on Earth.

Draw a line along the equator on the globe.

In the map below, color the three continents that the equator goes through.

You could tell your child that because the equator is hot all year round, there are no distinct seasons there. No spring, summer, fall, or winter. However, there are still cold places, such as high up in the snow-capped mountains of Ecuador.

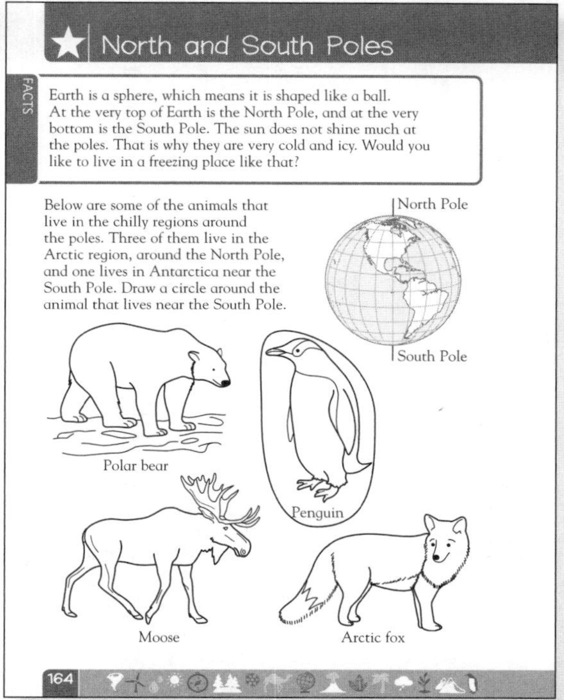

North and South Poles

FACTS

Earth is a sphere, which means it is shaped like a ball. At the very top of Earth is the North Pole, and at the very bottom is the South Pole. The sun does not shine much at the poles. That is why they are very cold and icy. Would you like to live in a freezing place like that?

Below are some of the animals that live in the chilly regions around the poles. Three of them live in the Arctic region, around the North Pole, and one lives in Antarctica near the South Pole. Draw a circle around the animal that lives near the South Pole.

Share with your child that the North Pole is in the middle of the ice-covered Arctic Ocean, while the South Pole lies on land, on the continent of Antarctica. The nearest land to the North Pole is more than 400 miles away!

Oceans

FACTS

Most of Earth is covered by water, and most of Earth's water is found in oceans. Oceans are the largest bodies of water in the world. There are five oceans on Earth—the Pacific Ocean, the Atlantic Ocean, the Indian Ocean, the Arctic Ocean, and the Southern Ocean.

Circle the animals that live in the ocean.

Ask your child if he or she knows the difference between freshwater and saltwater. If you have visited the beach, ask him or her to describe the animals and plants that live in and around the sea.

166

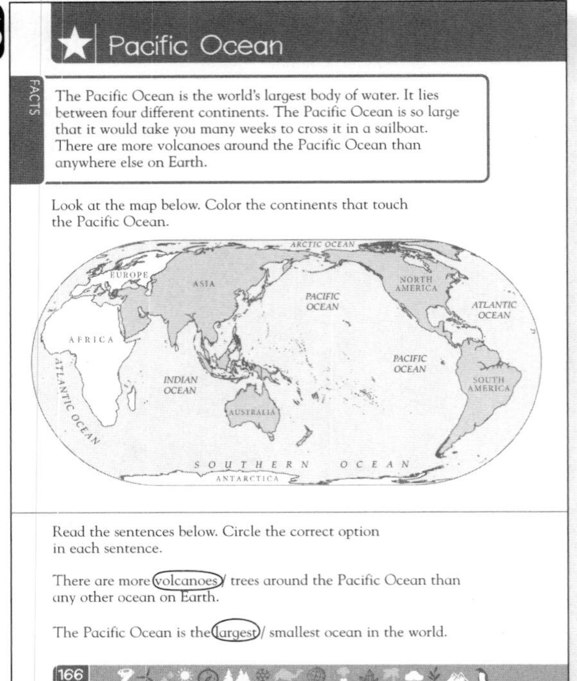
Pacific Ocean

FACTS

The Pacific Ocean is the world's largest body of water. It lies between four different continents. The Pacific Ocean is so large that it would take you many weeks to cross it in a sailboat. There are more volcanoes around the Pacific Ocean than anywhere else on Earth.

Look at the map below. Color the continents that touch the Pacific Ocean.

Read the sentences below. Circle the correct option in each sentence.

There are more volcanoes / trees around the Pacific Ocean than any other ocean on Earth.

The Pacific Ocean is the largest / smallest ocean in the world.

Your child may be interested to know that the Pacific Ocean contains the Mariana Trench. With a depth of almost 7 miles, the trench is the deepest part in all of the world's oceans.

167

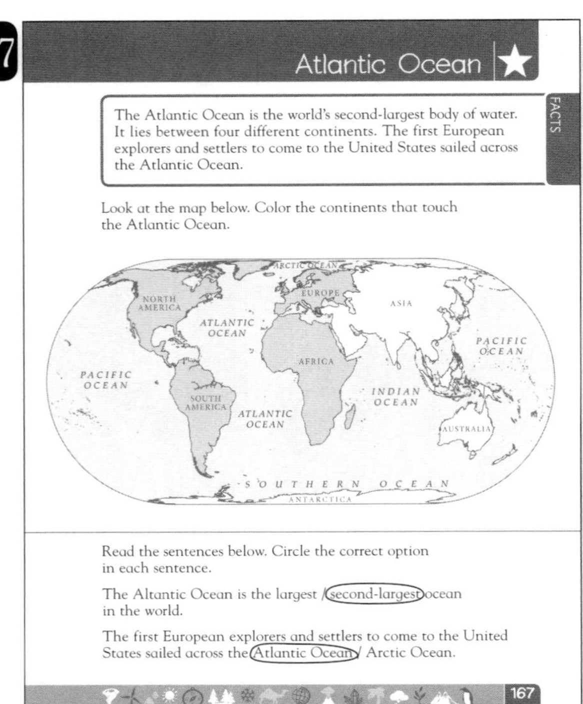
Atlantic Ocean

FACTS

The Atlantic Ocean is the world's second-largest body of water. It lies between four different continents. The first European explorers and settlers to come to the United States sailed across the Atlantic Ocean.

Look at the map below. Color the continents that touch the Atlantic Ocean.

Read the sentences below. Circle the correct option in each sentence.

The Altantic Ocean is the largest / second-largest ocean in the world.

The first European explorers and settlers to come to the United States sailed across the Atlantic Ocean / Arctic Ocean.

After completing the activity on this page, cover the book and ask your child if he or she can remember the names of three of the four continents that touch the Atlantic Ocean. Help your child if he or she cannot remember.

168

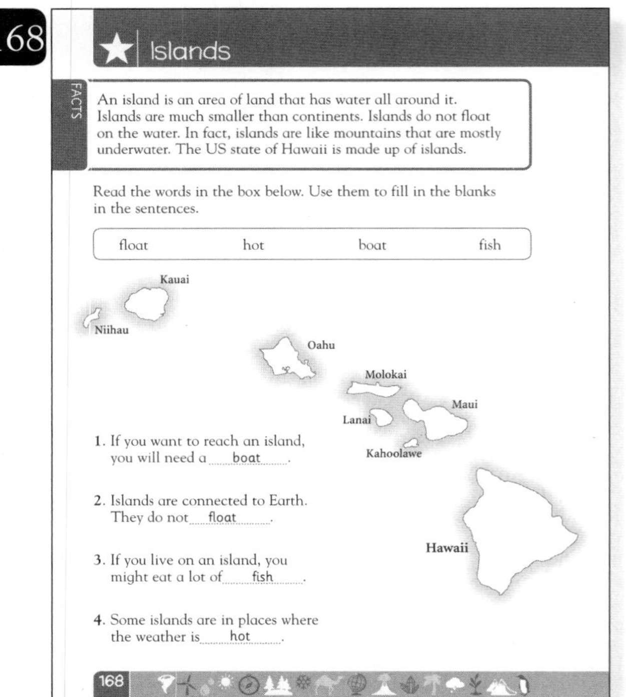
Islands

FACTS

An island is an area of land that has water all around it. Islands are much smaller than continents. Islands do not float on the water. In fact, islands are like mountains that are mostly underwater. The US state of Hawaii is made up of islands.

Read the words in the box below. Use them to fill in the blanks in the sentences.

float	hot	boat	fish

1. If you want to reach an island, you will need a boat.
2. Islands are connected to Earth. They do not float.
3. If you live on an island, you might eat a lot of fish.
4. Some islands are in places where the weather is hot.

Expand your child's knowledge by discussing any islands you may have visited, read about, or seen on television. You could also mention some well-known islands, such as the British Isles, Japan, Cuba, Puerto Rico, and Easter Island.

169

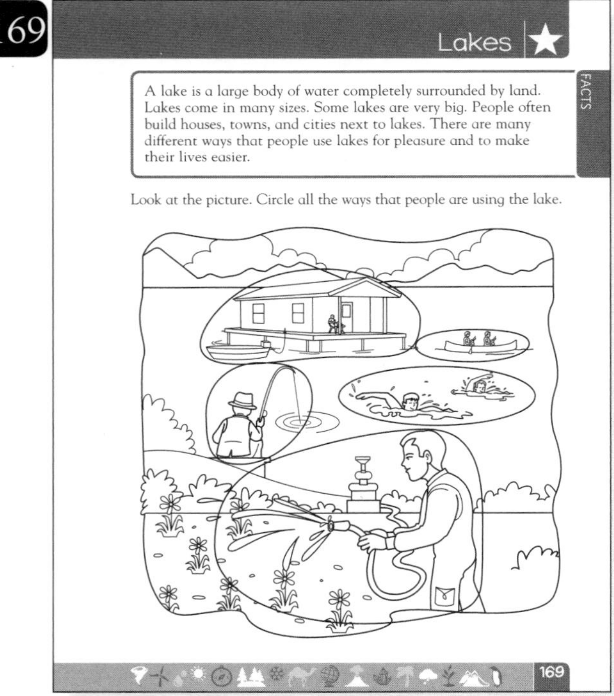
Lakes

FACTS

A lake is a large body of water completely surrounded by land. Lakes come in many sizes. Some lakes are very big. People often build houses, towns, and cities next to lakes. There are many different ways that people use lakes for pleasure and to make their lives easier.

Look at the picture. Circle all the ways that people are using the lake.

You could expand on the topic of lakes by telling your child about the five Great Lakes—Superior, Michigan, Huron, Erie, and Ontario—on the border between the United States and Canada. They are among the biggest lakes in the world.

Rivers
FACTS
Water always flows from high places to low places. A large amount of running water is called a river. A small amount of running water is called a stream. Some rivers are very long and very wide. Their water can move very quickly, too. Streams are usually much smaller than rivers.
Write an R in the box next to the picture of the river, and write an S in the box next to the picture of the stream.
R
S
170

Ask your child if he or she knows the names of some rivers. If not, mention the river nearest to where you live and how people use it. You could also mention some of the world's largest rivers, such as the Amazon, Mississippi, and Nile Rivers.

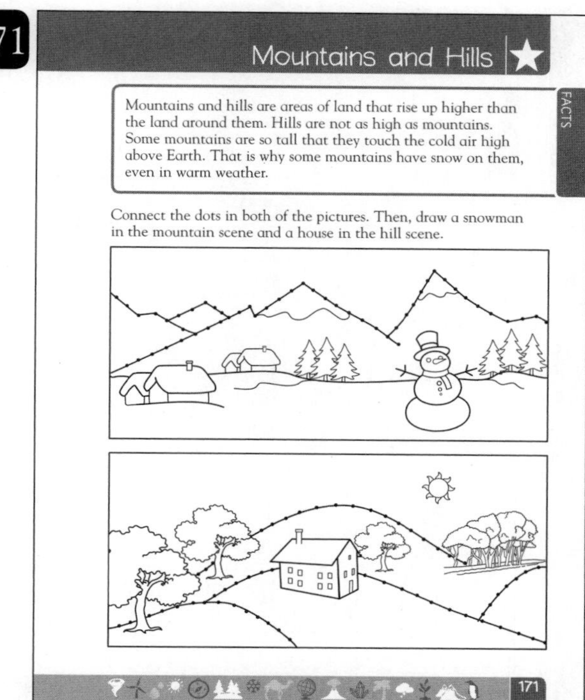

171
Mountains and Hills
FACTS
Mountains and hills are areas of land that rise up higher than the land around them. Hills are not as high as mountains. Some mountains are so tall that they touch the cold air high above Earth. That is why some mountains have snow on them, even in warm weather.
Connect the dots in both of the pictures. Then, draw a snowman in the mountain scene and a house in the hill scene.
171

Next time you travel with your child, point to some hills and animals that might live there. If you are lucky enough to see mountains, point to them, too. Tell your child the name of the tallest mountain in your country or continent, if you know it.

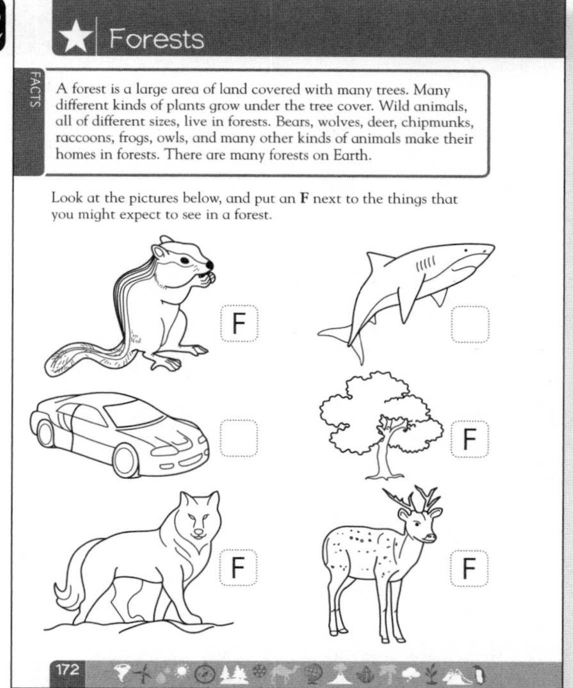

Forests
FACTS
A forest is a large area of land covered with many trees. Many different kinds of plants grow under the tree cover. Wild animals, all of different sizes, live in forests. Bears, wolves, deer, chipmunks, raccoons, frogs, owls, and many other kinds of animals make their homes in forests. There are many forests on Earth.
Look at the pictures below, and put an F next to the things that you might expect to see in a forest.
F
F
F
F
172

Explain to your child that people often built towns near forests because the trees provided the wood for buildings and furniture.

173
Jungles
FACTS
Jungles are very rainy and wet parts of Earth. Because of all the rain, jungles can support the growth of lots of different kinds of plants. Most of Earth's plants and animals are found in jungles. They are often very hot places. Jungles are usually hard places for people to live in.
Look at the pictures below and put a J next to the things that you might expect to see in a jungle.
J
J
J
J
J
173

Jungles include the tropical forests that are home to a huge number of different plants and animals. You could also explain to your child that many jungles are under threat as the trees are being cleared to make farmland or for timber.

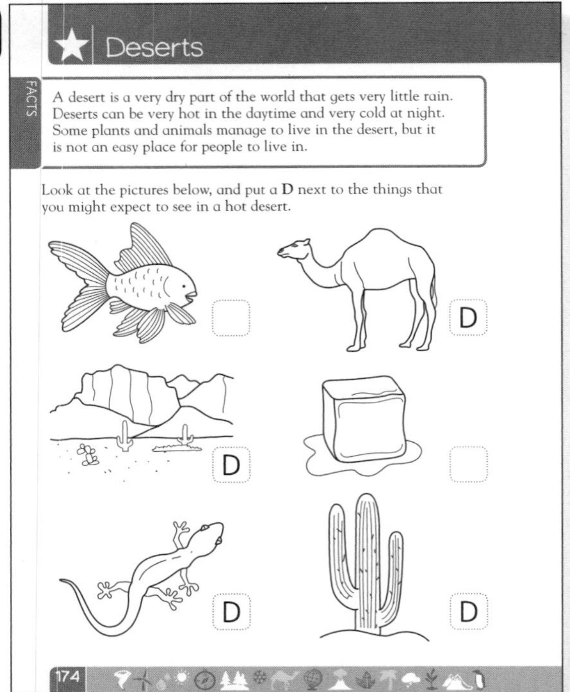

Deserts
FACTS
A desert is a very dry part of the world that gets very little rain. Deserts can be very hot in the daytime and very cold at night. Some plants and animals manage to live in the desert, but it is not an easy place for people to live in.
Look at the pictures below, and put a D next to the things that you might expect to see in a hot desert.
D
D
D
D
174

Use books or the internet to find out about one of the deserts in North America, such as the Mojave Desert. What kind of animals and plants live there? Are there any towns in the desert?

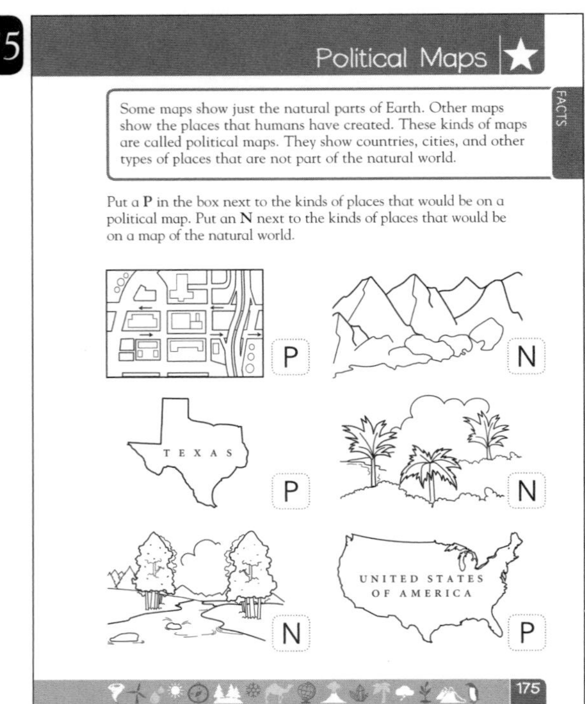

After working through this page, introduce your child to an atlas—if you have one at home. Show him or her the city or town you live in.

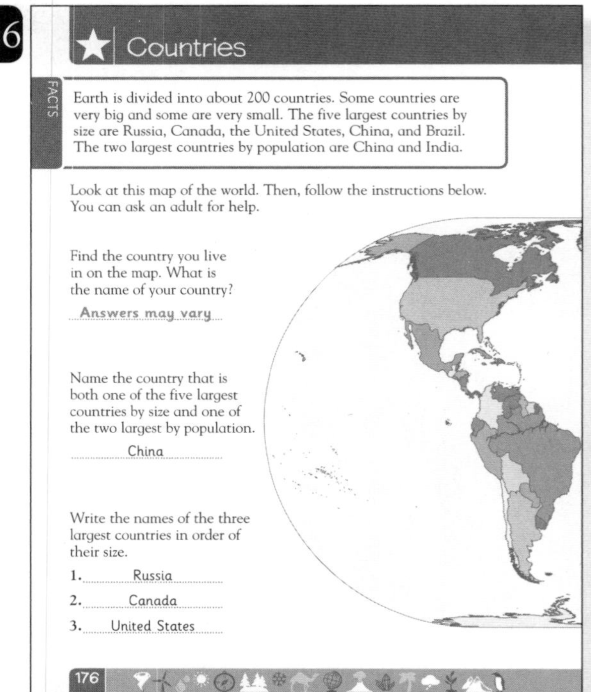

Countries
FACTS
Earth is divided into about 200 countries. Some countries are very big and some are very small. The five largest countries by size are Russia, Canada, the United States, China, and Brazil. The two largest countries by population are China and India.
Look at this map of the world. Then, follow the instructions below. You can ask an adult for help.
Find the country you live in on the map. What is the name of your country?
Answers may vary
Name the country that is both one of the five largest countries by size and one of the two largest by population.
China
Write the names of the three largest countries in order of their size.
1. Russia
2. Canada
3. United States
176

Looking at the map above, ask your child if he or she knows names of countries other than his or her own. Point to where they are on the map. You could also point to countries you have visited or have friends or relatives in.

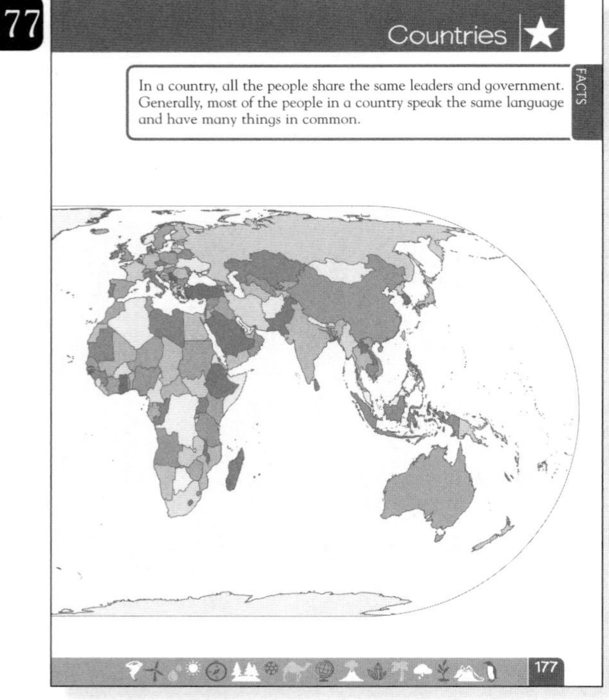

Countries
FACTS
In a country, all the people share the same leaders and government. Generally, most of the people in a country speak the same language and have many things in common.
177

178

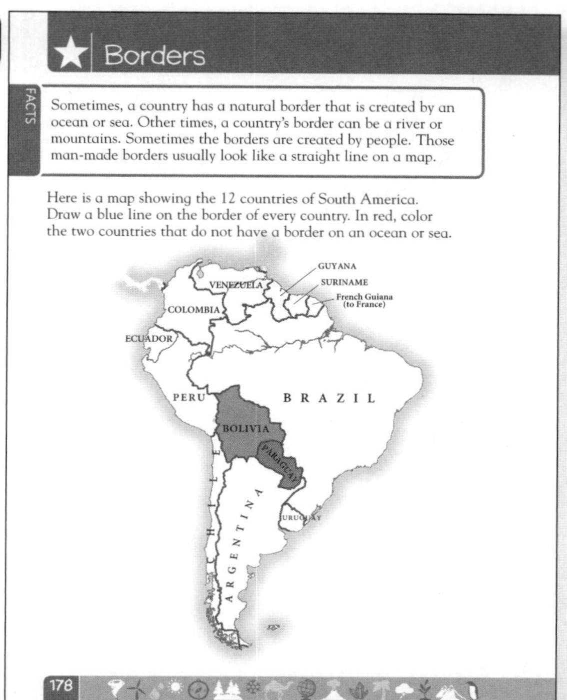

Borders

FACTS

Sometimes, a country has a natural border that is created by an ocean or sea. Other times, a country's border can be a river or mountains. Sometimes the borders are created by people. Those man-made borders usually look like a straight line on a map.

Here is a map showing the 12 countries of South America. Draw a blue line on the border of every country. In red, color the two countries that do not have a border on an ocean or sea.

Find a map of your state or country in an atlas or on the internet. With your child, decide whether its borders are political (man-made) or natural.

179

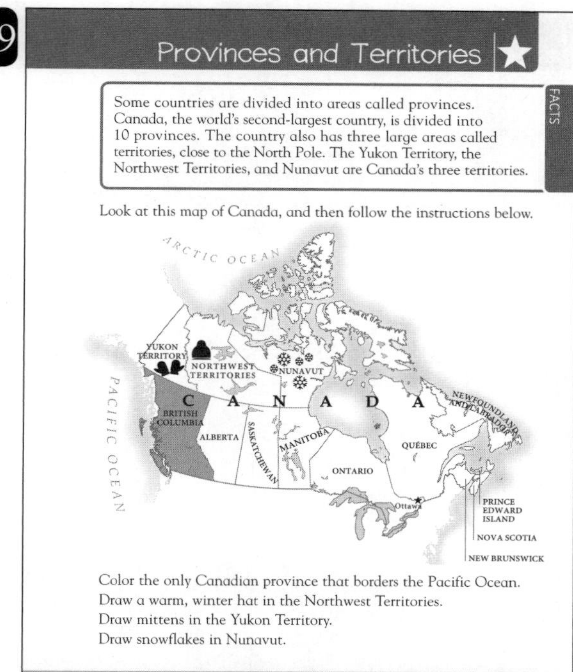

Provinces and Territories

FACTS

Some countries are divided into areas called provinces. Canada, the world's second-largest country, is divided into 10 provinces. The country also has three large areas called territories, close to the North Pole. The Yukon Territory, the Northwest Territories, and Nunavut are Canada's three territories.

Look at this map of Canada, and then follow the instructions below.

Color the only Canadian province that borders the Pacific Ocean.
Draw a warm, winter hat in the Northwest Territories.
Draw mittens in the Yukon Territory.
Draw snowflakes in Nunavut.

As an extension to this page, give your child some more facts about Canada. These may include: it has the longest coastline of any country; much of it is covered in ice; and its border with the United States is the longest border between any two countries in the world.

180

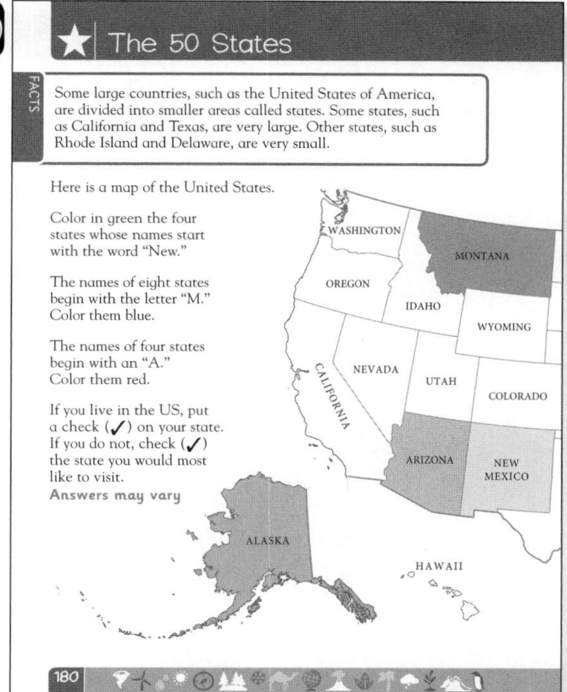

The 50 States

FACTS

Some large countries, such as the United States of America, are divided into smaller areas called states. Some states, such as California and Texas, are very large. Other states, such as Rhode Island and Delaware, are very small.

Here is a map of the United States.

Color in green the four states whose names start with the word "New."

The names of eight states begin with the letter "M." Color them blue.

The names of four states begin with an "A." Color them red.

If you live in the US, put a check (✓) on your state. If you do not, check (✓) the state you would most like to visit.

Answers may vary

After looking at the map of the United States, close the book and encourage your child to recall the names of at least five states. Give hints if your child cannot remember any names.

181

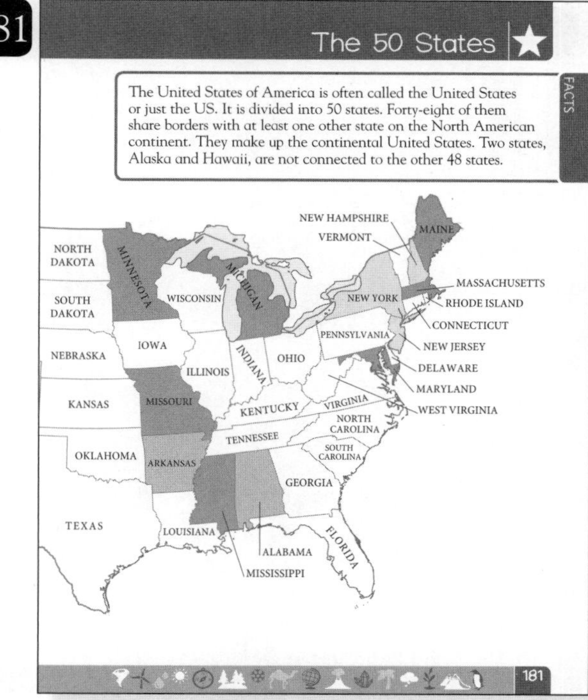

The 50 States

FACTS

The United States of America is often called the United States or just the US. It is divided into 50 states. Forty-eight of them share borders with at least one other state on the North American continent. They make up the continental United States. Two states, Alaska and Hawaii, are not connected to the other 48 states.

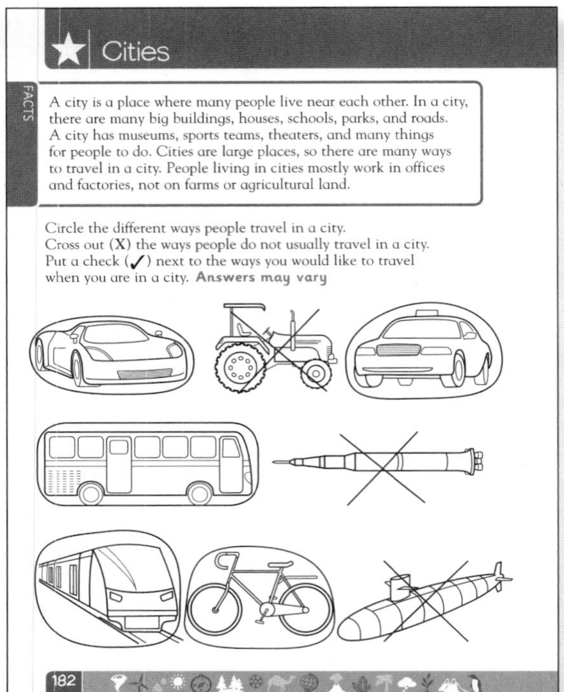

Cities

FACTS

A city is a place where many people live near each other. In a city, there are many big buildings, houses, schools, parks, and roads. A city has museums, sports teams, theaters, and many things for people to do. Cities are large places, so there are many ways to travel in a city. People living in cities mostly work in offices and factories, not on farms or agricultural land.

Circle the different ways people travel in a city.
Cross out (X) the ways people do not usually travel in a city.
Put a check (✓) next to the ways you would like to travel when you are in a city. **Answers may vary**

182

Ask your child to think of more differences between the city and the country. In addition to the differences between the buildings and transportation, ask him or her about the animals and plants you might see outside the city.

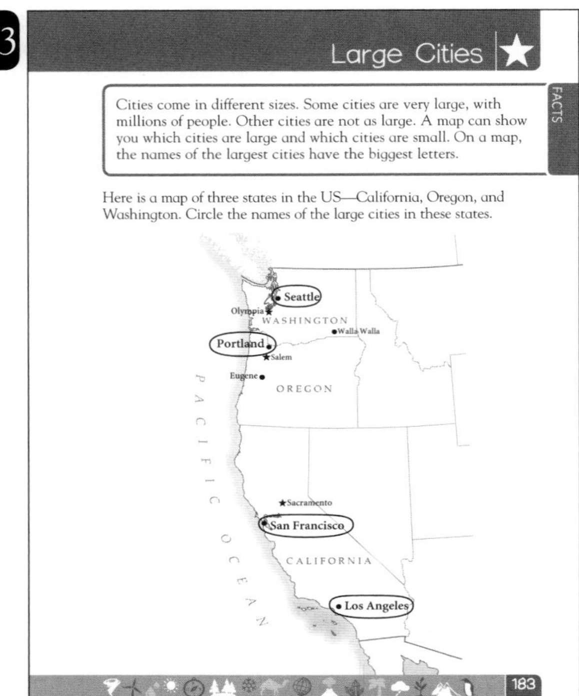

Large Cities

FACTS

Cities come in different sizes. Some cities are very large, with millions of people. Other cities are not as large. A map can show you which cities are large and which cities are small. On a map, the names of the largest cities have the biggest letters.

Here is a map of three states in the US—California, Oregon, and Washington. Circle the names of the large cities in these states.

183

Ask your child if he or she can think of some good things about living in a big city. Then ask if he or she can think of any drawbacks to city life.

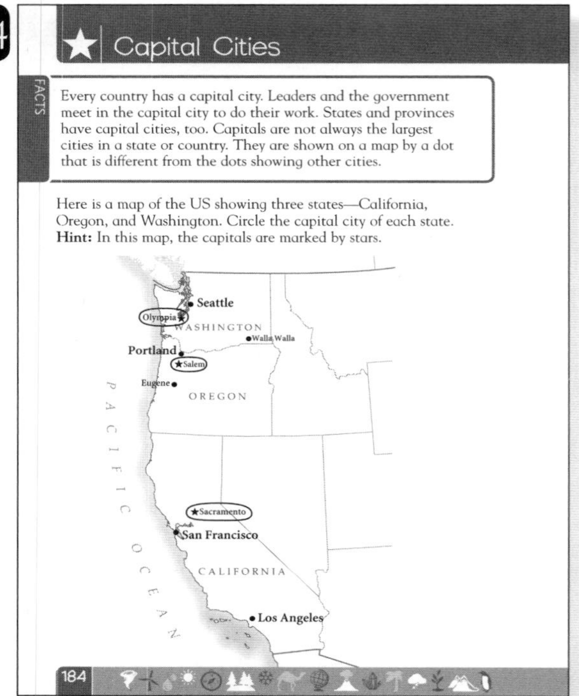

Capital Cities

FACTS

Every country has a capital city. Leaders and the government meet in the capital city to do their work. States and provinces have capital cities, too. Capitals are not always the largest cities in a state or country. They are shown on a map by a dot that is different from the dots showing other cities.

Here is a map of the US showing three states—California, Oregon, and Washington. Circle the capital city of each state. **Hint:** In this map, the capitals are marked by stars.

184

As extra information, you could tell your child that none of the five most populated cities in the United States—New York, Los Angeles, Chicago, Houston, and Philadelphia—is a state capital. Ask them if they know the capital of the United States.

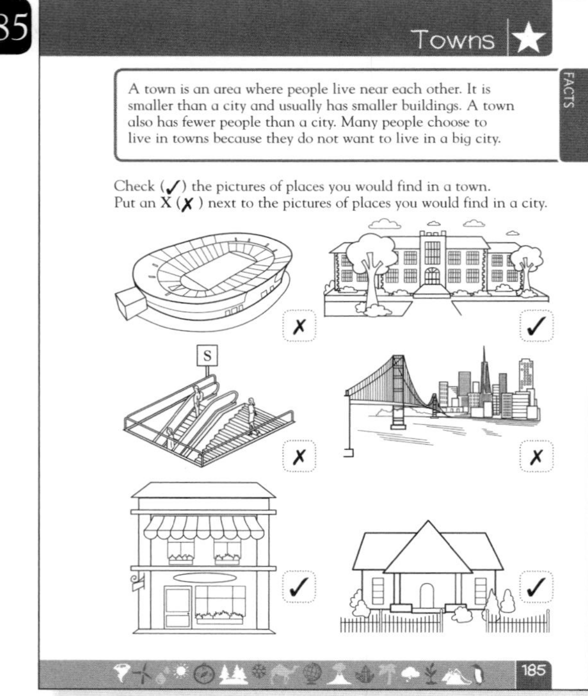

Towns

FACTS

A town is an area where people live near each other. It is smaller than a city and usually has smaller buildings. A town also has fewer people than a city. Many people choose to live in towns because they do not want to live in a big city.

Check (✓) the pictures of places you would find in a town.
Put an X (✗) next to the pictures of places you would find in a city.

185

Invite your child to think of some of the good things about living in a town. Then, ask if he or she can think of any drawbacks to life in a town.

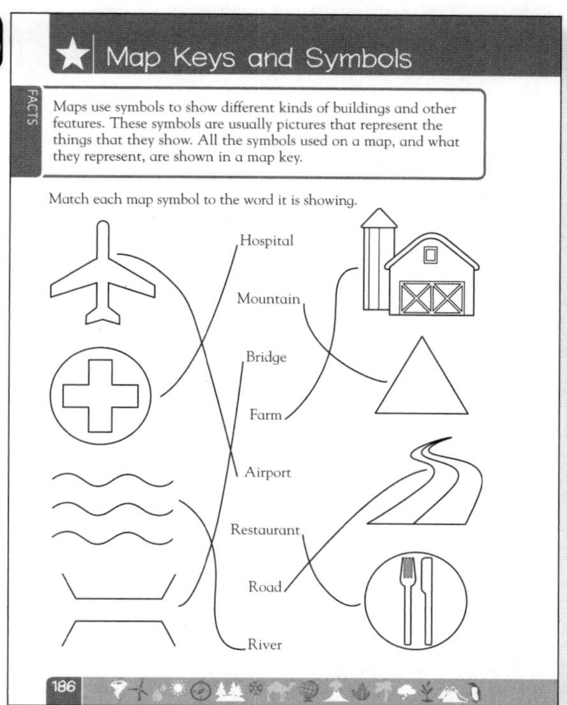

★ Map Keys and Symbols

FACTS

Maps use symbols to show different kinds of buildings and other features. These symbols are usually pictures that represent the things that they show. All the symbols used on a map, and what they represent, are shown in a map key.

Match each map symbol to the word it is showing.

Hospital
Mountain
Bridge
Farm
Airport
Restaurant
Road
River

186

Next time you're outside with your child, point out road signs with symbols on them, such as a bicycle, bus, pedestrians, or an uppercase **P** or **H**. Ask your child if he or she can figure out what the signs are referring to.

187

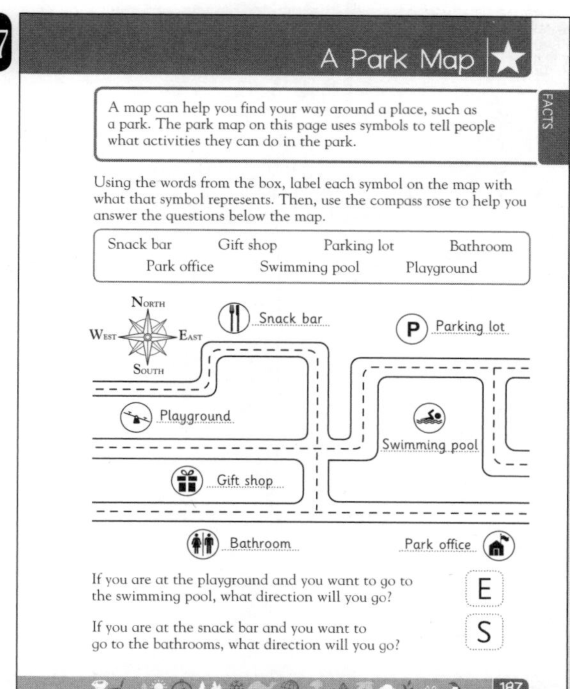

A Park Map ★

FACTS

A map can help you find your way around a place, such as a park. The park map on this page uses symbols to tell people what activities they can do in the park.

Using the words from the box, label each symbol on the map with what that symbol represents. Then, use the compass rose to help you answer the questions below the map.

Snack bar	Gift shop	Parking lot	Bathroom
Park office	Swimming pool	Playground	

If you are at the playground and you want to go to the swimming pool, what direction will you go? E

If you are at the snack bar and you want to go to the bathrooms, what direction will you go? S

187

On your next visit to a park, study the park's map and accompanying key with your child. Ask your child to then direct you to the places you want to visit in the park.

188

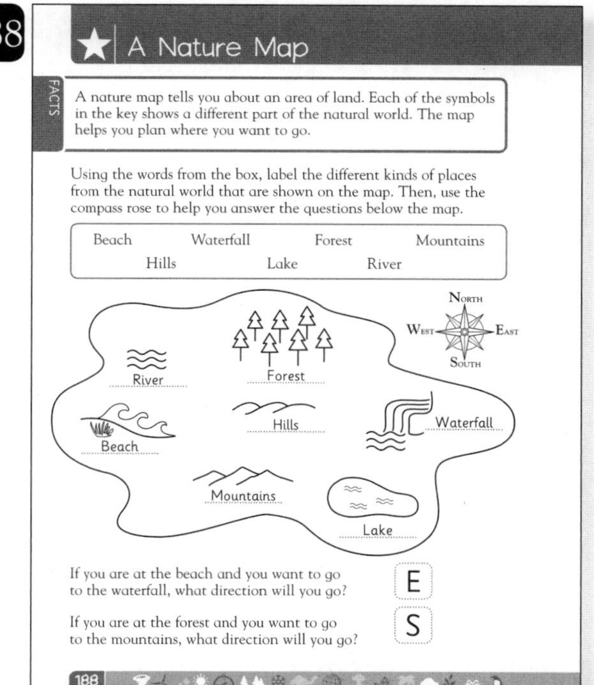

★ A Nature Map

FACTS

A nature map tells you about an area of land. Each of the symbols in the key shows a different part of the natural world. The map helps you plan where you want to go.

Using the words from the box, label the different kinds of places from the natural world that are shown on the map. Then, use the compass rose to help you answer the questions below the map.

Beach	Waterfall	Forest	Mountains
Hills	Lake	River	

If you are at the beach and you want to go to the waterfall, what direction will you go? E

If you are at the forest and you want to go to the mountains, what direction will you go? S

188

As an extra fun exercise, ask your child to draw his or her own symbol for a volcano.

189

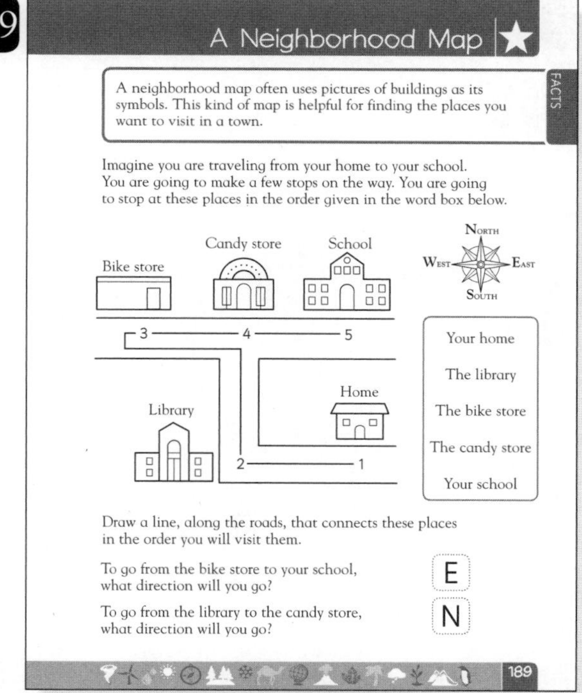

A Neighborhood Map ★

FACTS

A neighborhood map often uses pictures of buildings as its symbols. This kind of map is helpful for finding the places you want to visit in a town.

Imagine you are traveling from your home to your school. You are going to make a few stops on the way. You are going to stop at these places in the order given in the word box below.

Your home
The library
The bike store
The candy store
Your school

Draw a line, along the roads, that connects these places in the order you will visit them.

To go from the bike store to your school, what direction will you go? E

To go from the library to the candy store, what direction will you go? N

189

To start a memory game, ask your child to tell you about his or her journey to school each day, describing some of the buildings along the route. If this is too difficult, offer hints.

190

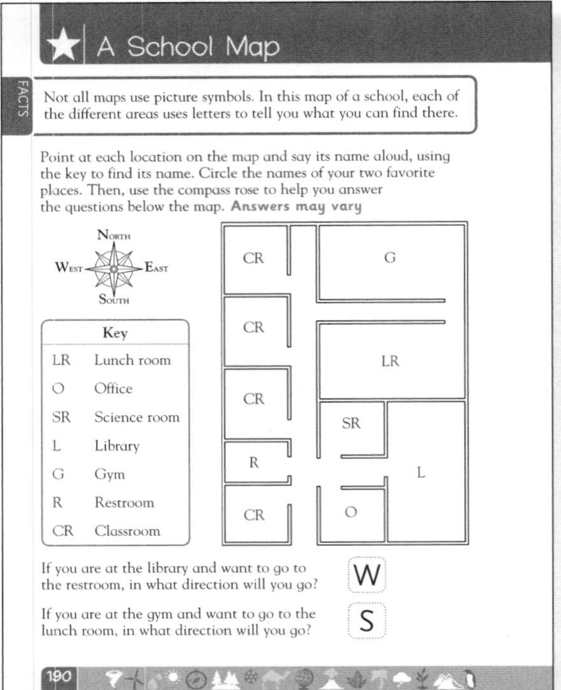

A School Map

FACTS

Not all maps use picture symbols. In this map of a school, each of the different areas uses letters to tell you what you can find there.

Point at each location on the map and say its name aloud, using the key to find its name. Circle the names of your two favorite places. Then, use the compass rose to help you answer the questions below the map. **Answers may vary**

Key	
LR	Lunch room
O	Office
SR	Science room
L	Library
G	Gym
R	Restroom
CR	Classroom

If you are at the library and want to go to the restroom, in what direction will you go? **W**

If you are at the gym and want to go to the lunch room, in what direction will you go? **S**

190

Invite your child to describe all the different rooms in which he or she has classes in at school. Ask him or her to describe the location, such as "upstairs" or "next to the playground" of each classroom.

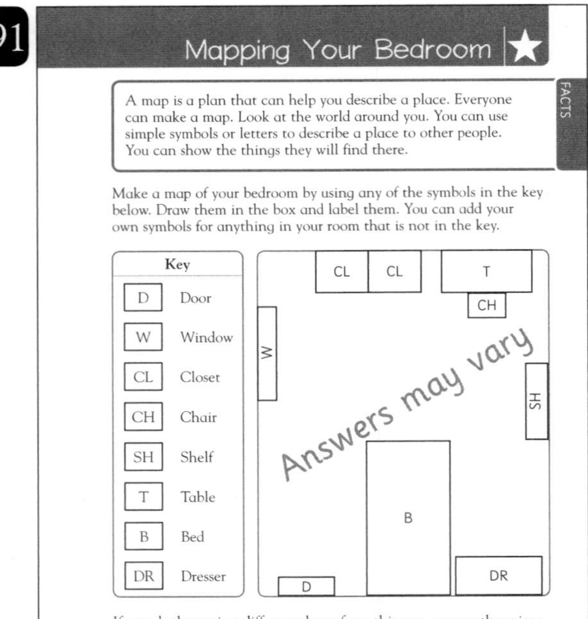

191

Mapping Your Bedroom

FACTS

A map is a plan that can help you describe a place. Everyone can make a map. Look at the world around you. You can use simple symbols or letters to describe a place to other people. You can show the things they will find there.

Make a map of your bedroom by using any of the symbols in the key below. Draw them in the box and label them. You can add your own symbols for anything in your room that is not in the key.

Key	
D	Door
W	Window
CL	Closet
CH	Chair
SH	Shelf
T	Table
B	Bed
DR	Dresser

If your bedroom is a different shape from this one, use another piece of paper to draw walls that match the shape of your bedroom.

191

As an extra exercise, let your child draw a map of his or her ideal, or "dream," bedroom. It can be any size and include anything your child wants in it. Encourage his or her imagination.

192

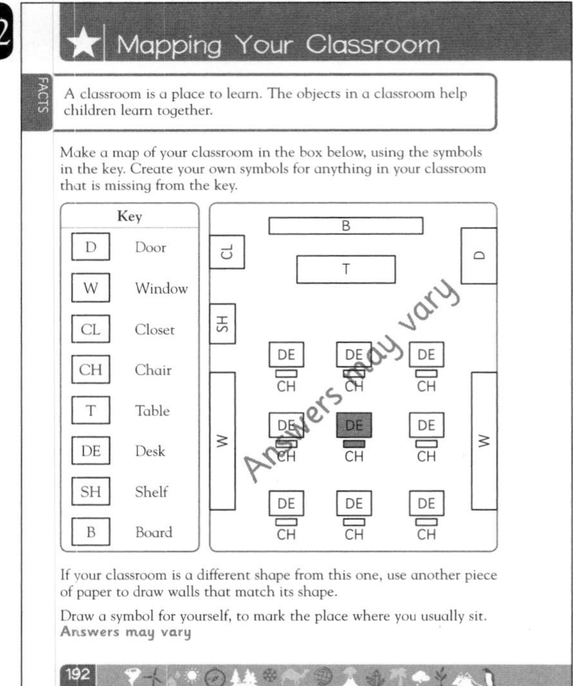

Mapping Your Classroom

FACTS

A classroom is a place to learn. The objects in a classroom help children learn together.

Make a map of your classroom in the box below, using the symbols in the key. Create your own symbols for anything in your classroom that is missing from the key.

Key	
D	Door
W	Window
CL	Closet
CH	Chair
T	Table
DE	Desk
SH	Shelf
B	Board

If your classroom is a different shape from this one, use another piece of paper to draw walls that match its shape.

Draw a symbol for yourself, to mark the place where you usually sit. **Answers may vary**

192

Are all the classrooms in your child's school the same? Ask your child to think of some differences between the various classrooms in which he or she has classes.

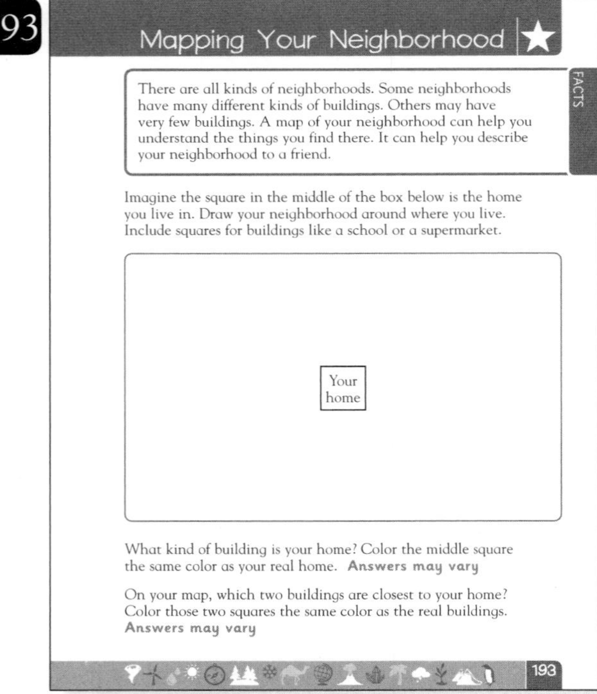

193

Mapping Your Neighborhood

FACTS

There are all kinds of neighborhoods. Some neighborhoods have many different kinds of buildings. Others may have very few buildings. A map of your neighborhood can help you understand the things you find there. It can help you describe your neighborhood to a friend.

Imagine the square in the middle of the box below is the home you live in. Draw your neighborhood around where you live. Include squares for buildings like a school or a supermarket.

What kind of building is your home? Color the middle square the same color as your real home. **Answers may vary**

On your map, which two buildings are closest to your home? Color those two squares the same color as the real buildings. **Answers may vary**

193

Discuss differences between your neighborhood and that of a friend or relative. Are all neighborhoods the same?

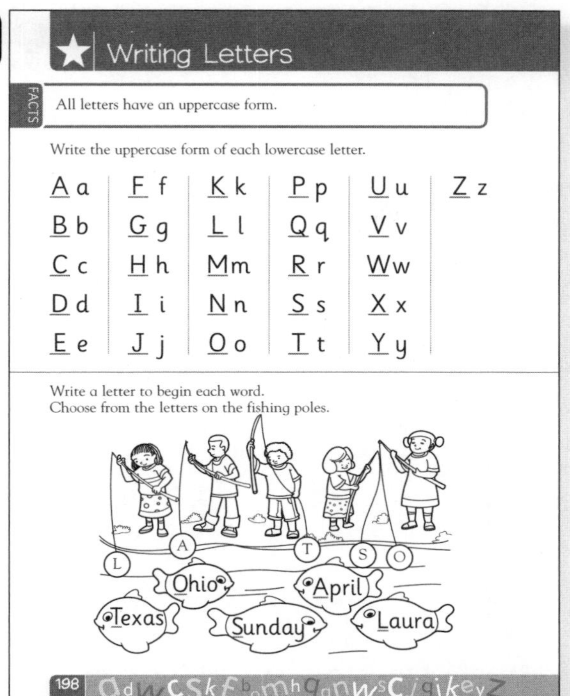

Writing Letters

FACTS: All letters have an uppercase form.

Write the uppercase form of each lowercase letter.

A a	F f	K k	P p	U u	Z z
B b	G g	L l	Q q	V v	
C c	H h	M m	R r	W w	
D d	I i	N n	S s	X x	
E e	J j	O o	T t	Y y	

Write a letter to begin each word.
Choose from the letters on the fishing poles.

Invite your child to suggest other words that start with uppercase letters. For instance, names of cities or names of people they know.

199

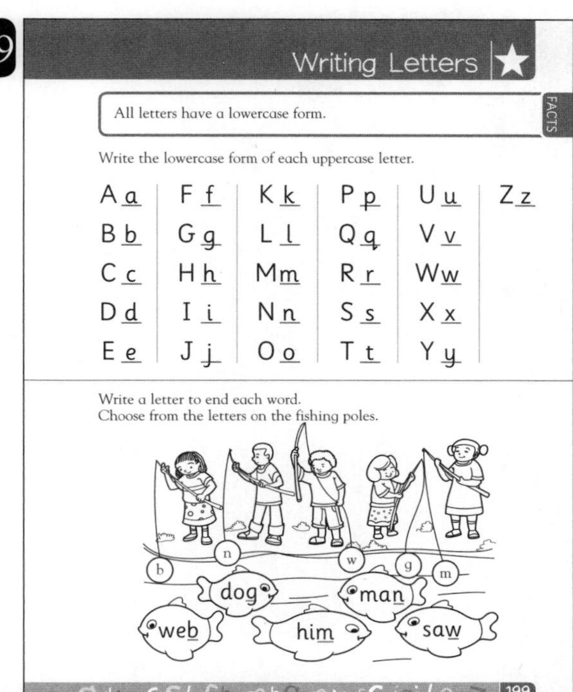

Writing Letters

FACTS: All letters have a lowercase form.

Write the lowercase form of each uppercase letter.

A a	F f	K k	P p	U u	Z z
B b	G g	L l	Q q	V v	
C c	H h	M m	R r	W w	
D d	I i	N n	S s	X x	
E e	J j	O o	T t	Y y	

Write a letter to end each word.
Choose from the letters on the fishing poles.

For extra practice, have your child come up with other lowercase words that start with the same letters as those on the fishing poles.

Capital Letters

FACTS: Uppercase letters are also called capital letters.
Use capital letters at the beginning of a sentence.

Read each sentence below. Underline the word that needs a capital letter. Write the word, using correct capitalization, in the space below the sentence.

the girl fed the cat.

The

snow falls in the winter.

Snow

a monkey eats fruit.

A

rockets zoom through the sky.

Rockets

quiet mice are hard to find.

Quiet

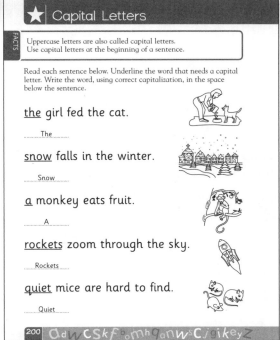

Regularly point out examples of how capital letters are used: on street signs and in titles of books, magazines, and articles.

Capital Letters

FACTS: Use a capital letter at the beginning of the name of a person, place, day of the week, or month of the year.

Complete each line below.

My full name is Answers may vary.

The people in my family are Answers may vary.

The day of the week today is Answers may vary.

The month is Answers may vary.

My friend's name is Answers may vary.

The name of my school is Answers may vary.

The city or town where I live is Answers may vary.

Provide spelling support for this activity if your child asks for it. Some children may, however, prefer to sound out and write words themselves; correct spelling isn't the focus of this activity. Just be sure that your child uses correct capitalization.

202

Creating a Character

FACTS

A character is a person or an animal in a story.

Pick one word from each column that could describe a character.
Combine the three words to create a character!

huge	monkey	cook
tiny	snake	dancer
purple	ant	detective
silly	horse	firefighter
upside-down	elephant	movie star

My character is a Answers may vary.

Draw your character below. Tell a story about your character.

Answers may vary

Answers may vary

If your child enjoys this activity, work together to create more characters on separate pieces of paper.

203

Describing a Character

FACTS

Every story is about a character.

Think of your favorite character from a book or movie.
Complete the sentence and answer the questions that follow.

My favorite character is Answers may vary.

What does your character look like? Answers may vary

What does your character do? Answers may vary

What do you like best about your favorite character?

Answers may vary

Draw your character below.

Answers may vary

You may wish to demonstrate how to do this activity for your child using a character that is familiar to you both.

204

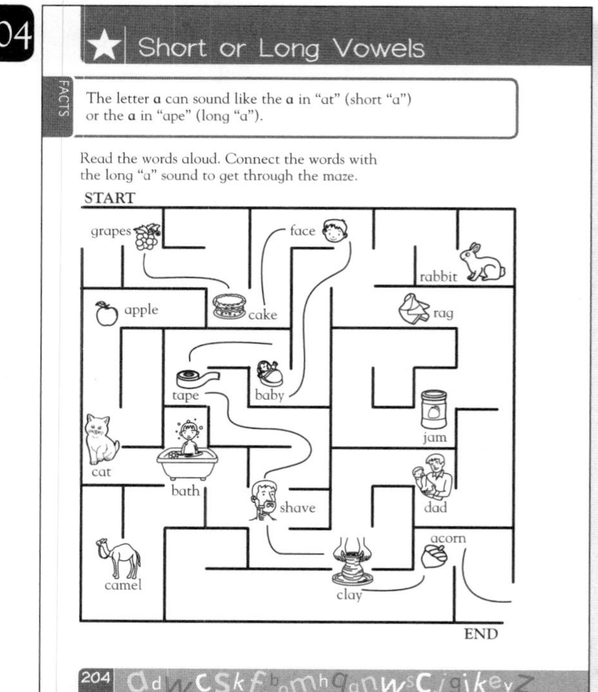

Short or Long Vowels

FACTS

The letter **a** can sound like the **a** in "at" (short "a") or the **a** in "ape" (long "a").

Read the words aloud. Connect the words with the long "a" sound to get through the maze.

Invite your child to name other examples of a short and a long "a."

205

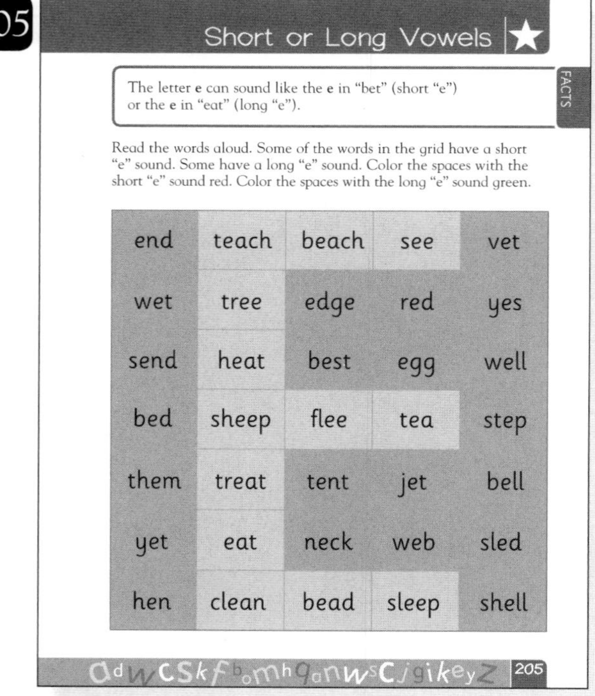

Short or Long Vowels

FACTS

The letter **e** can sound like the **e** in "bet" (short "e") or the **e** in "eat" (long "e").

Read the words aloud. Some of the words in the grid have a short "e" sound. Some have a long "e" sound. Color the spaces with the short "e" sound red. Color the spaces with the long "e" sound green.

end	teach	beach	see	vet
wet	tree	edge	red	yes
send	heat	best	egg	well
bed	sheep	flee	tea	step
them	treat	tent	jet	bell
yet	eat	neck	web	sled
hen	clean	bead	sleep	shell

Invite your child to name other examples of a short and a long "e."

206

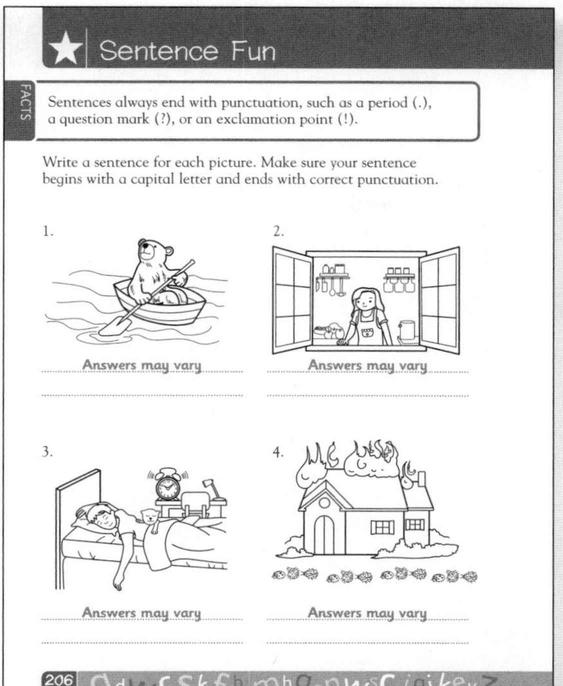

Sentence Fun

FACTS

Sentences always end with punctuation, such as a period (.), a question mark (?), or an exclamation point (!).

Write a sentence for each picture. Make sure your sentence begins with a capital letter and ends with correct punctuation.

1. Answers may vary

2. Answers may vary

3. Answers may vary

4. Answers may vary

206

Review your child's sentences for correct capitalization and punctuation.

207

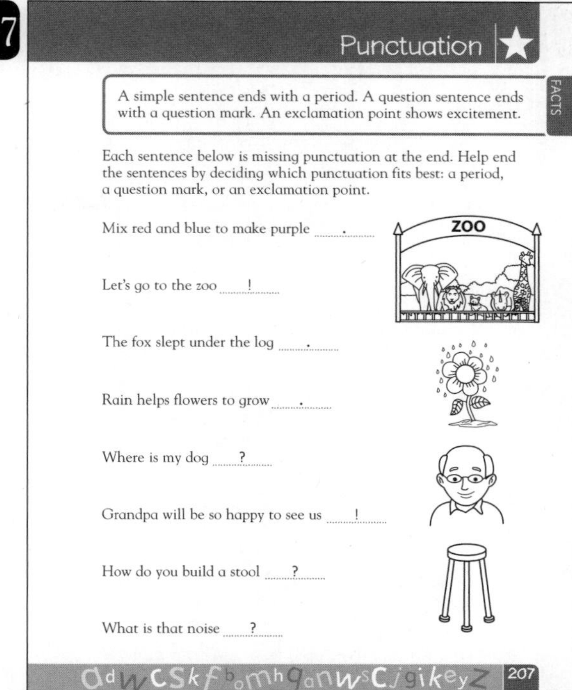

Punctuation

FACTS

A simple sentence ends with a period. A question sentence ends with a question mark. An exclamation point shows excitement.

Each sentence below is missing punctuation at the end. Help end the sentences by deciding which punctuation fits best: a period, a question mark, or an exclamation point.

Mix red and blue to make purple .

Let's go to the zoo !

The fox slept under the log .

Rain helps flowers to grow .

Where is my dog ?

Grandpa will be so happy to see us !

How do you build a stool ?

What is that noise ?

207

Find examples of printed sentences in books that end in periods, question marks, or exclamation points. Read them aloud so your child can hear the difference in the expression of these types of sentences.

208

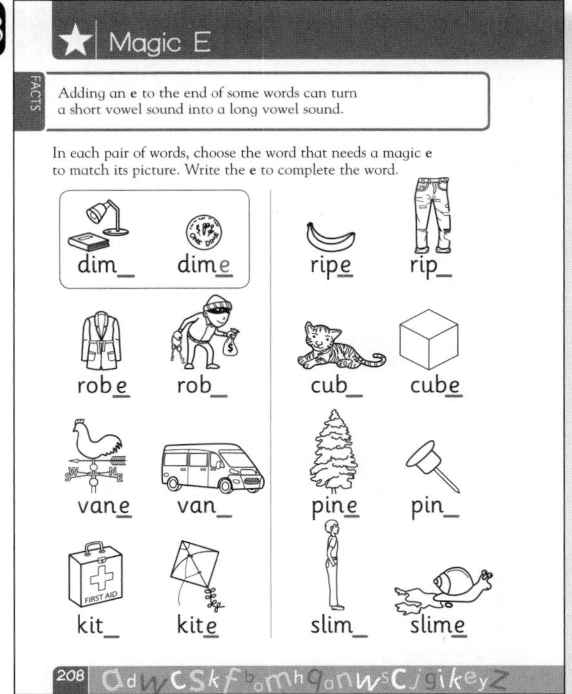

Magic E

FACTS

Adding an **e** to the end of some words can turn a short vowel sound into a long vowel sound.

In each pair of words, choose the word that needs a magic **e** to match its picture. Write the **e** to complete the word.

dim_ dime

ripe rip_

robe rob_

cub_ cube

vane van_

pine pin_

kit_ kite

slim_ slime

208

Does someone in your family have a "magic **E**" in their name? Demonstrate it to your child.

209

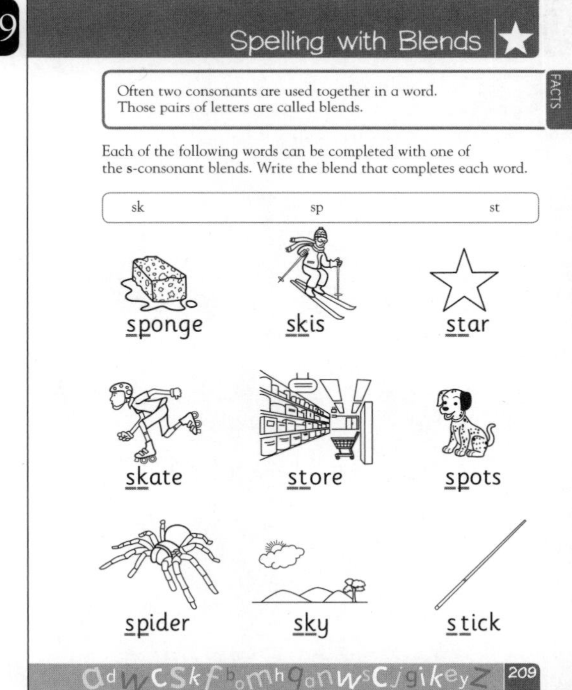

Spelling with Blends

FACTS

Often two consonants are used together in a word. Those pairs of letters are called blends.

Each of the following words can be completed with one of the s-consonant blends. Write the blend that completes each word.

sk sp st

sponge skis star

skate store spots

spider sky stick

209

Encourage your child to think of other words with **sk**, **sp**, and **st** consonant blends.

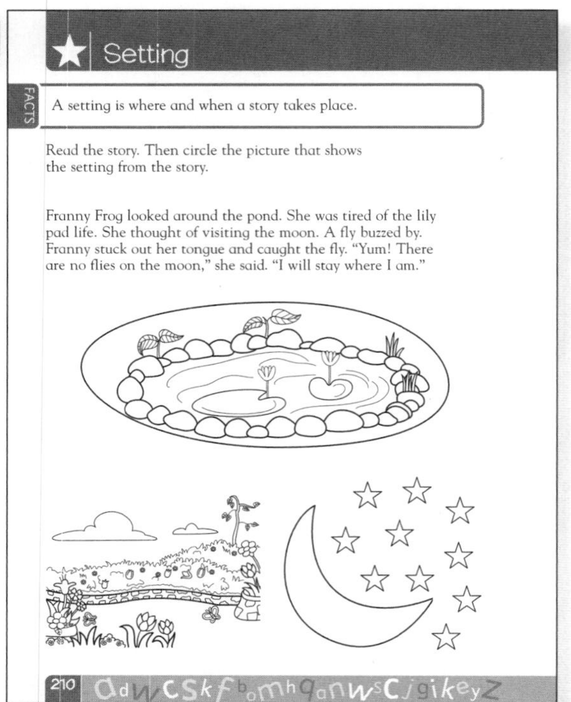

Setting

FACTS A setting is where and when a story takes place.

Read the story. Then circle the picture that shows the setting from the story.

Franny Frog looked around the pond. She was tired of the lily pad life. She thought of visiting the moon. A fly buzzed by. Franny stuck out her tongue and caught the fly. "Yum! There are no flies on the moon," she said. "I will stay where I am."

As you read books to your child, point out details about the setting. Talk to your child about how the setting adds to the story.

211

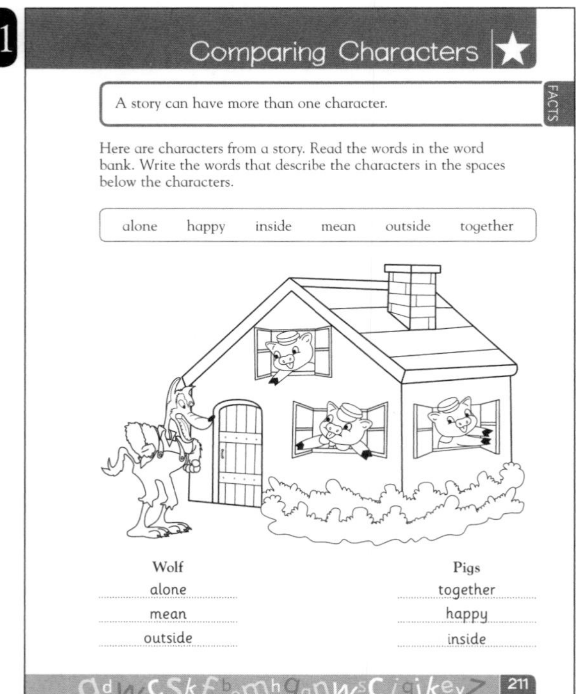

Comparing Characters

FACTS A story can have more than one character.

Here are characters from a story. Read the words in the word bank. Write the words that describe the characters in the spaces below the characters.

alone	happy	inside	mean	outside	together

Wolf	Pigs
alone	together
mean	happy
outside	inside

Repeat this activity with characters from one of your child's favorite books.

212

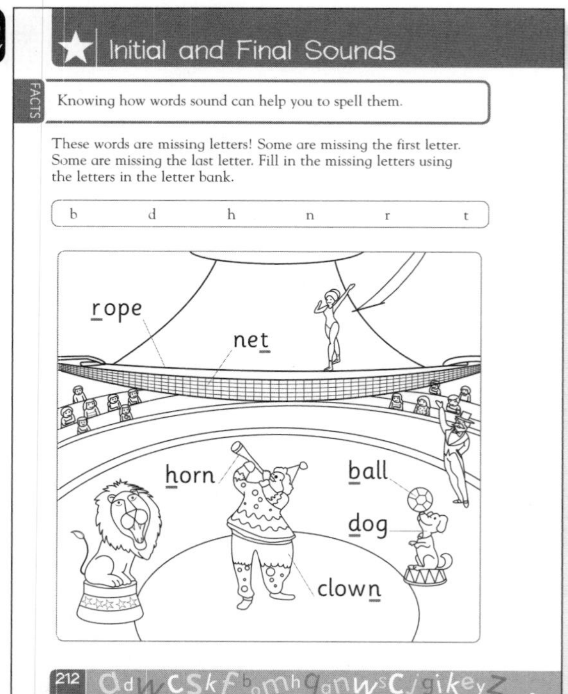

Initial and Final Sounds

FACTS Knowing how words sound can help you to spell them.

These words are missing letters! Some are missing the first letter. Some are missing the last letter. Fill in the missing letters using the letters in the letter bank.

b	d	h	n	r	t

After your child has completed each word, read each word aloud, paying attention to initial and final sounds.

213

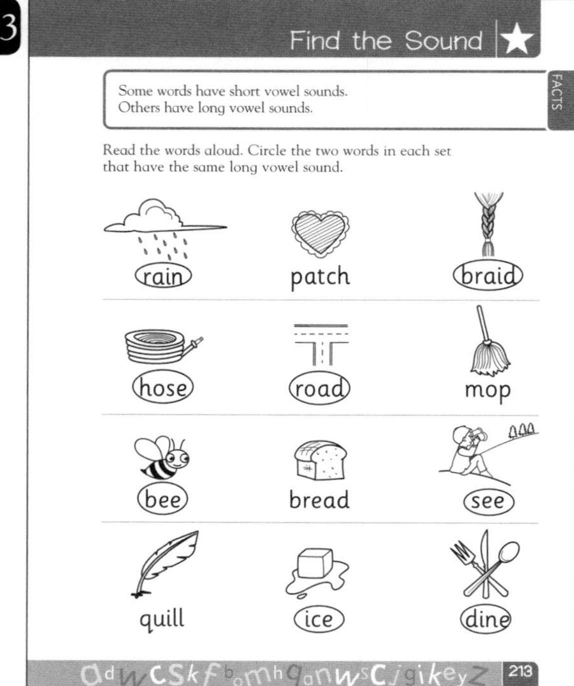

Find the Sound

FACTS Some words have short vowel sounds. Others have long vowel sounds.

Read the words aloud. Circle the two words in each set that have the same long vowel sound.

rain	patch	braid
hose	road	mop
bee	bread	see
quill	ice	dine

If your family's names have short or long vowels, point those out to your child. Challenge your child to say if the vowels are short or long.

Pronouns
Pronouns are words that can take the place of nouns in a sentence.
Circle the pronoun in each sentence. Then write the pronoun.
My dog is small and fluffy.
My
Where are you going?
you
They went to the movies.
They
Jane gave her a book.
her
He needs new shoes.
He
I like to bake cookies.
I
We sang together.
We
214

Have your child say a sentence that uses a pronoun instead of a proper name.

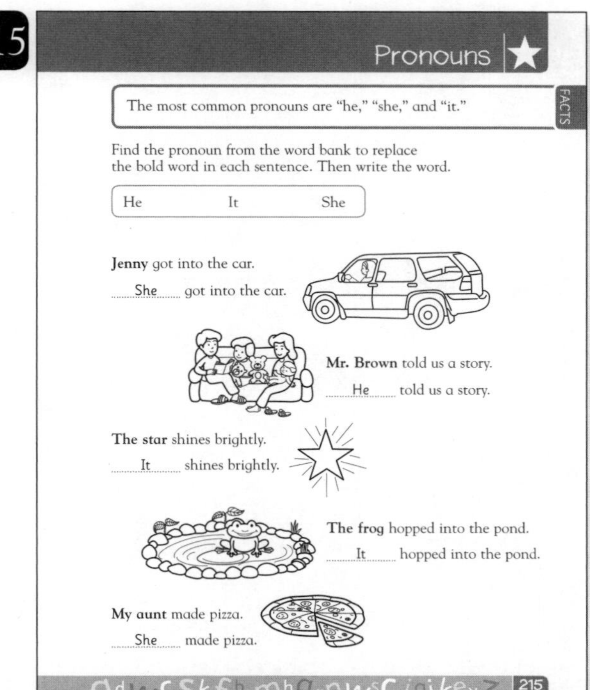

215
Pronouns
The most common pronouns are "he," "she," and "it."
Find the pronoun from the word bank to replace the bold word in each sentence. Then write the word.
He It She
Jenny got into the car.
She got into the car.
Mr. Brown told us a story.
He told us a story.
The star shines brightly.
It shines brightly.
The frog hopped into the pond.
It hopped into the pond.
My aunt made pizza.
She made pizza.
215

When you read with your child, be on the lookout for pronouns. Ask your child to whom or to what the pronoun refers.

Words that convey time and order are called temporal words. Ask your child to retell other stories using words such as "first," "second," "next," "then," "finally," and "last."

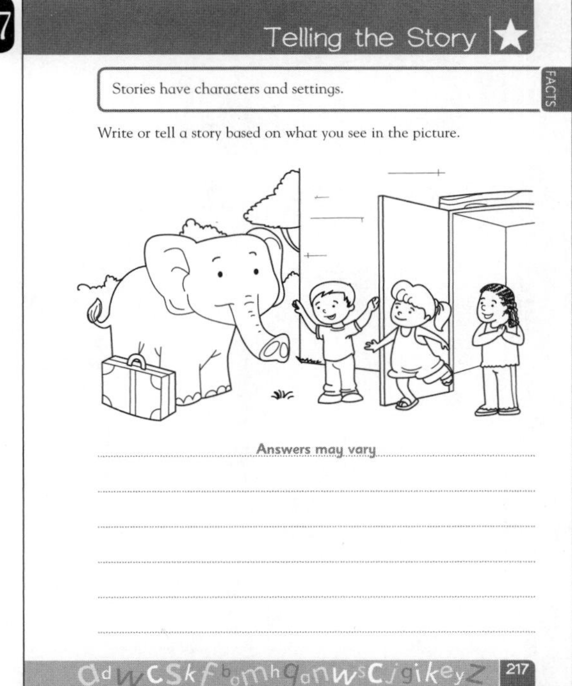

Check your child's writing for capitalization and punctuation. Don't worry about spelling.

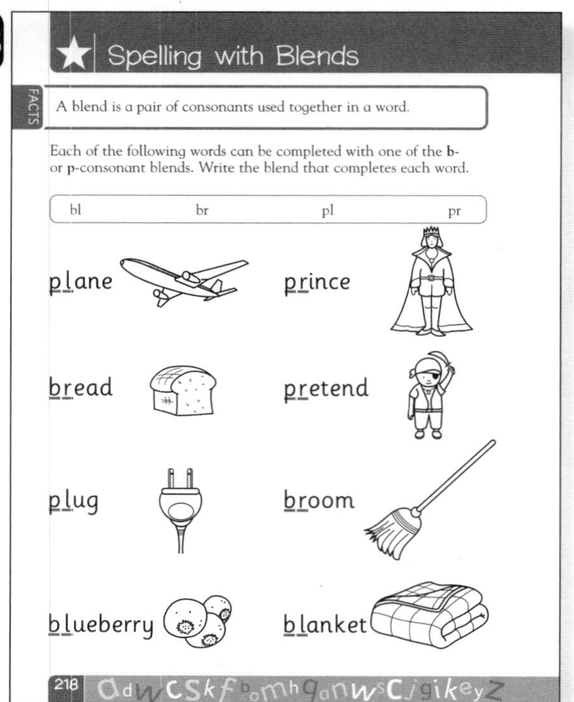

Encourage your child to think of other words with the **bl**, **br**, **pl**, and **pr** consonant blends.

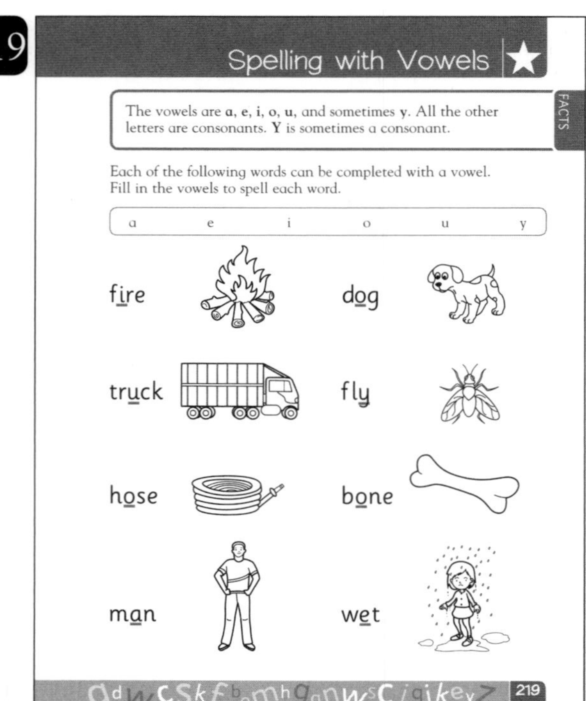

Explain to your child that every word has a vowel. In some instances, such as the words "why" and "spy," the letter **y** is considered a vowel.

Practice using verbs by giving your child verbs to demonstrate.

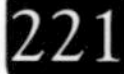

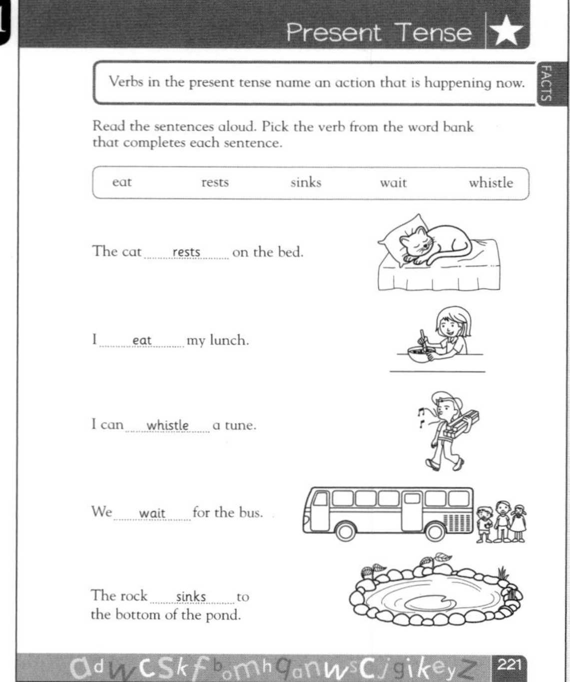

Present Tense
FACTS
Verbs in the present tense name an action that is happening now.
Read the sentences aloud. Pick the verb from the word bank that completes each sentence.
eat rests sinks wait whistle
The cat rests on the bed.
I eat my lunch.
I can whistle a tune.
We wait for the bus.
The rock sinks to the bottom of the pond.
221

After completing the activity on page 222, invite your child to come back to the verbs on this page. Help your child put them in the past tense.

222

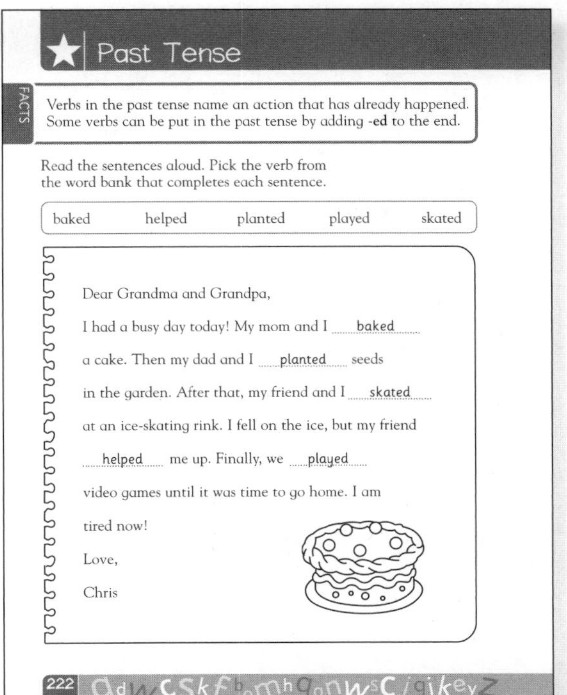

Past Tense

FACTS

Verbs in the past tense name an action that has already happened. Some verbs can be put in the past tense by adding **-ed** to the end.

Read the sentences aloud. Pick the verb from the word bank that completes each sentence.

baked	helped	planted	played	skated

Dear Grandma and Grandpa,

I had a busy day today! My mom and I baked a cake. Then my dad and I planted seeds in the garden. After that, my friend and I skated at an ice-skating rink. I fell on the ice, but my friend helped me up. Finally, we played video games until it was time to go home. I am tired now!

Love,

Chris

Ask your child to describe the previous day's activities using verbs in the past tense.

223

Future Tense

FACTS

A verb is a word that names an action. Verbs in the future tense name an action that has not yet happened but will happen later.

Verbs in the future tense are usually paired with "will." Complete each sentence by writing the verb in the future tense.

Dad will wash the car. (wash)

You will cook dinner tonight. (cook)

We will ride the bus to school tomorrow. (ride)

I will meet you at the park at 3:00 p.m. (meet)

James will visit his cousins next summer. (visit)

The chef will add salt to the soup if she needs to. (add)

Ask your child to say what may happen tomorrow, using verbs in the future tense.

224

My Favorite Book

FACTS

Books are written by authors. They have titles.

Stories are fiction, or made up. Books that are true are called nonfiction. What is your favorite book to read? Fill in the blanks.

The title of my favorite book is: Answers may vary

The author is: Answers may vary

The book is about: Answers may vary

Check one. My favorite book is:

☐ fiction ☐ nonfiction Answers may vary

A book's cover gives the reader an idea of what the book is about. Design a cover for your favorite book.

Answers may vary

When you read books with your children, point out the features on the cover: title, author, and illustrator. Invite your child to make predictions about the story based on the information on the cover. If the book is a familiar one, talk about why the cover illustration is (or is not) a good choice for the book.

225

My Day

FACTS

A diary is a record of what you did or felt during a day.

Fill in the blanks.

My Day

Write today's date: Answers may vary

Write the names of three people you saw today.

1. Answers may vary
2. Answers may vary
3. Answers may vary

Write three sentences describing what you did or how you felt today.

1. Answers may vary
2. Answers may vary
3. Answers may vary

This activity can be repeated regularly on separate pieces of paper. Tell your child that writing daily about one's thoughts and experiences is called keeping a diary, or journal. At this age, your child may not want to take on a daily diary, but using this activity as a template for regular practice can build writing skills.

226

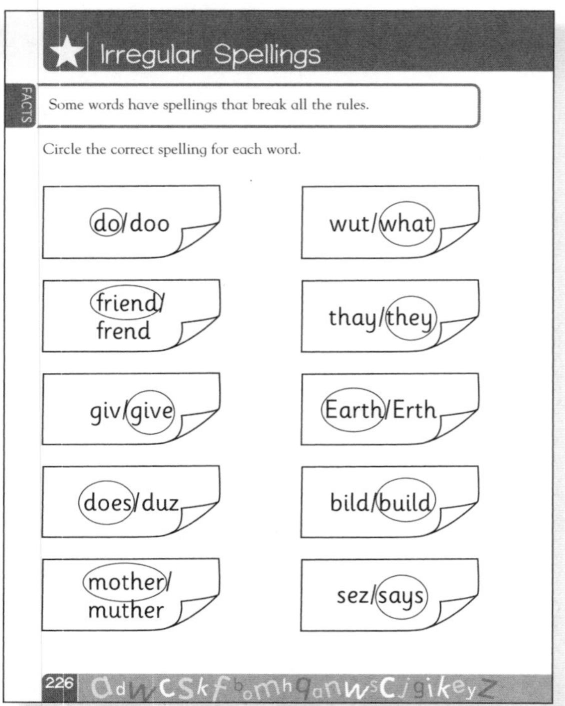

Irregular Spellings

FACTS: Some words have spellings that break all the rules.

Circle the correct spelling for each word.

do/doo	wut/what
friend/frend	thay/they
giv/give	Earth/Erth
does/duz	bild/build
mother/muther	sez/says

226

The only way to learn to spell words with irregular spellings is through repetition. Over time, your child will become familiar with them.

227

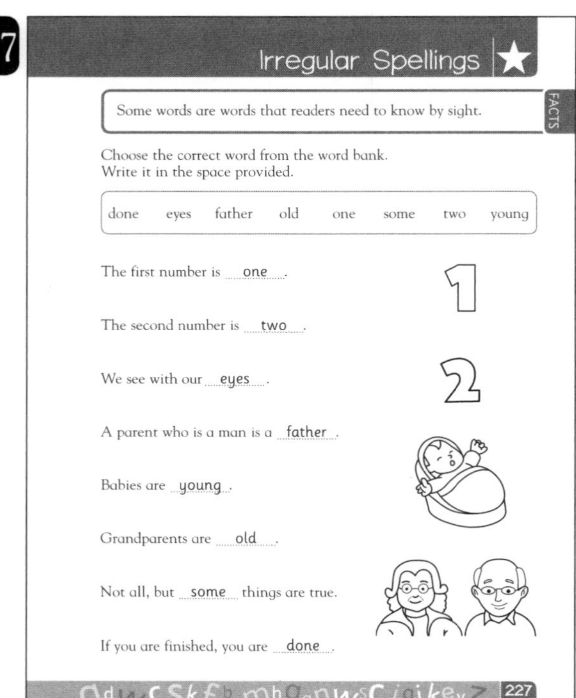

Irregular Spellings

FACTS: Some words are words that readers need to know by sight.

Choose the correct word from the word bank.
Write it in the space provided.

done eyes father old one some two young

The first number is one.

The second number is two.

We see with our eyes.

A parent who is a man is a father.

Babies are young.

Grandparents are old.

Not all, but some things are true.

If you are finished, you are done.

227

As your child becomes more adept at reading, he or she will begin to recognize words that have irregular spellings.

228

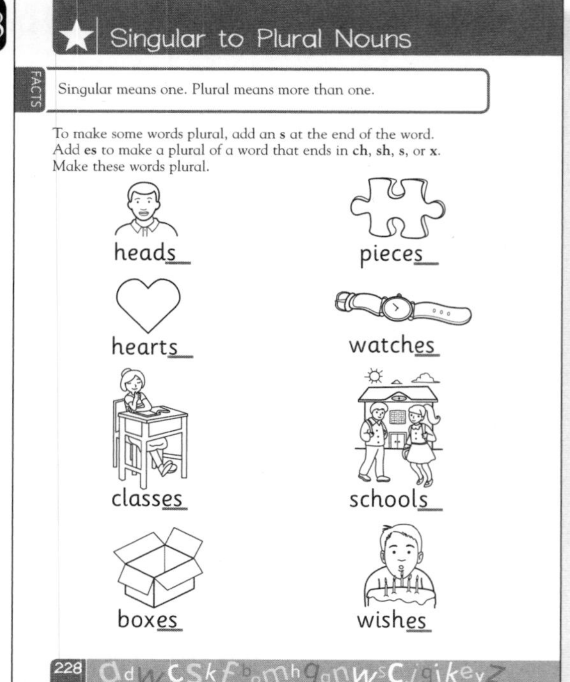

Singular to Plural Nouns

FACTS: Singular means one. Plural means more than one.

To make some words plural, add an **s** at the end of the word.
Add **es** to make a plural of a word that ends in **ch**, **sh**, **s**, or **x**.
Make these words plural.

heads	pieces
hearts	watches
classes	schools
boxes	wishes

228

Challenge your child to find examples of plural nouns printed around your house (such as on food packaging, game boxes, or the titles of books). Ask your child to name the singular noun.

229

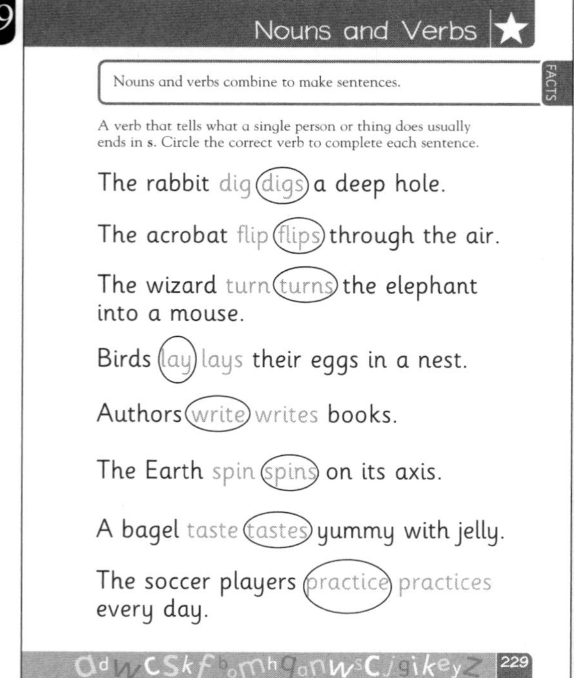

Nouns and Verbs

FACTS: Nouns and verbs combine to make sentences.

A verb that tells what a single person or thing does usually ends in **s**. Circle the correct verb to complete each sentence.

The rabbit dig digs a deep hole.

The acrobat flip flips through the air.

The wizard turn turns the elephant into a mouse.

Birds lay lays their eggs in a nest.

Authors write writes books.

The Earth spin spins on its axis.

A bagel taste tastes yummy with jelly.

The soccer players practice practices every day.

229

When a verb is properly matched to a noun (i.e., "Joe plays" versus "Joe play"), the noun and verb are in agreement.

230

Instructions

FACTS

Instructions tell us how to do something in a clear, logical order.

Think of something you know how to do well.
Then fill in the instructions below.

How to Answers may vary

First, Answers may vary

Next, Answers may vary

Then, Answers may vary

Finally, Answers may vary

Now you know how to Answers may vary

Read through the instructions of a favorite game or recipe together to give your child a real-world example of how instructions are presented.

231

Step-by-step Instructions

FACTS

Instructions use numbered steps or words like "first," "next," and "last" to help the reader understand the order of the instructions.

Read the instructions. Then underline the words that tell what items you need to complete the activity. Finally, answer the questions that follow.

1. Ask an adult to help you use the toaster.
2. Place a new piece of bread in the toaster. Turn on the toaster.
3. After about a minute, take the bread out of the toaster.
4. Place the toasted bread on a plate.
5. Use a knife to spread butter, jelly, or peanut butter on the toast.
6. Eat.

What do the instructions tell how to do?

The instructions tell how to make toast.

How many steps are there?

There are six steps.

Explain to your child how breaking up instructions into steps and numbering them can make the instructions easier to follow.

232

Conjunctions

FACTS

Conjunctions are words that join other words together.
Conjunctions include "and," "but," "or," "so," and "because."

Put each pair of sentences into the conjunction mixer!
Add "and" to make one sentence.

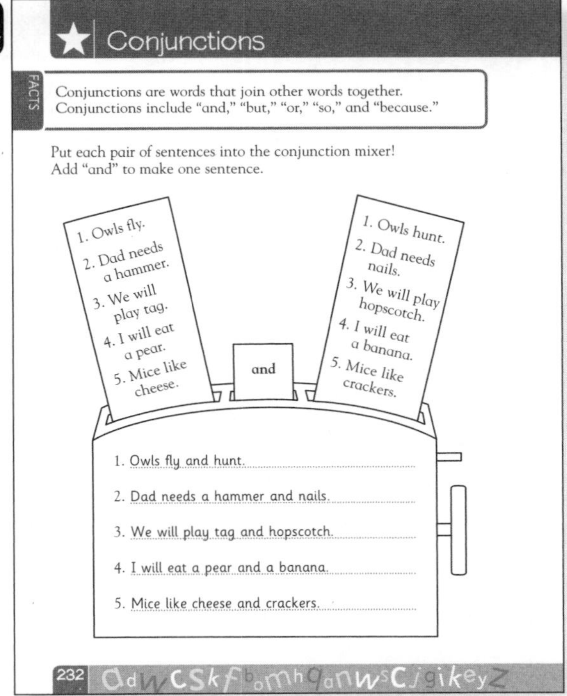

1. Owls fly.
2. Dad needs a hammer.
3. We will play tag.
4. I will eat a pear.
5. Mice like cheese.
and
1. Owls hunt.
2. Dad needs nails.
3. We will play hopscotch.
4. I will eat a banana.
5. Mice like crackers.
1. Owls fly and hunt.
2. Dad needs a hammer and nails.
3. We will play tag and hopscotch.
4. I will eat a pear and a banana.
5. Mice like cheese and crackers.

Invite children to come up with their own sentences based on the models given.

233

Conjunctions

FACTS

Conjunctions combine ideas.
"Because" gives a reason for an action or thought.

Put each pair of sentences into the conjunction mixer!
Add "because" to make one sentence.

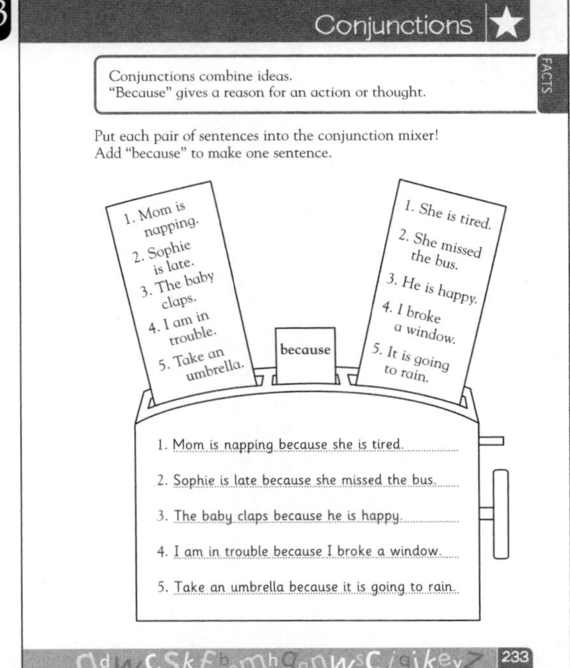

1. Mom is napping.
2. Sophie is late.
3. The baby claps.
4. I am in trouble.
5. Take an umbrella.
because
1. She is tired.
2. She missed the bus.
3. He is happy.
4. I broke a window.
5. It is going to rain.
1. Mom is napping because she is tired.
2. Sophie is late because she missed the bus.
3. The baby claps because he is happy.
4. I am in trouble because I broke a window.
5. Take an umbrella because it is going to rain.

Challenge your child to come up with a sentence with another conjunction, such as "but" or "so."

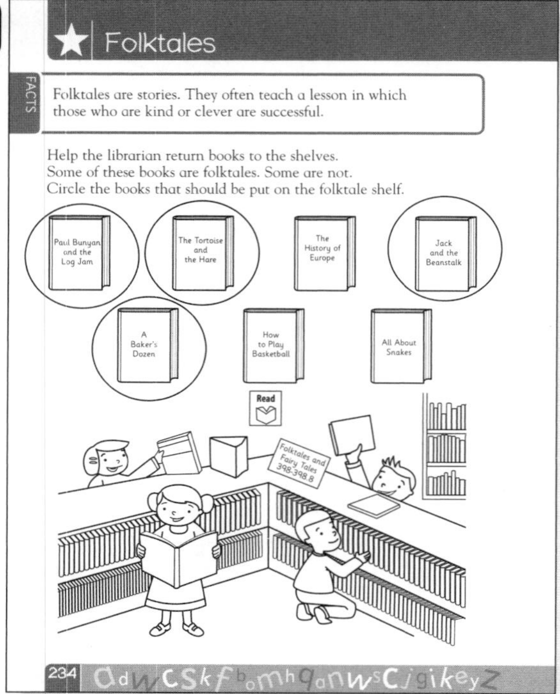

Folktales

FACTS

Folktales are stories. They often teach a lesson in which those who are kind or clever are successful.

Help the librarian return books to the shelves.
Some of these books are folktales. Some are not.
Circle the books that should be put on the folktale shelf.

Look in your local library for folktales to read with your child. The Dewey Decimal number for folktales told as stories is 398.2.

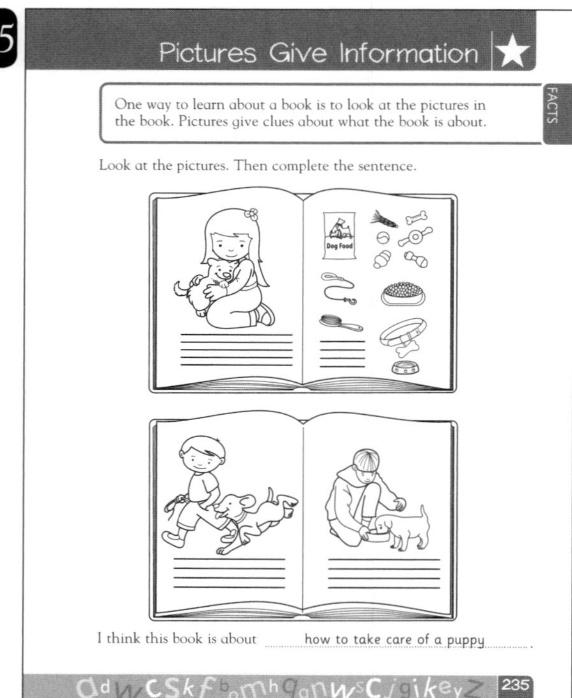

Pictures Give Information

FACTS

One way to learn about a book is to look at the pictures in the book. Pictures give clues about what the book is about.

Look at the pictures. Then complete the sentence.

I think this book is about how to take care of a puppy.

As you read books with your child, point out the information you find in pictures. By demonstrating this process, you expose your child to this type of thinking and learning.

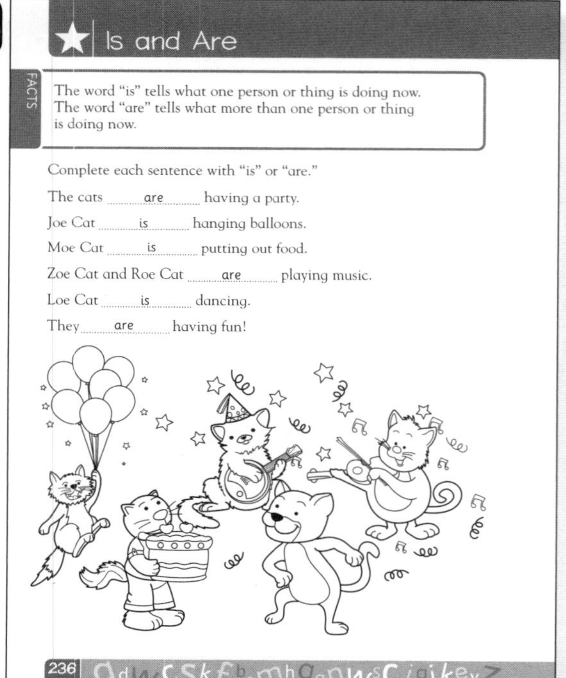

Is and Are

FACTS

The word "is" tells what one person or thing is doing now. The word "are" tells what more than one person or thing is doing now.

Complete each sentence with "is" or "are."

The cats are having a party.

Joe Cat is hanging balloons.

Moe Cat is putting out food.

Zoe Cat and Roe Cat are playing music.

Loe Cat is dancing.

They are having fun!

Invite your child to come up with original sentences using "is" and "are."

237

Word Endings

FACTS

Verbs can have endings that tell when the action took place. The verb on its own is called a root word.

Read the pairs of sentences. Use **-ing** to complete the root word that describes something happening now. Use **-ed** to complete the root word that describes something that has already happened.

Dad is cooking dinner.

Mom cooked dinner last night.

I sewed a button on my shirt last week.

It fell off, so I am sewing it again.

We watched a movie in school this morning.

Now we are watching a movie at home.

Stay on the lookout in your everyday life for printed words ending in **-ing** or **-ed**. Ask your child to name the root words of those words.

238

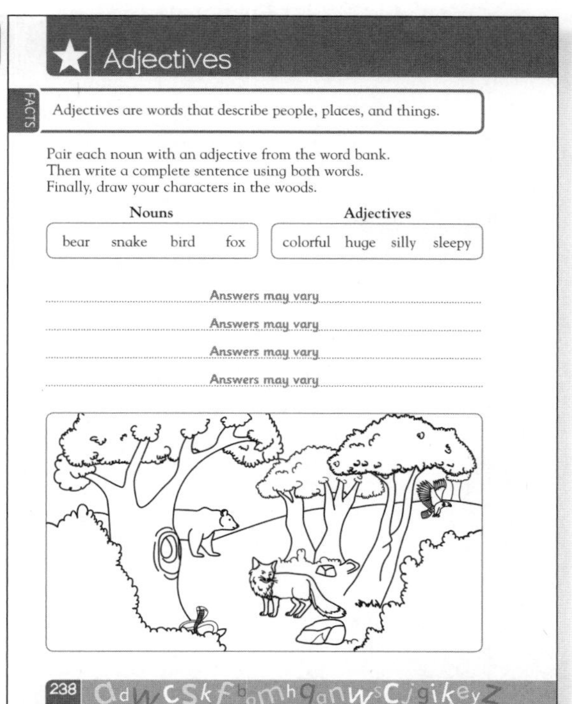

Adjectives

FACTS

Adjectives are words that describe people, places, and things.

Pair each noun with an adjective from the word bank.
Then write a complete sentence using both words.
Finally, draw your characters in the woods.

Nouns	Adjectives
bear snake bird fox	colorful huge silly sleepy

Answers may vary

Answers may vary

Answers may vary

Answers may vary

238

Ask your child to use adjectives to describe the things around you.

239

Prepositions

FACTS

A preposition relates a noun or a pronoun to another word in the sentence.

Complete each sentence with a preposition from the word bank.

behind beside in on over under

Answers may vary

The bird is in the tree.

The bird is under the tree.

The bird is on the tree.

The bird is beside the tree.

The bird is over the tree.

The bird is behind the tree.

239

There are many songs and rhymes to help children understand prepositions. Look online for prepositional rhymes and songs to share with your child.

240

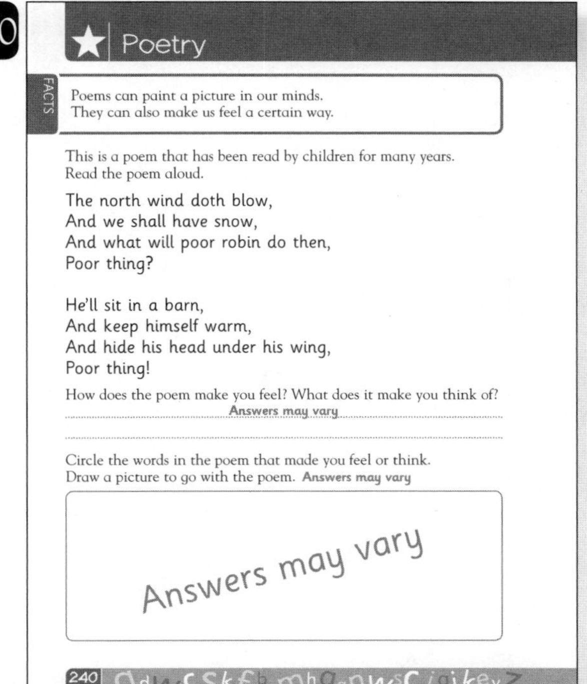

Poetry

FACTS

Poems can paint a picture in our minds.
They can also make us feel a certain way.

This is a poem that has been read by children for many years.
Read the poem aloud.

The north wind doth blow,
And we shall have snow,
And what will poor robin do then,
Poor thing?

He'll sit in a barn,
And keep himself warm,
And hide his head under his wing,
Poor thing!

How does the poem make you feel? What does it make you think of?
Answers may vary

Circle the words in the poem that made you feel or think.
Draw a picture to go with the poem. Answers may vary

Answers may vary

240

Look in your local library for poems to read with your child. Poetry will be found among the 800s in your library.

241

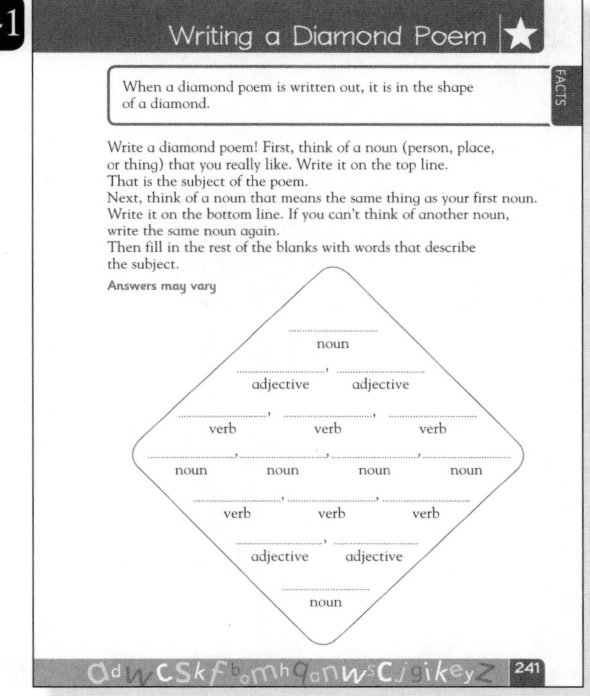

Writing a Diamond Poem

FACTS

When a diamond poem is written out, it is in the shape of a diamond.

Write a diamond poem! First, think of a noun (person, place, or thing) that you really like. Write it on the top line.
That is the subject of the poem.
Next, think of a noun that means the same thing as your first noun.
Write it on the bottom line. If you can't think of another noun, write the same noun again.
Then fill in the rest of the blanks with words that describe the subject.

Answers may vary

noun

adjective, adjective

verb, verb, verb

noun, noun, noun, noun

verb, verb, verb

adjective, adjective

noun

241

If your child enjoys this activity, encourage him or her child to write more diamond poems on separate pieces of paper.

246

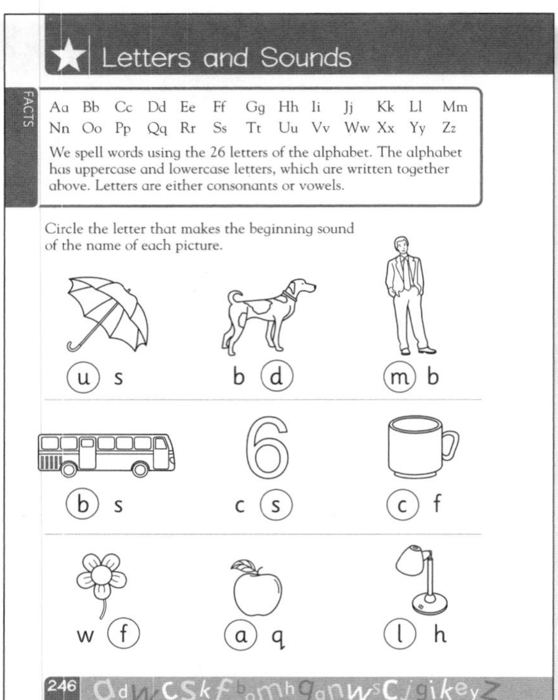

Letters and Sounds

FACTS

Aa Bb Cc Dd Ee Ff Gg Hh Ii Jj Kk Ll Mm
Nn Oo Pp Qq Rr Ss Tt Uu Vv Ww Xx Yy Zz

We spell words using the 26 letters of the alphabet. The alphabet has uppercase and lowercase letters, which are written together above. Letters are either consonants or vowels.

Circle the letter that makes the beginning sound of the name of each picture.

u s | b d | m b

b s | c s | c f

w f | a q | l h

246

Ask your child to say the beginning sounds of his or her name and to identify the letter. Next, help your child to make the sound of each beginning letter on this page.

247

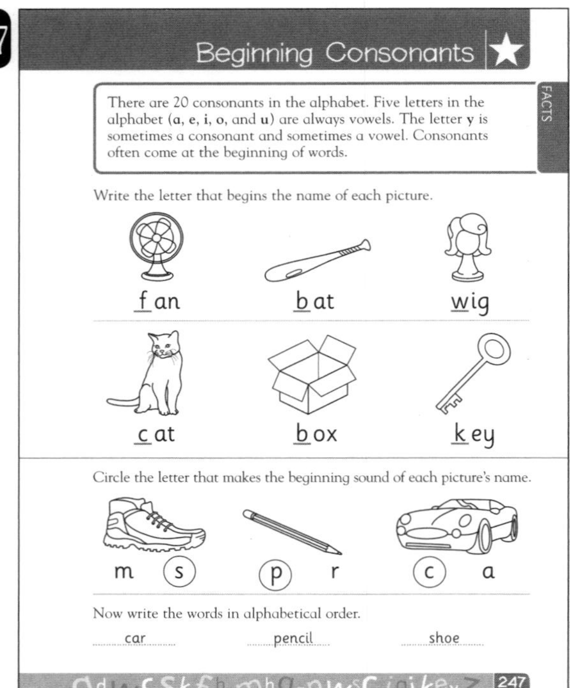

Beginning Consonants

FACTS

There are 20 consonants in the alphabet. Five letters in the alphabet (**a**, **e**, **i**, **o**, and **u**) are always vowels. The letter **y** is sometimes a consonant and sometimes a vowel. Consonants often come at the beginning of words.

Write the letter that begins the name of each picture.

fan | bat | wig

cat | box | key

Circle the letter that makes the beginning sound of each picture's name.

m s | p r | c a

Now write the words in alphabetical order.

car | pencil | shoe

247

Continue to reinforce beginning consonant sounds. You might want to explain that different letters can make the same sound in some words, such as **c** and **k** in "cut" and "kind."

248

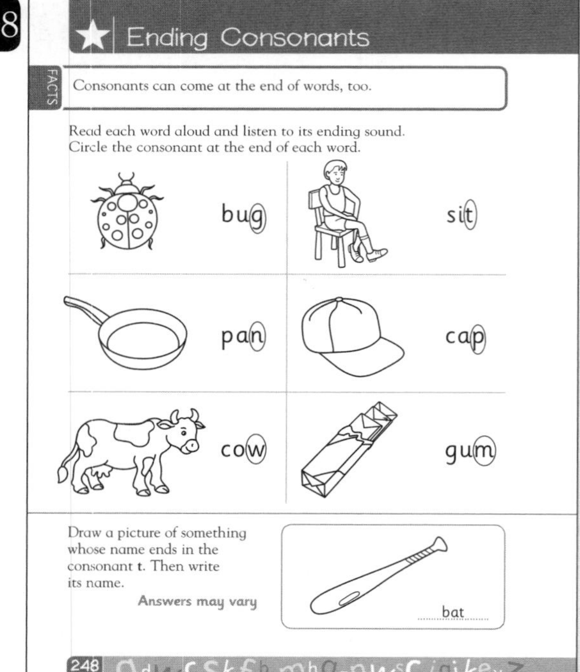

Ending Consonants

FACTS

Consonants can come at the end of words, too.

Read each word aloud and listen to its ending sound. Circle the consonant at the end of each word.

bug | sit

pan | cap

cow | gum

Draw a picture of something whose name ends in the consonant **t**. Then write its name.

Answers may vary

bat

248

Say a word and let your child identify the ending sound. Next, say groups of three words with the same ending consonant and let your child identify the sound and the letter that makes the sound.

249

Consonant Blends

FACTS

Consonant blends are two or more consonants that come together to make one sound. Some consonant blends come at the beginning and others at the end of words. For example, say the word "glove." Listen to the "gl" sound at the beginning.

Read the name of the first picture aloud. Listen to the beginning blend. Then circle the name of the picture with the same beginning sound.

fruit | plane | frog | kite

clock | clown | globe | skunk

Read the name of the first picture aloud. Listen to the ending blend. Circle the name of the picture with the same ending sound.

ring | king | nest | salt

hand | sink | shelf | band

249

Find things with names that begin with consonant blends, such as a glove or a crayon. Let your child say the name aloud. Then help him or her identify and write the letters in the blend. Repeat with things that have names with ending blends, such as a belt or a lamp.

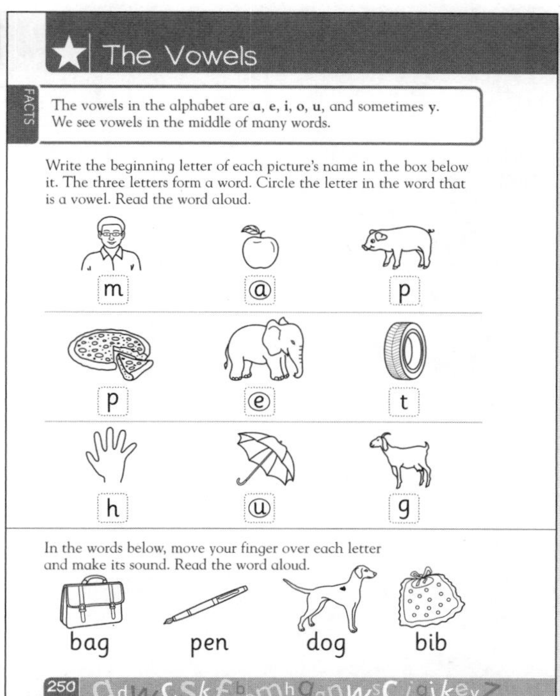

Say the word "dog." Then say the separate letter sounds of the word "d-o-g." After that, ask your child to say "dog." Then ask him or her to identify the letter that makes the middle sound of the word.

251
Missing Vowels
FACTS
The vowels a, e, i, o, and u each have a long sound and a short sound. When used as a vowel, y makes a long "i" sound or a long "e" sound.
Some vowels in the picture are missing.
Where in the world can they be?
Look at each word in the picture.
Write in its vowel, please!
sun
swing
nest
ball
bush
slide
rock
rope
251

Have your child listen carefully as you say these three words: "sun," "fun," and "cat." Let him or her identify which word has a different middle sound. Ask your child how that sound is different and which letter is associated with that sound.

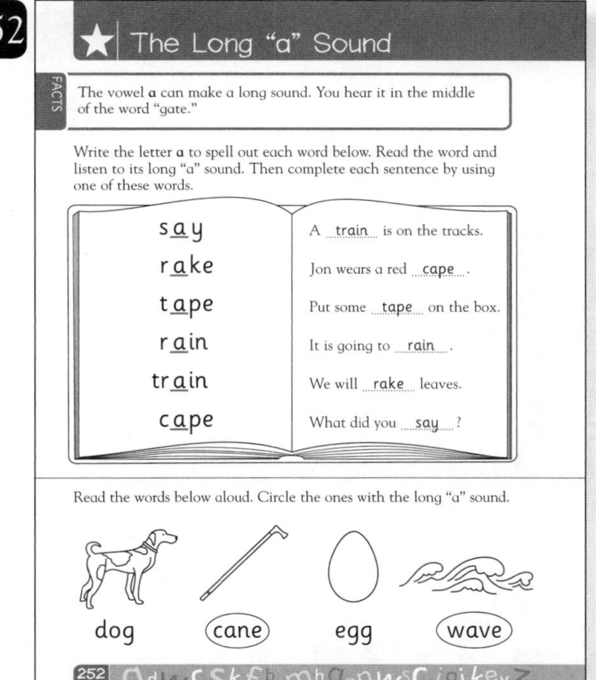

252
The Long "a" Sound
FACTS
The vowel a can make a long sound. You hear it in the middle of the word "gate."
Write the letter a to spell out each word below. Read the word and listen to its long "a" sound. Then complete each sentence by using one of these words.
say
rake
tape
rain
train
cape
A train is on the tracks.
Jon wears a red cape.
Put some tape on the box.
It is going to rain.
We will rake leaves.
What did you say?
Read the words below aloud. Circle the ones with the long "a" sound.
dog cane egg wave
252

Let your child write long "a" words on strips of paper. Use the strips to make a paper chain. Then go through each link of the chain together and read the long "a" words. Encourage your child to use the words in sentences.

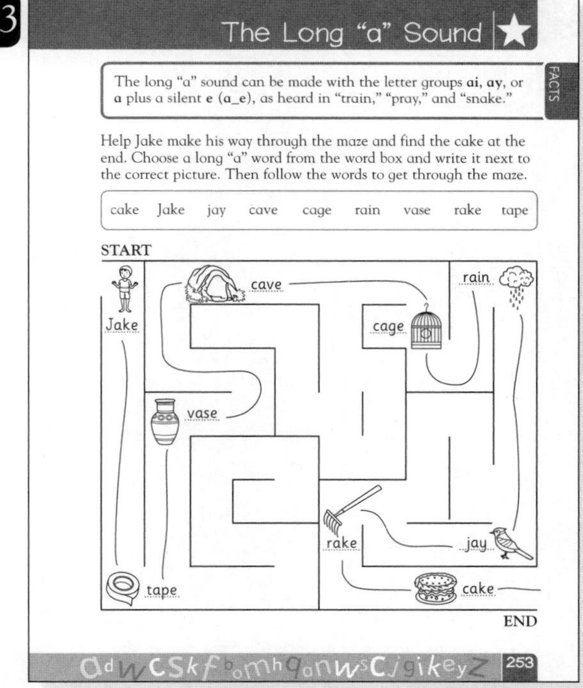

253
The Long "a" Sound
FACTS
The long "a" sound can be made with the letter groups ai, ay, or a plus a silent e (a_e), as heard in "train," "pray," and "snake."
Help Jake make his way through the maze and find the cake at the end. Choose a long "a" word from the word box and write it next to the correct picture. Then follow the words to get through the maze.
cake Jake jay cave cage rain vase rake tape
START
Jake
cave
rain
cage
vase
rake
jay
tape
cake
END
253

Write long "a" words from the same rhyming family, such as "rain" and "pain." Let your child create new words, such as "gain" and "main," by substituting the letter in front of the long "a" ending. Continue the activity using other long "a" endings, such as "ane," "ate," and "ake."

254

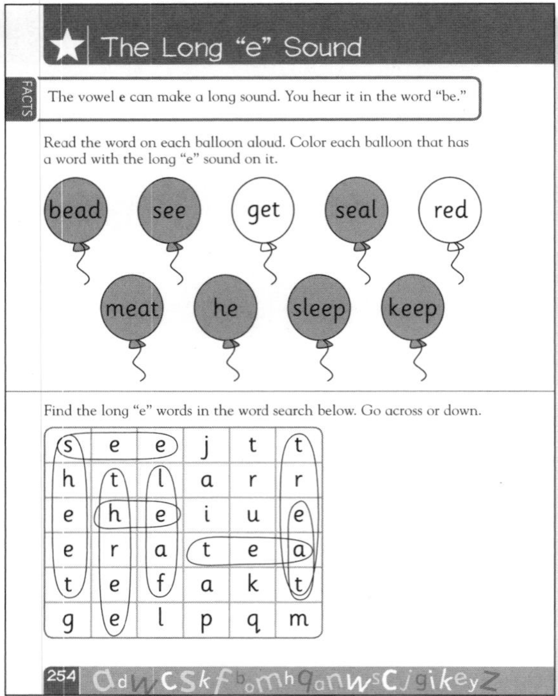

The Long "e" Sound

FACTS: The vowel **e** can make a long sound. You hear it in the word "be."

Read the word on each balloon aloud. Color each balloon that has a word with the long "e" sound on it.

bead see get seal red
meat he sleep keep

Find the long "e" words in the word search below. Go across or down.

s	e	e	j	t	t
h	t	l	a	r	r
e	h	e	i	u	e
e	r	a	t	e	a
t	e	f	a	k	t
g	e	l	p	q	m

Look through magazines or newspapers with your child to find long "e" words with various spellings, such as with letters **ee** or **ea**. Read the words aloud. Invite your child to draw a picture of something with a name that has a long "e" sound.

255

The Long "e" Sound

FACTS: The long "e" sound can be made by the letter groups **ea**, **ee**, **ey**, **ie**, or a lone **e** at the end of a short word.

Choose the correct long "e" word to finish each sentence. Then read the sentences aloud.

The name of the baseball team was the Sluggers.	**term**	**team**	**treat**
They were playing in a park near a big tree .	**see**	**tree**	**heel**
The green baseball field was very smooth.	**feel**	**green**	**treat**
The Sluggers could see that this would be a hard game.	**sail**	**see**	**she**
Each player took a turn at bat.	**Teach**	**Reach**	**Each**
Brittany threw the ball to me .	**me**	**we**	**he**
Tom hurt his knee .	**keep**	**peel**	**knee**

Take a walk through the house or neighborhood. Invite your child to look for things with names that have the long "e" sound. How many can he or she find? They might include a tree, feet, meat, beans, and a seat.

256

The Long "i" Sound

FACTS: The vowel **i** can make a long sound. You hear it in the middle of the word "hike."

Does each word in the table below have the long "i" sound? Check (✓) **Yes** or **No**.

Word	Yes	No	Word	Yes	No
line	✓		hit		✓
if		✓	bike	✓	
fire	✓		fix		✓
find	✓		hide	✓	
kite	✓		side	✓	

Read the clues and pick the correct long "i" word from the word box.

mice tires light bike smile

It shows you are happy. smile

You ride it. bike

There are four on a car. tires

They are little animals. mice

It helps us to see. light

On a piece of paper, make two columns. Label one column "Long i" and the other "Short i." Show simple words containing the letter **i**. Let your child read each word aloud and then write it in the correct column.

257

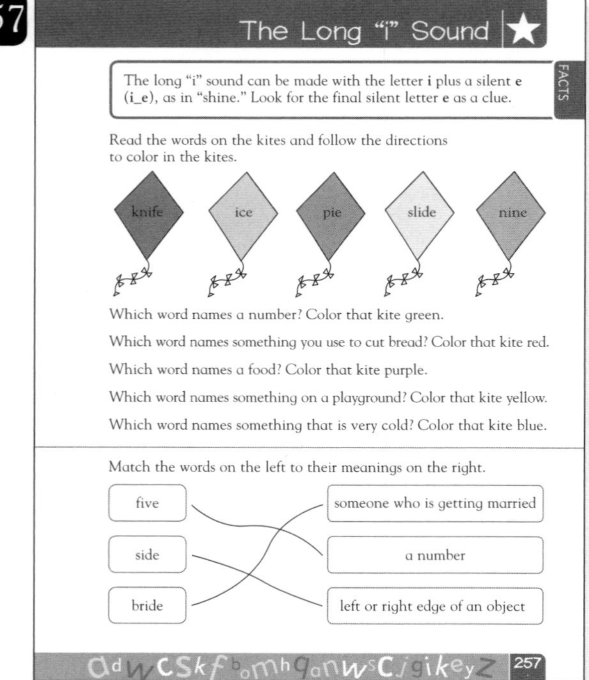

The Long "i" Sound

FACTS: The long "i" sound can be made with the letter **i** plus a silent **e** (i_e), as in "shine." Look for the final silent letter **e** as a clue.

Read the words on the kites and follow the directions to color in the kites.

knife ice pie slide nine

Which word names a number? Color that kite green.

Which word names something you use to cut bread? Color that kite red.

Which word names a food? Color that kite purple.

Which word names something on a playground? Color that kite yellow.

Which word names something that is very cold? Color that kite blue.

Match the words on the left to their meanings on the right.

five	someone who is getting married
side	a number
bride	left or right edge of an object

Tape a dime to the center of a piece of paper. Say the word "dime." Draw four lines radiating out from around the dime. Let your child write a long "i" word at the end of each line.

258

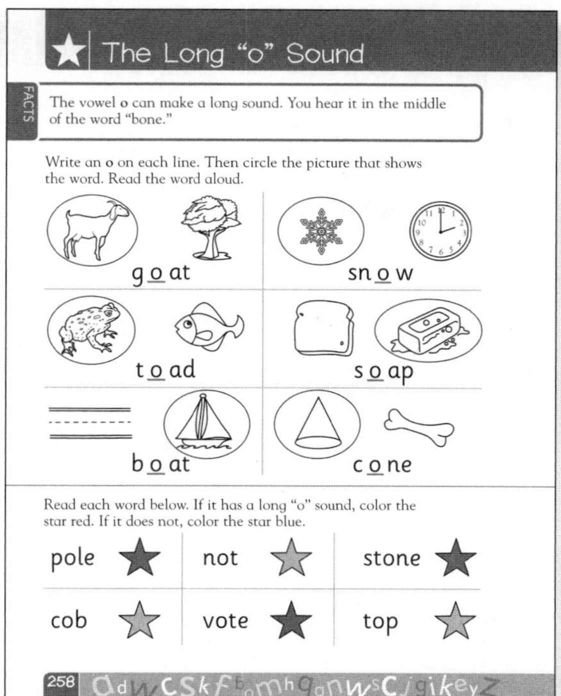

★ The Long "o" Sound

FACTS: The vowel **o** can make a long sound. You hear it in the middle of the word "bone."

Write an **o** on each line. Then circle the picture that shows the word. Read the word aloud.

g o at — sn o w — t o ad — s o ap — b o at — c o ne

Read each word below. If it has a long "o" sound, color the star red. If it does not, color the star blue.

pole	not	stone
cob	vote	top

258

Let your child use clay to model objects whose names have the long "o" sound, such as coat, boat, and rope. Have your child say each word aloud.

259

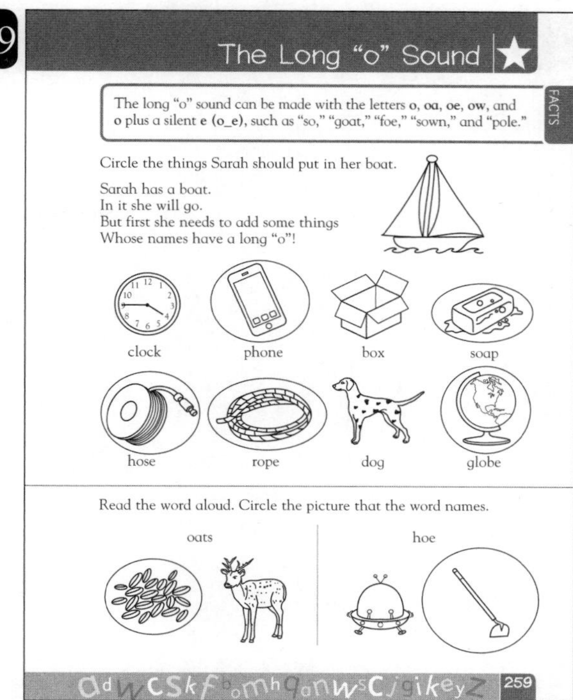

The Long "o" Sound ★

FACTS: The long "o" sound can be made with the letters **o**, **oa**, **oe**, **ow**, and **o** plus a silent **e** (**o_e**), such as "so," "goat," "foe," "sown," and "pole."

Circle the things Sarah should put in her boat.

Sarah has a boat.
In it she will go.
But first she needs to add some things
Whose names have a long "o"!

clock — phone — box — soap
hose — rope — dog — globe

Read the word aloud. Circle the picture that the word names.

oats — hoe

259

With your child, write silly rhymes using long "o" words. For example, "Silly goat put on a coat, jumped in the boat, and started to float!"

260

★ The Long "u" Sound

FACTS: The vowel **u** can make a long sound. You hear it in the middle of the word "rule."

Fill in the long "u" word to complete each sentence.

The baby is so cute ! — **cute** **bun**

The tube is filled with toothpaste. — **bug** **tube**

That dinosaur is huge ! — **huge** **hug**

Read the words below. Circle the words that have the same "u" sound as "rule."

just	tune	gut
June	run	bug
cane	rug	flute
sun	brute	tub

260

Say three words, two of which have the long "u" sound and another word that does not. For example, "blew," "flew," and "dog." Ask your child to identify the word that does not belong and to explain why.

261

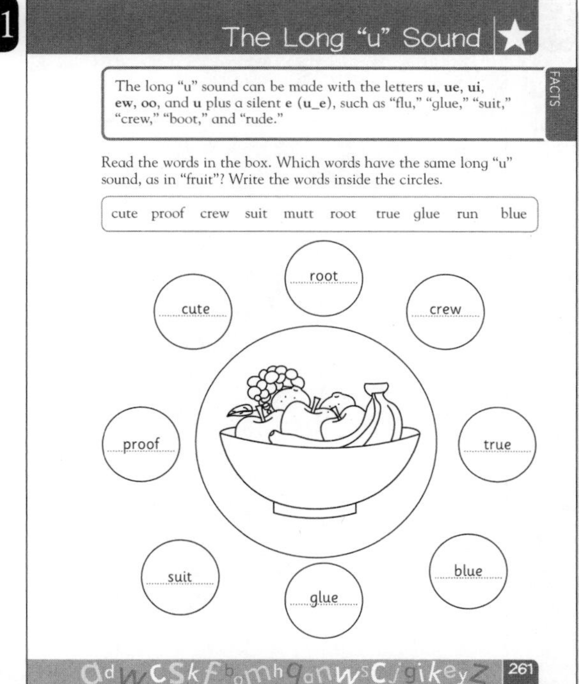

The Long "u" Sound ★

FACTS: The long "u" sound can be made with the letters **u**, **ue**, **ui**, **ew**, **oo**, and **u** plus a silent **e** (**u_e**), such as "flu," "glue," "suit," "crew," "boot," and "rude."

Read the words in the box. Which words have the same long "u" sound, as in "fruit"? Write the words inside the circles.

cute proof crew suit mutt root true glue run blue

root — cute — crew — proof — true — suit — blue — glue

261

Prepare word cards labeled "Long a," "Long e," "Long i," "Long o," and "Long u." Spread the cards on a table for your child to see. Say a simple word with a long vowel sound. Let your child identify the vowel sound by holding up the correct card.

262

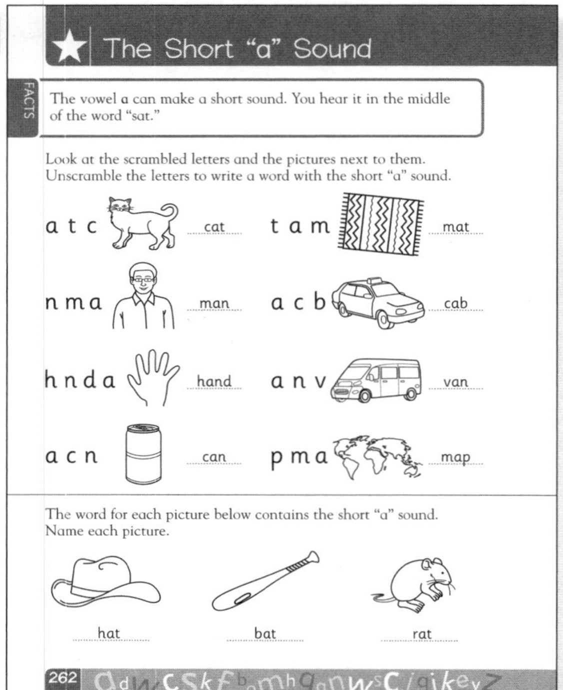

The Short "a" Sound

FACTS

The vowel a can make a short sound. You hear it in the middle of the word "sat."

Look at the scrambled letters and the pictures next to them. Unscramble the letters to write a word with the short "a" sound.

a t c	cat	t a m	mat
n m a	man	a c b	cab
h n d a	hand	a n v	van
a c n	can	p m a	map

The word for each picture below contains the short "a" sound. Name each picture.

hat bat rat

262

On paper strips, write simple words with short vowel sounds. Place the strips in a bag. Pick a strip and read the word. Let your child decide if it has the short "a" sound. When the bag is empty, review the short "a" word strips.

263

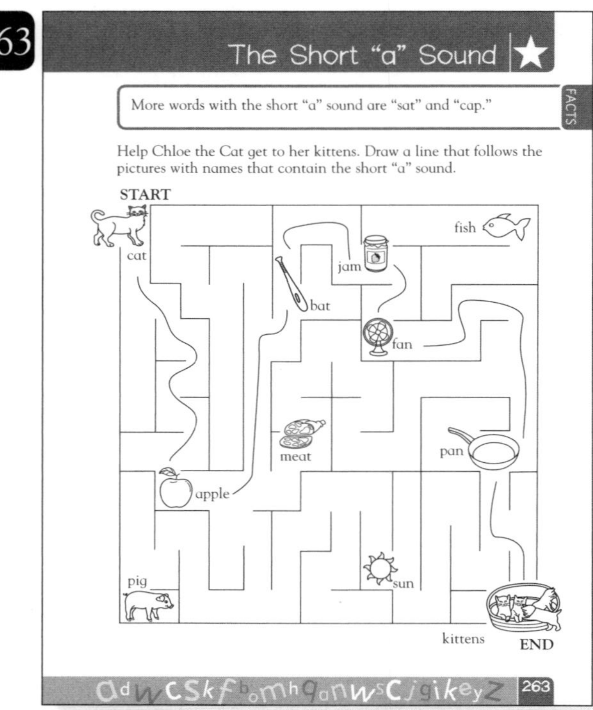

The Short "a" Sound

FACTS

More words with the short "a" sound are "sat" and "cap."

Help Chloe the Cat get to her kittens. Draw a line that follows the pictures with names that contain the short "a" sound.

263

Write short "a" words on index cards. Make two cards for each word. Mix them up and place the cards facedown. Let your child turn over pairs of cards to find each matching pair.

264

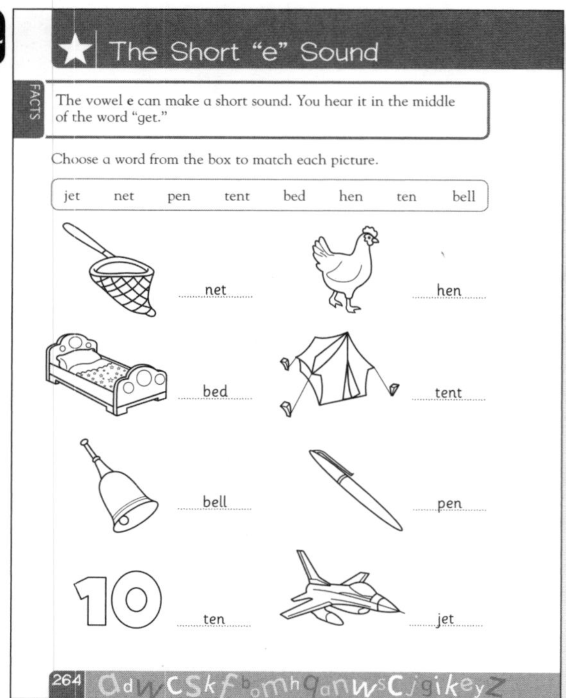

The Short "e" Sound

FACTS

The vowel e can make a short sound. You hear it in the middle of the word "get."

Choose a word from the box to match each picture.

jet net pen tent bed hen ten bell

net		hen	
bed		tent	
bell		pen	
10	ten		jet

264

Divide a piece of paper into four squares. In each square, write a short "e" word, such as "pet," "net," "men," or "steps." Invite your child to illustrate these words. Repeat with other short "e" words.

265

The Short "e" Sound

FACTS

More words with the short "e" sound are "pet," "let," and "went."

Hettie the Hen has lots of eggs! Look at the pictures and the words on each egg. If the word has the short "e" sound, color it yellow.

265

Play a game. Say, "I'm thinking of a word that has a short 'e' sound." Offer a clue. Say, "It starts with 'm' and rhymes with the word 'pet.'" Let your child say the words and encourage him or her to listen for the vowel sound.

266

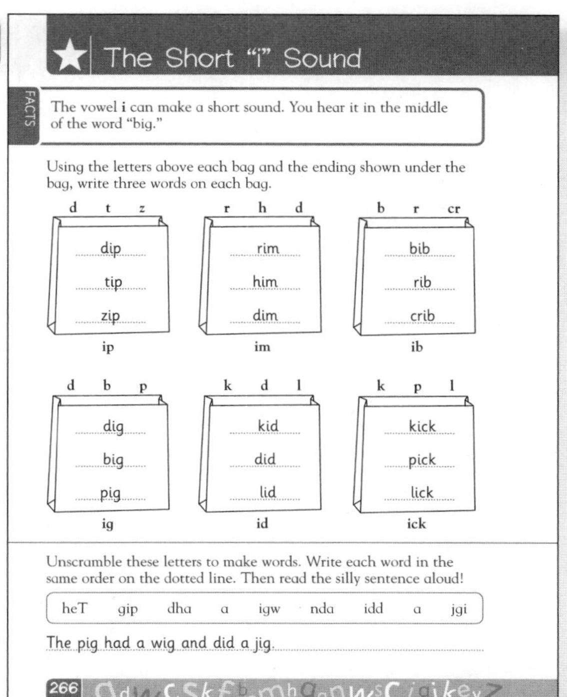

The Short "i" Sound

FACTS: The vowel **i** can make a short sound. You hear it in the middle of the word "big."

Using the letters above each bag and the ending shown under the bag, write three words on each bag.

d t z	r h d	b r cr
dip tip zip	rim him dim	bib rib crib
ip	im	ib

d b p	k d l	k p l
dig big pig	kid did lid	kick pick lick
ig	id	ick

Unscramble these letters to make words. Write each word in the same order on the dotted line. Then read the silly sentence aloud!

heT gip dha a igw nda idd a jgi

The pig had a wig and did a jig.

Review the short "i" sound. Ask your child to make up his or her own silly rhymes using short "i" words from this page as well as other short "i" words he or she can think of.

267

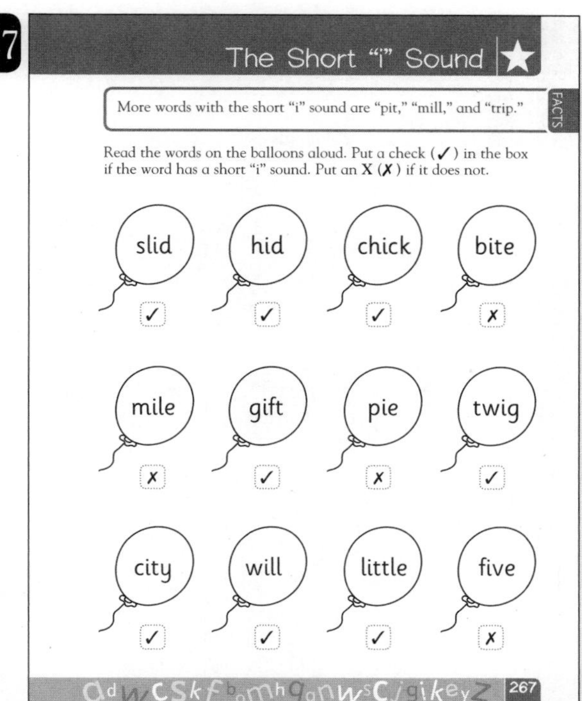

The Short "i" Sound

FACTS: More words with the short "i" sound are "pit," "mill," and "trip."

Read the words on the balloons aloud. Put a check (✓) in the box if the word has a short "i" sound. Put an **X** (✗) if it does not.

slid ✓	hid ✓	chick ✓	bite ✗
mile ✗	gift ✓	pie ✗	twig ✓
city ✓	will ✓	little ✓	five ✗

Write a list of simple words. Include some words with the short "i" sound. Let your child circle the words with a short "i" sound and then write them in alphabetical order.

268

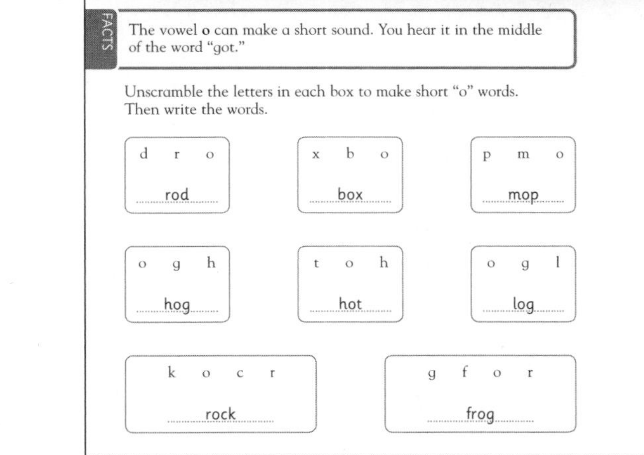

The Short "o" Sound

FACTS: The vowel **o** can make a short sound. You hear it in the middle of the word "got."

Unscramble the letters in each box to make short "o" words. Then write the words.

d r o	x b o	p m o
rod	box	mop
o g h	t o h	o g l
hog	hot	log

k o c r	g f o r
rock	frog

Choosing from the unscrambled short "o" words above, write the answer to each question.

Which word names an animal that croaks? frog

Which word means the opposite of cold? hot

Which word names something you use when fishing? rod

Draw a picture of a sock on a piece of paper. Around it, let your child draw pictures of items that have names that rhyme with the word "sock." They might include a rock, lock, dock, block, or clock. Encourage your child to use each word in a sentence.

269

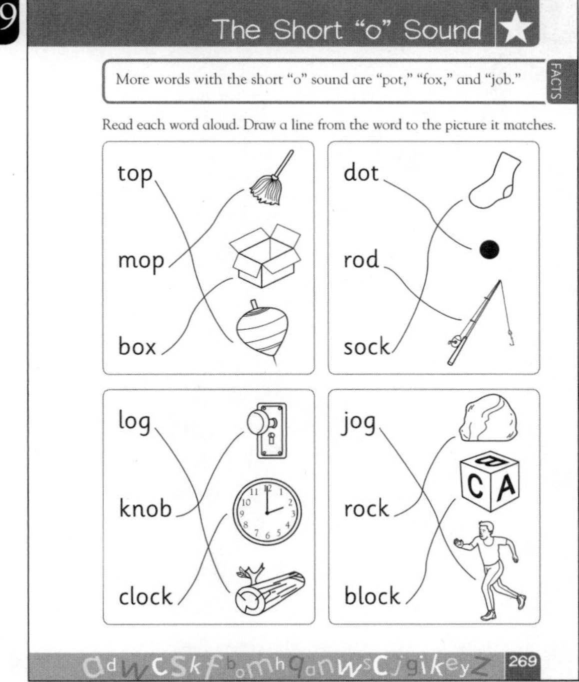

The Short "o" Sound

FACTS: More words with the short "o" sound are "pot," "fox," and "job."

Read each word aloud. Draw a line from the word to the picture it matches.

Read to your child the book *Hop On Pop* by Dr. Seuss. Discuss all the short-vowel words in the book. Have your child draw pictures to show the phrases in the book he or she enjoyed the most.

270

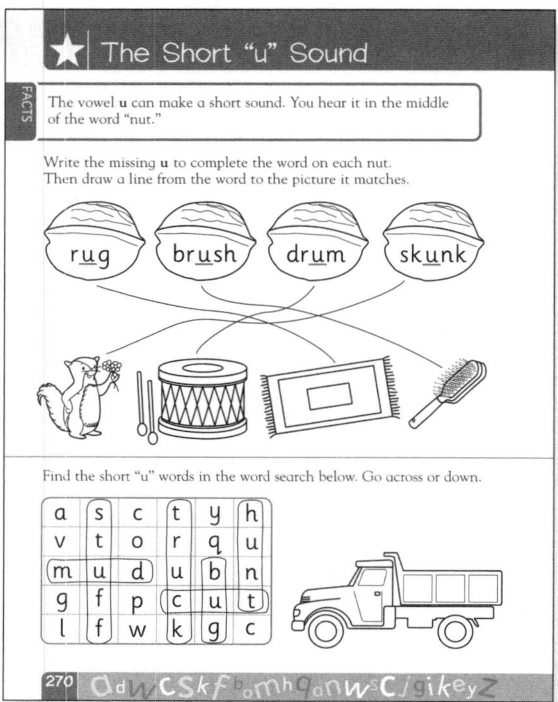

Make ladybugs by cutting out small red paper ovals and adding black dots to them. On each ladybug, write a short word that contains the vowel **u**. Hide the ladybugs and let your child find them. Then let your child read the word and tell you if the "u" sound is long or short.

271

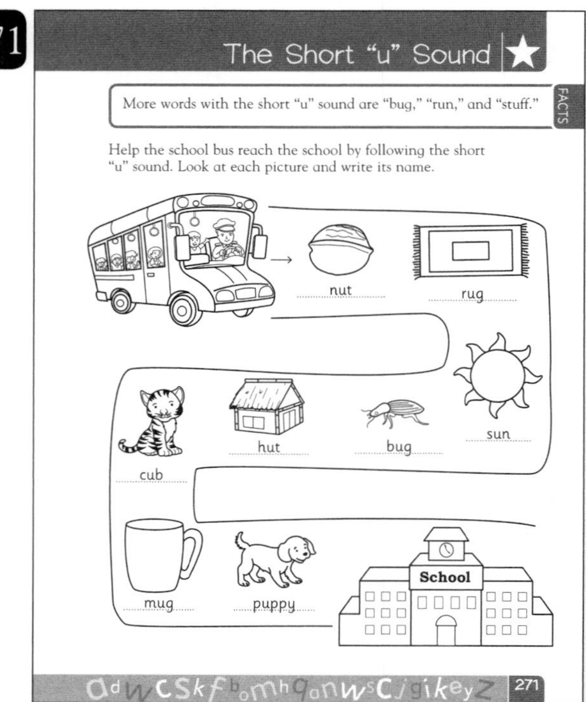

Give your child five index cards, each with a different vowel written on it. Say a list of words containing short vowel sounds. Let your child hold up the correct vowel card after listening to each word.

272

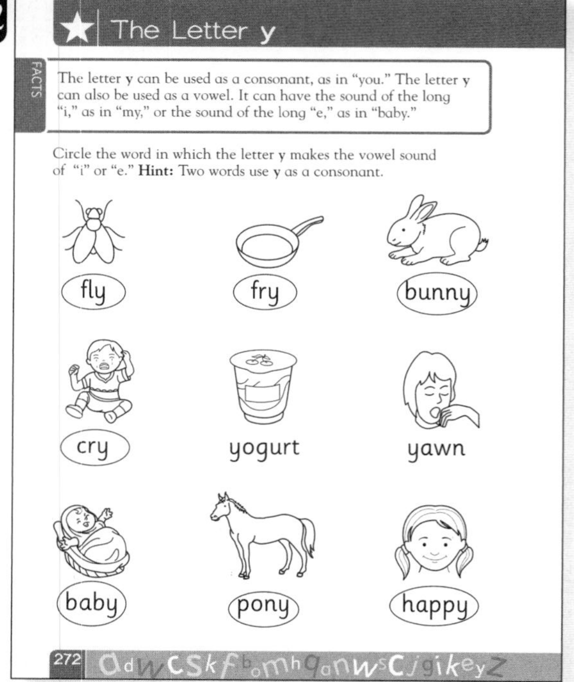

The Letter y
FACTS
The letter y can be used as a consonant, as in "you." The letter y can also be used as a vowel. It can have the sound of the long "i," as in "my," or the sound of the long "e," as in "baby."
Circle the word in which the letter y makes the vowel sound of "i" or "e." Hint: Two words use y as a consonant.
fly
fry
bunny
cry
yogurt
yawn
baby
pony
happy
272

Together, look in children's books and comic books for words that include the letter **y**. For each one you see, ask your child whether the letter is being used as a vowel or a consonant.

273

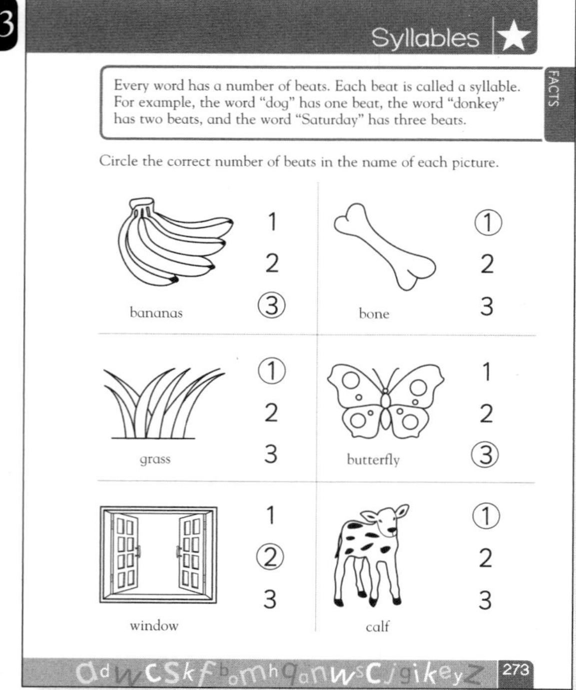

Syllables
Every word has a number of beats. Each beat is called a syllable. For example, the word "dog" has one beat, the word "donkey" has two beats, and the word "Saturday" has three beats.
FACTS
Circle the correct number of beats in the name of each picture.
bananas
bone
grass
butterfly
window
calf
273

Practice counting syllables with your child by clapping as you say the word to feel each beat.

274

Beginning Consonant Blends
FACTS
A blend is two or more consonant sounds used together. Some blends come at the beginning of words. For example, say the word "frog" and listen to the sound of the "fr" blend.
Say the name of the first picture. Listen to the beginning blend. Circle the pictures that have names that begin with the same blend sound.
glove
goat
globe
glue
crib
crayon
cat
crown
skate
skirt
smoke
skull
Say the name of each picture below. Circle the correct beginning blend.
gl pl fl
gr pr br
sq sk st
274

Cut out pictures of items whose names begin with blends, such as a flower, drum, and truck. On one set of index cards, write the name of each item. On a second set of cards, write the beginning consonant blend of each name. Let your child sort the cards and pictures into the correct groups.

275

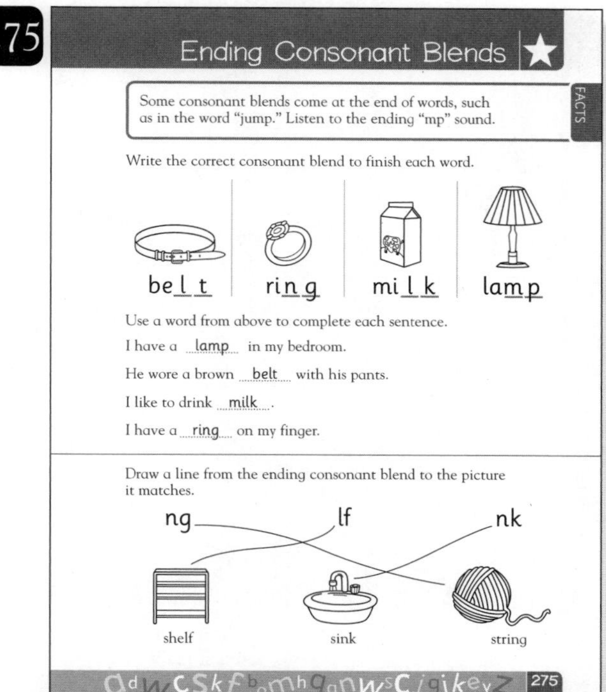

Ending Consonant Blends
FACTS
Some consonant blends come at the end of words, such as in the word "jump." Listen to the ending "mp" sound.
Write the correct consonant blend to finish each word.
belt
ring
milk
lamp
Use a word from above to complete each sentence.
I have a lamp in my bedroom.
He wore a brown belt with his pants.
I like to drink milk.
I have a ring on my finger.
Draw a line from the ending consonant blend to the picture it matches.
ng
lf
nk
shelf
sink
string
275

Write letter problems such as these for your child to combine to form a word:
ri + ng = ______
sa + lt = _______
Use any of the ending blends from this page to create these letter problems.

276

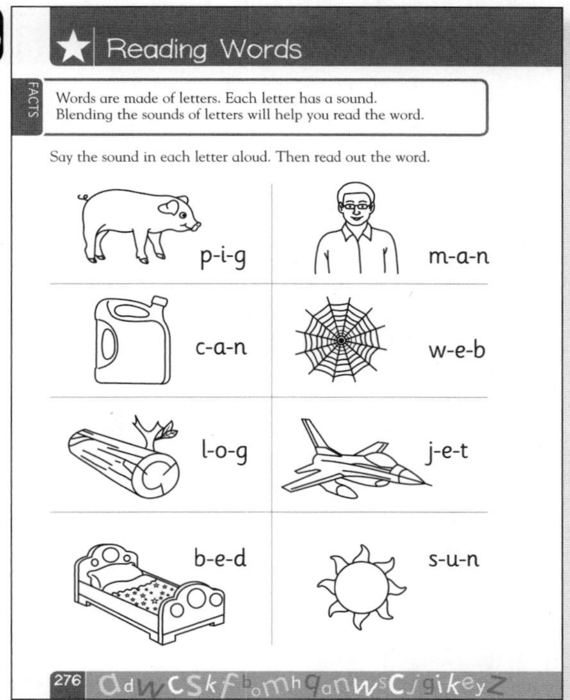

In large letters, write simple three- or four-letter words across a page with hyphens between each letter (such as "b-o-x" or "s-t-e-p.") Give your child a small toy car. Let him or her roll the car over each letter, saying its individual sound and then saying the complete word.

277

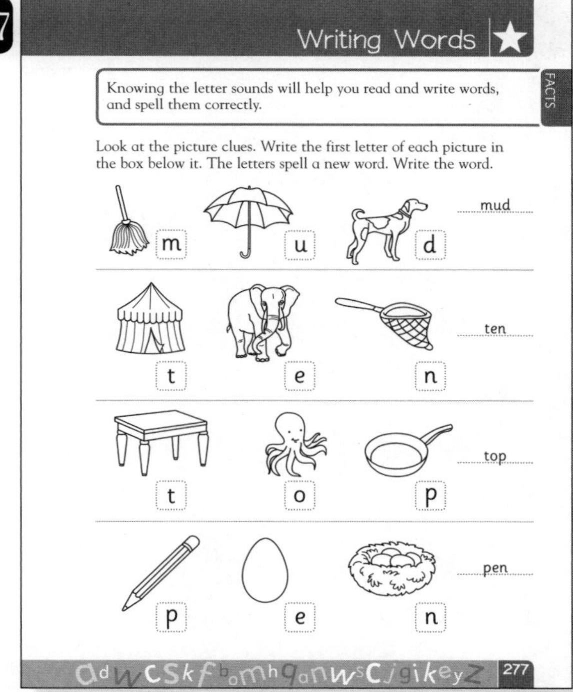

Writing Words
FACTS
Knowing the letter sounds will help you read and write words, and spell them correctly.
Look at the picture clues. Write the first letter of each picture in the box below it. The letters spell a new word. Write the word.
m u d
mud
t e n
ten
t o p
top
p e n
pen
277

Let your child read a word and then cut out pictures whose names begin with the letters found in the word he or she just read. Place the pictures in alphabetical order. For example, if the original word was "dog," you might have pictures of a **d**oll, an **o**ctopus, and a **g**oat.

278

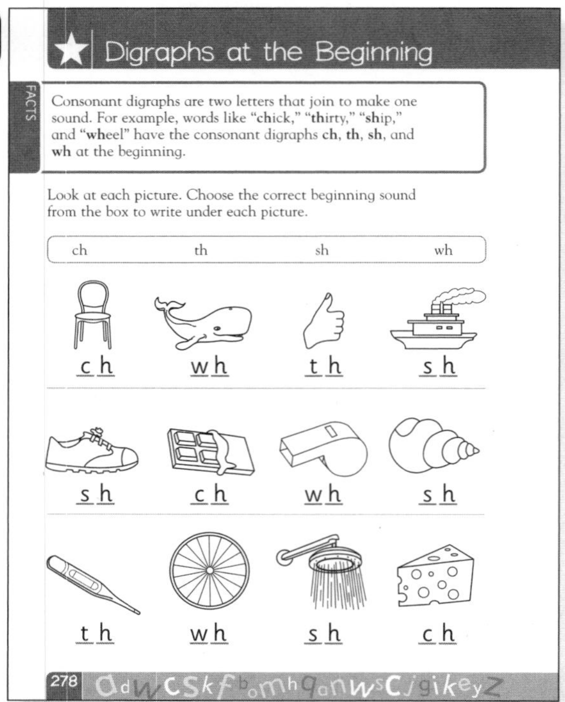

★ Digraphs at the Beginning

FACTS

Consonant digraphs are two letters that join to make one sound. For example, words like "**ch**ick," "**th**irty," "**sh**ip," and "**wh**eel" have the consonant digraphs **ch**, **th**, **sh**, and **wh** at the beginning.

Look at each picture. Choose the correct beginning sound from the box to write under each picture.

ch th sh wh

ch wh th sh

sh ch wh sh

th wh sh ch

278

Walk around a room with your child, pointing at items whose names begin with a digraph. These items might include a shadow, chain, chair, whistle, chin, chips, and shutters. Let your child say the name of each item and identify the beginning digraph sound and letters.

279

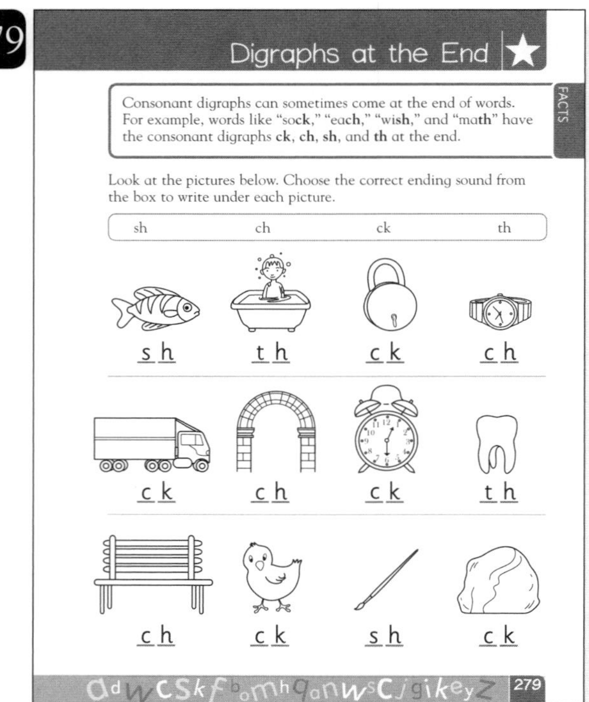

Digraphs at the End ★

FACTS

Consonant digraphs can sometimes come at the end of words. For example, words like "so**ck**," "ea**ch**," "wi**sh**," and "ma**th**" have the consonant digraphs **ck**, **ch**, **sh**, and **th** at the end.

Look at the pictures below. Choose the correct ending sound from the box to write under each picture.

sh ch ck th

sh th ck ch

ck ch ck th

ch ck sh ck

279

With your child, walk around a room pointing at items whose names end with a digraph found on this page, such as dish, couch, washcloth, and toothbrush. Let your child say the name of the item and identify the ending digraph sound and letters.

280

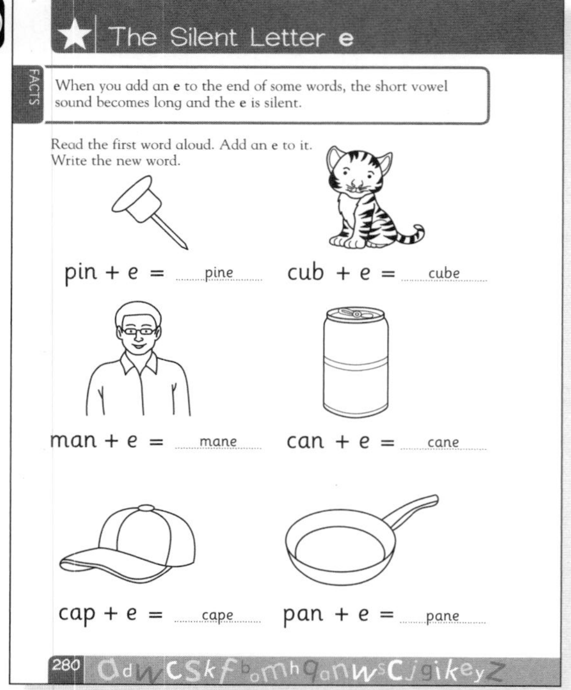

★ The Silent Letter **e**

FACTS

When you add an **e** to the end of some words, the short vowel sound becomes long and the **e** is silent.

Read the first word aloud. Add an **e** to it. Write the new word.

pin + e = pine

cub + e = cube

man + e = mane

can + e = cane

cap + e = cape

pan + e = pane

280

On paper strips, write more short-vowel words, such as "not," "tub," "sit," and "kit." On a small square of paper, write the letter **e**. Have your child read each short-vowel word. Then place the **e** at the end of that word. Let your child read the new word.

281

Vowel Teams ★

FACTS

You may have already noticed that two vowels often come together to make one long vowel sound. For example, **ai** in "pain," **ay** in "day," **ee** in "see," **ea** in "bead," **ie** in "lie," **oe** in "woe," and **oa** in "boat."

Circle the word that names each picture.

leak lean pie tie wear wheel

ray rain pay jay boat moat

sheep seal hoe foe goes toes

281

Review the vowel teams that make long vowel sounds. Write words with various vowel-team spellings, such as **ee**, **ea**, **ai**, **oa**, **ou**, and **oo**, on index cards. Let your child read each word and sort the cards by the vowel team they contain.

282

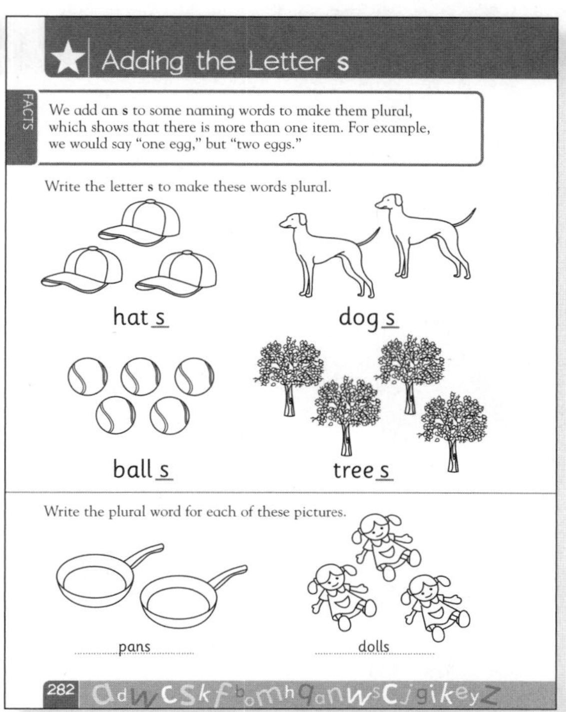

Adding the Letter s

FACTS

We add an **s** to some naming words to make them plural, which shows that there is more than one item. For example, we would say "one egg," but "two eggs."

Write the letter **s** to make these words plural.

hat s

dog s

ball s

tree s

Write the plural word for each of these pictures.

pans

dolls

282

Extend the exercise by teaching your child a few nouns with **-es** and irregular plurals, such as "fox/foxes," "child/children," and "mouse/mice."

283

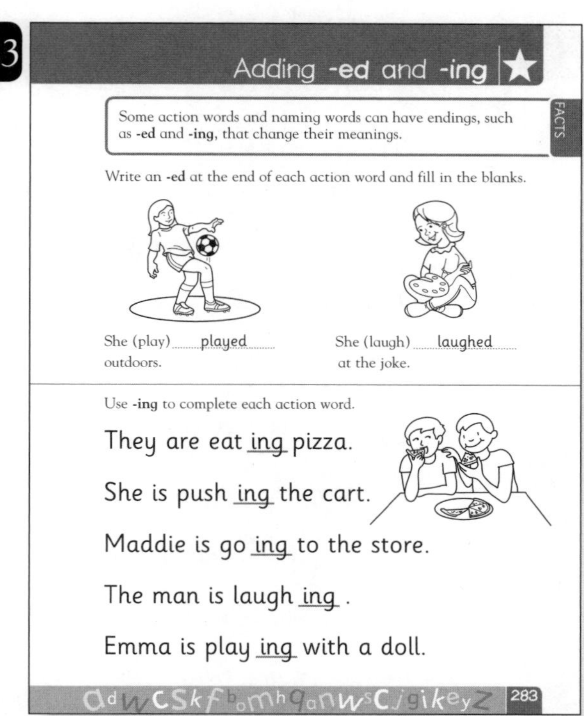

Adding -ed and -ing

FACTS

Some action words and naming words can have endings, such as **-ed** and **-ing**, that change their meanings.

Write an **-ed** at the end of each action word and fill in the blanks.

She (play) played outdoors.

She (laugh) laughed at the joke.

Use **-ing** to complete each action word.

They are eat ing pizza.

She is push ing the cart.

Maddie is go ing to the store.

The man is laugh ing .

Emma is play ing with a doll.

283

Write several sentences for your child. Have each sentence contain words ending in **-s**, **-ed**, or **-ing**. Ask your child to read each sentence and then circle any words that contain those endings.

284

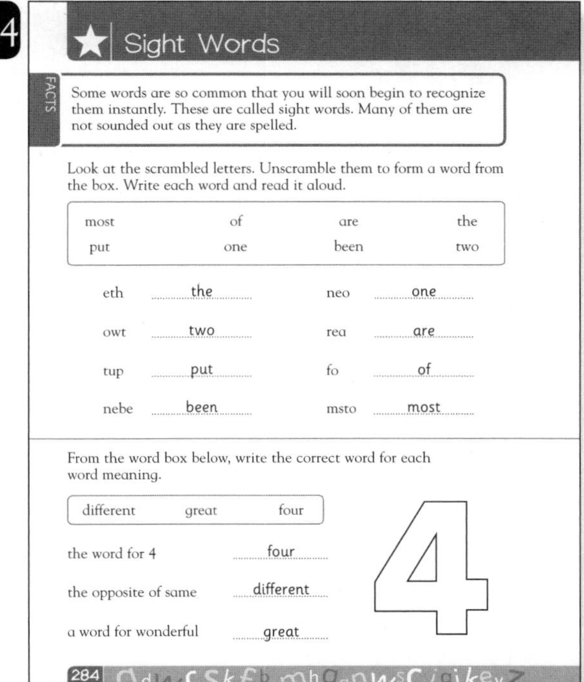

Sight Words

FACTS

Some words are so common that you will soon begin to recognize them instantly. These are called sight words. Many of them are not sounded out as they are spelled.

Look at the scrambled letters. Unscramble them to form a word from the box. Write each word and read it aloud.

most	of	are	the
put	one	been	two

eth	the	neo	one
owt	two	rea	are
tup	put	fo	of
nebe	been	msto	most

From the word box below, write the correct word for each word meaning.

different great four

the word for 4 four

the opposite of same different

a word for wonderful great

4

284

Reinforce the sight words on this page by making word cards and then help your child to form the letters out of clay. Then your child can touch each letter of the word to "feel" its spelling.

285

More Sight Words

FACTS

Sight words are also known as high-frequency words. Some more high-frequency words are "after," "again," "from," "once," and "thank."

Read each word aloud. Write each word on the basket that shows its beginning letter.

some	what	do	often	they
would	old	where	does	their
should	school	thought	different	only

w: what, where, would

t: their, they, thought

s: school, should, some

o: often, old, only

d: different, do, does

285

Encourage your child to use the sight words on this page to create his or her own oral sentences. Check to be sure that your child is using each word correctly.

286

What is a Sentence?

FACTS

A sentence is a group of words that expresses a complete thought. For example, "I like toast." is a complete sentence, but "The toy train" is not. Remember that a sentence always begins with a capital letter and ends with punctuation, which is very often a period (.).

Circle the words below that are complete sentences.

The girl is nice. Mows the lawn

No one else I know a secret.

Read each sentence below aloud. Underline the capital letter and circle the period at the end of each sentence.

I am six years old.

The puppy is cute.

We are playing with a ball.

This is a big and leafy tree.

286 adwcskfbomhqanwscjgikeyz

Prepare two cards one labeled "Sentence" and the other labeled "Not a Sentence." Read some sentences and phrases aloud to your child. Ask him or her to hold up the correct card to indicate which you read.

287

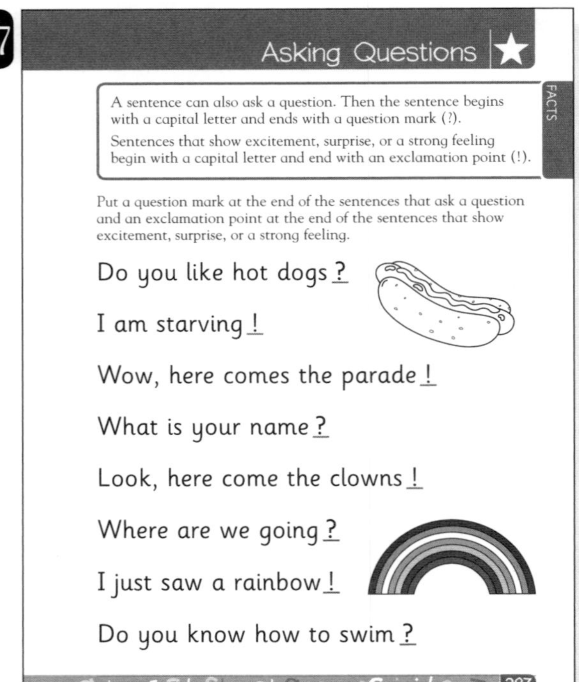

Asking Questions

FACTS

A sentence can also ask a question. Then the sentence begins with a capital letter and ends with a question mark (?).

Sentences that show excitement, surprise, or a strong feeling begin with a capital letter and end with an exclamation point (!).

Put a question mark at the end of the sentences that ask a question and an exclamation point at the end of the sentences that show excitement, surprise, or a strong feeling.

Do you like hot dogs ?

I am starving !

Wow, here comes the parade !

What is your name ?

Look, here come the clowns !

Where are we going ?

I just saw a rainbow !

Do you know how to swim ?

adwcskfbomhqanwscjgikeyz 287

Write a variety of telling, asking, and surprise sentences without their ending punctuation marks. Let your child read each sentence and add the correct punctuation mark.

288

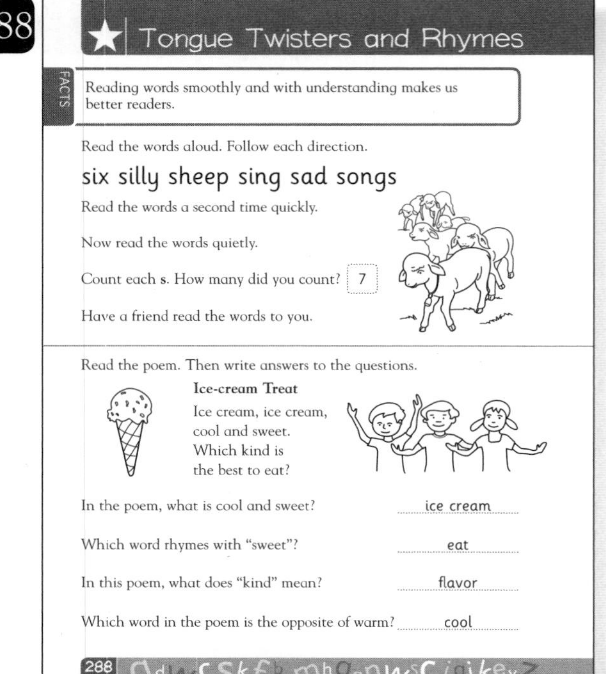

Tongue Twisters and Rhymes

FACTS

Reading words smoothly and with understanding makes us better readers.

Read the words aloud. Follow each direction.

six silly sheep sing sad songs

Read the words a second time quickly.

Now read the words quietly.

Count each **s**. How many did you count? 7

Have a friend read the words to you.

Read the poem. Then write answers to the questions.

Ice-cream Treat

Ice cream, ice cream,
cool and sweet.
Which kind is
the best to eat?

In the poem, what is cool and sweet? ice cream

Which word rhymes with "sweet"? eat

In this poem, what does "kind" mean? flavor

Which word in the poem is the opposite of warm? cool

288 adwcskfbomhqanwscjgikeyz

Help children become fluent readers by reading aloud to them regularly. Choose a variety of reading materials such as poems, magazine articles, fiction and nonfiction books, and riddles.

289

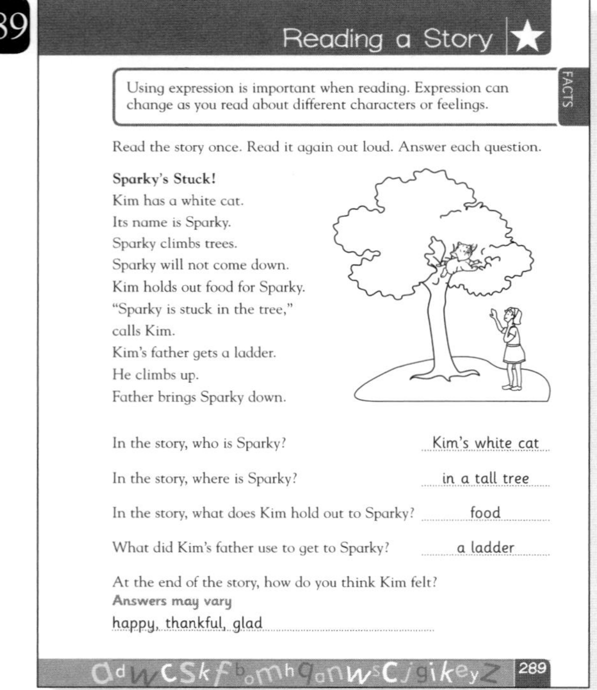

Reading a Story

FACTS

Using expression is important when reading. Expression can change as you read about different characters or feelings.

Read the story once. Read it again out loud. Answer each question.

Sparky's Stuck!

Kim has a white cat.
Its name is Sparky.
Sparky climbs trees.
Sparky will not come down.
Kim holds out food for Sparky.
"Sparky is stuck in the tree,"
calls Kim.
Kim's father gets a ladder.
He climbs up.
Father brings Sparky down.

In the story, who is Sparky? Kim's white cat

In the story, where is Sparky? in a tall tree

In the story, what does Kim hold out to Sparky? food

What did Kim's father use to get to Sparky? a ladder

At the end of the story, how do you think Kim felt?
Answers may vary
happy, thankful, glad

adwcskfbomhqanwscjgikeyz 289

As your child becomes familiar with reading, encourage him or her to practice reading aloud. Afterward, ask questions similar to those above to check your child's understanding of the text.

Practice Page

Practice Page